Law and Society
Recent Scholarship

Edited by Melvin I. Urofsky

A Series from LFB Scholarly

Universal Human Rights
Origins and Development

Stephen James

LFB Scholarly Publishing LLC
New York 2007

Copyright © 2007 by LFB Scholarly Publishing LLC

Library of Congress Cataloging-in-Publication Data

James, Stephen Andrew, 1965-
  Universal human rights : origins and development / Stephen James.
      p. cm. -- (Law and society recent scholarship)
  Includes bibliographical references and index.
  ISBN-13: 978-1-59332-209-0 (alk. paper)
  1. Human rights. 2. United Nations. General Assembly. Universal
Declaration of Human Rights. I. Title.
  K3240.J36 2007
  341.4'8--dc22

                                      2007018687

ISBN 9781593322090

Printed on acid-free 250-year-life paper.

Manufactured in the United States of America.

Contents

Acknowledgements

At the outset, I must acknowledge my debt to some of the leading human rights scholars whose work has influenced this book. I found the pioneering work of Paul Gordon Lauren and Johannes Morsink particularly valuable. I thank librarians at Princeton University (especially the Inter-Library Loan Service at the Firestone Library) in the U.S.A., and at the University of Melbourne, La Trobe University, Monash University, Victoria University (Melbourne) and Griffith University (Brisbane) in Australia.

I am grateful to those who taught me at the University of Melbourne, including David Tucker, David Wood, Stuart Macintyre and the late Lloyd Robson. I also acknowledge with appreciation those professors who taught me at Princeton University, including George Kateb, Alan Ryan, Walter Murphy, Alan Gilbert, Jennifer Hochschild and Gilbert Harman. Also at Princeton, Maurizio Viroli, Robert George and Charles Beitz provided insightful comments on my earlier research into human rights, jurisprudence and political philosophy. I give great thanks to Richard Falk for his inspirational teaching and research, friendly mentoring and helpful responses to my work over a number of years.

I thank the School of Law, Victoria University, for granting me supported leave under its Outside Studies Program (OSP). The OSP leave enabled me to take up appointments as a Visiting Fellow in the Key Centre for Ethics, Law, Justice and Governance at Griffith University, and as a Visiting Scholar in the Institute of International Law and the Humanities at the University of Melbourne during 2006–2007. Much of the additional research and writing of the book took place in the peaceful environment of the Key Centre. I thank its director, Ross Homel, as well as Charles Sampford, Howard Adelman and other Key Centre members. I benefited from insightful responses to the paper I presented in the Key Centre's seminar program in Semester

2, 2006. I also thank Rob McQueen of the Griffith University Law School for his friendly support (at Griffith University and as a colleague in the Law School at Victoria University). I am also grateful for the support given by administrative staff in Brisbane and Melbourne during my period of leave.

I thank Ian Britain for technical advice. Special thanks must be given to Richard McGregor for his meticulous copy-editing of the manuscript. I also thank Tania Sisinni for technical assistance in the preparation of the manuscript. And I thank Sasha James for securing books for me from near and far, and for other assistance.

Finally, I thank Leo Balk from LFB Scholarly Publishing for his support and advice, and Melvin Urofsky for detailed comments on the manuscript. Responsibility for this work naturally remains with the author.

Introduction

Thomas Buergenthal is Professor of Law at the George Washington University National Law Center in the U.S.A., where he is an international human rights scholar. As a young boy he lived through the Auschwitz Death March. He recounts how in January 1945, as a boy who had already survived the Polish Ghetto of Kielce and the Auschwitz concentration camp, he was marched in frigid weather to a train bound for another concentration camp in Sachsenhausen, Germany. The march left him with frostbite. He witnessed beatings and shootings, ate snow and grasped for scraps of bread to survive. His toes were later amputated. Having suffered through these experiences, and then having gone on to become one of the world's leading international law scholars, Buergenthal is able to provide us with an invaluable perspective on the meaning and significance of human rights and the consequences of their violation. On the occasion of a U.S. Holocaust Museum commemoration in 1995, he reflected that while some small relief had come to him over the years through the fading of his childhood memories, they were regularly restored by television images of various atrocities toward the end of the last century: the hollow faces of children starving in Africa, the tormented ones of Bosnian children. He implores us to embrace a universalistic and empathetic commitment to human rights:

> The suffering of those whose stories we read about today or whose corpses we see on television ... was our suffering not all that long ago. This is what we, the survivors, must feel in our bones, in our emotions, and in our hearts. Unless we can identify with today's victims and find ways to express our solidarity with them, to help them, our survival will have been nothing more than an act of random good luck of no lasting

significance. Only by universalizing its inhumanity does the suffering of our people acquire a meaning for the future.[1]

Like Buergenthal, this book understands human rights from a universalistic and "dignitarian" (to use legal scholar Mary Ann Glendon's term)[2] perspective. Given its already broad scope, this book does not propose either an exhaustive conceptualization of human rights, or a sustained philosophical defence of their universality.[3] Nevertheless, it is possible to provide a synopsis of this work's understanding of "human rights."

The conception of human rights in this book is consistent with the U.N.'s. That is, we are all entitled to human rights simply on the basis that we are human beings.[4] As dignitarian instruments, the Universal Declaration of Human Rights (1948) (UDHR), International Covenant on Civil and Political Rights (1966) (ICCPR) and International Covenant on Economic, Social and Cultural Rights (1966) (ICESCR) (which together are colloquially termed the International Bill of Rights) are based on a conception of a shared human nature and inherent human dignity.[5] As Glendon notes, for the drafters of the UDHR "what made universal human rights possible"

> ... was the *similarity* among all human beings. Their starting point was the simple fact of the common humanity shared by every man, woman and child on earth, a fact that, for them, put linguistic, racial, religious and other differences into their proper perspective. A strong emphasis on racial and cultural difference was, after all, one of the worst evils of colonialism and Nazism.[6]

University of London legal scholar Conor Gearty, while sceptical of some aspects of the global human rights regime, roots the universalism of human rights in "the simple insight that each of us counts, that we are equally worthy of esteem" as human beings.[7] Universalist human rights theorists have produced various lists of objects of rights: what every human being is entitled to simply as a human being. For the philosophers Alan Gewirth and Robert Churchill, it is whatever is necessary for reasonable success as a moral agent. For Gewirth, this means that everyone is entitled to "basic goods" (for example, life, freedom, corporal integrity), "nonsubstantive goods" without which one's capacity is reduced (such as clothing, food, healthcare, housing and other similar socio-economic goods) and "additive goods" that improve the quality of our lives (for example, education, involvement in the community). Another familiar classification involves a distinction between standard "liberal," *negative* rights (that bar the state, in particular, from interfering with the rights and liberties of individuals) and *positive* rights that require the state to allocate appropriate resources and take action to ensure that people enjoy goods such as an adequate standard of living, welfare, adequate food, clothing, healthcare and housing.[8] Gearty's categorization is distilled into two comparable human rights principles: what "should *not* be done" to us (prohibitions on killing, torture, racial discrimination and slavery, for example) and "what *ought* to be striven for" to facilitate human flourishing.[9] Similarly, these classifications are embodied in the architecture of the UDHR, which aims to protect – painting here with a broad brush – human dignity (Articles 1–2); civil rights (Articles 3–19); political, economic and social rights (Articles 20–26); and, finally, more communal and solidarist rights (Articles 27–28).[10]

As dignitarian instruments, the UDHR and the 1966 Covenants characterize humans as individuals and as social beings who are members of families and communities, toward whom they bear responsibilities. The state also has responsibilities to guarantee the myriad economic and social rights of the International Bill of Rights.[11]

It must be emphasized that the universality of human rights does not entail their uniformity. For example, the structure of the UDHR is, thanks to its framers, "flexible enough to allow for differences in emphasis and means of implementation," so that "its fertile principles … [can] be brought to life in a legitimate variety of ways" within the world's different cultures. In this respect, the adaptation, further elaboration and specification of the International Bill of Human Rights is analogous to a living constitution : it can evolve through legitimate interpretation (that is, within certain bounds) and through its application over time.[12]

This book gives an interdisciplinary account of the origins and development of universal human rights, and their incorporation in international law, from the earliest days until 1966, when the International Bill of Rights was in place. It evaluates historical, legal, political, theoretical (and sometimes philosophical) developments and literature, using the idea of universality as a theme. International legal scholar Balakrishnan Rajagopal has recently criticized mainstream human rights histories (especially those written from an international law perspective) for neglecting the important role of the Third World (and particularly the role of social movements, domestic struggles and anticolonial mobilizations within it) in the emergence of international human rights law and the global human rights regime.[13] His point is well made: there has been less attention in the literature to the Western resistance to, and Third World support of, international human rights.[14] This study goes a significant way toward redressing this deficiency. It develops the argument that the International Bill of Rights had diverse origins, benefiting greatly from non-Western contributions. Contrary to the view of scholars such as British political scientist Tony Evans,[15] the International Bill of Rights was not a Western hegemonic imposition, nor, in particular, an American imposition. Rather, it was concluded despite a long-standing pattern of Western – including American – resistance to universal human rights in international law.

Notes

[1] T. Buergenthal, "Remembering the Auschwitz Death March," *Human Rights Quarterly*, vol. 18 (1996), no. 4, pp. 874–876. I also rely on J. M. Pasqualucci, "Thomas Buergenthal: Holocaust Survivor to Human Rights Advocate," *Human Rights Quarterly*, vol. 18 (1996), no. 4, pp. 877–899, at pp. 877–880.
[2] M. A. Glendon, *A World Made New: Eleanor Roosevelt and the Universal Declaration of Human Rights* (New York: Random House, 2001), p. 227.
[3] The understanding of human rights in this book is reasonably consistent with Robert Churchill's excellent defence of their universality – see R. P. Churchill, *Human Rights and Global Diversity* (Upper Saddle River, New Jersey: Pearson Prentice Hall, 2006). See also W. J. Talbott, *Which Rights Should Be Universal?* (Oxford: Oxford University Press, 2005); and the useful discussion in A. Gutmann, "Introduction," in A. Gutmann (ed.), *Human Rights as Politics and Idolatry* (Princeton: Princeton University Press), pp. vii–xxviii.
[4] Glendon, *A World Made New*, p. 227; Churchill, *Human Rights and Global Diversity*, pp. xi–xii, 9, 42–43; C. A. Gearty, *Can Human Rights Survive?* (Cambridge: Cambridge University Press, 2006), ch. 1, especially pp. 4–6; M.

Ishay, *The History of Human Rights: From Ancient Times to the Globalization Era* (Berkeley, California: University of California Press, 2004), pp. 3–4.

[5] Glendon, *A World Made New*, pp. 175, 227. For the U.N. Charter, UDHR, ICCPR, ICESCR, and a number of other important international instruments (to be identified subsequently) I have commonly relied on the following sources: *Charter of the United Nations and Statute of the International Court of Justice* (New York: U.N. Office of Public Information, n.d. [1945]); I. Brownlie and G. S. Goodwin-Gill (eds.), *Basic Documents on Human Rights*, fourth edn. (Oxford: Oxford University Press, 2002); Center for the Study of Human Rights, Columbia University, *Twenty-five Human Rights Documents* (New York: Center for the Study of Human Rights, Columbia University, 1994); H. J. Steiner and P. Alston, *International Human Rights in Context: Law, Politics, Morals: Text and Materials*, second edn. (Oxford: Oxford University Press, 2002).

[6] Glendon, *A World Made New*, p. 232.

[7] Gearty, *Can Human Rights Survive?*, p. 4.

[8] Churchill, *Human Rights and Global Diversity*, especially pp. xi, 8–9, 17, 29–32; Glendon, *A World Made New*, especially p. 227; C. Sampford, "The Four Dimensions of Rights," in B. Galligan and C. Sampford (eds.), *Rethinking Human Rights* (Sydney: The Federation Press, 1997), pp. 50–71, at pp. 52–64.

[9] Gearty, *Can Human Rights Survive?*, pp. 5–8.

[10] Ishay, *The History of Human Rights*, pp. 3–4.

[11] Glendon, *A World Made New*, pp. 175, 227.

[12] Ibid., pp. 111, 230, 232. See also S. Power, *"A Problem From Hell": America and the Age of Genocide* (London: Harper Collins, 2002), p. 485 (for discussion of the Genocide Convention (1948) as a "living document").

[13] B. Rajagopal, *International Law from Below: Development, Social Movements, and Third World Resistance* (Cambridge: Cambridge University Press, 2003), especially pp. 35, 172, 174–176, 187–188, 246. See also E. Borgwardt, *A New Deal for the World: America's Vision for Human Rights* (Cambridge, Massachusetts: Belknap/Harvard University Press, 2005), pp. 57–59 (on human rights historians' neglect of group-based rights, duty-based traditions and non-Western developments).

[14] But see J. Rosenberg, *How Far the Promised Land? World Affairs and the American Civil Rights Movement from the First World War to Vietnam* (Princeton: Princeton University Press, 2006); P. G. Lauren, *The Evolution of International Human Rights: Visions Seen* (Philadelphia: University of Pennsylvania Press, 1998); and P. G. Lauren, *Power and Prejudice: The*

Politics and Diplomacy of Racial Discrimination, second edn. (Boulder, Colorado: Westview, 1996).

[15] For example in his *US Hegemony and the Project of Universal Human Rights* (London: Macmillan, 1996).

CHAPTER 1

Universal Human Rights: From the Earliest Days to 1939

Paul Gordon Lauren, in perhaps the first major history of human rights in the English language, insightfully surveyed a range of philosophical and religious "visions" of human dignity and human rights from ancient times to the eighteenth century and beyond. He concluded that these visions could not be attributed to any one society, form of government, culture or region. Every great religion, he observed, addressed in universalist fashion every person's value and dignity. Every one also proclaimed a human duty to relieve at least the innocent suffering of others, whoever they might be.[1]

Some commentators have been quick to point out that a conception of human dignity should not be equated with a conception of human rights.[2] This is accurate up to a point. Yet its accuracy is exaggerated by taking a narrow "liberal" conception of human rights as individualistic, largely "negative," civil and political rights held against the state. This view, which is sometimes characterized as the "Western" or "Enlightenment" understanding of human rights, is a crude one. It does not do justice to the great complexity of, for example, the natural law and Enlightenment heritage. In particular, this view fails to take proper account of the role that duties, social and economic rights, the interest of the community, group claims and, importantly, conceptions of inherent dignity have in that heritage. It also neglects the extent to which these dimensions of that heritage came to animate the International Bill of Rights. When that complexity is appreciated, the imagined gulf between long-standing religious and secular traditions in Western and non-Western civilizations is narrowed substantially. Thus, conceptions of human dignity elaborated in Hinduism, Buddhism,

7

Confucianism, Islam and Christianity remain relevant (despite various contrary and irreconcilable values) to the conceptualization of human rights. Human rights can in this way be succoured by notions of universal or common humanity, the worth of the person, the sanctity of human life, justice, equality, compassion, kindness, love, and various other virtues and moral stipulations.[3]

Religions and ancient civilizations have contributed much to understandings of human dignity and even identified human rights comparable to those found in various human rights instruments today.[4] But while many religions proclaimed that all humans were equal in the sight of God or before the universe, and were of one family, this universalism was an embryonic one. Often the universalist potential was not realized due to intolerance, racism, sexism, and so on. Samuel Murumba, whose work has focused on civilizational contributions to international human rights law, has referred to Hinduism's commitment to freedom for all humans from violence, want, exploitation, intolerance and fear. He has further given an account of early social welfare provisions under the Buddhist Emperor Asoka (third century B.C.E.). Moreover, drawing on Islamic scholars, he points to rights to life, respect, freedom, privacy, to a home, to "a means of living," to knowledge, freedom of movement, to equality, to freedom of conviction and expression, which have been considered compatible with the Qu'ran. He also describes the Islamic "welfare tax" (the *zakat*), which was imposed to assist the poor and unfortunate. But he does not really address values in Islam that might be in tension with human rights norms. Murumba also identifies notions of freedom, the rule of law, procedural justice, workers' rights, representative democracy, egalitarianism, "political accountability" of rulers, social welfare rights and so forth, from his rare survey of Sumerian, Babylonian, Egyptian, Indian, Chinese, Pacific (Oceanic), African, Islamic, Graeco-Roman, Judeo-Christian and European civilizations.[5] He describes the norms of international human rights as like a jigsaw puzzle, with pieces taken from every important culture and value system.[6]

One commentator has written that Elaine Pagels, an eminent historian of religion, "demolished" the idea that human rights were in existence before modern times.[7] But Pagels[8] identified human rights notions in equality, social justice and concern for the poor in Islam, as in Taoist, Confucian, Buddhist, Jewish and Christian understandings.

And she highlighted ancient Hebrew culture's valuation of the individual, its elaboration of the principle of equality among humans, and its corollary that rights are derived from a shared humanity. For Pagels, all these ideas contributed to the individualist foundation of "contemporary human rights theory."[9]

Moreover, this book argues that some of these early, diverse civilizational perspectives are even more relevant to, and compatible with, many provisions in present-day human rights documents, such as the UDHR, than Pagels might have perceived. This point becomes clearer when it is understood that her characterization of "contemporary human rights theory" is much too constricted, even as a representation of so-called Western, liberal conceptions. The range and breadth of provisions of the International Bill of Rights (including duties to society, limitations on rights, participation in society, cultural rights and self-determination) attest to communitarian, social and "solidarity" dimensions of international human rights law that Pagels misses in her portrayal of individual human rights as prior to, and outside of, society.

Natural law philosophy has also made a critical contribution to the development of international human rights law.[10] Natural law approaches can be traced back to ancient Greek and Roman Stoic philosophy and jurisprudence. In Plato's *Dialogues* one finds the notion of *nomos* (human customs and laws subject to change) being contrasted with *phusis* (immutable nature). Within that contrast one can find, also, a means to identify certain conduct as universally just or unjust, right or wrong.[11] Aristotle distinguished between conventional or legal notions of justice, and justice under natural law, "which everywhere has the same force and does not exist by people's thinking this or that."[12] So, also, Zeno of Citium referred to a "universal law" wherein every man was as a brother to his fellows.[13] Elements of classical Greek philosophy relevant to universal, eternal and transcendent natural law included the following: *isotimia* (citizens are entitled to respect on an equal basis), *isonomia* ("equality before the law"), *isokratia* (equal "political power"), *isopsephia* (equal suffrage), and *isopoliteia* (equality of "civil rights"). And natural law was the yardstick against which human law and behaviour were to be measured.[14]

Following in the footsteps of Aristotle's teleology, which identified reason as a key "inner principle" of human beings, the Roman Stoics argued that human nature was part of the natural order and, like it, was governed by reason (*logos*). The law of nature was the law of human nature, and that law was reason, or at least *right* reason. Through the instrument of this reason, natural law could be discerned and obeyed. Cicero, a Roman lawyer writing in the first century B.C.E., provided what became the classic synthesis of many of these ideas of a universal, unchanging, higher natural law to which all humans and their laws were subject, and which could be accessed through reason.[15] He observed that:

> True law is right reason in agreement with nature; it is of universal application, unchanging and everlasting ... It is a sin to try to alter this law ... We cannot be freed from its obligations by senate or people, and we need not look outside ourselves for an expounder or interpreter of it. And there will not be different laws at Rome or Athens, or different laws now and in the future, but one eternal and unchangeable law will be valid for all nations and at all times, and there will be one master and ruler, that is, God, over us all, for he is the author of this law ... and its enforcing judge.[16]

These ideas were the soil out of which grew the Roman conception of *jus gentium*, or the law of nations. This law prescribed rights and duties that were universal, and additional to any simply derived from state citizenship.[17] Importantly, especially considering a common criticism of Western human rights conceptions, duties had a vital place alongside rights.[18]

The Renaissance and Reformation brought an increasing focus on freedom and individual expression, and also on the ancient notion of a ruler's mandate (which can also be found in Confucian philosophy) – drawing attention to the fact that certain rulers may not have fulfilled their natural law obligations.[19]

Along with the nascent constitutionalism of the Magna Carta (1215), there was the renewed natural law philosophy of St. Thomas Aquinas, writing in the thirteenth century, which built on the earlier work of St. Augustine.[20] Just positive law was derived from natural law either as a logical deduction that prescribed the nature of the law or as a "determination" (*determinatio*) of general principles that left some scope for human choice in formulating laws, provided they did not breach the natural law.[21] For Aquinas there was also a sentiment of fellow feeling and reciprocal obligations among all members of humankind.[22]

In addition to early versions of the doctrine of humanitarian intervention in the sixteenth and seventeenth centuries, there was some protection given under treaty to religious freedom. For example, the Treaty of Westphalia (1648) proclaimed equal rights for Protestants and Roman Catholics.[23] In the sixteenth and seventeenth centuries, the leading advocates of universal human rights were the Dominican Francisco de Vitoria, Francisco Suarez and Alberico Gentili. Suarez identified rights to life and liberty based on natural law, and to which every "man," including any "Indian," was entitled. In his writings, he further recognized a right to property subject to natural law injunctions against theft or any other "undue taking of another's property." Gentili, who was appointed Professor of Civil Law at Oxford in 1587, advocated rights of self-defence, freedom (including liberty of conscience), and asylum for slaves fleeing from cruel masters. Asylum was also available for exiles or displaced persons who had left their own cities because of war. According to this surprisingly progressive and innovative doctrine, these people – whom we would probably call refugees or displaced persons – had rights to unoccupied lands for their livelihood and sustenance.[24]

Vitoria's doctrine is important for a number of reasons. First, according to J. B. Scott, an early historian of international law, Vitoria expanded the notion of the community of Christians so that all people, regardless of their civilization or geographical location, could be included within its embrace.[25] Second, positive law was judged against a universal law of nations that could be accessed through the employment of human reason.[26] Third, and in consequence, as Vitoria observed, "if there were any law which without any cause took away rights conferred by natural and divine law, it would be inhumane and unreasonable and consequently it would not have the force of law."[27] Fourth, Vitoria continued that individuals would have to be held accountable for the necessarily sinful violations of international law, since, on his view, states themselves could not act sinfully. Individuals thus had obligations under international law not to offend that law through their actions.[28] This foreshadows the Nuremberg principle, and bears on the debate over whether individuals could be "subjects" under international law, one to which I return later in this chapter. Fifth, as an ideal at least, Vitoria espoused equal rights for all peoples, Christian, pagan, or aboriginal, "irrespective of race, or colour or religion."[29] Finally, Vitoria identified a number of important kinds of rights such as freedom of conscience ("unbelievers who have never received the faith, like Gentiles and Jews, are in no wise to be compelled to do so")[30] and conscientious objection, to use a modern phrase, to an unjust war ("if a subject is convinced of the injustice of a war, he ought not to serve in it, even on the command of his prince").[31] One should also note, as does the classical historian Charles Lavery, that "Time and again … Victoria makes the existence of rights dependent on the fulfillment of duties."[32]

Grotius was an important figure in the seventeenth century. Lavery has even argued that by the time of Grotius there was "a definite doctrine of human rights" in existence.[33] Grotius' chief contribution regarding human rights was his reinvention of a natural law doctrine independent of divine origins. In his *On the Law of War and Peace* (1625), he developed his view that all nations could be judged in accordance with a natural law that did *not* depend upon (though it did not deny!) the existence of God; but rather upon the requirements of rationality. As Grotius reiterated in this major work:

> What we have been saying [about the foundation of natural law] would have a degree of validity even if we should concede that which cannot be conceded without the utmost wickedness, that there is no God, or that the affairs of men are of no concern to Him.[34]

This, then, helped to make possible a secular natural law approach.[35] As Grotius said:

> The law of nature … is unchangeable – even in the sense that it cannot be changed by God … [E]ven God, then, cannot cause that two times two should not make four, so that He cannot cause that that which is intrinsically evil be not evil.[36]

Grotius, moreover, identified a number of specific human rights such as the right of personal integrity and autonomy ("by nature … a man's life is his own, not indeed to destroy but to safeguard; also his own are his body, limbs, reputation, honor and the acts of his will"),[37] of self-defence, to private property and of freedom of religion.[38]

In the seventeenth century both political practice and liberal philosophy came to stress natural rights. Individual natural rights were deduced from natural law, and were ideals whose function was to legitimize limitations on the sovereignty of the state or government, a sovereignty that had been imagined and celebrated by philosophers such as Thomas Hobbes, Niccolò Machiavelli and the Frenchman Jean Bodin. In terms of political reality, one could see opposition to absolutism (justified, for example, in the idea of the "divine right" of kings) in revolts in France and Spain, in the Petition of Right in England (1628), in the English Revolution and the Leveller movement (which sought protection of the natural rights to life, property, representative government, religious freedom and rule of law, as well as a ban on conscription). Such an opposition was also evident in the *Habeas Corpus Act* (1679) and, ultimately, in the 1689 Bill of Rights. This bill included freedom of speech and protection from "cruel and unusual punishment," all on the basis of "ancient" and "undoubted" rights. And in terms of philosophy, around this time John Locke made his seminal contribution to natural rights theory in his *Second Treatise*.[39]

In the eighteenth century there was a confluence of philosophies of natural rights that the Lockean tradition continued to support. In particular it nourished that aspect focusing on the right of revolution in the face of tyranny (when the tyrant or despotic government has broken the social contract between ruler and ruled by trampling on rights it was established to preserve). In Immanuel Kant's metaphysics one finds the categorical imperative, which mandated universal respect for the intrinsic worth of all persons, and thus the prohibition on their being used as a means only.[40] His Third Definitive Article in *Perpetual Peace* recalls Cicero, albeit resting on a different foundation, and might also remind today's reader of some of Martin Luther King, Jr.'s ringing words:

> The peoples of the earth have thus entered into a universal community, and it has developed to the point where a violation of rights in *one* part of the world is felt *everywhere*. The idea of a cosmopolitan right is therefore not fantastic and overstrained; it is a necessary complement to the unwritten code of political and international right, transforming it into a universal right of humanity.[41]

Natural law continued to be developed in a similar direction during the Enlightenment, captured perhaps in the notion of faith in human reason, a phrase that seems to bridge the religious and the secular, and in the possibility of perfecting human arrangements.[42] Among the important philosophers of the time were Jean-Jacques Rousseau, Voltaire, the Baron de Montesquieu, and the Marquis de Condorcet,[43] who, in "Natural Law" in the *Encyclopédie* (1755), exhorted:

Tell yourself often: I am a man, and I have no other true, inalienable *natural rights* than those of humanity.[44]

The *philosophes* espoused principles that they held to be universal, and, like the Stoics before them, they believed that these principles ruled over the cosmos and human society alike. Among these principles was the supremacy of human reason. They wielded it skilfully against the hierarchies, social and economic barriers and injustices and, especially, against the intolerant religious dogmas of their times. The universal and inalienable "rights of man" became their secular creed.[45] For example, Voltaire defended religious freedom in his *Treatise on Toleration* (1763), Cesare Beccaria (a criminologist and economist) protested against torture, executions and cruel punishments in *On Crimes and Punishments* (1764), and the revolutionary Abbé Raynal, in his *Philosophical and Political Theory of Settlements and Trade of the Europeans* (1770), condemned slavery because it violated natural rights.[46]

But the nobility of these philosophies was often distorted by an unfulfilled universalism both in theory and in practice. As with ancient natural law ideals, these philosophies coexisted with radical inequalities, racism and sexism; slavery and the slave trade being among the monstrous hypocrisies of the time. Montesquieu, Diderot, Condorcet, Voltaire and the American revolutionary Thomas Jefferson each gave voice at various times to racist prejudices. Racism was also bolstered by pseudo-scientific theories of race and racial hierarchies that ranked non-whites as inferior. And these views strengthened imperialist, colonialist and segregationist schemes, and even gave further impetus to the trade of human beings across the seas.[47]

The ideals, and indeed the distortions, of the Enlightenment had a practical impact in the American and French revolutions, and in the constitutional norms and structures that crystallized from them.

Foreshadowing the constitutional outcomes of the American Revolution were rights protections in a number of colonial constitutional documents such as those of Pennsylvania, Maryland, Delaware, North and South Carolina, New Jersey, New York, New Georgia and Massachusetts.[48] Most important of all was the Virginia Declaration of Rights (1776) drafted by George Mason. The Virginia declaration, which predated the Declaration of Independence, proclaimed freedoms of the press and religious expression, and provided that no one must be denied their liberty except under the law.[49] It declared that "all men are by nature equally free and independent, and have certain inherent rights."[50]

The American founding fathers drew upon Lockean philosophy and the writings of the *philosophes* to justify the Revolution and to guide the creation of the new polity.[51] Thomas Jefferson, for instance, had read both Locke and Montesquieu, and described the American colonists as a "free people claiming their rights as derived from the laws of nature and not as the gift of their Chief Magistrate."[52] In the Declaration of Independence he wrote:

> We hold these truths to be self-evident, that all men are created equal, that they are endowed by their creator with certain unalienable rights, that among these are Life, Liberty and the pursuit of Happiness – That to secure these rights, Governments are instituted among Men, deriving their just powers from the consent of the governed. That whenever any Form of Government becomes destructive of these ends, it is the right of the People to alter or abolish it.[53]

The drafters of the American Constitution had also naturally been influenced by the Virginia declaration, and sought to protect a similar set of rights. With amendments to that constitution, now known as the Bill of Rights, freedoms of religion, expression, press and assembly, and due process of law were included. There was also protection against unreasonable search and seizure and an immunity against self-incrimination.[54] But, tragically, it was not really until the Civil War period that slavery came to be seen as incompatible with the equality of "men"; and the United States, as elsewhere, continues to struggle with this legacy and with other manifestations of racism.[55]

There were a number of important cross-pollinations between French and American philosophers of the eighteenth century, some of which have been mentioned above.[56] The American Revolution was naturally a stimulant to the French Revolution, as rebels rose up against the old regime.[57] Again, the French Revolution was heavily influenced by the rationalism of the Enlightenment thinkers who criticized absolutism, venal privileges, inequalities, repression and religious superstitions as against reason. The natural rights of Locke were combined with the radical popular sovereignty of Rousseau (though his concept of the "general will," notoriously, has authoritarian or conservative implications as well).[58] Principles from the English and American revolutions were emulated in the French Declaration of the Rights of Man and the Citizen (1789). The declaration stated that "men are born and remain free and equal in rights" and (Article 2) that "the aim of every political association is the preservation of the natural and imprescriptible rights of man"; including "Liberty, Property, Safety and Resistance to Oppression."[59] Article 4 elaborated upon "Liberty," which meant

> being able to do anything that does not harm others: thus the exercise of the natural rights of every man has no bounds other than those that ensure to the other members of society the enjoyment of these same rights. Those bounds may be determined only by Law.[60]

Specifically, liberty included the right to free speech, freedom of association, religious freedom, freedom to hold opinions and freedom from arbitrary arrest and confinement.[61] Other protections included "due process" and "presumption of innocence" rights.[62] These rights were possessed by individuals on the basis of their humanity, not because they were under the law of a state. They were naturally universal, inherent and inalienable.[63] Many of these rights were entrenched in the 1791 constitution, and further efforts were also made for poverty relief and for the provision of public education at no cost.[64]

Despite the ostensible universalism of the declaration, there was much debate in the French National Assembly about whether it should apply to "people of colour" and to slaves in France or in French colonies.[65] Philosophers such as Montesquieu, Rousseau and Diderot had opposed slavery. Consistent with this opposition, initially the

National Assembly had given citizenship to those of colour, and abolished slavery in the colonies, but these decisions were shortly to be reversed. It was rare indeed for the rhetoric of the declaration to be applied to indigenous peoples living within the French Empire.[66] When in 1794 France abolished slavery it was arguably the first among the European nations to do so. However, it was re-established by Napoleon and was not ended until 1848.[67]

The declaration did not extend to French women either, as human rights were denied to their English and American sisters. Women were excluded despite the best efforts of advocates such as Abigail Adams, wife of the second U.S. President John Adams. In 1792, in *A Vindication of the Rights of Woman*, Mary Wollstonecraft in England demanded that women be given all the "rights of humanity," including fuller benefits of education.[68]

The denial to women of the rights in the French declaration is well demonstrated by the tragic case of the French playwright and pamphleteer Olympe de Gouges. She wrote a "Declaration of Rights for Women and female Citizens" (1791) as a critique of the constitution of 1791. Her call for human rights for women was refused by the National Assembly.[69] De Gouges was executed in 1793, women's clubs for political discussion were dismantled, and even small gatherings of women were not allowed.[70]

De Gouges' declaration is a fascinating document and, as Hannelore Schröder, a historian of the French Revolution, notes, should seem radical even to our eyes. It did, however, include men, and thus is seen by Schröder as *"really ... the general, universal declaration of human rights for all humankind."*[71] In this respect de Gouges was in accord with the *philosophe* Condorcet who argued that "Either no individual of the human race has genuine human rights or else we all have the same ..."[72] Consequently, de Gouges condemned those Enlightenment men who sought "the right to equality for themselves only, while at the same time in deepest ignorance rule despotically over a sex which is in possession of all intellectual capabilities."[73] Women were "born free" and remained "equal with man in all rights concerned" (Article I). In Lockean tenor, she declared that the "[g]oal and purpose of uniting to a social body, is to secure the inalienable rights of women as well as men," such as "liberty, security, property and especially *the right to resistance* against repression." Article III recasts the popular sovereignty of the *philosophes*:

> Sovereign power has its origins in the nation. This is a social
> body *of women and men*, nothing else. No government, no
> individual may exercise power if it does not originate from the
> people, i.e. women and men.

This was elaborated still further by Article VI, which called for the
equal participation of women in (a) representative (form of)
government: "laws have to be the expression of [the] common will
(volonté generale [*sic*]) which comes into being only *if all female and
male* citizens participate through their representatives." That was so,
also, in relation to the creation of the nation's constitution (see Article
XVI of de Gouge's declaration):

> A society in which these basic human Rights of Women are
> not guaranteed, does not have a constitution at all ... [I]f the
> *majority* of the population has not participated in drafting the
> constitution, *there is no constitution.*[74]

The declaration was also important in forging reciprocal
connections between rights and duties, and in identifying their
relevance to political participation and to social and economic justice.
Article XIII, for example, argued that the fulfilment of the duty to pay
taxes gave rise to a right of access to the public service, trades,
professions and other means of income.[75]   Articles XIV and XV
stressed that the principles of "no taxation without representation" and
the control of public expenditure were related and applied as much to
women as to men. How could women exercise such control if they
lacked an equal opportunity to participate in government? Article XVII
stated that "Property belongs to both sexes, collectively or
individually."[76]

Charles Lavery has examined the writings of a number of leading
international law scholars in the sixteenth, seventeenth and eighteenth
centuries. He tabulated a great range of rights subscribed to by the
various scholars, including inherent personal rights, civic and social
rights. Almost without exception, the scholars he examined supported
rights to liberty, life and religious expression.[77] But Lavery stressed that
for these scholars duties were also important and indeed could not be
separated from rights. Nor were all rights (for example, ownership
rights) absolute, but rather limited in accordance with a medieval

conception of the common good, which treated others' needs with due reverence.[78] For Lavery, "the law of nations was written under the light of natural law," a light that illuminated human rights. But he is then provoked to ask:

> [W]hat happened at the end of the nineteenth century to these right[s] of man? Why did they vanish so suddenly from the international scene?[79]

We may begin an answer by referring to the augmentation of positivist thinking, of *realpolitik*, sovereignty, nationalism, imperialism and colonization in the nineteenth century. Nevertheless, there were countervailing forces that contributed to re-emergent internationalist, and at times universalist, norms and institutions, albeit with partial and inconsistent outcomes. In any event, these countervailing forces demonstrate that it is an exaggeration for Lavery to use the word "vanish." Here I will focus on three main areas: the "abolition" of the slave trade, ad hoc humanitarian intervention and the debate in international law over the status of individuals.

Opposition to the slave trade grew primarily out of a religious critique of the practice as inhumane, a critique that also included Muslim and Buddhist perspectives.[80] The Society for the Abolition of the Slave Trade in Britain was established in 1807 to protect the "common rights of humanity." Britain passed an *Act for the Abolition of the Slave Trade* that made it "illegal to trade in, purchase, sell, barter, or transport any human cargo for the purpose of slavery."[81] In the U.S.A., an *Act to Prohibit the Importation of Slaves* provided for the forfeit of ships and cargo, as well as fines and imprisonment as sanctions for those transporting persons from Africa for the purpose of slavery. These schemes were limited to national jurisdictions and difficult to enforce. In time, opponents of the slave trade recognized the need for an international approach.[82] At the Congress of Vienna (1814–1815) delegates signed the Eight Power Declaration against the slave trade, which stated that the trade was "repugnant to the principles of humanity and universal morality." In the Treaty of Ghent the U.S.A. and Britain condemned the slave trade as "irreconcilable with the principles of humanity and justice."[83]

Despite these treaties between diverse states, the slave trade (let alone slavery in general) had not yet been made illegal nor were there adequate enforcement measures against it.[84] Later treaties were backed by British naval force, and in 1890 the General Act for the Repression of the African Slave Trade was agreed by the Great Powers of Europe, the U.S.A., Scandinavia, the Ottoman and Persian empires, the Congo and Zanzibar. The Act committed the signatories to repress slave trading, punish slave traders, liberate and protect slaves, and exchange information.[85] This convention and the international governance it established later became something of a model when states began planning for the League of Nations and the U.N.[86]

Early advocates of a limited right of what we would now call humanitarian intervention included Alberico Gentili, Hugo Grotius and the Swiss diplomat and jurist Emmerich de Vattel. Gentili referred to the defence of a "common law of humanity" whose violation injured everyone, and Grotius and Vattel to the protection of subjects from a tyrant. These principles can be compared with the Lockean notion of the right of resistance when the social contract has been breached.[87] They were an amalgam of liberalism and cosmopolitanism:

> [I]f a prince, by violating the fundamental laws, gives his subjects a lawful cause for resisting him; if, by his insupportable tyranny, he brings on a national revolt against him, any foreign power may rightfully give assistance to an oppressed people who asked for its aid.[88]

The importance of religious freedom and toleration to humanitarian intervention was signalled early on by treaties "guaranteeing" equality of rights and freedom of conscience for Roman Catholics and Protestants in Europe (for example, the Treaty of Westphalia of 1648 and the Treaty of Utrecht of 1713).[89] The peace established by the Congress of Vienna embodied, also, protections for religious freedom and an ideal of non-discrimination against religious "minorities" within national borders. For example, the Federative Constitution of Germany (1815) emphasized the need for action to protect Jews' civil rights.[90]

As potential customary international law, humanitarian intervention was derived not merely from natural law but from the practice of states.[91] This practice of interventions by major European powers in the cause of protecting various religious minorities persecuted *by their own states* (a fact about such persecutions that distinguished them from venerable international law protections of aliens) was tainted by one-sidedness and by commercial interests and motivations.[92] Even so, the emergence of such a doctrine of humanitarian intervention was important in corroding the sovereign shield of "domestic jurisdiction" which hid a state's mistreatment of even its own citizens. It helped to recover the sense of a universal community, morality and law that the emerging positivism of the nineteenth century suppressed.

Of particular concern to the intervening powers was the mistreatment of various religious minorities, especially Christians, in areas such as Crete, Syria, Russia, Romania, some Balkan states and the Ottoman Empire.[93] Following massacres of Greek Orthodox Christians by the military forces of Sultan Abdul-Aziz in 1827, the London Treaty was concluded between Great Britain, France and Russia, providing formal authority for collective military intervention to prevent further slaughter. In 1860, in response to a massacre of thousands of Christian Maronites by Muslim Druze in Syria, a number of European powers intervened militarily and, further, established an International Commission. Anticipating a number of features of international and regional governance and international law in the following century, the commission was established to investigate persecutions and to seek possible punishment of wrongdoers. Again, atrocities against Christians in the 1870s, this time in the Balkans, made their tragic imprint upon the Treaty of Berlin (1878). This treaty supported international rights to religious freedom, non-discrimination on the basis of religion, and the protection of ethnic minorities (with direct reference to the fate of Armenians persecuted by Circassians and Kurds). The Treaty stated that in the Ottoman Empire

> differences in religious creeds and confessions shall not be alleged against any person as a ground for exclusion or incapacity in matters relating to the enjoyment of civil and political rights, admission to public employments, functions and honors, or the exercise of various professions and industries in any locality whatsoever.[94]

The dark mood in Europe and the Ottoman Empire in response to the thousands who had died and suffered as the result of religious persecution in the nineteenth century could not simply be lifted by a positive evolution in the norms and practices of international law. In hindsight, however, positive and significant evolutions in international law can indeed be discerned.

An absolutist conception of state sovereignty was challenged, individuals' flesh-and-blood humanity was recognized. It was also recognized that the persecution of those individuals was often based on their race, ethnicity, religion or other collective identity. This latter recognition is an important refutation of the crude view that human rights notions were obsessively focused on individuals and paid scant attention to collective identity. These so-called "second" or even "third generation" rights were pursued alongside the "first generation" rights: which should lead us to reassess the orthodox chronology, at least as far as international human rights law and enforcement is concerned. After all, one of the earliest protections of human rights reflected in international law norms and practice were rights to religious freedom and non-discrimination. These rights are characteristically complex, hybrid individual/group human rights claims. This is a feature, also, of the international community's piecemeal concern with the protection of minorities that came to the fore in the interwar years.

By 1921 at least one international law scholar, E. C. Stowell of American University, was prepared to argue that the "legality of humanitarian intervention" had the support of scholars such as Hugo Grotius, the London barrister and Cambridge University professor John Westlake, Henry Wheaton, a diplomat from the USA, the German legal and political scholar Johann Caspar Bluntschli "and many others."[95] He defined the doctrine as emanating from limitations in the very nature, one might say, of state sovereignty. Here was an interesting inversion given the common justification in sovereignty's name of the very abuses intervention was often said to be a response to:

> Humanitarian intervention may be defined as the reliance upon force for the justifiable purpose of protecting the inhabitants of another state from treatment which is so arbitrary and persistently abusive as to exceed the limits of that authority within which the sovereign is presumed to act with reason and justice.[96]

Edwin Borchard, of Yale Law School, also rested his explanation of humanitarian intervention on an understanding of sovereignty. His explanation reflected an uneasy relationship between a theory of sovereignty's supposedly "absolute" nature and its limitation on "the grounds of humanity":

> ... [W]here a state under exceptional circumstances disregards certain rights of its own citizens, over whom presumably it has absolute sovereignty, the other states of the family of nations are authorized by international law to intervene on the grounds of humanity. When these "human" rights are habitually violated, one or more states may intervene in the name of the society of nations and may take such measures as to substitute at least temporarily, if not permanently, its own sovereignty for that of the state thus controlled.[97]

We come now to a phase in the history of international human rights law that is sometimes taken misleadingly as the *starting* point: the status of the individual under international law in the nineteenth century. It is misleading because, as this book has so far emphasized, the rights of individuals were much in evidence in international law doctrine of the sixteenth to eighteenth centuries. By taking the nineteenth century as a starting point, one both dramatizes the achievement of respect for individual human beings in the mid-twentieth century, presenting a linear view of progress, and underestimates the earlier revolution (or counter-revolution) represented by the positivist backlash against the natural law–infused international law of earlier centuries. A number of scholars have recognized this. Indeed, prior to the middle of the nineteenth century, the conventional understanding of international law was enlivened by the natural law view that it was properly concerned with individual human beings: with their rights, duties, welfare and dignity. Of course, accordingly, individuals were also regarded as subjects of international law. Thus individuals were recognized under international law as having the capacity to form and be subject to legal relations. International law was not, then, merely a creation by and for states alone.[98]

However, even when it has been examined in a critical light, the state-centric view of nineteenth-century international law as typical of all international law, or even defining it, nevertheless carries the weight of orthodoxy. It is a weight which tends to lean against allegedly "unrealistic", or aspirational notions such as human rights. This is consistent with positivism more generally, which distinguishes between law as it is and law as it should be. But, importantly, the state of international human rights in the nineteenth century ought not to be treated in isolation from earlier international law, lest that law be misrepresented. Yet there is no doubt that the growth of positivism, of the nation-state, sovereignty and domestic jurisdiction in the nineteenth century diminished the available rights claims of individuals under international law.

In the nineteenth century, as in earlier times, the development of international law was influenced by the philosophical context. Natural law and natural rights were subject to utilitarian critiques by Jeremy Bentham, historicist critiques on the part of the German legal scholar F. K. von Savigny and English legal historian Sir Henry Maine, positivist critiques by John Austin and others, Marxist and socialist critiques, and to those of German Idealism.[99] The English Idealist philosopher F. H. Bradley, for example, was able to declare in 1894 that

> The rights of the individual are today not worth serious consideration ... The welfare of the community is the end and is the ultimate standard.[100]

The doctrine of sovereignty seemed to have become paramount in the nineteenth century, and affected the question of whom or what could be accorded "personality" under international law. A legal person can have "legal relations" and can possess rights and owe duties under the law. In present-day liberal-democratic legal systems all people have personality, whereas in the past, slaves, for example, lacked it. Animals, however, continue to lack "legal personality." Laws can be made to benefit animals – for example, to prohibit cruelty toward them – but animals do not possess rights under the law, even in modern legal systems.[101]

The dominant view in the nineteenth century was that international law concerned principally, or even only, "a body of rules which ... regulates the conduct of the States in their intercourse with one another," to quote the legal philosopher Hans Kelsen.[102] While the international law scholar Lassa Oppenheim noted that individuals were important to the law of nations because they were "the personal basis of every State," paradoxically they themselves lacked international legal personality because they "belonged" to a state. Only states were subjects of international law, whereas individuals, according to Oppenheim, were

> *objects* of the Law of Nations [, which] recognises the personal supremacy of every state over its subjects at home and abroad, [so] these individuals appear just as much objects of the Law of Nations as the territory of the States does in consequence of the recognised territorial supremacy of the States.[103]

This explanation is hardly a model of clarity. Oppenheim refers to the *personal* supremacy of every state, but it is not clear what he means by this other than the supremacy of a state's ruler within its *own* exclusive jurisdiction described by its territorial boundaries. Interestingly, also, in Oppenheim's account individuals are simultaneously *subjects* of the state (in the sense of being under its rule, owing it allegiance and being given a recognized identity) and *objects* under international law.[104] Oppenheim further notes that only states have rights because "the Law of Nations ... impose[s] the duty on all the members of the Family of Nations to grant certain privileges to such foreign heads of States and diplomatic envoys, and certain rights to such foreign citizens as are on their territory."[105] This explanation is also rather unclear. The bold claims for state sovereignty and state rights seem in some sense to be undermined by their derivation from supra-national international law *duties*. Could not the law of nations then *impose* different duties, with different consequent rights, or different obligations altogether? One answer might be that the duties are *self-imposed* in that, in accordance with the voluntarist or consensual approach to international law, states are bound only by obligations they freely adopt through a discretionary exercise of sovereign power, any agreement from which is always able to be revoked by a relevant state. But this would seem to contradict the ordinary coercive meaning of "impose[s]" in Oppenheim's formulation.

It fell to Hersch Lauterpacht, the famous Cambridge international law scholar, to revise Oppenheim's classic international law text. To one section of it, he added the following:

> [I]t cannot be said that the doctrine of the "rights of mankind" is altogether divorced from practice ... [T]he State is bound to

respect certain fundamental rights of aliens resident within its
territory ... [and there was] the principle and practice of
humanitarian intervention in defence of human rights
ruthlessly trampled upon by the State ...[106]

Still, there had been criticism of the new positivist "classical" doctrine
that displaced the naturalistic classical international law of the sixteenth
to eighteenth centuries. The new "classical" doctrine has been
described by the international legal scholar K. Partsch as follows:

To the extent that international law concerns itself with the
interests of individuals, it does so not by creating rights and
duties of individuals as such but rather by obliging States to
treat individuals in a certain manner.

On this view, states may have duties from which individuals benefit,
but individuals do not possess rights per se. But Partsch, for instance,
also refers to the "sociological school" of international law, based in
France, which defended an inverse picture of the role of the individual
in international law. The individual was the "object" of international
legal order in the very different sense that the individual was the end at
which it ought to aim, and might "even be considered its exclusive
subject," or exclusive subject matter.[107] Instead of being neglected or
even trampled on, according to this French school the welfare of
individuals was the *raison d'être* of public international law. Here,
then, was an interesting subversion of the usual meaning of individuals
as "objects" under international law. And it is a perspective that
harkens back to the earlier naturalist international law discussed earlier.

An outline of the doctrine of international legal personality of
individuals as it applies in international law has often been followed in
conventional textbooks by an exploration of the doctrine of state
sovereignty. It is not clear, however, why the one ought necessarily to
follow from the other. Why would the classification of individuals as
the "objects" of international law somehow justify an unlimited state
sovereignty within an exclusive territorial jurisdiction? Perhaps the
association of the two is due to the connotations of "objects" versus
"persons." On a Kantian view, this makes sense – things and "objects"
may be used instrumentally, but persons ought not to be. This takes
one back to Oppenheim's equation of a state's own citizens with its

territory. A citizen thus *belongs* to his or her state in a sharper fashion than even sentiment, culture or nationalist ideology might suggest. The relationship is a quasi-proprietary one. These interpretations are given some support by international lawyer Peter Malanczuk's conclusion that individuals lacked personality under the international law of the nineteenth century and were, rather, in a similar position in this regard to animals under municipal (national) legal systems today.[108]

It is true that, despite the doctrine of humanitarian intervention, states had great freedom of action under international law in this period in relation to their own citizens. But it is interesting that stress was laid on what *harm* states could do to their own citizens with impunity, rather than on how they might seek to advance their citizens' interests. In other words, there was a reiteration of the connections between the subject–object distinction, state sovereignty, "domestic jurisdiction" and abuses perpetrated on citizens, which reinforced the view that such actions were not the concern of international law. The legal validity of these actions could not be impugned even if their moral legitimacy could be challenged. In orthodox accounts, how a state treated its own citizens was a matter of exclusive, impervious "domestic jurisdiction," one that international law could not penetrate.[109]

Given that this was the predominant view of state sovereignty under international law in the nineteenth century, were there any exceptions, or is there a basis for qualifying it in any way? Limited recognition of individuals under international law in the nineteenth century came in the form of the imposition of "direct responsibility" upon individuals in relation to piracy *jure gentium* and slave trading.[110] Another challenge to a sole focus on states, and to state sovereignty, was the "universality principle," which had grown out of piracy and slave trading as crimes "against international society":

> [O]ffenders ... can thus be punished by international tribunals or by any state at all. Jurisdiction to hear the charge is not confined to, for example, the state on whose territory the act took place, or national state of the offender.[111]

Under customary international law and treaty, the universality principle now arguably applies to torture, genocide, war crimes, crimes against peace and crimes against humanity and non-discrimination.[112]

Writing in 1941, the scholar F. S. Dunn argued, at the optimistic end of the spectrum, that individuals were not without power to seek the protection of international law for their various interests. He cited, in support of this conclusion, diplomatic protections of citizens abroad, the doctrine of neutrality (which in wartime enabled the continuation of social and economic intercourse between neutral and other states), treaties dealing with private persons' interests and rights, and tribunal cases involving individuals.[113] The tenor of Dunn's argument seems to follow from a kind of methodological individualism – that abstractions such as "the state" can never really do anything, that any action must in reality be undertaken by some flesh-and-blood person. It should be noted that Dunn's view contradicts the orthodox approach that if there is no protest by "the state of nationality," an individual will not usually have standing to prosecute the violation of an international treaty.[114]

But both Lauterpacht and Rosalyn Higgins, an eminent British international lawyer, have made the point that one ought to distinguish the holding of a right and the procedural ability of individuals to enforce that right themselves.[115] For all sorts of reasons, they argue, one might have the former but not the latter. Higgins, for instance, has said that "the weakness of the positivist view on the place of individuals [in international law] is that it fails to distinguish between the possession of rights and duties and the procedural capacity to sue and be sued on them." She describes international law as a "decision-making process" in which individuals participate. On this view, international law is and means different things to different participants. Some international law simply has more relevance to some actors, including individuals, than others. So, for Higgins,

> the topics of minimum standard treatment of aliens, requirements as to the conduct of hostilities and human rights, are not simply exceptions conceded by historical chance within a system of rules that operates as between states. Rather, they are simply part and parcel of the fabric of international law, representing the claims that are naturally made by individual participants in contradistinction to state participants.[116]

Lauterpacht, writing in 1955, further noted that states sometimes give individuals, regardless of whether they are subjects of the state or aliens, "international rights *stricto sensu*." These rights are not at all dependent on domestic legislation, and they may be pursued by individuals in their own right in "international tribunals."[117]

It is important to note that human rights are not being defined here as the conferral of personality on individuals under international law. Rather, that conferral is a necessary but not a sufficient condition. Treating individuals as subjects rather than objects of international law is emblematic of a shift from an approach focused on international law as the law between and of states to a more human-oriented international law. Not only are the subjects of international law not limited to states as actors – it includes individuals who can hold rights and owe duties – but international law should take as one of its chief measures of success how well it serves the interests of humankind. To this end, also, international law has come to represent a more supranational kind of law, making national law subordinate to it in relevant contexts, and consequently shrinking the domain of exclusive state sovereignty. More generally, the extension of legal personality to individuals under international law mirrors developments in liberal-democratic states whereby the rights and benefits associated with legal recognition (for example, equality of treatment, freedom of movement, suffrage and so on) have been progressively conferred, as a result of painful struggle, on disfavoured persons. The story of the progressive, but clearly imperfect, conferral of rights upon women and people of colour is evidence of these developments.

Conversely, the denial of the recognition of legal personality, history shows, creates an environment in which people are more likely to be dehumanized (subject to abuses, deprivations, depredations and atrocities) at the hands of the state or of those who *have* been granted recognition by the law and are in positions of power over others. We will revisit this truth later in the book when I discuss the importance of the Nazi regime's denial of legal personality to Jews prior to the Holocaust. But, to reiterate, while the recognition involved in the conferral of legal personality on individuals is a critical part of the evolution of international human rights, one must remember that it is a necessary but not a sufficient condition for the fulfilment of human rights protection. Such legal recognition is not enough: states or their agents could conceivably recognize an individual legally and still act abusively toward him or her. Nevertheless, the conferral of legal personality at least recognizes one's humanity and personhood, and suggests, though it does not guarantee, access to redress through the law and legal institutions such as courts. More generally, as suggested above, the notion of an individual as a subject resonates with Kantian anti-utilitarian principles. Unlike an object, humans are not mere chattels, cannot be used like so much brute matter, or valued only in an instrumental sense. Karl Marx, in his critique of capitalism, was another philosopher, albeit from a very different perspective, who condemned the commodification of human beings, and their exploitation for profit by the bourgeoisie.[118]

Many scholars, particularly after World War II, have noted the irony that according to a prominent view of international law in the nineteenth century a state had an almost untrammelled "right" to mistreat its own citizens but *not* foreign nationals within its territory. This was explained in a way that was consistent with principles of state sovereignty, nationality, the subject–object dichotomy and the rights of states. Unlike a state's own citizens, foreign nationals were almost like moving pieces of their own state's territory, to recall Oppenheim's metaphor. For one state to harm another state's citizen was to harm that latter *state's* interest; such a state could then ask for reparation for the injury. The right lay with the state not the individual harmed. It could choose not to pursue such a claim at all, and the individual victim would have no recourse under international law.[119] It is illuminating to quote from Oppenheim[120] at some length:

> If, as stated, individuals are never subjects but always objects of the Law of Nations, then nationality is the link between this law and individuals. It is through the medium of their nationality only that individuals can enjoy benefits from the exercise of the Law of Nations ... [I]f individuals who possess nationality are wronged abroad, it is their home state only and exclusively which has a right to ask for redress, and these individuals themselves have no such right ... [I]ndividuals enjoy benefits from this law *not as human beings but as subjects of such States* as are members of the Family of Nations ...

Stateless persons fared even worse. According to Oppenheim, stateless persons enjoyed "no protection whatever" under the law of nations for any mistreatment by the state within which they lived.[121]

Under the law of state responsibility, a state was not bound to admit aliens to its territory, but if it did then it would be required to be "civilised" toward them in accordance with an international minimum standard.[122] Breaches of this standard will trigger the wrongdoing state's responsibility, and allow the alien's state to make a claim against it for "compensation" or other form of redress. This is known as a right to "diplomatic protection." The standard could be violated through the unlawful killing, imprisonment or other mistreatment of an alien (or by "looting" or otherwise damaging her property). A state could also fail to meet the standard by being complicit in unduly severe law-and-order measures that kept the peace but at the cost of due process and the rule of law, or with regard to corruption or maladministration in the justice system.[123]

But whether the "plaintiff" state does make a claim at all, and if so on what terms, is a matter for the state itself and not the individual victim.[124] There may, for instance, be countervailing interests, motivations and pressures, economic, strategic and even moral, which convince the state not to pursue its claim: "In these respects, the injured individual is at the mercy of his/her national state."[125] In the event of a successful action by a claimant state, the wrongdoing state must cease the offending action and provide the former with satisfactory reparation, which could include compensation, commitments to desist from the offending action and various forms of restitution.[126]

Jan Herman Burgers, a Dutch international relations historian, has noted that many historical accounts of human rights are unsatisfactory because they make a great leap from the putative natural rights climax of the eighteenth century to the Holocaust and the San Francisco conference of 1945.[127] I agree with the tenor of Burgers' complaint, and further stress that the period 1900 to 1939, in particular, must not be neglected.

In this period there were some significant gains for human rights ideas, law and institutions, despite the continuation of racism, imperialism, colonialism and the defence of state sovereignty. Interestingly, given the common negative characterization of the human rights of the early to mid-twentieth century as being simply European, Western and focused on "traditional" (that is, so-called "Enlightenment") civil and political rights for individuals, a closer historical analysis reveals a much wider international drive for human rights, an emerging anticolonialism (with regard for self-determination and the condition of indigenous peoples), an entrenchment of anti-slavery provisions, a regard for economic and social rights (evidenced by the creation of the International Labor Organisation (ILO)) and for collective rights, especially for certain minorities.

From the turn of the century until the outbreak of World War I, certain developments helped advance the cause of human rights. One dimension of these was an outcome of internationalization. Intergovernmental groups and auxiliary scholars elaborated various conceptions of human rights, and sought their realization through practical measures of various kinds.[128] For instance, in 1901 the *Ligue des droits de l'homme* sought the advancement of "liberty, equality, fraternity and justice" for "all humanity," with special attention to "religious and ethnic persecution," indigenous peoples' rights, the victims of oppressive regimes, and to socio-economic inequality.[129] In terms of universality, it is important to note that the *Ligue* was interested in human rights violations wherever they were committed. China, France, Algeria, the Ivory Coast, the Ottoman Empire, Senegal, Indochina, the Balkans, the Congo and Madagascar all received its attention.[130] Support for human rights in China in this period was reflected in Kang Youwei's promotion in *The Book of Great Harmony* of the principles of equality and individual liberties and freedoms as part of humanity's universal, natural rights.[131]

In the early twentieth century there was also a consolidation of custom relating to international humanitarian intervention. There were state diplomatic protests in relation to Romanian and Russian oppression of Jews, against Morocco's cruel punishment of political prisoners, against Peru's and Belgium's mistreatment of aboriginal peoples, and against the Turks for persecuting Christians and Armenians.[132] Importantly, in relation to the treatment of Christians in the Ottoman Empire, the Turkish government was required to allow a foreign military force on its soil to ensure the safety and welfare of the minority.[133] Despite his staunch defence of state sovereignty, even Oppenheim conceded that "should a State venture to treat its own subjects or a part thereof with such cruelty as would stagger humanity, public opinion of the rest of the world would call upon the Powers to exercise intervention for the purpose of compelling such State to establish a legal order of things within its boundaries sufficient to guarantee to its citizens an existence more adequate to the ideas of modern civilization."[134]

Another significant event in this period was the creation of the International Association for the Protection of Labor (IAPL), which ultimately formed the ILO in 1919. In 1906 the IAPL fostered two conventions, one relating to the safety and working conditions of women, the other relating to the dangerous match-manufacturing industry. In that same year, the International Office of Public Health was formed.[135]

Transnational movements emerged to combat racism. Critical among them were those that drew upon a pan-African solidarity in opposition to racial discrimination and imperialism. Harvard-educated African American W. E. B. Du Bois and the Jamaican-born visionary Marcus Garvey were central figures, and their activism was reflected in the African Congress of 1900 in London, the formation of the National Association for the Advancement of Colored People (NAACP) in the U.S.A., and the Universal Races Congress in 1911. They pointed out the hypocrisies that stained Christian and American egalitarian constitutional rhetoric alike.[136] These movements included the Western Anti-Imperialist League, and leftists of various kinds, such as E. D. Morel, who criticized French and Belgian practices in the Congo, and Henry Nevinson who condemned human rights abuses in Angola and São Tomé.[137]

Just prior to World War I, there was a rather strange cross-pollination of ideas relating to self-determination and proposals for open international diplomacy.[138] The views of Lenin, and of the Bolsheviks more generally, on these issues had a strong influence on the views of U.S. President Woodrow Wilson.[139] Wilson was also influenced by the leftist "progressive internationalism" within the Democratic Party.[140] Further influences included the Women's Peace Party and the League to Enforce Peace, which stressed the self-determination of peoples, equality of states, and "collective security" to which Wilson referred in his speeches.[141] Mention should also be made of the role of Alejandro Alvarez, who helped to found and then led the American Institute of International Law. In 1917 he produced for the institute a draft declaration on international law that in part addressed international human rights.[142]

The Great War has been seen by scholars as pivotal in the emergence of "total war." An important aspect of it was the erosion of the distinction between combatants and non-combatants, the extension of the war to civilians as a matter of military strategy. Perhaps somewhat ironically, the "realist" E. H. Carr described this phenomenon in his classic work *The Twenty Years' Crisis*. He emphasized that an international moral code sought to protect human beings from "*unnecessary* death or suffering"; although he sarcastically pointed out that "necessity" was a test easily satisfied by the rationalizations of nation-states in their own interest. Carr argued that attacks on civilians could "in fact promote important military objectives," so less and less death and suffering could be considered, on this view, "unnecessary." "Modern conditions of warfare" since 1914, said Carr, "are doing much to break down in one important point, *a previously existing and effective sense of universal obligation.*"[143]

Carr identified an attack on civilian morale as one form of justification of the exception concerning the pursuit of "a military objective."[144] As evidence of this view, Carr quoted a statement from an unnamed British Chief of Staff in January 1918:

> Long-distance bombing will produce ... its maximum moral effect only if visits are constantly repeated at short intervals so as to produce in each area bombed a sustained anxiety. It is this recurrent, as opposed to isolated spasmodic attacks, which interrupts industrial production and undermines public confidence.[145]

This justification was later used in World War II in relation to the massive bombing of civilian areas. In practical terms, the atrocities in Belgium, the Germans' use of heavy artillery against Paris and the British economic blockade of Germany bear out Carr's observations in this regard.[146] The circumstances of the Belgian atrocities concerned the German army's slaughter of hundreds of Belgian citizens who were resisting the German invasion. Many thousands died as a result of the British blockade, and a number of scholars see it as a morbid prelude to "total war."[147] More specifically, for the philosopher and psychologist Jonathan Glover it represented a grim dawn for "the power of mass killing at a distance." It was a psychological and ethical precedent for the normalization of the saturation bombing of civilians that was to come in future wars.[148] It is interesting to note, in contrast, the ruling Kaiser's, and many other Germans', grave objections to the drowning of innocent civilians that led to the rejection of suggested military plans to blockade Britain by submarines.[149]

The experience of World War I galvanized the work of many international law "idealists" and peace activists, and made the Marxist and socialist critiques of imperialism more acute. Additionally, the war accentuated the issue of race, highlighting, for example, the injustice of black American troops dying at the front for a country that did not treat them as worthy of an equal life of dignity at home. Almost one-third of U.S. armed forces were black, yet these "heroes" were often subject to segregation and other forms of discrimination within their own country. Similarly, at both the 1917 and 1918 Imperial war conferences, Indian delegates urged that racial inequality within the Empire be addressed.[150]

At the end of the war, there were a number of other important developments relevant to international human rights law. First, there emerged a regime for the protection of the rights of various minorities. Second was the debate over the ill-fated non-discrimination clause proposed for the Covenant of the League of Nations. Third, there was the system of "mandates" that gave some structure to the paternalistic protection of "native" inhabitants in so-called dependent territories.[151] Finally, there was a push, particularly by the British, to try military and political leaders of the Ottoman Empire for crimes against humanity over the massacre of perhaps one million Armenians. This push anticipated developments at Nuremberg at the end of World War II.[152]

The minorities regime[153] sought to respond to some of the elements of earlier peace treaties, which had contained clauses protecting religious freedom, as well as to the sporadic forms of international humanitarian intervention discussed above.[154] With the collapse of a number of empires at the end of World War I, the maps of European territory were redrawn and new states emerged.[155] The imperfect idealism of President Wilson's "Fourteen Points," including the notions of self-determination for peoples, liberation of persecuted minorities and equal sovereignty for all states – small or large – was given greater impetus by these circumstances.[156] The fact that the persecution of a racial, linguistic or religious minority could trigger intervention by an interested state, escalating into international conflict, was uppermost in the minds of statesmen gathered in Paris at the end of the Great War.[157] While there were hopes among some, and fears among others, that a human rights regime would apply to all minorities, this did not eventuate.[158] Instead, international protection was given only to minorities in the territory of *defeated* states (as well as in new states created at the end of the war).[159]

There were four main innovative and significant aspects of this regime. First, it went beyond religious freedom to embrace a range of other civil and political rights. Second, while focused on the protection of minorities, a number of provisions had much wider human rights implications – guaranteeing, for example, the right to life and liberty to all *inhabitants* in the relevant territories.[160] Third, the regime was not purely individualistic. In addition to a developing notion of equality of treatment, or non-discrimination, the regime also advanced collective cultural and social rights of minorities. It was not simply a liberal-individualist regime, but had collective elements. For example, rights were included for substantial minorities to educate themselves, and to learn and use their native tongue, all with the support of a fair share of the relevant state's resources. Under the regime, minority schools and cultural organizations were subsidized by the state. Collective rights included for minority groups facilitated their physical preservation, strengthened their confidence in their own identity, and helped to maintain that confidence. The maintenance of a group's healthy esteem if you like.

The autonomy of minorities within this "devolutionist" arrangement is evident in their right to seek public positions, in their right to use their own language in official forums such as courts, in their authority to establish and maintain indigenous charities, and in their right to freely practice their religions.[161] This anticipates some of the protections now to be found in the Universal Declaration of Human Rights (1948) and the 1966 human rights covenants.[162] This approach also has some similarities with various contemporary forms of internal self-determination, autonomy and cultural pluralism in some Western, and other, states (for example, the accommodation of Amish groups and Native Americans in the U.S.A., the policy of "multiculturalism," as well as support for indigenous-language and cultural education, in Australia). Fourth, the obligations toward minorities were guaranteed under the processes and institutions of the League of Nations.[163]

The League's minorities regime provided for a complex set of rights and constitutionalist protections that were not limited to minorities or even to nationals. Nationals, or state citizens,[164] were to have equality before the law and a common set of political and civil rights, with no discrimination on the grounds of religion, language or race. Those nationals who also belonged to a particular minority were guaranteed more collectivist rights related to the use of their native tongue and the creation and maintenance of religious and social bodies (for example, schools). From a universalist perspective, an even more important feature of the minorities regime was that it reached beyond them. It gave all those living in a relevant country comprehensive civil liberties with no discrimination related to nationality, birth, language, religious identity or race.[165] The intricate instruments protecting minorities included: "special minorities treaties" that bound Poland, Romania, Greece, the Serbo–Croat–Slovene state and Czechoslovakia; clauses regarding minorities in the peace treaties concluded with Bulgaria–Hungary, Turkey and Austria; "general declarations," upon being admitted to the League, made by Lithuania, Latvia, Albania, Iraq and Estonia; Finland's declaration concerning the Aaland Islands; as well as treaties for Danzig, Memel and Upper Silesia.[166] The League had a system of monitoring and enforcement of the international obligations owed to various minorities within the regime's purview. Institutions were created, such as a minorities committee (which could help resolve disputes), minorities commissions and tribunals, and the office of Director of the Minorities Section. A victimized minority could also petition the League in relation to an alleged breach of a minority treaty. There were also procedures that allowed for human rights violations to be brought before the Permanent Court of International Justice (PCIJ).[167] But it seems that minorities had "no standing as such" before the council or the PCIJ.[168] There were various stages through which a minority's grievance might progress. First, the secretary-general of the League would assess the merits of a complaint. If the secretary-general found it credible then she or he could recommend that the council appoint an ad hoc Minorities Committee. It could investigate the complaint and attempt to achieve a settlement agreeable to the parties. If this was unsuccessful the grievance could be submitted to "the Council as a whole" or the PCIJ.[169]

Member states that found themselves obliged under the regime complained that they were being unfairly targeted, and some of them urged a universal regime in which – following the precedent of state practice regarding humanitarian intervention – minorities would be protected as a matter of universal human rights. Indeed, unsuccessful attempts were made in 1925, 1930 and 1932 to achieve such an extension of the regime. The lack of success in this regard meant that the regime remained a partial one. It was limited to Europe, and the victorious powers were exempt. Further, the regime's effectiveness was hampered by the weakness of its supervisory mechanisms and the defensiveness of new states in relation to the League's supervisory role regarding minority questions. Adolf Hitler's cynical use of minority interests as a pretext to undermine states of strategic interest to him further eroded the regime.[170]

Even so, Pablo de Azcárate, who had been Director of the Minorities Section of the League of Nations, concluded that it was relatively successful during the interwar period. Moreover, according to Azcárate, the provisions that applied to all inhabitants in a relevant state were a model for universal human rights:

> Three of the human rights – life, liberty, and religious freedom – were assured ... in an absolute and general form ... This ... places the guarantee of these three human rights above all national considerations and on the human plane, the only one consonant with their universal character. In this sense there is reason to consider this clause of the minorities treaties [protecting the above rights] as a genuine precedent for any attempt to establish an international guarantee of human rights.[171]

Though leading states were reluctant to comply fully with its demands, the minorities regime was a significant improvement on the early notion of the "standard of civilization" in international law, which placed more burdens on non-Western countries. In limiting state sovereignty, and in placing demands upon some Western states in relation to European minorities, the regime represented progress – it "brought the standard of civilization back home," as the political scientist Jack Donnelly has acutely observed.[172]

E. H. Carr, a celebrated pioneer of the discipline of International Relations, famously characterized the leading forces and perspectives of the interwar period as utopianism versus realism. To a certain extent this is a helpful characterization, despite inconsistencies, ambiguities and other weaknesses in Carr's argument, which I will not pursue here.[173] It is notable that in a book focusing on idealism and utopianism in the interwar years, Carr himself makes, according to my reckoning, only one brief mention of "human rights."[174] Perhaps this is because of the overwhelming preoccupation of scholars, statesmen and the public with "peace" after the carnage of the war. And yet statesmen certainly did recognize a link between oppression at home and warmongering abroad.[175] Later, W. E. Rappard (Director of the Mandates Section of the League of Nations in the 1920s and on the commission between 1925 and 1945), writing at the end of World War II, similarly concluded that:

> Mindful of the recent past, conscious of the intimate connection which undoubtedly existed between intolerant internal and the bellicose external policies of their defeated foes, and realizing that no lasting peace was possible except between free nations composed and governed by free citizens … [the UN's founders] have sought to protect the world community against war by protecting its individual members against oppression.[176]

A brief discussion of Wilsonian idealism at Versailles will help to elucidate emerging notions of the equality of nations, democracy and self-determination relevant to human rights. Self-determination, the equality of nations, open diplomacy and international morality were some of the keynotes of Wilson's rhetoric. In an address to Congress in 1917, upon the U.S.A.'s declaration of war, Wilson announced:

> We are at the beginning of an age … in which it will be insisted that the same standards of conduct and of responsibility for wrong shall be observed among nations and their governments that are observed among individual citizens of civilized states.[177]

This advocacy was echoed many times in other statements by the President and by Prime Minister Lloyd George of Great Britain. In some of these, the importance of "human rights above all other rights"[178] was proclaimed, while at other times more specific references were made to the "equality of nations," large and small, "upon which peace must be founded if it is to last."[179] Audiences were reminded by these statesmen of what, to paraphrase H. G. Wells, the allies were fighting for: democracy and the self-determination of nations.[180] Notably, it was as a publicist or propagandist that Wells came up with the poetic, but at the same time rather ambiguous, expression of "making the world safe for democracy."[181]

How large was the gap between these ideals and the reality of the experience at Versailles? The Peace Conference at Versailles built upon the trend toward quasi-universal conferences of nations, strengthened by the meetings at the Hague.[182] With 32 states meeting at Versailles, around three-quarters of the global population could be said to be represented there. The countries represented went well beyond the confines of Europe or the Western world. So-called "Powers with general interests" were France, the British Empire, Japan, Italy and the U.S.A. "Powers with special interests" was a category comprising Australia, Brazil, Belgium, Canada, Cuba, China, Greece, the Czecho-slovak Republic, Haiti, Guatemala, Honduras, Hedjaz (which later became Saudi Arabia) and South Africa. Finally, certain powers could attend "sessions" of the conference in which the agenda particularly affected them (Bolivia, Ecuador and Uruguay were in this class).[183] Consistent with the other ideals discussed above, Wilson aspired to have plenary sessions involving all the delegates present at Versailles originating discussions and making "final decisions," but this happened only at the early meetings. Overall, the Great Powers dominated. The Council of Ten, and then the Council of Four (U.K., France, U.S.A., Italy), were the decisive coalitions: with vigorous, secret meetings on a daily basis between the heads of state of the Council of Four.[184]

This view seems generally to be accepted by scholars.[185] The international lawyer R. P. Anand concluded that having achieved victory in the war, the leading powers wanted to consolidate their superiority in the League of Nations. His view was that the conference failed to respect the principle of equality of nations in terms of procedure and representation. Anand noted that the peace treaty with Germany was the result of the Great Powers, and there was a hierarchy even within plenary sessions. The most crucial commissions, for example, had only great power delegates.[186] The international relations historian Andrew Williams concluded that the Covenant of the League of Nations was a product of Great Power deliberations and interests, and that it was "relatively painlessly drafted, mainly by [Lord Robert] Cecil by mid-February 1919."[187] Williams made the further point that the British were better prepared for Versailles than the Americans, an important part of the explanation for their dominance.[188] Even U.S. Secretary of State Robert Lansing criticized the conduct of Wilson at Versailles in the following fashion: in his efforts to "make the world safe for democracy, he abandoned international democracy and became the advocate of international autocracy."[189] One example of the undermining of Woodrow Wilson's principle of applying the same morality to nations as nations did to individuals was the President's changes to the covenant to satisfy conservative opinion in the U.S.A, so that so-called "domestic" disputes could not be examined by the League.[190] These changes were consistent with American resistance to international, universal human rights on the basis of racial politics.[191] This resistance was evident in the attitude of the U.S. Senate and the U.S.A.'s ultimate failure to become a member of the League.[192]

Japan was keen not only to be admitted to the society of "civilized" states – a goal formally fulfilled as, in part, a response to its demonstration of military prowess in the Russo-Japanese War (as well as to its internal legal, constitutional and institutional reforms during the Meiji Restoration), and because of its participation in World War I – but also to have itself and its citizens treated as civilized, and in a civilized fashion. Racism, embodied in Western imperialism and in domestic politics, in particular the demeaning and exclusivist immigration policies in Britain, the U.S.A., Canada, and Australia ("White Australia Policy"), remained barbs causing pain and dishonour to Japan at Versailles. Japan sought to hold the Allied powers to account for their rhetoric during the war about the equality of nations, the unity of humankind, about international democracy and so forth. It sought to include a guarantee of racial equality, and it was bitterly aggrieved when its efforts failed.[193] If Japan were to succeed in relation to racial equality it would have to overcome views of the kind expressed by the British Foreign Office:

> Japan is the only non-white first-class Power. In every respect, except the racial one, Japan stands on a par with the great governing nations of the world. But however powerful Japan may eventually become, the white races will never be able to admit her equality. If she can enforce her claim she will become our superior, if she cannot enforce it she remains our inferior; but equal she can never be. There is therefore, at present in practical politics no solution to the racial question.[194]

During World War I, Germany exploited for propaganda purposes the mistreatment of African Americans in the United States. It even dropped propaganda material from aircraft over black troops in the field.[195] Many people of colour held hopes that, as one veteran put it, "As this hath been no white man's war neither shall it be a white man's peace".[196] The President of the National Association for the Advancement of Colored People (NAACP), Moorfield Story, put this telling question: "Mr President, why not make America safe for democracy?"[197] Du Bois trusted that "[w]hat we cannot achieve before the choked conscience of America, we have an infinitely better chance to accomplish before the organised Public Opinion of the World." A Pan-African Congress was held in mid-February 1919, bringing together in Paris delegates from the French West Indies, Haiti, Liberia and from other non-Western countries. It agreed upon resolutions addressing the welfare and human rights of dependent peoples in the developing world regarding land and other resources, labour conditions, education, health and culture.[198] Less hopeful, the Japanese newspaper *Asahi* editorialized:

> No other question is so inseparably and materially interwoven with the permanency of the world's peace as that of unfair or unjust treatment of a large majority of the world's population … If the discrimination wall is to remain standing then President Wilson will have spoken of peace, justice and humanity in vain, and he would have proven after all only a hypocrite.[199]

In support of this view, thirty-seven Japanese NGOs held a meeting in Tokyo from which emerged the Association for the Equality of Races.[200] Racism in Japan ought not be forgotten here. The British and Americans had, for example, been variously described in Japanese publications of the time as bestial, devilish, fiendish, monstrous and primitive – as "hairy, twisted-nosed savages."[201] The Japanese delegation pushed for an equality of races clause to be included in the Covenant of the League of Nations, as follows:

> The equality of nations being a basic principle of the League of Nations, the High Contracting Parties agree to accord, as soon as possible, to all alien nationals of States members of the League, equal and just treatment in every respect, making

no distinctions either in law or fact, on account of their race or nationality.[202]

But the "choked consciences" of the U.S.A., Great Britain and its Dominions could not withstand racist influences and domestic constituencies with vested interests in segregation and restrictive immigration based on race.[203]

Despite the fact that there was a majority in favour of the clause, President Wilson, in the Chair of the Commission of the League of Nations, insisted on unanimity, an insistence on very shaky ground legally.[204] The Australian Prime Minister, William Morris "Billy" Hughes, threatened that Australia would not join the League if such a clause were included.[205] Wilson himself had expressed racist views, was weak in his opposition to segregation, failed to support "anti-lynching" laws, was anxious about Asian immigration to the west of the U.S.A., and was sure the Senate would not ratify a covenant including a racial equality clause (the Senate later more than vindicated his views on this).[206]

The mandates system under the League of Nations steered a perilous course between imperialism and self-determination. According to international lawyer Richard Falk, Robert Lansing (U.S. Secretary of State) characterized it as a form of self-determination *"within* the colonial order."[207] The fifth of Wilson's Fourteen Points was as follows:

> A free, open-minded, and absolutely impartial adjustment of all colonial claims, based on a strict observance of the principle that in determining all such questions of sovereignty the interests of the populations concerned must have equal weight with the equitable claims of the government whose title is to be determined.[208]

Reflecting this point, at least in part, the colonies of the defeated powers Germany and Turkey were not to be annexed outright,[209] but were to be assisted by the victorious powers, as "mandatories,"[210] to obtain independence. The mandatories were to administer the territories, respecting "the well-being and development of such peoples" living there as a "sacred trust of civilisation."[211] The territories were graded paternalistically according to their supposed readiness and suitability for independence. There was a hierarchy of Class A, B and C mandates. The Class A mandates of Transjordan, Syria, Iraq and Palestine, formerly under Turkish rule, were characterized under the regime as closest to independence. In the Class B category were the African regions of the Cameroons, Togoland and Tanganika, previously colonies under German rule. They were seen as less ready for self-determination. But slavery was prohibited and all Class B inhabitants were granted freedom of conscience and religion, even if this could be restricted in the name of public order. Class C mandates (South West Africa, New Guinea, Nauru, Caroline Islands) guaranteed some rights to individuals but were administered as part of the administering powers' own territory. Under Article 22 of the covenant, "advanced states" (taking into account their wealth, proximity and experience) would act as mandatories for the League. Mandatories were to act as guardians for the territorial populations under their tutelage.[212]

The contribution of the mandates system to the protection of human rights was mixed. In one publication, Paul Gordon Lauren concluded that the system was largely hypocritical, a thinly veiled imperialism. But despite its paternalism, English political scientist Scott Davidson has drawn attention to the role of the covenant in compelling mandatories to do their best to eliminate religious or racial discrimination.[213] In contrast, Richard Falk has concluded that even the limited principles reflected in the language of the clause were rarely fulfilled.[214] Certainly, the regime allowed the Allied powers to extend their control over new peoples. But its virtues included some fostering of moves toward independence,[215] as well as some monitoring of the conduct of mandatories through the council and the Permanent Mandates Commission.[216] This included the right of an inhabitant of a mandate to petition the commission in relation to an alleged violation of rights under the mandate.[217] For example, in 1922 there was criticism of South Africa following a petition in relation to its treatment of tribal peoples in South-West Africa.[218]

While Lauren would be unlikely to agree with Davidson that the mandates system was "perhaps, one of the major humanitarian achievements"[219] of the League, he recognized some progress, as well as the "heroic efforts" of the Mandates Commission.[220] Indeed, Lauren seems somewhat inconsistent in his evaluation of the mandates system.[221] Falk has provided an acute and balanced assessment of the mandates system as a "holding operation" that delayed decolonization while at the same time providing a contrary impetus towards its realization.[222]

During the interwar years a wide range of organizations were active in promoting human rights.[223] It is important to note the philosophical diversity of these organizations, countering the notion that such initiatives were exclusively European or Western. Human rights organizations included the *Ligue pour la défense des droits de l'homme*, the *Deutsche Liga für Menschenrechte* (which was linked with fourteen other human rights leagues), the *Fédération internationale des droits de l'homme* (which had a representative from China) and the China League for Civil Rights. A number of intellectuals pressed the cause of human rights through existing professional and scholarly societies and created other bodies to further that cause. The Chilean Alvarez, the Russians Mandelstam and Mirkine-Guetzévitch, the Greek Frangulis and the Englishman H. G. Wells were among them.[224]

The International Law Institute commissioned Mandelstam to carry out a study of minorities' human rights, and of human rights generally, in 1921. The International Diplomatic Academy (founded in 1926) established a commission to study human rights, and passed an important resolution in November 1928, which was endorsed by the International Federation of Leagues for the Defense of the Rights of Man and of the Citizen on November 11, 1931. The resolution supported the generalization of rights under the minorities regime to all persons, and a global convention on human rights under the aegis of the League. The International Law Institute produced a Declaration of the International Rights of Man. This declaration referred to every state's duty to recognize the equal right of every individual on its territory to life, liberty, property, freedom of religion and the right to use their native tongue. The French League of Human Rights drafted a Complement to the Declaration of the Rights of Man and of the Citizen (July 1936) that reflected socialist principles. The International Union of Associations for the League of Nations passed a resolution in favour of the general protection of human rights and of humanitarian intervention. It also drew attention to the League's responsibility to respond to the violation of Jews' human rights in Germany.[225]

In addition to these organizations were individuals and bodies concentrating their human rights activism on issues of race, anticolonialism and slavery. Mohandas Gandhi and Jawaharlal Nehru in India, Sukarno in the Dutch East Indies (now Indonesia), and Ho Chi Minh in Vietnam, for example, sought the liberation of their respective lands from colonial rule. The "Colored International," founded in 1925, sought to end racial discrimination in the immigration policies of "white nations." It included representatives from Japan, China, India, the Philippines, East Indies, the Malay states, Egypt and Turkey. W. E. B. Du Bois and Marcus Garvey were key figures in a number of organizations that sought to hold various countries to account for their abuse of people of colour, and which established links with countries such as Liberia and Ethiopia. The Pan-African Association, the Universal Negro Improvement Association and the African Communities League were also active organizations.[226]

The latter two bodies announced proudly that they represented "six million members scattered in Africa, the West Indies, South and Central America, North America, Europe, and Asia." Their Petition of the Negro Race (May 23, 1923) declared that

> [T]he four hundred million Negroes of the world are no longer disposed to hold themselves as serfs, peons, and slaves, but that it is their intention to look forward to the higher benefits of human liberty, human rights, and true democracy.[227]

The NAACP's Harvard-educated lawyer Moorfield Story "felt the Negroes were being badly treated, denied the equal chance that every human being ought to have ..." Du Bois declared that "Racial slander must go. Racial prejudice will follow. Steadfast humanity must come. The domination of one people by another ... be the subject people black or white, must stop." "We have got to help make a world where there will be less kicking around," implored the NAACP's Roy Wilkins, and "where a man won't be lynched because he is black [or] beaten and spat upon because he is a Jew ..." The "job" of making this world a reality, he urged, was "not for one color, one race [or] one nation ... [but] for all men ... who want a voice in shaping the kind of world in which we must live." Other entreaties to the League on the question of racial inequality came from Australasia, France, India, Cuba and North America.[228] But little assistance was forthcoming from most League members. The League was deaf to the grievances of Garvey, Maori leader T. W. Ratana and the Iroquois leader Deskaheh.

And there was a Western boycott of the ILO's International Emigration Commission because of the relatively strong influence anticipated from Japan, China and India.[229]

The League continued to chip away at the institution of slavery in all its evil incarnations. Mandatories, for instance, were obliged under the covenant to outlaw slavery in their respective territories, and treaties were concluded in the British, French and Belgian territories to this end. The League also created a Temporary Slavery Commission, which investigated slavery practices and reported to the council of the League. Finally, in 1926, the International Convention on the Abolition of Slavery and the Slave Trade was drafted. Signatories were obliged to end slavery and forced labour in all its varieties within their territories. Other lesser abuses of worker rights were addressed by the new ILO, which developed a Labor Charter. This charter began to outline the dimensions of a decent standard of living (such as the eight-hour day and an end to child labour), as well as the rights of association and equal pay for women.[230]

The Health Organization of the League of Nations built on concerns related to a better standard of living by seeking to address the quality of water, sewerage and sanitation infrastructure and services, and housing in the world. Achieving progress in these areas was vital to realizing a "right of all people" to a "minimum level of decent health." The ILO and the International Federation of Trade Unions also concerned themselves with these critical domains.[231]

The interwar years also saw efforts to improve the conditions of life for women, children and refugees. Apart from NGOs such as the Women's International League for Peace and Freedom, *Association féminine internationale*, *Union internationale des ligues féminines catholiques*, and the International Woman Suffrage Alliance, there were important conferences in the Americas relating to women and human rights: for example, the Fifth Conference of the American Republics (Santiago, Chile, 1923) and their 1928 conference at which the Inter-American Commission on Women (1928) was created. The Inter-American Commission passed the Lima Declaration in Favor of Women's Rights and endorsed a Defense of Human Rights document calling for equality of civil and political as well as employment rights. Women were able to take part in the council, assembly, commissions and secretariat of the League of Nations. And the League supported a study on the protection of the human rights of women at the "joint request" of delegations of women from Argentina, Bolivia, Cuba, the Dominican Republic, Haiti, Honduras, Mexico, Panama, Peru and Uruguay. The study made use of reports from Africa, the Americas, Asia, Europe, and the Pacific.[232] The League's Advisory Committee for Child Welfare directed its efforts towards early infant health, starvation, homelessness, orphans and "illegitimacy." In 1924, a Declaration of the Rights of the Child was signed by 50 nations.[233] In relation to refugees, Red Cross and Red Crescent societies sought to assist these vulnerable persons with food, clothes, shelter, healthcare and employment.[234]

The League of Nations found in favour of Franz Bernheim, a German Jew, over his 1933 complaint under one of the minorities treaties regarding his discriminatory dismissal under anti-Semitic Nazi laws. But in November 1938 Nazis beat and killed Jews and attacked synagogues and Jewish businesses across Germany and Austria. That the League only responded weakly to *Kristallnacht* did not augur well for the human rights of Jews across Europe. Consistent with this weakness, Switzerland, Britain, the U.S.A., U.S.S.R., France, and Latin American countries were unreceptive to any significant Jewish immigration as the Nazi threat intensified.[235]

Notes

[1] P. G. Lauren, *The Evolution of International Human Rights: Visions Seen* (Philadelphia: University of Pennsylvania Press, 1998), pp. 1, 2, 5. See also: S. K. Murumba, "The Cultural and Conceptual Basis of Human Rights Norms in International Law," Ph.D. thesis, Law, Monash University, Melbourne, 1986, summary of thesis (unpaginated); see also pp. 168–170, ch. 6; L. B. Sohn, "The New International Law: Protection of the Rights of Individuals Rather than States," *American Law Review*, vol. 32 (1982), no. 1, pp. 1–64, at p. 1; Sompong Sucharitkul, "A Multi-Dimensional Concept of Human Rights in International Law," *Notre Dame Law Review*, vol. 62 (1987), pp. 305–317, at p. 306; G. Best, "Whatever Happened to Human Rights," *Review of International Studies*, vol. 16 (1990), no. 1, pp. 3–18, at p. 4; K. Vasak and P. Alston (eds.), *The International Dimensions of Human Rights* (Westport, Connecticut/Paris: Greenwood Press/UNESCO, 1985; English edn.), p. xv; K. Mühlahn, "China, the West and the Question of Human Rights: A Historical Perspective," *asien*

afrika lateinamerika, vol. 24 (1996), pp. 287–303, at p. 288; K. Minogue, "The History of the Idea of Human Rights," in W. Laqueur and B. Rubin (eds.), *The Human Rights Reader*, rev. edn. (New York: Meridian/Penguin, 1990), pp. 1–17, at p. 5; C. Lavery, "The Classical Doctrine of Human Rights in International Law," Ph.D. dissertation, Department of Political Science, University of Chicago, 1950, pp. 328–329.

[2] A leading account along these lines is J. Donnelly, *Universal Human Rights in Theory and Practice* (Ithaca, New York: Cornell University Press, 1989).

[3] Lauren, *The Evolution of International Human Rights*, pp. 5–10.

[4] Id. See also Murumba, "The Cultural and Conceptual Basis of Human Rights Norms in International Law"; M. R. Ishay, *The History of Human Rights: From Ancient Times to the Globalization Era* (Berkeley: University of California Press, 2004), ch. 1; and the various contributions to I. Bloom and W. L. Proudfoot (eds.), *Religious Diversity and Human Rights* (New York: Columbia University Press, 1996) which emphasize liberal (in the broad sense), egalitarian, tolerant, compassionate and humanitarian dimensions of Judaism, Hinduism, Buddhism, Confucianism, Christianity and Islam.

[5] Murumba, "The Cultural and Conceptual Basis of Human Rights Norms in International Law," pp. 91–92, 95, 98–99, 100, 105–109, 112, 114, 170, 177, 184, 188, 190 (where he tabulates the results of his inquiry), and *passim*. On ancient India, see, further, N. Singh, "History of the Law of Nations: Regional Developments: South Asia and South-East Asia," in R. Bernhardt (ed.), *Encyclopedia of Public International Law* (Amsterdam: Max Planck-Institut/Elsevier Science B.V., 1995), vol. 2, pp. 824–839. On China, see, for example, Wang Tieya, "International Law in China: Historical and Contemporary Perspectives," in *Recueil des Cours de l'Académie du droit international de la Haye* (hereinafter *Rd.C.*), vol. 221, 1990/II, pp. 195–369. On Africa, see, for example, T. O. Elias, *Africa and the Development of International Law*, second rev. edn., by R. Akinjide (Boston: Martinus Nijhoff, 1988); F. C. Okoye, *International Law and the New African States* (London: Sweet and Maxwell, 1972); and Y. Makonnen, *International Law and the New States of Africa* (New York/Addis Ababa: Ethiopian National Agency for UNESCO, 1983). For a critical account of "Islamist" human rights instruments in certain states, see A. E. Mayer, *Islam and Human Rights: Traditions and Politics* (Boulder, Colorado: Westview Press, 1991).

[6] Murumba, "The Cultural and Conceptual Basis of Human Rights Norms in International Law," p. 188.

[7] K. Sellars, *The Rise and Rise of Human Rights* (Phoenix Mill: Sutton Publishing, 2002), pp. vii–viii.

[8] E. Pagels, "The Roots and Origins of Human Rights," in A. H. Henkin (ed.), *Human Dignity: The Internationalization of Human Rights* (Dobbs Ferry, New York: Oceana Publications, 1979), pp. 1–8.

[9] Ibid., and especially p. 4 (from which page the quotation is taken). See also Bloom and Proudfoot (eds.), *Religious Diversity and Human Rights.*

[10] See Lavery, "The Classical Doctrine of Human Rights in International Law," especially at p. 334.

[11] S. Buckle, "Natural Law," in P. Singer (ed.), *A Companion to Ethics* (Oxford: Blackwell, 1999), pp. 161–162, and *passim.*

[12] Ibid., p. 162 (quoting Aristotle's *Nicomachean Ethics*).

[13] Lauren, *The Evolution of International Human Rights*, p. 12. See also Ishay, *The History of Human Rights*, p. 23.

[14] Lauren, *The Evolution of International Human Rights*, p. 12.

[15] Buckle, "Natural Law," pp. 162–164; Lauren, *The Evolution of International Human Rights*, pp. 12–13.

[16] Quoted in Buckle, "Natural Law," p. 164.

[17] Lauren, *The Evolution of International Human Rights*, p. 13.

[18] Ibid., pp. 12–13.

[19] Ibid., p. 13. On Confucianism, see Lauren, *The Evolution of International Human Rights*, pp. 6–7, 10.

[20] Ibid., p. 13. On Augustine, see, further, J. Haldane, "Medieval and Renaissance Ethics," in Singer (ed.), *A Companion to Ethics*, pp. 133–146, at pp. 135–138.

[21] See M. Davies, *Asking the Law Question: The Dissolution of Legal Theory*, second edn. (Sydney: Lawbook Co., 2002), pp. 77–79; Buckle, "Natural Law," pp. 165–166; J. W. Harris, *Legal Philosophies* (London: Butterworths, 1990), ch. 2; R. George, "Natural Law and International Order," in D. R. Mapel and T. Nardin (eds.), *International Society: Diverse Ethical Perspectives* (Princeton: Princeton University Press, 1998), ch. 3 (especially pp. 62–64, on *determinatio*); M. Charlesworth, "Augustine and Aquinas: Church and State," in D. Muschamp (ed.), *Political Thinkers* (South Melbourne, Victoria: Macmillan, 1986), pp. 43–50; R. Cotterrell, "The Appeal of Natural Law," in R. Cotterrell, *The Politics of Jurisprudence* (London: Butterworths, 1989), ch. 5; B. Bix, "Natural law theory," in D. Patterson (ed.), *A Companion to Philosophy of Law and Legal Theory* (Oxford: Blackwell, 1996), pp. 223–240.

[22] Lauren, *The Evolution of International Human Rights*, p. 13.

[23] Ibid., p. 314, note 90. See, generally, Lauren, *The Evolution of International Human Rights*, pp. 62–71.

[24] See, generally, Lavery, "The Classical Doctrine of Human Rights in International Law," especially chs. 1, 2 and 4 (especially pp. 55, 56, 68, 90 and 92–93. The quotations from Suarez's writings come from pp. 55, 56). See also Lauren, *The Evolution of International Human Rights*, pp. 29, 63. I also rely here on Ishay, *The History of Human Rights*, p. 99; and R. Tuck, *The Rights of War and Peace: Political Thought and the International Order from Grotius to Kant* (Oxford: Oxford University Press, 1999), pp. 9, 16–17.

[25] Lavery, "The Classical Doctrine of Human Rights in International Law," pp. 10–11.

[26] Ibid., pp. 11–13.

[27] Vitoria, quoted in ibid., p. 13.

[28] Lavery, "The Classical Doctrine of Human Rights in International Law," p. 15.

[29] Ibid., p. 20; and pp. 19–20.

[30] Vitoria, quoted in ibid., p. 25.

[31] Vitoria, quoted in ibid., p. 28.

[32] Lavery, "The Classical Doctrine of Human Rights in International Law," p. 39.

[33] Ibid., p. 104.

[34] Buckle, "Natural Law," pp. 167–168.

[35] Ibid. For somewhat differing accounts of Grotius' secular natural law theory, see P. Malanczuk, *Akehurst's Modern Introduction to International Law*, seventh edn. (London: Routledge, 1997), p. 16; R. Piotrowicz and S. Kaye, *Human Rights in International and Australian Law* (Chatswood, N.S.W.: Butterworths, 2000), p. 12. Cf. Samuel Pufendorf's "equality of right" of all men, based on a common possession of reason – see Lavery, "The Classical Doctrine of Human Rights in International Law," pp. 169–170, 172; and ch. v.

[36] Quoted in W. J. Bajor, "Discussing 'Human Rights': An Anthropological Exposition on 'Human Rights' Discourse," Ph.D thesis, Department of Social Anthropology, University of St. Andrews, Scotland, 1997, p. 27.

[37] Quoted in Lavery, "The Classical Doctrine of Human Rights in International Law," pp. 119–120; and see ch. v.

[38] Ibid., ch. v.

[39] Lauren, *The Evolution of International Human Rights*, pp. 14–15; and pp. 14–28, 28–36. The characterization of natural rights and constitutionalism in this section has been influenced by: T. Blackshield and G. Williams, *Australian*

Constitutional Law and Theory: Commentary and Materials, third edn. (Sydney: The Federation Press, 2002), chs. 1 and 2; P. Parkinson, *Tradition and Change in Australian Law* (Sydney: Law Book Company, 1994); M. Forsyth and M. Keens-Soper (eds.), *The Political Classics: A Guide to the Essential Texts from Plato to Rousseau* (Oxford: Oxford University Press, 1988, 1992); Muschamp (ed.), *Political Thinkers*; J. A. Camilleri and J. Falk, *The End of Sovereignty? The Politics of a Shrinking and Fragmenting World* (Aldershot: Edward Elgar, 1992); and by readers collated by the author (in conjunction with his colleagues) for the course BLB1118 Constitutional Law, Victoria University, Melbourne, Australia. The quotations come from Lauren, *The Evolution of International Human Rights*, pp. 14–15. On Bodin, see also Lauren, *The Evolution of International Human Rights*, pp. 26–27. See also D. Zarat, "Tradition, Human Rights, and the English Revolution," in J. N. Wasserstrom, L. Hunt, and M. B. Young (eds.), *Human Rights and Revolutions* (Lanham, Maryland: Rowman and Littlefield, 2000), pp. 43–58, especially at pp. 43–46.

[40] Lauren, *The Evolution of International Human Rights*, p. 15.

[41] Kant, quoted in T. Dunne, "Liberalism," in J. Baylis and S. Smith (eds.), *The Globalization of World Politics: An Introduction to International Relations* (Oxford: Oxford University Press, 1997), p. 150.

[42] B. Weston, "Human Rights," *Human Rights Quarterly*, vol. 6 (1984), no. 3, pp. 257–283, at p. 259.

[43] Lauren, *The Evolution of International Human Rights,* pp. 15–16. See also Weston, "Human Rights"; Ishay, *The History of Human Rights*, pp. 81, 110.

[44] Quoted in Lauren, *The Evolution of International Human Rights*, p. 16.

[45] Weston, "Human Rights," p. 259.

[46] Lauren, *The Evolution of International Human Rights*, p. 16; Ishay, *The History of Human Rights*, pp. 87, 113.

[47] Lauren, *The Evolution of International Human Rights*, pp. 25, 29, 30; P. G. Lauren, *Power and Prejudice: The Politics and Diplomacy of Racial Discrimination*, second edn. (Boulder, Colorado: Westview, 1996), pp. 17, 22–23. See also Mühlahn, "China, the West and the Question of Human Rights," p. 290; and M. Svensson, *The Chinese Conception of Human Rights: The Debate on Human Rights in China, 1898-1949* (Lund, Sweden: Lund University Press, 1996), pp. 47–48 (on rights theorists who have used the idea of rights to "defend the absolute state and endorse slavery"). On the paradoxes of the French Revolution and human rights, see, further, L. Hunt, "The Paradoxical

Origins of Human Rights," in Wasserstrom, Hunt and Young (eds.), *Human Rights and Revolutions*, pp. 3–17.

[48] H. Lauterpacht, *International Law and Human Rights* (London: Stevens and Sons, 1950; reprinted Hamden, Connecticut: Archon Books, 1968), p. 88.

[49] S. Davidson, *Human Rights* (Buckingham: Open University Press, 1993), p. 4; Lauren, *The Evolution of International Human Rights*, p. 17.

[50] Quoted in Lauren, *The Evolution of International Human Rights*, p. 17. For the influence of John Locke, and of the natural law and natural rights traditions, on the American Revolution, see eminent historian Michael Zuckert's "Natural Rights in the American Revolution: The American Amalgam," in Wasserstrom, Hunt and Young (eds.), *Human Rights and Revolutions*, pp. 59–76 (see pp. 60–61 for a useful discussion of rights provisions in American colonial constitutions).

[51] Davidson, *Human Rights*, p. 3.

[52] Weston, "Human Rights," p. 259 (the quotation comes from this page); Ishay, *The History of Human Rights*, p. 80.

[53] Davidson, *Human Rights*, p. 3.

[54] Ibid., p. 4. See, further, "Bill of Rights (Virginia)," in Baron F. M. Van Asbeck (ed.), *The Universal Declaration of Human Rights and Its Predecessors (1679–1948)* (Leiden: Brill, 1949), pp. 33–36.

[55] Lauren, *Power and Prejudice*, pp. 35, 36; Lauren, *The Evolution of International Human Rights*, p. 31.

[56] One should also note the importance of Thomas Paine's *Rights of Man* (1791–1792) which popularized the notion of human rights for the English working class – N. O'Neill and R. Handley, *Retreat from Injustice: Human Rights in Australian Law* (Annandale, NSW: The Federation Press, 1994), p. 8; and Lauren, *The Evolution of International Human Rights*, pp. 15–22 (especially at p. 20, where he notes that Paine "introduced the specific expression 'human rights,' perhaps for the first time"). According to Svensson, *The Chinese Conception of Human Rights*, p. 51, Paine also developed something of a notion of "welfare rights." See also Lauren, *The Evolution of International Human Rights*, pp. 15–22, 307 (note 67).

[57] Davidson, *Human Rights*, p. 4.

[58] Weston, "Human Rights," pp. 259–260. See also Lauren, *The Evolution of International Human Rights*, pp. 15–20.

[59] Davidson, *Human Rights*, p. 5 (the quotation comes from this page); Weston, "Human Rights," p. 260.

[60] Quoted in Davidson, *Human Rights*, p. 5. See also Weston, "Human Rights," p. 260.

[61] Weston, "Human Rights," p. 260.

[62] Davidson, *Human Rights*, p. 5.

[63] Id.

[64] Lauren, *The Evolution of International Human Rights*, p. 18.

[65] C. Wright, "Revolution, Emancipation, and the State Definition of Human Status," *History of European Ideas*, vol. II (1989), pp. 51–82, at p. 56.

[66] Lauren, *The Evolution of International Human Rights*, pp. 30–32; Wright, "Revolution, Emancipation, and the State Definition of Human Status," p. 62; Lauren, *Power and Prejudice*, pp. 20–25.

[67] Wright, "Revolution, Emancipation, and the State Definition of Human Status," pp. 71, 62, and *passim*.

[68] Lauren, *The Evolution of International Human Rights*, p. 32 (the quotation comes from this page); Ishay, *The History of Human Rights*, pp. 96, 110.

[69] H. Schröder, "The Declaration of Human and Civil Rights for Women (Paris, 1791) by Olympe de Gouges," *History of European Ideas*, vol. II (1989), pp. 263–271, at pp. 265–266; Hunt, "The Paradoxical Origins of Human Rights," p. 12.

[70] Schröder, "The Declaration of Human and Civil Rights for Women (Paris, 1791) by Olympe de Gouges," p. 266; Hunt, "The Paradoxical Origins of Human Rights," p. 11–12; Ishay, *The History of Human Rights*, pp. 106, 110–112, 328.

[71] Schröder, "The Declaration of Human and Civil Rights for Women (Paris, 1791) by Olympe de Gouges," p. 266 (emphasis in original).

[72] Quoted in Lauren, *The Evolution of International Human Rights*, p. 18.

[73] Quoted in Schröder, "The Declaration of Human and Civil Rights for Women (Paris, 1791) by Olympe de Gouges," p. 267. See also Lauren, *The Evolution of International Human Rights*, pp. 18, 32.

[74] Quoted in Schröder, "The Declaration of Human and Civil Rights for Women (Paris, 1791) by Olympe de Gouges," pp. 268–269 (emphasis in original).

[75] Schröder, "The Declaration of Human and Civil Rights for Women (Paris, 1791) by Olympe de Gouges," p. 269.

[76] Quoted in id.

[77] Lavery, "The Classical Doctrine of Human Rights in International Law", p. 319; and table on p. 318.

[78] Ibid., p. 324; and pp. 316–338.

[79] Ibid., p. 326; 329–338; 334–335 (the quotations come from pp. 326 and 334–335 respectively).

[80] Lauren, *The Evolution of International Human Rights*, p. 38.

[81] Ibid., p. 39.

[82] Id.

[83] Lauren, *The Evolution of International Human Rights*, pp. 40–42.

[84] Ibid., pp. 42–43.

[85] Ibid., pp. 43–45.

[86] Ibid., p. 45.

[87] Ibid., pp. 63, 15; Tuck, *The Rights of War and Peace*, p. 191.

[88] Vattel, quoted in Lauren, *The Evolution of International Human Rights*, p. 63.

[89] Lauren, *The Evolution of International Human Rights*, pp. 64, 314 (note 90).

[90] Ibid., p. 64.

[91] Ibid., p. 69.

[92] Ibid., p. 69, 63.

[93] Weston, "Human Rights," p. 270.

[94] Lauren, *The Evolution of International Human Rights*, pp. 65–68.

[95] E. C. Stowell, *Intervention in International Law* (1921), extracted in Laqueur and Rubin (eds.), *The Human Rights Reader*, p. 173; M. Koskenniemi, *The Gentle Civilizer of Nations: The Rise and Fall of International Law, 1870–1960* (Cambridge: Cambridge University Press, 2002), pp. 12, 17, 30, 40, 46–47.

[96] Stowell, *Intervention in International Law* (1921), extracted in Laqueur and Rubin (eds.), *The Human Rights Reader*, p. 172.

[97] E. Borchard, quoted in ibid., p. 74. See also L. B. Sohn, "The New International Law: Protection of the Rights of Individuals Rather than States," pp. 4–5; D. McGoldrick, *The Human Rights Committee: Its Role in the Development of the International Covenant on Civil and Political Rights* (Oxford: Clarendon Press, 1991), p. 3.

[98] See K. J. Partsch, "Individuals in International Law," in Bernhardt (ed.), *Encyclopedia of Public International Law*, pp. 957–962, especially at p. 958; M. Shaw, *International Law*, fourth edn. (Cambridge: Cambridge University Press, 1997), pp. 182–183; Malanczuk, *Akehurst's Modern Introduction to International Law*, p. 100. Cf. F. S. Dunn, "The International Rights of Individuals," *Proceedings of the American Society of International Law* (1941) (April 25), pp. 14–22 (including discussion), at pp. 14–15.

[99] Weston, "Human Rights," p. 261; M. D. A. Freeman, *Lloyd's Introduction to Jurisprudence*, seventh edn. (London: Sweet and Maxwell, 2001), pp. 905–906.

[100] Quoted in Weston, "Human Rights," p. 261; A. Bullock and S. Trombley (eds.), *The New Fontana Dictionary of Modern Thought*, third edn. (London: Harper Collins, 2000), pp. 94, 412.

[101] Malanczuk, *Akehurst's Modern Introduction to International Law*, p. 91.

[102] Quoted in R. Higgins, "Conceptual Thinking about the Individual in International Law," *British Journal of International Studies*, vol. 4 (April 1978), no. 1, pp. 1–19, at p. 2 (note 2). See also Koskenniemi, *The Gentle Civilizer of Nations*, p. 240.

[103] L. Oppenheim, *International Law: A Treatise* (1912), Sections 288, 290, extracted in Laqueur and Rubin (eds.), *The Human Rights Reader*, pp. 164–165.

[104] On individuals as "objects" of international law, see: Lauren, *The Evolution of International Human Rights*, p. 27; Davidson, *Human Rights*, p. 7; H. Lauterpacht, "The Subject of the Law of Nations," 63 *Law Quarterly Review* (October 1947), pp. 438–460, at pp. 439–440; A. V. Freeman "Response [to F. S. Dunn]," *Proceedings of the American Society of International Law*, (1941) (April 25), pp. 19–20.

[105] Oppenheim, *International Law: A Treatise* (1912), extracted in Laqueur and Rubin (eds.), *The Human Rights Reader*, pp. 164–165.

[106] Ibid., p. 169.

[107] Partsch, "Individuals in International Law," p. 958. See also E. I. Hambro, attributing to G. Scelle the view "that individuals and individuals only are subjects of international law" – quoted in E. I. Hambro, "Individuals before International Tribunals," *Proceedings of the American Society of International Law*, (1941), pp. 23–29 (including discussion), at p. 23.

[108] Malanczuk, *Akehurst's Modern Introduction to International Law*, p. 91.

[109] J. Driscoll, "The Development of Human Rights in International Law," extracted in Laqueur and Rubin (eds.), *The Human Rights Reader*, p. 41. To similar effect, see: Shaw, *International Law*, p. 200; Lauren, *The Evolution of International Human Rights*, pp. 26–27; Oppenheim, *International Law: A Treatise* (1912), Sections 288, 290 extracted in Laqueur and Rubin (eds.), *The Human Rights Reader*, p. 197; T. J. Farer, "The United Nations and Human Rights: More than a Whimper," in R. P. Claude and B. H. Weston (eds.), *Human Rights in the World Community: Issues and Action* (Philadelphia: University of Pennsylvania Press, 1989), pp. 194–206, at p. 194; Freeman, "Response [to Dunn]", p. 19.

[110] Shaw, *International Law*, pp. 184, 200–202, 423, 470.

[111] Ibid., p. 184. See also Shaw, *International Law*, pp. 200–202, 423, 470.

[112] Ibid., pp. 204, 470–474; and see also pp. 212–215.

[113] Dunn, "The International Rights of Individuals," pp. 15–16. See also Borchard, "Historical Background of International Protection of Human Rights," pp. 112–117, especially at p. 113.

[114] Shaw, *International Law*, p. 183.

[115] See, for example, Lauterpacht, "The Subjects of the Law of Nations," pp. 438–460 and especially at pp. 440–441, 450–459; Higgins, "Conceptual Thinking about the Individual in International Law."

[116] Higgins, "Conceptual Thinking about the Individual in International Law," pp. 3–6.

[117] H. Lauterpacht, "Revision of Oppenheim," extracted in Laqueur and Rubin (eds.), *The Human Rights Reader*, p. 168.

[118] On the progressively inclusive nature of human rights, see, further, generally, Ishay, *The History of Human Rights*. On the important links between recognition, personality and human dignity, see, generally, J. Glover, *Humanity: A Moral History of the Twentieth Century* (London: Jonathan Cape, 1999); E. Brems, *Human Rights: Universality and Diversity* (The Hague: Martinus Nijhoff Publishers/Kluwer Law International, 2001), pp. 328–331 (discussing philosopher Charles Taylor's work on recognition). For further treatments of the status of individuals under international law, see: P. Alston, "The 'Not-a-Cat' Syndrome: Can the International Human Rights Regime Accommodate Non-State Actors?," in P. Alston (ed.), *Non-state Actors and Human Rights* (Oxford: Oxford University Press, 2005), ch. 1, especially at pp. 17–20; F. Volio, "Legal Personality, Privacy, and the Family," in L. Henkin (ed.), *The International Bill of Rights: The Covenant on Civil and Political Rights* (New York: Columbia University Press, 1981), ch. 8, especially pp. 185–188; P. Sieghart, *The International Law of Human Rights* (Oxford: Oxford University Press, 1983), pp. 10–13, 15, 17, 18; T. Meron, *The Humanization of International Law* (Leiden/Boston: Martinus Nijhoff, 2006), pp. 315–316 (on the present-day acceptance by some international legal scholars of individuals as *subjects*).

[119] Farer, "The United Nations and Human Rights: More than a Whimper," p. 194; Lauren, *The Evolution of International Human Rights*, pp. 27, 314 (note 88), Davidson, *Human Rights*, p. 8; Sohn, "The New International Law"; Freeman, "Response [to Dunn]," p. 19.

[120] Oppenheim, *International Law: A Treatise* (1912), Section 291, extracted in Laqueur and Rubin (eds.), *The Human Rights Reader*, p. 166 (emphasis added).

[121] Id. See also Freeman, "Response [to Dunn]," p. 19. On the present-day status of the stateless, see Malanczuk, *Akehurst's Modern Introduction to International Law*, p. 24.

[122] Malanczuk, *Akehurst's Modern Introduction to International Law*, pp. 256, 260. See also Davidson, *Human Rights*, pp. 7-8.

[123] Malanczuk, *Akehurst's Modern Introduction to International Law*, pp. 256–257, 261.

[124] Ibid., p. 257; see also pp. 258–260.

[125] Ibid., p. 257; see also, pp. 263, 267–268; Sohn, "The New International Law," p. 4.

[126] Malanczuk, *Akehurst's Modern Introduction to International Law*, p. 270 (discussing Articles 6, 10(2) of the Draft Articles on State Responsibility, 1980).

[127] J. H. Burgers, "The Road to San Francisco: The Revival of the Human Rights Idea in the Twentieth Century," *Human Rights Quarterly*, vol. 14 (November 1992), no. 4, pp. 447–477, at pp. 447–448.

[128] Lauren, *The Evolution of International Human Rights*, pp. 74–75.

[129] Ibid., p. 75.

[130] Id.

[131] Id. See, further, on the human rights debate in China, J. N. Wasserstrom, "The Chinese Revolution and Contemporary Paradoxes," in Wasserstrom, Hunt and Young (eds.), *Human Rights and Revolutions*, pp. 19–40, especially at p. 23.

[132] Lauren, *The Evolution of International Human Rights Visions Seen*, p. 76.

[133] Id.

[134] Oppenheim, *International Law: A Treatise* (1912), Section 292, extracted in Laqueur and Rubin (eds.), *The Human Rights Reader*, p. 167.

[135] Lauren, *The Evolution of International Human Rights*, pp. 75–76.

[136] Ibid., pp. 77–78; see also pp. 110, 128; J. Rosenberg, *How Far the Promised Land? World Affairs and the American Civil Rights Movement from the First World War to Vietnam* (Princeton: Princeton University Press, 2006), pp. 22, 92–94.

[137] Lauren, *The Evolution of International Human Rights*, p. 78.

[138] A. Williams, *Failed Imagination? New World Orders of the Twentieth Century* (Manchester: Manchester University Press, 1998), pp. 4, 7, 22.

[139] Ibid., pp. 4, 22.

[140] Ibid., p. 33.

[141] Ibid., pp. 32–34.

[142] Burgers, "The Road to San Francisco," pp. 450–451.

[143] E. H. Carr, *The Twenty Years' Crisis: 1919–1939: An Introduction to the Study of International Relations*, second edn. (London: Macmillan, 1946; reprinted 1954, 1962), pp. 154, 155 and footnote 1, p. 155 (emphasis added).

[144] Ibid., p. 136.

[145] Id.

[146] Carr, *The Twenty Years' Crisis*, pp. 136, 131; S. Robson, *The First World War* (London and New York: Longman, 1998), pp. 9, 37–39; Glover, *Humanity*, pp. 64–66, 69, 77–79, 95.

[147] Robson, *The First World War*, p. 37; Glover, *Humanity*, pp. 64–66.

[148] Glover, *Humanity*, pp. 64–66.

[149] Robson, *The First World War*, pp. 37–39. See also Carr, *The Twenty Years' Crisis*, p. 131 ("Blockade in time of war may cause as much suffering as a series of air raids.").

[150] Lauren, *The Evolution of International Human Rights*, pp. 84–85; see also pp. 82–92. On the segregation of, discrimination toward, and other mistreatment of black soldiers in the U.S. army during World War I, see Rosenberg, *How Far the Promised Land?*, pp. 52, 58–60.

[151] Burgers, "The Road to San Francisco," p. 449. The requirement of "just treatment" of native inhabitants was to be found in Article 23 of the Covenant – Burgers, "The Road to San Francisco," p. 449.

[152] See, generally, Bass, *Stay the Hand of Vengeance: The Politics of War Crimes Tribunals* (Princeton: Princeton University Press, 2000). See also Lauren, *The Evolution of International Human Rights*, pp. 87, 94.

[153] In surveying this regime, I have drawn principally on the following sources: Williams, *Failed Imagination?*, especially pp. 4, 7–8, 22, 33–52; Pablo de Azcárate, "Protection of Minorities and Human Rights," *The Annals of the American Academy of Political and Social Science*, vol. 243 (January 1946), pp. 124–128; M. G. Johnson, "The Contributions of Eleanor and Franklin Roosevelt to the Development of International Protection for Human Rights," *Human Rights Quarterly*, vol. 9 (1987), no. 1, pp. 19–48, especially pp. 19–20; Lauren, *Power and Prejudice*, especially pp. 118–126; Burgers, "The Road to San Francisco," especially pp. 449–450; J. Donnelly, "Human Rights: A New Standard of Civilization?," *International Affairs*, vol. 74 (1998), no. 1, pp. 1–24, at pp. 10–11; I. Brownlie, *Principles of Public International Law*, fourth edn. (Oxford: Clarendon Press, 1990), pp. 565–566, and ch. xxiv; H. Tolley, Jr., *The U.N. Commission on Human Rights* (Boulder, Colorado: Westview, 1987), p. 2; Lauren, *The Evolution of International Human Rights*, pp. 94–95,

115–116, 126–127; Weston, "Human Rights," pp. 270–271; F. Ermacora, "The Protection of Minorities Before the United Nations," in *Rd.C.*, vol. 182, 1983/IV, pp. 257–370, especially at pp. 258–263; H. J. Steiner and P. Alston, *International Human Rights in Context: Law, Politics, Morals: Text and Materials*, second edn. (Oxford: Oxford University Press, 2000), pp. 93–96, 112; R. P. Anand, "Sovereign Equality of States in International Law," in *Rd.C.*, vol. 197, 1986/II, pp. 17–228, at pp. 80–91; R. A. Falk, *Human Rights Horizons: The Pursuit of Justice in a Globalizing World* (London/New York: Routledge, 2000), pp. 97–125; S. Carruthers, "International History 1900–1945," in J. Baylis and S. Smith (eds.), *The Globalization of World Politics: An Introduction to International Relations* (Oxford: Oxford University Press, 1997), pp. 49–69, especially at pp. 54–55; Shaw, *International Law*, pp. 218–219.

[154] See Steiner and Alston, *International Human Rights in Context*, pp. 93–94.

[155] Id. See also Lauren, *The Evolution of International Human Rights*, p. 94; Azcárate, "Protection of Minorities and Human Rights," p. 124; Shaw, *International Law*, p. 218.

[156] See Williams, *Failed Imagination?*; Anand, "Sovereign Equality of States in International Law"; Falk, *Human Rights Horizons*; Steiner and Alston, *International Human Rights in Context*; Johnson, "The Contributions of Eleanor and Franklin Roosevelt to the Development of International Protection of Human Rights."

[157] Steiner and Alston, *International Human Rights in Context*, pp. 93–94.

[158] Burgers, "The Road to San Francisco," pp. 449–450; Lauren, *Power and Prejudice*, pp. 119–122; Lauren, *The Evolution of International Human Rights*, p. 115; Falk, *Human Rights Horizons*, pp. 104–105, 257.

[159] See Steiner and Alston, *International Human Rights in Context*, pp. 94–95; Donnelly, "Human Rights," p. 11; Lauren, *The Evolution of International Human Rights*, p. 115.

[160] Burgers, "The Road to San Francisco," p. 450. Tolley, Jr. (*The U.N. Commission on Human Rights*, p. 2) makes an overstatement claiming that the regime provided "comprehensive human rights norms and supervisory machinery." Cf. Azcárate ("Protection of Minorities and Human Rights," p. 124; see also pp. 125–127) who argued that the regime was a "precedent for the establishment of an international statute of human rights."

[161] Lauren, *The Evolution of International Human Rights*, p. 115; Ermacora, "The Protection of Minorities before the United Nations," p. 259; Azcárate, "Protection of Minorities and Human Rights," pp. 125–126; Davidson, *Human*

Rights, p. 11; P. Thornberry, "Self-Determination, Minorities, Human Rights: A Review of International Instruments," in C. Ku and P. F. Diehl (eds.), *International Law: Classic and Contemporary Readings* (Boulder, Colorado/London: Lynne Rienner, 1998), pp. 135–153, at p. 137. The term "devolutionist" is Michael Ignatieff's – see M. Ignatieff, "Human Rights as Politics and Idolatry," in A. Gutmann (ed.), *Human Rights as Politics and Idolatry* (Princeton: Princeton University Press, 2001), pp. 3–98, at p. 30. See also Burgers, "The Road to San Francisco," p. 450; Brownlie, *Principles of Public International Law*, pp. 565–566; Tolley, Jr., *The U.N. Commission on Human Rights*, p. 2; Steiner and Alston, *International Human Rights in Context*, pp. 93–95.

[162] See, for example, Article 27, International Covenant on Civil and Political Rights (1966) (ICCPR) in Center for the Study of Human Rights, Columbia University, *Twenty-five Human Rights Documents* (New York: Columbia University, 1994), p. 23. See also Davidson, *Human Rights*, p. 11.

[163] Azcárate, "Protection of Minorities and Human Rights," pp. 126–127; Donnelly, "Human Rights," p. 10; Brownlie, *Principles of Public International Law*, pp. 565–566; Lauren, *The Evolution of International Human Rights*, p. 116 (see also pp. 114–117).

[164] Steiner and Alston, *International Human Rights in Context*, p. 94.

[165] Burgers, "The Road to San Francisco," p. 450.

[166] Shaw, *International Law*, p. 218 (note 140). For a complete list of the relevant instruments, see Ermacora, "The Protection of Minorities Before the United Nations," pp. 258–260; and the discussion in Azcárate, "Protection of Minorities and Human Rights." See also Steiner and Alston, *International Human Rights in Context*, pp. 93–96.

[167] Lauren, *The Evolution of International Human Rights*, p. 116; Steiner and Alston, *International Human Rights in Context*, pp. 95–96. On the *international* nature of obligations under the regime, see Donnelly, "Human Rights," p. 10; Brownlie, *Principles of Public International Law*, pp. 565–566; Shaw, *International Law*, p. 218.

[168] Shaw, *International Law*, p. 219.

[169] Lauren, *The Evolution of International Human Rights*, pp. 114–116, and especially at p. 116.

[170] Burgers, "The Road to San Francisco," p. 450 (Burgers here also records that the League merely "hoped" that states not bound under the regime would comply, citing the League's Assembly resolution of September 21, 1922 to that

effect); Lauren, *The Evolution of International Human Rights*, pp. 115, 127, 126, 115; Shaw, *International Law*, p. 219.

[171] Azcárate, "Protection of Minorities and Human Rights," pp. 24, 126 (the quotation is from this page); A. W. B. Simpson, *Human Rights and the End of Empire: Britain and the Genesis of the European Convention* (Oxford: Oxford University Press, 2001), p. 127. See also Lauren, *The Evolution of International Human Rights*, pp. 115, 126–127.

[172] Lauren, *Power and Prejudice*, p. 120; Burgers, "The Road to San Francisco," p. 450; Donnelly, "Human Rights," pp. 10–11.

[173] See Carr, *The Twenty Years' Crisis*. See also D. Long and P. Wilson (eds.), *Thinkers of the Twenty Years' Crisis: Inter-war Idealism Reassessed* (Oxford: Clarendon Press, 1995).

[174] Carr, *The Twenty Years' Crisis*, p. 226.

[175] See, generally, Long and Wilson (eds.), *Thinkers of the Twenty Years' Crisis*, pp. 303, 305, 306. See also W. E. Rappard, "Human Rights in Mandated Territories," *The Annals of the American Academy of Political and Social Science*, vol. 243 (January 1946), pp. 118–123, at p. 119.

[176] Rappard, "Human Rights in Mandated Territories," p. 119; Simpson, *Human Rights and the End of Empire* , p. 145 (note 194).

[177] Quoted in Carr, *The Twenty Years' Crisis*, p. 153.

[178] President Wilson, quoted in ibid., p. 234.

[179] President Wilson, quoted in Anand, "Sovereign Equality of States in International Law," p. 81.

[180] The allusion is to H. G. Wells' *The Rights of Man or What Are We Fighting For?* (London: Penguin, 1940), cited in Lauren, *The Evolution of International Human Rights*, p. 152. In a war message to congress, President Wilson said the U.S.A. would fight "for democracy, for the right of those who submit to authority to have a voice in their own governments for the rights and liberties of small nations, for a universal dominion of right by such a concert of free peoples as shall bring peace and safety to all nations and make the world itself at last free" – quoted in Anand, "Sovereign Equality of States in International Law," p. 81. In a first draft of the League of Nations Covenant, Article 1, Colonel House, one of Wilson's advisers, wrote in part that "[t]he same standards of honour and ethics shall prevail internationally and in affairs of nations as in other matters" (quoted in Carr, *The Twenty Years' Crisis,* p. 153). The clause was not included in the first document (Carr, *The Twenty Years' Crisis*, p. 153). Prime Minister Lloyd George declared on Christmas Day 1917 that "equality among nations, small as well as great, is one of the fundamental

issues the country and her Allies were fighting to establish in this war" – quoted in Anand, "Sovereign Equality of States in International Law," p. 81.

[181] Robson, *The First World War*, p. 21.

[182] C. Reus-Smit, *The Moral Purpose of the State: Culture, Social Identity, and Institutional Rationality in International Relations* (Princeton: Princeton University Press, 1999), p. 145. See also Donnelly, "Human Rights," p. 9; R. Henig, *Versailles and After: 1919–1933* (London/New York: Routledge, 1995) p. 9 (Wilson "sought to construct ... a more just and equitable system of international relations, based on clear principles of international law and centred on a universal association of nations working through agreed procedures to maintain world order.").

[183] Henig, *Versailles and After*, pp. 1, 74.

[184] Ibid., pp. 13–14.

[185] See, for example, Carr, *The Twenty Years' Crisis*, p. 104. See also Reus-Smit, *The Moral Purpose of the State*, p. 146; Williams, *Failed Imagination?*, pp. 59–60.

[186] Anand, "Sovereign Equality of States in International Law," pp. 82, 83, 84.

[187] Williams, *Failed Imagination?*, p. 60.

[188] Ibid., p. 54.

[189] Quoted in Anand, "Sovereign Equality of States in International Law," p. 85.

[190] Henig, *Versailles and After*, p. 16.

[191] Lauren, *Power and Prejudice*, pp. 118–124; Lauren, *The Evolution of International Human Rights*, pp. 100–101, 124–125, 127–128.

[192] Williams, *Failed Imagination?*, pp. 40–41, 63, 69, 190.

[193] P. G. Lauren, "First Principles of Racial Equality: History and the Politics and Diplomacy of Human Rights Provisions in the United Nations Charter," *Human Rights Quarterly*, vol. 5 (1983), no. 1, pp. 1–26 at pp. 2–3; Lauren, *Power and Prejudice*, chs. 3 and 4 and especially at p. 120; Anand, "Sovereign Equality of States in International Law"; Lauren, *The Evolution of International Human Rights*, chs. 3 and 4; Williams, *Failed Imagination?*, pp. 261–262.

[194] Confidential memorandum (1921) quoted in Lauren, "First Principles of Racial Equality," p. 3.

[195] Lauren, *Power and Prejudice*, pp. 80–81.

[196] Quoted in ibid., p. 81.

[197] Quoted in Lauren, *The Evolution of International Human Rights*, p. 101. See also M. L. Dudziak, *Cold War Civil Rights: Race and the Image of American Democracy* (Princeton: Princeton University Press, 2000), p. 7.

[198] Du Bois quoted in Dudziak, *Cold War Civil Rights*, p. 7; Rosenberg, *How Far the Promised Land?*, pp. 56–57.

[199] Quoted in Lauren, *The Evolution of International Human Rights*, p. 100.

[200] Id.

[201] Glover, *Humanity*, p. 175.

[202] The clause was proposed by Baron Makino. It is quoted in Anand, "Sovereign Equality of States in International Law," p. 89.

[203] Lauren, *The Evolution of International Human Rights*, pp. 100–101.

[204] Ibid., p. 101; Lauren, *Power and Prejudice*, pp. 94–100.

[205] Lauren, *The Evolution of International Human Rights*, p. 100.

[206] Ibid., p. 100–101; Lauren, *Power and Prejudice*, p. 89; and Lauren, *The Evolution of International Human Rights*. See also Lauren, *Power and Prejudice*, pp. 17, 22–23; Mühlahn, "China, the West and the Question of Human Rights," p. 290; Svensson, *The Chinese Conception of Human Rights*, pp. 47–48.

[207] Falk, *Human Rights Horizons*, p. 105. See, generally, on mandates, Weston, "Human Rights," pp. 270–271; Lauren, *The Evolution of International Human Rights*, pp. 102–103, 114, 117–118; Lauren, *Power and Prejudice*, pp. 104, 124–125; Williams, *Failed Imagination?*, pp. 40, 51–52; Rappard, "Human Rights in Mandated Territories," pp. 118–123; Shaw, *International Law*, p. 160; Davidson, *Human Rights*, p. 10.

[208] Quoted in Falk, *Human Rights Horizons*, pp. 104–105.

[209] Shaw, *International Law*, p. 160.

[210] Weston, "Human Rights," pp. 270–271.

[211] Shaw, *International Law*, p. 160.

[212] Falk, *Human Rights Horizons*, p. 105; Shaw, *International Law*, p. 160. The quotation is from Shaw, *International Law* (quoting Article 22 of the Covenant of the League of Nations), p. 160. Piotrowicz and Kaye, *Human Rights in International and Australian Law*, pp. 17–18.

[213] Lauren, *The Evolution of International Human Rights*, p. 102. See also Lauren, *Power and Prejudice*, pp. 104, 124. Davidson, *Human Rights*, p. 10.

[214] Falk, *Human Rights Horizons*, p. 105.

[215] Id.

[216] See Kaye and Piotrowicz, *Human Rights in International and Australian Law*, pp. 17–18; Rappard, "Human Rights in Mandated Territories."

[217] Kaye and Piotrowicz, *Human Rights in International and Australian Law*, p. 18.

[218] Lauren, *The Evolution of International Human Rights*, p. 117.

[219] Davidson, *Human Rights*, p. 10.

[220] Lauren, *The Evolution of International Human Rights*, p. 129.

[221] For instance, Lauren, ibid., p. 117–118, wrote that "the majority of members of the League sought to distance themselves from the old practice of direct, no-questions-asked, colonial annexation and abuse of native peoples by the powerful, working instead to develop a greater sense of moral responsibility for the rights of indigenous and dependent peoples wherever they might be around the world." Cf. Lauren, *The Evolution of International Human Rights*, p. 102 and Lauren, *Power and Prejudice*, pp. 104, 124.

[222] Falk, *Human Rights Horizons*, pp. 105, 103 (Falk also refers to President Wilson's failure to meet with members of anticolonial movements – see p. 105).

[223] The following account is drawn mainly from two sources: Lauren, *The Evolution of International Human Rights*, chs. 3 and 4; and Burgers, "The Road to San Francisco."

[224] Lauren, *The Evolution of International Human Rights*, pp. 108, 110–113; Burgers, "The Road to San Franciso," pp. 450–454, 464–468.

[225] Burgers, "The Road to San Francisco," pp. 450–454, 464–468; Lauren, *The Evolution of International Human Rights*, chs. 3 and 4, and especially pp. 108, 110–113. I rely principally upon Burgers' account.

[226] Lauren, *The Evolution of International Human Rights*, pp. 109–110, 128; Ishay, *The History of Human Rights*, pp. 192, 214, 219–220; Rosenberg, *How Far the Promised Land?*, pp. 83–84, 99.

[227] Lauren, *The Evolution of International Human Rights*, p. 128.

[228] Id. Story, Du Bois and Wilkins are quoted in Rosenberg, *How Far the Promised Land?*, pp. 21, 28, 119.

[229] Lauren, *The Evolution of International Human Rights*, pp. 128, 129, 135; Lauren, *Power and Prejudice*, pp. 121–125.

[230] Lauren, *The Evolution of International Human Rights*, pp. 118, 96–97.

[231] Ibid., pp. 120, 112.

[232] Ibid., pp. 106–107, 113–114, 118–119; and ch. 4.

[233] Ibid., pp. 118–120.

[234] Ibid., pp. 121–123.

[235] Ibid., pp. 131–135; Lauren, *Power and Prejudice*, pp. 132–133; Bullock and Trombley (eds.), *The New Fontana Dictionary of Modern Thought*, p. 400; Rosenberg, *How Far the Promised Land?*, p. 113; Lord Russell, *The Scourge of the Swastika: A Short History of Nazi War Crimes* (London: Cassell, 1954), pp. 226–229; E. Borgwardt, *A New Deal for the World: America's Vision for*

Human Rights (Cambridge, Massachusetts: Belknap/Harvard University Press, 2005), p. 98. See also Burgers, "The Road to San Francisco," pp. 455–459. For a fuller account of the Bernheim case, see Simpson, *Human Rights and the End of Empire*, pp. 142–143.

CHAPTER 2

World War II and its Aftermath

World War II is notorious for the massive scale of human rights violations that took place during it.[1] In addition to the Rape of Nanking leading up to the war, the sometimes appalling treatment of POWs, and of course the Holocaust, there was extensive aerial bombardment of cities where it was not possible to pretend to distinguish between civilians and combatants. The Allies' nuclear bombardments of Hiroshima and Nagasaki were the most extreme cases. But, according to one estimate, area bombing of Germany killed more than 300,000 non-combatants. A firestorm from incendiary bombs on the night of July 27, 1943 killed 40,000 people in Hamburg. And by the commencement of the area bombardment of Germany, 30,000 British had been killed by German bombing. In early 1945, a fire bombing of Tokyo killed approximately 100,000 people in one night.[2] As a matter of Allied self-interest, none of these bombardments were made part of the postwar war crimes prosecutions. The end of defeating the forces of Nazism and Fascism was thought by some to justify the use by the Allies of these extraordinary means of warfare.[3] And the German wehrmacht had no compunction in using almost unlimited means of warfare. The war is yet another demonstration of the fact that the history of international law is not a simple one of linear progress; regression is always possible. As Edwin Borchard, reflecting on the war shortly after its end expressed it:

> [T]he legal limitations thrown around war by several hundred years of practice seem to be abolished – we play havoc with established maritime law ... we drop all pretense of chivalry, we approve postwar forced labor, we annihilate the enemy country and many of its citizens ... [W]e concurrently exterminate civilians wholesale by the use of the atomic bomb.[4]

The Allies fought to defeat Nazi Germany whose leading ideologies were based on anti-Semitism and "Aryan" supremacy. There is thus considerable tragic irony in racism on the part of the Allies. Segregation in the American armed forces[5] as well as at home was perhaps the leading example of this racism, but racial stereotyping of the Japanese enemy was also ironic given that such stereotyping was the stock-in-trade of Nazi ideology. Allied attitudes on race had real consequences for the policies adopted during the war and further "coloured" Allied countries' ambivalence toward human rights and, in particular, toward any international legal recognition of the equality of races. China took up the cause of racial equality at Dumbarton Oaks and, like Japan at Versailles, left that meeting empty-handed.

The existence of a tenacious Allied racism is important because it demonstrates that the principle of equality and non-discrimination was ultimately one recognized through difficult struggle in the face of opposition that often came from Western powers such as the U.K., the U.S.A., Canada and Australia.[6] This shows that another critical aspect of human rights was not imposed by hegemonic Western states, but rather ultimately given recognition *in spite of* those states. Success in the struggle was due largely to the activism of various NGOs as well as a number of smaller states.

Rather than a simple tale of human rights emerging in response to the "outrages" of the Holocaust which "shocked the conscience" of humankind, what is more remarkable is the persistence of, for example, British and American anti-Semitism and racism during and after the war, with the images of Auschwitz, Dachau and Belsen still clear in the public mind.[7] The following examples tell of these attitudes: the turning out of port of one thousand Jewish refugees by the U.S.A., the passivity of many Christian churches amid the Holocaust, the anti-Semitism of Churchill, Stalin and many British and American officials, the Allies' prevention of the immigration of Chinese and Indians during World War II, the continued defence of the British Empire, and the internment of people of Japanese "descent" in Mexico, Canada and the U.S.A. One American draftee, in words that anticipate some of the comments of Malcolm X and Mohammed Ali in reference to the Vietnam War, summed up the absurd hypocrisies with this exasperated plea: "Just carve on my tombstone ... Here lies a black man, killed fighting a yellow man, for the protection of a white man."[8]

A particular question related to these matters of prejudice is whether the Allies did enough to respond to the persecution of Jews in Europe. Allied efforts fell well short in many ways: restrictive and discriminatory immigration systems continued to exclude Jews; asylum was often not given to Jewish escapees; serious rescue plans were not implemented; neutral states were not used as a conduit for humanitarian aid; and those who purchased so-called "exit visas" to assist Jews were even prosecuted for "trading with the enemy."[9] In February 1943 a British M.P., Eleanor Rathbone, stressed that the West could bring pressure to bear on German satellite countries in order to push them to arrange for the evacuation of Jews to "safe havens." But, according to the historian Richard Breitman, officials from the U.K. actually "feared that the Nazis *might* release large numbers of Jews" who would then be unwelcome in Britain. In contrast, in Hungary, American military action and other pressures prevented the deportation of Jews and demonstrated that such an approach could have saved many Jewish lives elsewhere.[10] Breitman's study provides further evidence of the weakness of the British and American responses to atrocities committed against Jews in Europe. By late 1941, British intelligence personnel knew of Nazi Germany's systematic killing of Jews. This knowledge came from British deciphering efforts in 1941 that revealed "dozens of open reports" of Nazi massacres under the direction of "Higher SS and Police Leaders," and conducted by "the Order Police and Waffen-SS." In February 1942 the World Jewish Congress, London, gave a long report (entitled "Jews in Nazi Europe: February 1933 to November 1941") to the British Foreign Office. The report described in detail the course of various Nazi atrocities before and in the early years of World War II. The British Ministry of Information, in its "Third Report on Jewry" (January 22, 1942) wrote that the "Germans clearly pursue a policy of extermination against the Jews ... [An official German document] states the only things Jewish that will remain in Poland will be Jewish cemeteries." British officials also had access to information about the Auschwitz concentration camp, but either failed to examine the intelligence properly or refused to believe the accounts.[11]

In the face of this kind of scepticism, a Polish Jew, Szmul Zygielbojm, who was working for the Polish National Council in London, distributed a comprehensive report on behalf of the Jewish Socialist Bund, which was operating clandestinely in Poland. The report included details of the Nazis use of *Einsatzgruppen* (travelling killing corps) in Eastern Europe, including Lithuania and Poland during the summer of 1941:

> ... men, fourteen to sixty years old, were driven to a single place, a square or a cemetery, where they were slaughtered or shot by machine guns or killed by hand grenades. They had to dig their own graves. Children in orphanages, inmates in old-age homes, the sick in hospital were shot, women were killed in the streets. In many towns the Jews were carried off to "an unknown destination" and killed in adjacent woods.

The report described the use of gas vans in Chelmno, Poland, to kill one thousand people daily during the period from the winter of 1941 to March 1942. It estimated that some 700,000 Jews had already been killed, and it demonstrated an understanding of the massive scale of Hitler's extermination plan. In that same year, a compatriot of Zygielbojm, the Jewish diplomat Jan Karski, made his way under cover, with his life in peril, into the Warsaw ghetto, and smuggled copies of documents out by secreting microfilm in a key. He cabled what he had found to the World Jewish Congress in a desperate and distraught telegram packed with abbreviated descriptions of deportations, killings of women and children and death camps. But when Karski repeated the substance of his cable in a meeting with Justice Felix Frankfurter of the U.S. Supreme Court, the only response the judge could muster was "I don't believe you."

The British and the Americans also received reliable intelligence regarding the Holocaust from U.S. embassies maintained in Berlin, Budapest, Bucharest and Vichy France. In November 1942, Rabbi Wise (a personal associate of FDR) told a press conference in Washington, D.C. that he and the State Department had credible intelligence that at least two million Jews had already been killed by the Nazi regime. But this flood of information met with incredulity, apathy, timidity and even anti-Semitic hostility on the part of the Allies. Very little was done. In a suicide note written during May 1943, despairing of the world's inaction, Zygielbojm wrote:

> Responsibility for this crime of mudering the entire Jewish population of Poland falls in the first instance on the perpetrators, but indirectly also it weighs on the whole of

humanity, the peoples and governments of the Allied states, which so far have made no effort toward a concrete action for the purpose of curtailing this crime. By passive observation of this murder of defenseless millions and of the maltreatment of children, women, and old men, these countries have become the criminals' accomplices ...

He took his own life on May 12, 1943.[12]

In July 1941 the British Ministry of Information gave advice on how the "Nazi threat" ought to be presented to the public: "[H]orror stuff [about Nazi atrocities] must be used sparingly and must deal always with treatment of indisputably innocent people. Not with violent political opponents. And not with Jews."[13] This almost seems to call into question the innocence of Jewish victims of Nazi atrocities. It strategically appeals to any anti-Semitism among the British people. The advice is further illuminated by an understanding of official British wariness of singling Jews out as a "separate people." This wariness was due to the anticipated (or imagined) foreign policy effects of doing so: including, for example, the implications for Palestine, and the possibly negative reactions of Arab leaders. There was even, ironically, the fear on the part of the British administration that mentioning the persecution of Jews would lend credence to Nazi propaganda that – in a pejorative characterization designed to appeal to anti-Semitic resentments – the Allies were really waging war "on behalf of the Jews" of the world. Pushing the interests of Jewish victims further into the background was the overriding pressure on the Allies to prevail in the war.[14] On October 18, 1943, Winston Churchill, speaking of the time devoted to postwar planning, colourfully referred to the apocryphal Mrs Glasse's "recipe for jugged hare: 'First catch your hare.'"[15] The war had to be won by the Allies first and foremost, on this view.

This motivation also proved important in undermining the ostensible mission of the U.S. War Refugee Board that FDR established in January 1944. The board was instructed to take "all measures within its [U.S.] policy to rescue victims of enemy oppression in imminent danger of death" and to give "relief and assistance consistent with successful prosecution of the war."[16] However, the War Department opposed any humanitarian commitments that might impede the goal of winning the war as soon as possible. But the Allies did at least make some declarations in 1942 concerning commitments to punish anyone who had committed atrocities during the war. On December 17, 1942, for example, there was the joint Allied Declaration Condemning the German Policy of Extermination of the Jewish Race and the denial to Jewish persons of "the most elementary human rights."[17]

A variety of scholars, activists, professional bodies, social movements and what would now be called national and international NGOs contributed to the development and defence of international human rights during World War II. Such actors made contributions in their own right as well as by responding critically to official human rights proposals and general plans for international organization, especially in the Atlantic Charter, at Dumbarton Oaks, at the San Francisco conference, and during the drafting of the Universal Declaration of Human Rights.

The English novelist, futurist, "utopian," socialist and publicist H. G. Wells wrote a letter to *The Times* on October 23, 1939, suggesting the need for the Allies to clarify their war aims, and to make human rights protection a chief outcome of any ultimate victory in the war. There was, he wrote an "extensive demand for a Statement of War Aims on the part of the young and old, who want to know more precisely what we are fighting for." British officials had until then avoided detailed statements of war aims that could, as they thought, restrict *realpolitik* and unhelpfully elevate expectations regarding the nature of international relations at war's end. Although it is true that the U.K. Foreign Secretary, Lord Halifax, had spoken vaguely in 1939 of "the rights of peoples to decide their own destinies." In conjunction with a committee of eminent citizens, including Lord Sankey (formerly the Lord Chancellor and the sole lawyer on the committee) and Norman Angell (Nobel Peace Prize winner for 1933), Wells wrote a number of articles on human rights for the English *Daily Herald* newspaper. Ultimately he wrote the book *The Rights of Man or What Are We Fighting For?*, which was distributed in some 48 countries and translated into many languages. His "Declaration of Rights" included a non-discrimination clause and various rights to freedom of speech (broadly conceived), to humane imprisonment, to freedom of movement, to protection from violence (including torture), compulsion or intimidation, and to housing, medical care, education and work. There were also rights to conscientious objection, and freedoms of discussion, association and worship. It was translated into Arabic, Esperanto, Hindi and Swahili. Wells then actively promoted these rights, contacting Franklin and

Eleanor Roosevelt, the former Czech leader Eduard Beneš (who had also been a co-founder of the *Académie diplomatique internationale* in 1926), anti-imperialist leader Jawaharlal Nehru and Mohandas Gandhi of India, and various Chinese philosophers. And in 1940 he undertook a lecture tour around the U.S.A. From these experiences, Wells learnt the importance of paying attention to the variety of philosophies in the world (and in particular to the ways in which rights and duties were related to each other) in the construction of any charter proclaiming universal human rights.[18]

In August 1940 a British War Aims Committee was established in response to growing public demand. Both Lord Halifax and Harcourt Johnstone (Secretary for the Department of Overseas Trade) developed rough statements of British war aims. Halifax wrote of "the absolute value ... of every human soul," "the moral principle of respect for personality and conscience," of the need for "equal opportunity" and of the upholding of democracy. Interestingly, Johnstone's plan set out not only the rights but also the "duties of citizens," including "the duty to give due service to the community." Surprisingly – given the much more conservative stance of most British officials – his list of rights included "the right of freedom from discrimination on the grounds of race" and, quite remarkably (in light of generally prevailing views), on the grounds of sex. Given President Roosevelt's famous "Four Freedoms" speech the following year, it is of note also that, in a paper dated December 4, 1940, Halifax spoke of "[t]he right to live without fear, either of injustice or of want," and of "[t]he social principle of individual liberty, based on equal opportunity, economic security and the rule of law."[19]

Although this book does not endorse Burgers' conclusion that before World War II "the idea of giving human rights an international status was only advocated by [*sic*] some limited circles,"[20] NGOs were certainly very active in the war. There were League of Nations Associations, the Atlantic Charter Society (London), the Movement for Federal Union, the International League for the Rights of Man, World Citizens Association, and the Commission to Study the Organization of Peace (CSOP), among others.[21] The CSOP, in its fourth report (May 1944), entitled *International Safeguard of Human Rights*, was very prescient in its recommendations, given what we know about the later course of events in the development of human rights. The CSOP made four main recommendations: that a United Nations conference on human rights be organized, that a "permanent" United Nations commission on human rights be established to fashion standards and means of protecting human rights, that the main civil rights be incorporated in "national constitutions" with teeth for enforcing them, and that individuals and groups be given a right to petition the human rights commission for relief "after exhausting local remedies."[22] The CSOP report predictably took the Axis powers to task for gross human rights abuses, but also condemned the "double standards" of the Allies.[23]

.   In 1944 the American Law Institute published its *Statement of Essential Rights*, which was produced by a committee of advisers drawn from diverse cultures around the world.[24] It set for itself the task of ascertaining "how rights ... on which all can unite can be expressed in a manner acceptable to their different traditions and cultures."[25] Although carrying the name of the *American* Law Institute, this appellation should be understood in its broadest sense, since jurists from Latin America and from all over the world had a significant impact, including the former President of Panama, Ricardo J. Alfaro, Huh Shih (Chinese Ambassador to the U.S.A. from 1938 to 1941), Henri Laugier, former Dean of Algiers University and Indian businessman K. C. Mahindra. It listed a range of civil and political, social and economic rights, and was to become an important model for the initial draft of the UDHR.[26] The statement included rights to education, sound conditions of work, adequate housing and food, and social security. It also included a general protection clause.[27]

The international labour movement also played an important role in the development of human rights standards. The 26th session of the International Labor Conference was held in Philadelphia in April 1944.[28] Forty-one countries approved the Declaration of Philadelphia. The declaration proclaimed rights to "material well-being" and "spiritual development" in "freedom and dignity," "economic and social security and equal opportunity."[29] Other commitments declared at Philadelphia included the following: the achievement of "full employment" and the raising of the standard of living; a minimum "living wage"; better working conditions, and social security measures (including a "basic income in case of inability to work"); comprehensive medical care; child and maternity welfare; and "equality of educational and vocational opportunity."[30]

This conference was influential in the development of a right to work for the UDHR, as was the private initiative of the French sociologist Georges Gurvitch's *La Déclaration des droits sociaux*. This declaration included the social rights of workers (Articles X–XXXII), of consumers and users (XXX–XLVIII) and of the common man (XLIX–LVIII). There were, additionally, "Social Duties and Social Rights Concerning Property" (XLIII–XLVIII). Specific worker rights included the "right to labour," to strike, and to create and join unions. Historian Brian Simpson conceded that "in spite of its long-winded and repulsive style" many of the rights Gurvitch's declaration recognized could later be found in the UDHR, such as the right to work under humane conditions, to form and participate in trade unions, to recreation and rest, to social security and to an adequate standard of living, and to participate fully "in cultural life."[31] In February 1945, the so-called Chapultepec Conference (the Inter-American Conference on Problems of War and Peace) was held. At the conference labour groups, social organizations and educational bodies continued discussion of human rights along the lines that had been pursued at Philadelphia.[32]

Anticolonial movements continued to press their twin causes of self-determination and equality of treatment of humans, regardless of race. The Institute of Pacific Relations demanded that the Allies provide economic and political justice for all persons regardless of race. The Pan-African and Universal African Movements, and the Council on African Affairs, continued similar forms of advocacy during the war, and the American National Association for the Advancement of Colored People (NAACP) poetically captured the twin causes in their "Double-V" campaign: victory over the Axis enemies abroad, and the triumph over racism at home.[33] Historian Penny M. Von Eschen has drawn attention to a humanitarian universalism that encompassed African American, pan-African, and other human rights campaigns:

> [Africans and African Americans were engaged in] articulating links between movements in Africa and the struggles of African-Americans for civil and economic rights in the United States … In their specific interpretations of … [World War II] and anticolonial struggles, black intellectuals and journalists in the United States, Britain, West Africa, and the Caribbean elaborated a conception of democracy that focused on the struggles of black peoples and their potential democratic transformations, yet also embraced a universalism that linked all struggles for democracy and independence.[34]

Or, as the celebrated African American poet Langston Hughes put it[35] in 1942, with U.S. segregation laws squarely in mind:

> From Harlem to India to Africa's land
> Jim Crow started his last stand.
> Our battle yet is far from won,
> But when it is, Jim Crow'll be done!

On January 6, 1941, President Roosevelt made his famous "Four Freedoms" speech to Congress. His motivation in doing so was partly to reinforce American support for the Allied effort, in particular to encourage support of the Lend-Lease funding scheme for Britain and the Allies,[36] but was also consistent with his domestic New Deal agenda, which expanded the role of the state in social security in response to the Great Depression.[37] He proclaimed "four essential freedoms", of speech and expression and of worship, as well as freedoms from want and from fear "everywhere in the world." He proclaimed that "Freedom ... means the supremacy of human rights everywhere."[38] Burgers argues that the Four Freedoms "formula was entirely of his own making."[39] A distinctive aspect of this formula was its recognition of economic and social rights as well as a broad interpretation of freedom from fear that identified the threats of aggressive war and the spread of weapons of mass destruction.[40] But Roosevelt also meant by "freedom from fear" that people ought to be free from any oppression from their own state.[41]

In contrast, British political scientist Tony Evans has argued that freedom from want "did not mean freedom from economic deprivation or a right to social welfare" but, rather, the dismantling of barriers to global free trade.[42] He bases this view largely on one passage of Roosevelt's speech to Congress in 1941, namely: "The third is freedom from want – which translated into world terms, means economic understandings which will secure every nation a healthy peacetime life ..."[43] But Evans is unable to show that this was merely a camouflage for free trade policies, nor to reconcile his view with Roosevelt's New Deal policies which, he recognized, "increased the role of the federal government in civil rights and welfare issues ... [and] alarmed many conservative groups."[44] On Evans' view, these groups should be a liberal (in the strict sense of the word), capitalist constituency that Roosevelt would be eager to appeal to not alienate. Therefore, the better view is that Roosevelt's advocacy of economic and social rights was not insincere[45] and did not dovetail with a unidimensional commitment to global free trade. As Burgers argues, such a "restrictive interpretation" distorts what Roosevelt meant by "freedom from want." Roosevelt repeatedly emphasized the philosophy of the New Deal in which governments were to be held accountable not only for civil and political rights but also for their performance in advancing the welfare of citizens. This commitment was evident in Roosevelt's strong call for an "Economic Bill of Rights," particularly in his State of the Union speech to Congress on January 11, 1944.[46]

One of the influences on FDR's advocacy of economic and social rights seems to have been the very progressive draft national bill of rights produced by the U.S. National Resources Planning Board (NRPB) in January 1943. It included the following rights: the right to work; to "fair pay"; to "adequate food, clothing, shelter and medical care"; "to security with freedom from fear of old age, want, dependency, sickness, unemployment and accident"; "to equality before the law, with equal access to justice in fact"; "to education for work"; "to rest, recreation and adventure" and more. Many of these rights have not to this day been recognized or even modestly realized in the U.S.A.[47] The very progressive nature of these rights was too much even for Roosevelt's administration, which hastened the board's end in 1944 by denying it funding. As historian Brian Simpson noted, the NRPB's "combination of socialism and hedonism" was a bitter pill that the Congress was not prepared to swallow.[48] Thus it was that Roosevelt's generally progressive views did not preclude official American ambivalence toward, and indeed resistance to, international legal recognition of human rights, and, ironically, specifically on the question of the protection of economic and social rights. This ambivalence, indeed often hostility, was reflected in later debates during the drafting of the UDHR and in the subsequent years of the Cold War. And even at the time of the Four Freedoms speech the U.S.A. was a strong defender of the principles of inviolable state sovereignty and non-intervention in the domestic matters of states.[49]

The Atlantic Charter of 1941, formally known as the Anglo-American Eight Point declaration, (August 14, 1941)[50] was initially drafted by Prime Minister Churchill, then adapted by Roosevelt and his entourage. The Charter made reference to a right of democratic self-determination for all peoples, to "improved labor standards, economic advancement, and social security" and to the "freedom from fear and want." The Charter also drew attention to the need for "a wider and permanent system of general security" in the world, which would "afford to all nations the means of dwelling in safety within their own boundaries." The Charter received the support of the ILO and was an important influence on New Zealand's Prime Minister Peter Fraser and Deputy Prime Minister Walter Nash. It especially influenced Fraser's thinking in regard to conditions of labour and social security.[51]

Furthermore, the apparent universalism of the Charter's proclamations inspired various dependent and oppressed peoples around the world, and gave them a focal point through which to concentrate the energies of their critique of colonialism. The heat from this concentration was felt acutely by those who continued to defend imperial power, notably Prime Minister Churchill. He made it clear that the Charter "had no reference to the internal affairs of the British Empire." In a speech on November 10, 1942, he wanted to "make this clear, in case there should be any mistake in any quarter. We mean to hold our own. I have not become the King's First Minister in order to preside over the liquidation of the British Empire." This attitude was representative of Britain's hostility toward self-determination, particularly on the part of the Colonial Office. Britain wanted to retain the British Empire, but ultimately in a paternalistic fashion it hoped to act as a trustee: bringing about the transition of suitable colonies toward Dominion status but not full independence in the American sense of the term. Britain did not want the deceased League of Nations mandates system reincarnated in any other scheme for international monitoring and enforcement. As Churchill noted in a minute of January 8, 1943, Britain could tolerate foreign states having "a means of expressing their reasonable and legitimate interest in colonial territories *without* affecting … [Britain's] sovereignty or exclusive authority, or allowing them to meddle in constitutional questions, or establishing international bodies possessing powers of interference divorced from responsibility." Moreover there was some basis for Britain to question the bona fides of the U.S.A. as an advocate for colonial peoples, given that state's desire to secure military bases on Pacific islands.[52] Still, the Charter managed to inspire many in the developing world. One person undaunted by the cynical clawing back from the Charter by Western states was the South African lawyer Nelson Mandela. His attitude exemplified the hope that it could encourage, a hope that could, however, deepen the deflation experienced by dependent peoples if its principles were not ultimately taken seriously and applied without discrimination:

> The Atlantic Charter of 1941 ... reaffirmed faith in the dignity of each human being and propagated a host of democratic principles. *Some in the West saw the Charter as empty promises, but not those of us in Africa.* Inspired by the Atlantic Charter and the fight of the Allies against tyranny and oppression, the ANC [African National Congress] created its own Charter, called African Claims, which called for full citizenship for all Africans ... and the repeal of all discriminatory legislation. We hoped that the government and ordinary South Africans would see that *the principles they were fighting for in Europe were the same ones we were advocating at home.*[53]

The Charter became useful as a reference point for criticizing the double standards of the Allied powers in relation to race and colonialism. Racial segregation in the U.S.A., racist immigration laws in Allied countries and the plight of indigenous peoples in the colonies were exposed to light.[54]

The Charter was followed on January 1, 1942 by the Declaration of the United Nations (a term coined by FDR and used at that time to refer to the Allied states) which 26 and ultimately 46 countries signed. In addition, foreign affairs ministers of the American republics supported the Charter and the Declaration.[55] The signatories, including Haiti, Cuba, India and China, were exhorted to win the war to provide a "decent life, liberty, independence and religious freedom" to all individuals. The relevant states pledged to adhere to the Charter and to "preserve human rights and justice in their own lands as well as in other lands."[56] But poverty and racial and sexual discrimination in signatory states embarrassed the Allies and frustrated anti-colonial activists and human rights proponents generally.[57]

Even conservative politicians such as the Republican American Wendell Wilkie saw at least the strategic danger of failing to establish greater protection of human rights at home.[58] This kind of perception was at times used by human rights supporters to enhance a pragmatic argument for skeptical domestic audiences: to win their support for the "idealism" of human rights by showing that better human rights conditions on the domestic front were indeed in "the national interest." As Wilkie conceded, "[t]he defense of democracy against the forces that threaten it from without has made some of its failures to function at home glaringly apparent. Our very proclamations of what we are fighting for have rendered our own inequities self-evident. When we talk of freedom and opportunity for all nations the mocking paradoxes in our own society become so clear they can no longer be ignored."[59] But even this strategic concern was insufficient to prevail at this stage over the British and American administrations' shared commitment to a strong notion of state sovereignty and their consequent resistance to *international* guarantees of human rights.[60] These obstacles are well reflected in a speech by U.S. Secretary of State Cordell Hull on July 23, 1942. He noted that "advances – in political freedom, in economic betterment, in social justice, in spiritual values – can be achieved by each nation *primarily through its own ... wise policies and actions. They can be made only where there is acceptance and cultivation of the concepts and spirit of human rights and human freedom.*"[61] Moreover, Britain (and, more specifically, England), including its aristocratic civil service, which was variously enamoured with Austinian positivism, Benthamite utilitarianism, Diceyan constitutionalism and Burkean conservativism, was often sceptical about what it deemed the extravagant declarations of human rights of the "Continental" or American variety.[62] As J. L. Brierly (Professor of International Law at Oxford from 1922 to 1947, and author of the standard British text on the subject) noted, "[a]n English lawyer is perhaps not well qualified to judge the probable effect in other countries of a mere declaration; he comes to such a question with an ineradicable distrust of attempts to create rights without creating remedies for their violation."[63] There is in Brierly's statement the assumption that really only domestic remedies were likely to be effective and appropriate. In a House of Lords debate, Lord Chancellor Simon emphasized that "[i]t is the existence in this country of ... effective practical remedies of procedure which have secured ... important rights, and not any declaration at all."[64] And in a sardonic response by the British Foreign Office to the American Carnegie peace commission's (CSOP's) report on "The International Safeguard of Human Rights," one H. St. L. B. Moss wrote that "once [its] generalities have been left behind and the possibilities of international pressure [have been] envisaged, [there will be] a degree of interference with municipal law that no State, and certainly no Great

Power, is likely to tolerate. It is hard to imagine the US 'recognizing the rights of individuals' e.g. negroes in the South 'to petition the United Nations Commission on Human Rights' to obtain redress."[65]

Yet there were developments in the U.S.A., U.K., Australia and New Zealand that fostered economic and social rights under the umbrella of an emerging welfare state, one that emerged out of the stormy days of the Great Depression. In the U.S.A. there were various schemes, laws and bodies associated with the New Deal and in the U.K. there was the Beveridge Report (1942), which proved to be the blueprint for a "universal" welfare state. Despite various anti-communist "Red Scares" in Australia in the first half of the twentieth century there was at this time a much more utilitarian attitude to "what the government could do for us," to twist President John F. Kennedy's subsequent exhortation. Even in the U.S.A., where the socialist tradition was and is much weaker, and where state intervention at that time, and thereafter during the Cold War, might well be branded "communistic," developments favourable to domestic economic and social rights emerged. With FDR's sponsorship, New Deal social legislation was introduced and an "Economic Bill of Rights" was mooted. Roosevelt created an Advisory Committee on Postwar Foreign Policy with a Subcommittee on Political Problems. Sumner Welles was its Chair. The subcommittee identified various goals for postwar organization, including the advancement of the principle of equality, of decolonization and of the welfare of indigenous peoples (a surprisingly progressive concern).[66]

The U.S. State Department, circa 1942, additionally established a Special Subcommittee on Legal Problems to discuss formulations for an international bill of rights.[67] It drew on the classic bills of rights as well as on formulations from the *Fédération internationale des droits de l'homme, Institut de droit international*, American Institute of International Law and the CSOP. In addition to the so-called classic civil and political rights, the subcommittee recommended commitments to equal protection under the law, and socio-economic rights such as a minimum standard of living and a right to education.[68] Importantly, or at least so it seemed on the face of it, the subcommittee proposed that the international bill of rights end with the following paragraph:

These human rights shall be guaranteed by and constitute a part of the supreme law of each state and shall be observed and enforced by its administrative and judicial authorities without discrimination on the basis of nationality, language, race, political opinion or religious belief, *any law or constitutional provision to the contrary notwithstanding.*[69]

Such a declaration seemed to augur a substantial erosion of U.S. state sovereignty, but U.S. State Department official Durward Sandifer, a lawyer on the subcommittee, pressed for an international bill of rights that would not have legal sanction or enforcement mechanisms.[70] His view held sway with the U.S.A. and with the other Great Powers, as we will see, at Dumbarton Oaks. It is ultimately reflected in the fact that the UDHR was originally proclaimed as only a non-binding declaration, a point ironically emphasized by no less a figure than Eleanor Roosevelt. In classified advice, Sandifer urged that having a bill of rights without enforcement provisions:

> … would represent the simplest and least complicated method of putting an international bill of rights into effect … *It is a device used many times in the past.* States agree on the adoption of new rules of law or a formulation of existing rules and proclaim them to the world in a formal international agreement. Reliance is placed primarily upon the good faith of the contracting parties … Such a procedure has the advantage of provoking the minimum of opposition, which is important in a step as radical in character as giving universal legal recognition to individual human rights.[71]

International Relations Realists would no doubt utter an exasperated "Of course, of course!" to this apparent Machiavellianism. Yet there are ambivalences here, hinting that avoiding provocation of resistance to human rights with legal force was a tactical choice by human rights proponents. The achievement of even "in principle" recognition of international human rights by the U.S.A. could be put in jeopardy if the more radical step of providing enforcement provisions were taken. Certainly the legal subcommittee put the view that "[t]he necessity of prohibiting any discrimination … requires no comment. It is the heart of any modern bill of rights, national or international."[72] But it was Sandifer again who concluded that state racial segregation laws need not be disturbed by any international ban on discrimination. This view was purported to be based on federal and constitutional principles, and, more plausibly, at least in terms of nation-state motivation, on arguments about national sovereignty.[73] The idea that the U.S.A. could make an international commitment to non-discrimination and retain laws for racial segregation is not only contradictory, but also reinforces the view that Sandifer's comments were more about the maintenance of good international standing than a prudent, tactical move to introduce the legal recognition of international human rights without causing unnecessary domestic controversy. However, an international bill of rights that would not cause much anxiety for serious violators of human rights would be if not a completely hollow then certainly a rather disappointing achievement.

Sandifer's views were made more explicit and heartily endorsed by U.S. Secretary of State Cordell Hull who stated that any human rights bill "requiring a derogation of national sovereignty" would "meet the opposition" of the U.S.A.[74] The commitment of the U.S.A. to human rights principles without any challenge to or change in American laws, which this kind of view on its best characterization seems to suppose, can be reconciled only if a brand of American constitutional chauvinism is accepted: that the U.S. Constitution, legal system and culture *already* protected the relevant human rights at the highest level, setting the standard for other states and cultures. This perception is not dissimilar to England's traditional view of the "genius of the common law," the English "Constitution," and Parliament in guaranteeing the rights of "freeborn Englishmen." For example, English constitutional theorist A. V. Dicey was, in the nineteenth century, to entrench an English legal antagonism toward the "Continental" and American fetish for bills of rights and formal constitutional codifications (an inverse of American scepticism toward "non-American" ways of realizing rights). Similarly, a long-serving prime minister of Australia, in the postwar decades, R. G. Menzies, summed up his faith in the English constitutional tradition by proclaiming that "responsible government" in the Westminster tradition was effectively Australia's Bill of Rights.[75]

In addition to the Special Subcommittee on Legal Problems, a Special Subcommittee on International Organization wrestled with similar conundrums. This special subcommittee produced a model for "international organization" under which a wide range of rights were to be protected: civil, political, economic and social (the latter encompassing public provision of education and guarantees of "minimum standards of well-being"). Crucially, a non-discrimination and equal protection clause was included, prohibiting discrimination on the basis of religion, race, language, nationality or political views or affiliations. The subcommittee concluded that the non-discrimination clause was "fundamental because without it no person's rights are assured and those of all may be undermined." However, the U.S. domestic politics of race and segregation ensured that enforcement measures were not included in the subcommittee's draft.[76]

In 1944 representatives of the U.S.A., U.K. and the U.S.S.R. met for talks on postwar organization at Dumbarton Oaks. China was not present for the first part of the talks, but was later invited by the Great Powers to attend.[77] China's leader, Chiang Kai-Shek, emphasized that "without the participation of Asiatic peoples, the conference will have no meaning for half of humanity."[78] The draft charter for the United Nations which emerged from the talks only included one rather weak and vague provision on human rights:

> [T]he Organization should facilitate solutions of international economic, social and other humanitarian problems and promote respect for human rights and fundamental freedoms.[79]

It is interesting to observe that the provision included reference to economic, social and other humanitarian problems, given later American resistance to the notion of economic rights during the Cold War.

The U.S.S.R. and the U.K, in the name of state sovereignty, resisted the inclusion of this or any other general human rights obligations in the United Nations charter. There was some support for a general provision that the postwar organization would be "required to promote the observance of human rights,"[80] but we must recall here my discussion of Sandifer's classified advice. When it came to racial equality, or to binding legal obligations, the U.S.A. showed its true position in being as intransigent as the other Great Powers. As Benjamin Cohen, FDR's personal representative, wrote in an early proposed clause for the Charter, "[t]he International Organization should refrain from intervention in the internal affairs of any state, it being the responsibility of each state to see that conditions prevailing within its jurisdiction do not endanger international peace and security, and to this end, to respect the human rights and fundamental freedoms …"[81] The Chinese put forward the following proposal for the United Nations postwar organization:

1. The International Organization shall be universal in character, to include eventually all states.

2. The principle of equality of all states and all races shall be upheld.[82]

The proposal was defeated by a united front of the Great Powers. The Soviet Union stressed that human rights should not be the focus of an "international *security* organization."[83] The U.S.A., with the more conservative Secretary of State Cordell Hull and his Undersecretary Edward Stettinius at the helm – replacing Sumner Welles – opposed the inclusion of any racial equality clause, for reasons already discussed, thus departing from the more sympathetic position prior to Dumbarton Oaks.[84]

As we have noted, the British Prime Minister Winston Churchill did not accept that the Atlantic Charter or Declaration of the United Nations (January 1, 1942) applied to people in British colonies, bluntly declaring: "Why be apologetic about Anglo-Saxon superiority ... ? We are superior."[85] This imperialist spirit was also evident at Dumbarton Oaks where the interests of the British Empire and of restrictive national immigration polices meant the rejection of China's proposal.[86] Sir Alexander Cadogan, the leader of the British group, sent a telegram to the British Foreign Office:

Discussion has taken place ... on racial equality ... Argument strongly advanced is that it would be against our interest and tradition as a liberal power to oppose the expression of a principle denial of which figures so prominently in Nazi philosophy and is repugnant to the mass of British and American relations in a sphere of greatest delicacy by supplying ammunition to critics who accuse us of reactionary policy in the Far East.[87]

In a fashion reminiscent of Sandifer, Cadogan continued:

Recognition of the principle commits us to nothing more than we have always stood for. But there might be a revival of the quite unfounded fears of 1919 that immigration problems are

involved. These are, of course ... matters of domestic
jurisdiction ... We may be sure that if it were thought that such
questions were involved by the recognition of the principle, the
United States Delegation would oppose it.[88]

That is exactly what happened. None of the Great Powers supported
China's proposal, and the U.S. Senate resolved that if the U.S.A. were to
be part of any particular international organization it would only do so if
a robust domestic jurisdiction clause were agreed to. So the draft charter
emphasized the rights of states rather than of individuals, did not refer to
race or to colonies, and gave no human rights functions to the proposed
General Assembly or Security Council.[89] Countering the view that
rights were imposed by the Western states on the non-Western world, at
Dumbarton Oaks China alone was prepared to surrender sovereignty in
the name of human rights![90]

    Criticism of the Dumbarton Oaks proposals centred around the lack
of inclusivity of the process,[91] the grievances of the developing world
(colonialism, racism, the denial of self-determination) and the weakness
of its sole provision on human rights. Many of these issues were
discussed at the Inter-American Conference on Problems of War and
Peace, held in Mexico City in March 1945. Latin American states were
particularly disappointed not to have been invited to Dumbarton Oaks
when earlier the U.S.A. had promised consultation regarding the
character of postwar organization. Twenty Latin American states
produced a Final Act of the Conference that called for an international
declaration of human rights (including the rights of women and children
and a declaration of economic and social rights), the punishment of war
crimes and an end to racial discrimination. Innovatively, many of the
states stressed the interconnections between the international rights and
duties of nations and individuals. Cuba prepared a Draft Declaration of
the International Rights and Duties of Man. An inter-American
convention on human rights was also contemplated. Other states that
were influential in the critique of the Dumbarton Oaks proposals
included India, Australia and New Zealand. Australia and New Zealand
agreed to a joint position in November 1944. They wanted more say for
smaller powers, an international trusteeship for indigenous peoples and
express human rights (in particular, social welfare and economic
rights).[92] In their joint declaration of January 29, 1944, the two
governments proclaimed that as a result of the Atlantic Charter "

'trusteeship' ... is applicable in broad terms to all colonial territories in the Pacific and elsewhere ... [for] the welfare of the natives peoples and their social, economic and political development."[93] The stage was now set for the 1945 San Francisco Conference. Before turning my attention to that conference (in the next chapter), I want to discuss the implications of the postwar war crimes trials (and some of their predecessors) for the development and justification of universal human rights.[94]

The war crimes trials that followed in the wake of World War II were certainly procedurally imperfect and partial in their almost exclusive focus on the abominations of the vanquished.[95] Yet the trials made massive contributions to strengthening universalist dimensions of international humanitarian and human rights law. Moreover, even "victors' justice" – if one concedes this characterization as accurate – was an achievement in the context of more visceral forces for revenge. Even "victors' *justice*" was far removed from vengeful injustice, from victors' vengeance. Indeed the victors were at times reluctant to hold the trials at all. Of special significance is the fact that there were some non-Western dimensions of the war crimes trials and their precedents, often neglected, which can be discerned in the Ottoman trials following the Great War, and in the trials in the Far East at the end of World War II.[96]

As far as the augmentation of universalist dimensions of international humanitarian law is concerned, the World War II war crimes trials clarified and extended earlier notions of "the laws of humanity"[97] and "crimes against humanity."[98] These notions, as the political scientist Gary Bass has demonstrated in his important archivally based work, have a much longer history than has been commonly recognized. For instance, "crimes against humanity" were not created – let alone fabricated – at Nuremberg, but rather can be traced back to at least the time of the Turkish massacre of Armenians in 1915.[99] They figured prominently, also, in various speeches and reports made by prominent British officials (such as Prime Minister Asquith, Lloyd George and Attorney-General Frederick Smith) during and after the Great War.[100] Indeed the basic principle behind crimes against humanity goes back to the calls for humanitarian intervention in the nineteenth century.

A noted American international legal scholar, Professor Quincy Wright,[101] who had held positions at Harvard, Minnesota and Chicago, drew attention to possible analogies between the prosecution of crimes against humanity and cooperation on an international scale in relation to "universally recognized crimes" such as "murder, rape, mayhem, arson, piracy, robbery, forgery, counterfeiting, embezzlement and theft." Wright further emphasized the references in the Hague Convention IV on Land Warfare (1907) to the "laws of humanity," noting that the victims of their violation could be nationals, not only aliens.

Respecting the jurisdiction to try alleged offenders for crimes against humanity, the postwar trials at Nuremberg, in the Far East and elsewhere clarified and strengthened the so-called "universality principle." Departing from territorial bases of jurisdiction, notions of untrammelled state sovereignty, domestic jurisdiction and the depiction of individuals as mere objects of international law, this principle provided that there was universal jurisdiction to try war criminals. Any state could prosecute and try any person anywhere for a crime alleged to have been committed against anyone, regardless of nationality.[102] Those persons committing crimes against humanity do just that – they threaten the community of humankind and make themselves, in the age-old phrase, *"hostis humani generis."* They are enemies of humankind.[103] These principles of customary international law have come to be incorporated in the 1949 Geneva Conventions and have been vindicated in both the Israeli *Eichmann* case (1962) (whatever other defects this case displayed), and in the American case of *Filartiga v Peña-Irala* (1980), in which a Paraguayan citizen successfully sued in the U.S.A. a Paraguayan ex-policeman, who was illegally in the U.S.A. at the time, for the torture death of his brother in Paraguay.[104]

Immediate precursors to the Nuremberg trials included the Moscow Declaration (November 1, 1943), the Yalta Conference (February 11, 1945) where the leaders of the Big Three declared their "inflexible purpose to ... bring all war criminals to just and swift punishment", and the Berlin Conference (August 2, 1945) where these powers "regarded it as a matter of great importance that the trial of those major criminals should begin at the earliest possible date."[105] In the Moscow Declaration, which followed the creation of a United Nations War Crimes Commission (UNWCC) in October 1943, Roosevelt, Stalin and Churchill said that Germans

> responsible for, or having taken a consenting part in the ... atrocities, massacres and executions, will be sent back to the

countries in which their abominable deeds were done in order that they may be judged and punished according to the laws of these liberated countries and of the free governments which will be created therein.[106]

This view is consistent with that of the American international lawyer Willard B. Cowles (Judge Advocate General's Department) which he expressed in 1945: "... every independent State has jurisdiction to punish war criminals in its custody regardless of the nationality of the victim, the time it entered the war, or the place where the offence was committed."[107] The Moscow Declaration provided that "major criminals, whose offences have no particular geographical localization" – or, more accurately, were so widespread and of such a notoriously gross nature, would be "punished by the joint decision of the Governments of the Allies."[108]

The Nuremberg Charter (Article 6) attached to the Agreement for the Establishment of an International Military Tribunal – signed by the U.S.A., France, the U.K. and the U.S.S.R. on August 8, 1945 – provided for three offences: crimes against peace, war crimes and crimes against humanity. Twenty-two alleged senior German offenders were tried in the main trial, with three acquitted, but many others were tried in other contexts. The most important developments at Nuremberg in terms of international human rights law were the reinforcement of the notion of individual responsibility on the part of the leaders for the planning, carrying out and involvement in an illegal war; and on the part of anyone – military and political leaders and subordinates – engaged in the "systematic" mistreatment of "any civilian population." Such a systematic mistreatment could be a crime against humanity, regardless of the discredited doctrines of sovereign immunity, "superior orders" or authorization by "local laws." In this we can see a universalistic approach: a crime against humanity, for example, is a crime against humanity *as such*.[109] As Geoffrey Robertson, the famous Australian human rights lawyer, has explained at length:

These were not war crimes against enemy soldiers, but against German civilians ... who were regarded as pseudo-humans. They were not committed because of the exigencies of war, but because of the vicious racism of Nazi leaders. Unlike the crimes of pirates and slavetraders, the traditional targets of individual responsibility in international law, they did not need any international or transborder element to attract jurisdiction: these were crimes that the world could not suffer to take place anywhere, at any time, because they shamed everyone. They were not, for that crucial reason, crimes against Germans (which therefore only Germans should punish); they were crimes against humanity, because the very fact that a fellow human could conceive and commit them diminishes every member of the human race.[110]

The Nuremberg Charter provided for "an international military tribunal for the trial of war criminals whose offences have no particular geographical location." Article 7 of the Charter provided that "The official position of defendants, whether as Heads of States or responsible officials in Government Departments, shall not be considered as freeing them from responsibility or mitigating punishment." Article 8 of the Charter stated, in part, that "the fact the defendant acted pursuant to the order of his Government or of a superior shall not free him from responsibility, but may be considered in mitigation of punishment ..." On individual responsibility, the tribunal proclaimed that "the very essence of the Charter is that individuals have international duties which transcend the national obligations imposed by the individual state ... if the state in authorizing action moves outside its competence in international law."[111]

But the achievement of the Nuremberg Charter could not have been predicted, even given the record of Nazi abominations during World War II. The path to Nuremberg was a rocky one indeed, with much ambivalence, resistance and even outright opposition from Western states, and their national populations, along the way. This history is a less well known, less commonly told, account, drowned out by the deafening chorus that the Allies were meting out "victors' justice" to the Nazis. Moreover, Gary Bass has amply demonstrated that the Western resistance to the proposals to try Nazis for war crimes had early precedents in the post–World War I experience. The U.S.A., for example, despite the internationalism of President Woodrow Wilson, was alternatively lukewarm, neutral or even hostile toward the plans for the trial of Germans at the end of the Great War – let alone a trial of its political leaders.[112] President Wilson and Secretary of State Robert Lansing maintained that the U.S.A.'s neutrality meant that it should favour "the policy of avoiding all protests on account of inhuman methods of warfare by belligerents which are in violation of international law."[113] While Lansing admitted, for example, that the German bombardment of Antwerp, Belgium, had been "an outrage against humanity," he then cautioned that "[i]f we begin to make protests general in nature as to violations of civilized and humane methods of slaughter where are we going to stop?" Indeed. Consistent with this approach, there was no American protest when Germany invaded Belgium; and a Zeppelin attack on London in 1915 was dismissed by President Wilson as "none of our business."[114]

On the proposed trial of Wilhelm II (1859–1941), Wilson was equally unenthusiastic. "I am not convinced", he said, "that the Kaiser was personally responsible for the war or the prosecution of it ... The Kaiser was probably the victim of circumstance and environment. In a case of this sort you can't with certainty put your finger on the guilty party."[115] Official American outrage tended to be reserved for American victims, especially those who had fallen to Germany's submarine warfare.[116] The 1919 Peace Conference Commission on the Responsibility of the Authors of the War and the Enforcement of the Penalties was chaired by Robert Lansing, whom President Wilson directed to write a minority report against the High Tribunal and the trial of Wilhelm II. The upshot was that the U.S.A. would not be involved in any war crimes tribunal.[117] Despite more than sixty thousand Australian soldiers dying in World War I, Prime Minister W. M. "Billy" Hughes was even more blunt in his opposition to war crimes trials: "You cannot indict a man for making war. War has been the prerogative of the right of all nations from the beginning, and if you say, well, as a result of this war, millions have died, you can say that much of Alexander and of Moses and of almost anybody."[118]

Another example of American reluctance regarding the prosecution of international criminals is the U.S.A.'s response to the Turkish massacre of Armenians in 1915. Giving the rationalization that the Armenians were undermining the Turkish war effort by rendering aid to the Russians, the Turkish Government arranged for the killing of Armenian community leaders, and of Armenian soldiers in the Ottoman forces, and also exposed many Armenian citizens to a "death march" across the Ottoman Empire. It has been estimated that approximately one million Armenians died as the result of this Turkish "ethnic cleansing."[119]

Within the Allied war crimes commission American representatives opposed inquiry into violations of "the laws of humanity" and the prosecution of Turkish crimes against humanity. Ultimately this position was reflected in the Treaty of Lausanne (1923), which gave amnesty to those accused of the Armenian massacre.[120] Christopher Blakesley has reminded his readers of the encouragement this weak response gave to Adolf Hitler as his genocidal plans took shape, reportedly asking sarcastically, "And who now remembers the Armenians?"[121]

In contrast to the American response, as far back as 1915 war crimes trials were formally a British war aim that had been endorsed by cabinet. Winston Churchill and British prime ministers Asquith and Lloyd George were at times strong advocates for the trial of the German Emperor Wilhelm II and of others accused of crimes under international law.[122] But, ultimately, the escape of Wilhelm II and the Crown Prince to the Netherlands in 1918 (which state refused to surrender them to the Allies), the limited success of the trials at Leipzig of German and Austrian defendants in the German Supreme Court (*Reichsgericht*) in 1920,[123] and of the Ottoman Empire's trials (1918–1923), soured official feeling toward war crimes trials. That was how Leipzig and Constantinople came to be "forgotten," a repressed memory that precluded their being much noticed as precedents for the trial of war crimes at Nuremberg.[124]

Despite resounding Allied condemnations between 1943 and 1945 of Axis war crimes, Allied commitment to trials of any sort (and to seeking the justice due to those who had suffered crimes against humanity, especially Holocaust victims) often wavered. Following the lead of antagonistic American and British public opinion, there was substantial support among Allied officials in Britain, the U.S.A. and, less surprisingly, the U.S.S.R., for military executions of at least the major German criminals without any trial whatsoever.[125]

Abandoning his positive stance toward war crimes trials at the Great War's end, Prime Minister Winston Churchill came up with a list of 50 Nazis who would upon capture be shot without trial. The British Foreign Secretary, Anthony Eden, claimed that "the guilt of such as Himmler is so black that they fall outside and go beyond the scope of any judicial process." Lord Chancellor Simon chimed in that the "question of the fate of the Nazi leaders ... is a political, not a judicial, question. It would not rest with judges, however eminent or learned, to decide finally a matter like this, which is of the widest and most vital public policy."[126] In part their opposition was due to what they considered the proposed trial's unprecedented nature, and the lack of a clear foundation for it in international law, which would thus render any convictions in violation of the *nullum crimen sine lege* ("no crime without law") maxim against retrospective criminalization and punishment. However, paradoxically and ironically, despite rhetoric from some Allied leaders, the opposition was also coloured, as Gary Bass has shown, by *precedents* such as Leipzig and Constantinople (which to their minds had turned out disastrously), as well as by the usual pressures of public opinion on politicians (especially in democracies) amid understandably raw desires for revenge.[127]

At a foreign ministers conference in Moscow in November 1943, U.S. Secretary of State Cordell Hull seethed that if he could have his way he "would take Hitler and Mussolini and Tojo and their accomplices and bring them before a drumhead court martial, and at sunrise the following morning there would occur an historic incident."[128] In 1944, General Dwight Eisenhower expressed his desire, in a very unfortunate turn of phrase, to "exterminate all of the [German] General staff," numbering some 3500 people, including all members of the Gestapo and many senior Nazi Party members.[129]

These kinds of sentiments were ultimately reflected in the American Morgenthau Plan of September 5, 1944 which came close to final approval. The plan was named after its chief proponent, Henry Morgenthau, Jr., U.S. Treasury Secretary, and had garnered the support of Roosevelt and Churchill. "A list of the arch criminals whose obvious guilt has generally been recognized" by the Allies was to be made; the list was to be given to the "military authorities"; and persons on the list were to be identified and apprehended. Then, according to the plan, "the person identified [by an officer at the rank of at least a General] shall be put to death by firing squads made up of soldiers of the United Nations [that is, of the Allies]."[130]

It is reasonably common to find criticisms directed at the Nuremberg trial for the alleged dubiousness in law of its charges of crimes against peace and crimes against humanity, but less commonly noted is the Allies' own ambivalence toward a trial for the perpetrators of the Holocaust and their at least initial lack of enthusiasm for the notion of crimes against humanity. Although there were precedents for such crimes to be tried under international law, the post–World War I experience of war crimes trials deterred the Allies from pursuing such methods and helped to suppress even the existence of those precedents. Rather, Allied, and especially American, emphasis was on punishing Nazi Germany for instigating World War II.[131]   Prosecutor Robert Jackson, in the trial of the major German defendants, stressed the necessary nexus between Nazi atrocities and the preparations for and conduct of a war of aggression. This nexus continued some time after Nuremberg to be an element that would have to be proved to establish a crime against humanity.[132]   At Nuremberg, Jackson argued that:

> [t]he reason that this program of extermination of Jews and destruction of the rights of minorities becomes an international concern is this: it was part of a plan for making illegal war. Unless we have a war connection as a basis for reaching them, I would think we have no basis for dealing with atrocities. They were part of the preparation for war in so far as they occurred inside of Germany and that makes them our concern.[133]

The possible foundation for prosecution of crimes against humanity in their own right, on the basis of the precedent of the Leipzig and Constantinople trials, was lost in Allied amnesia.

Furthermore, there was only limited reference to the atrocities against Jews in official Allied speeches. For instance, the Moscow Declaration only indirectly referred to the Holocaust as "the slaughters inflicted on the people of Poland" and made no explicit remarks regarding Jews.[134] The relative weakness of the Allied response generally to the Holocaust – the meagre efforts to assist European Jews, Britain's failure to receive Jewish children escaping Vichy and its refusal to bomb the access to the Auschwitz camp because it would risk "valuable" (that is, British) lives[135] – was an important factor in the emphasis on Nazi aggression. But so were anti-Semitism, purported doubts about the legality of any trial, and, at times, a lingering attachment to older notions of state sovereignty. This continuing attachment was a particularly tragic irony, given that the shield of sovereignty had done so much to protect, hide and sustain the atrocities committed against German nationals, and especially, Jews. D. B. Somervell, Britain's Attorney-General, had, for instance, said that "the primary … justification for punishing Hitler and his colleagues is the policy which they have pursued in bringing about and conducting the war."[136] And the British Foreign Office resisted any expansion of the brief of the United Nations War Crimes Commission to include the investigation of Nazi crimes committed against German nationals.[137] As Bass concluded, "this hedging was a step *back* for Britain which had not hesitated in 1915 to condemn the Ottoman Empire for atrocities against Armenians who were Ottoman subjects."[138]

Ultimately, however, the advocacy of Henry Stimson (the U.S. Secretary of War and the so-called "architect of Nuremberg") for a trial won out with President Truman and the Allies. Important support came from U.S. Supreme Court Justices Felix Frankfurter (despite, or in atonement for, his earlier scepticism about reports of massacres of Jews) and Robert Jackson.[139] Significantly, Stimson was successful because he found a way to channel public and official animus against Germany and the Nazis. He did this through conspiracy charges, the notion of corporate criminal liability (which included the German "government," the Nazi Party and other "terror organizations") and by use of the category of "crimes against the peace."[140] For the sake of justice, the "nightmarish reports" from Allied forces coming out of the liberated camps at Dachau and Belsen in April 1945 forced the Holocaust into the brief of the Nuremberg trial.[141]

Still, there were critical deficiencies at Nuremberg. The sound principles and serviceable trial processes were not applied at all to the Allied side. This was largely due to the tribunal's exclusion of *tu quoque* ("I did it, but so did you") evidence.[142] In addition, no traditional war crimes on the part of the Allies were put to trial, including submarine warfare, "wanton destruction," mistreatment of POWs, and Allied bombings of civilian targets – indeed even *Axis* bombings were excluded to avoid heightening Allied embarrassment.[143] We "left out of our draft the destruction of villages and towns of Germany," conceded prosecutor Robert Jackson, because, he admitted, "I think you will have great difficulty distinguishing between the military necessity for that kind of destruction as distinguished from some done by the Germans, assuming the war to be legitimate. It seems to me that those subjects invite recriminations that would not be useful in the trial."[144] Allied crimes against humanity, particularly by the Soviets (who notoriously blamed the massacre of Polish officers in Katyn Forest on the Nazis), were not tried either.[145] Another kind of improper selectivity was evident in the immunity granted to Nazi scientists and business leaders whose skills could serve the East or the West in a Cold War world.[146]

The International Military Tribunal for the Far East (the Tokyo Tribunal) was set up in 1946 to try Japanese officials and soldiers for crimes against peace, traditional war crimes and crimes against humanity – including death marches, forced labour, torture, killings and massacres. The pattern for the horrendous conduct of Japanese forces during the war was set by the "Rape of Nanking" in 1937, in which Japanese soldiers committed scores of thousands of rapes of Chinese women and girls, and killed more than 200,000 civilians in the Chinese capital. Japan was a signatory to, but had not ratified, the 1929 Geneva Convention for the humane treatment of POWs, and their soldiers were products of a brutal, fascistic, military regime of hierarchy and unqualified demands for obedience. One outcome of this was the appalling treatment of POWs by the Japanese: 36,375 out of a total of 132,784 POWs perished – almost 28 per cent (with more than 35 per cent of Australian POWs, the highest percentage of Allied troops, dying in Japanese captivity).[147] One scholar has described the character and conduct of the Japanese military during World War II as follows:

> ... its armed forces ... had become exceptionally authoritarian ... men were trained to blindly follow orders without question. Beatings had become a common method of enforcing discipline. Surrender had become the supreme disgrace ... [Japanese] forces during World War II generally behaved with utter barbarity. The contempt that Japanese forces now felt towards POWs and civilians in occupied territories resulted in extensive incidents of war crimes and atrocities ... torture, murder, rape and other cruelties ...[148]

As with Nuremberg, the Allied prosecution team (led by the American Joseph Keenan) and the Tokyo Tribunal concentrated their efforts on Japanese responsibility for aggression. Thirty-six of the 55 charges related to crimes against peace. Again, the application of the category of crimes against peace was skewed.[149] Judges Rabinod Pal (India) and Bernard Röling (Netherlands) drew attention to Allied violations of the laws of war, especially its bombings (including the use of atomic bombs), which had not come within the purview of the trials. Röling reflected that "[i]t was horrible that we went there [Japan] for the purpose of vindicating the laws of war ... and yet saw every day how the Allies had violated them dreadfully."[150]

Loss of Western resolve in the prosecution and trial of Japanese war crimes was evident in the deal struck not to prosecute Japan's Emperor Hirohito despite his significant command of Japanese national and foreign policy,[151] and in American pressure for the winding up of the Australian war crimes trials of Japanese. With the support of the American General Douglas MacArthur – in charge of occupied Japan– the need to maintain some political stability and unity in occupied Japan led to a decision to preserve a place for the Emperor in peacetime and for the indefinite future. After all, the strategic value of Japan to the West in the emerging Cold War was well understood by the U.S. administration. The prosecution thus dutifully steered away from any responsibility on Hirohito's part for war crimes.[152] When the Tokyo Tribunal delivered its judgment in November 1948, American pressure was brought to bear on Australian military authorities to wind up their proceedings against the Japanese. The U.K. terminated its war trials program in December of that year.[153]

While obviously imperfect, the trial of war crimes in the Far East moved some way beyond Nuremberg in the cultural diversity of the Tokyo Tribunal's bench (including judges from India, the Philippines, China and the U.S.S.R.),[154] in the ready availability of Japanese lawyers for the defence[155], and in the geographical reach of the trials. Trials were conducted in the Far East and Pacific by the U.S.A., U.K., Australia (in Morotai, Labuan, Wewak, Rabaul, Darwin, Singapore, Hong Kong, Manus), the Netherlands, France, the Philippines and China. There were well over two thousand trials across the region.

Additionally, countries such as China had an important role in international declarations on war crimes such as the January 1942 St James Palace Declaration and the Cairo Declaration of December 1943, and in the Far Eastern and Pacific Sub-Committee of the United Nations War Crimes Commission (UNWCC) established in August 1942 (China's Ambassador to the U.K. was its first Chair). The Far-Eastern and Pacific Sub-Commission of the UNWCC was based in Chungking, China.[156] The prosecutors in these various trials sought justice for a diverse range of victims across the Far Eastern region, including Chinese nationals, indigenous peoples, Manchurians, Formosans and Koreans.[157]

War crimes trials were not at all the exclusive preserve of Western powers. More than 20,000 Japanese and Germans were convicted in trials held across Asia, the Pacific and Europe, "conducted by almost every country that had fought or been occupied by the Germans or the

Japanese."[158] In this respect, these war crimes trials welded a link between the faltering Constantinople trials held in the Ottoman Empire at the end of the Great War and international criminal justice at the end of World War II. Under pressure admittedly, the Ottoman administration took an initially active role in investigating the killing of Armenians and the mistreatment of British POWs.[159] The administration drew up lists of offenders, with little regard for their governmental position or official status and power. Indeed, Turkey recognized the category of crimes against humanity, arrested alleged offenders and secured convictions of at least two high-ranking officials – among the first convictions of their kind.

The Ottoman minister of the interior compiled a list of 60 persons accused of responsibility for the Armenian massacres. In February 1919, Turkish authorities arrested around 50 prominent leaders and citizens, including the grand vizier Said Halim Pasha; justice, finance, public works, interior, public instruction, and foreign affairs ministers; the governor of Lebanon; and former directors of police and intelligence.[160] In convicting a lieutenant governor of the Yozgat district, and the commander of the Yozgat police (who, respectively, received punishments of 15 years hard labour and the death penalty),[161] for deporting Armenians, the Ottoman war crimes court announced that "[a]ll these facts are against humanity and civilization. They are never compatible in any manner to human considerations. Moslem supreme justice consider [*sic*] these events as murder, pillage, robbery, and crimes of enormous magnitude."[162]

Raphael Lemkin, a Polish Jew who studied linguistics and law at the University of Lvov, and who was fluent in several languages, made his way to New York where he invented the word "genocide" from Ancient Greek and Latin roots.[163] He made the prohibition of genocidal conduct his life's obsession. As with Hersch Lauterpacht,[164] members of his family had been killed by the Nazis, and he was similarly convinced that warped positivistic conceptions both of international concern and sovereignty needed to be drastically refashioned. It was, he thought, contrary to "civilization" and good sense "that selling a drug to an individual is a matter of worldly concern, while gassing millions of human beings might be a problem of internal concern."[165] Consequently, for Lemkin, sovereignty meant matters such as "conducting an independent foreign and internal policy, building schools, construction of roads ... all types of activity directed towards the welfare of people," not "the right to kill millions of innocent people."[166]

Lemkin's early lobbying for a genocide convention met with indifference when, working as an international law adviser for the U.S. War Department in 1944, he sought out FDR's Vice-President Henry Wallace, and then wrote a memorandum to FDR. Lemkin turned to the representatives of developing countries, from whom he received a much more positive reception. He was able to persuade representatives from Panama, Cuba and India, with the support of Saudi Arabia, to fashion a draft resolution on genocide for consideration by the U.N. General Assembly. He initiated and facilitated an international committee against genocide that was linked to groups in 28 countries and thereby claimed to act on behalf of more than 200 million people. Furthermore, China played a pivotal role in the development of the Genocide Convention. China's draft convention, for example, was adopted for consideration in 1948 in preference to a U.S. one.[167] China also supported an expansive conception of genocide, consistent with Lemkin's view, that went beyond physical destruction of a group to incorporate cultural genocide. It promoted, also, the notion of universal jurisdiction and of the idea of having an international court to adjudicate upon allegations of genocide.[168] In a similar vein, Lemkin had argued that those persons who instigate and commit acts of genocide "should be punished wherever they were caught, regardless of where the crime was committed, or the criminals' nationality or official status."[169] To China's contribution were added those of Brazil, Egypt, Iran and Uruguay, all of which had seats on the drafting committee.[170]

In stark contrast, despite some early U.S. support for the passage of the Genocide Convention, particularly among lawyers in the State Department, and sporadically from President Truman, it was savagely criticized in the Senate and by a number of private organizations, most notoriously by the American Bar Association (ABA). There was an alliance between sections of the Senate and the ABA that killed the possibility of U.S. ratification of the Convention.[171]

The ABA was at the time an almost exclusively white organization, with very few African American members. In its opposition to the Convention, the ABA was motivated by xenophobic, racist isolationism. The ABA's president, Frank Holman, and its Committee on Peace and Law, chaired by one Alfred T. Schweppe, depicted the Convention as part of a communist plot of U.N. "world government"; not surprisingly finding in this strategy firm allies in Senators John Bricker (who later sought to weaken the presidential power in relation to treaties) and the ubiquitous Joseph McCarthy.[172] The Convention would, in their view, interfere with the constitutional rights of states and threaten freedom of speech. But it was the improbable threat to state Jim Crow segregation laws that was, at the end of the day, the real reason for their opposition to the Convention. In fully paranoid, or simply cynical, flights of imagination, the ABA even suggested that the lynching of a single African American, or the running out of town of a few "Chinamen" (to use Schweppe's ugly hypothetical) could constitute genocide under the treaty, as could causing "mental harm" to blacks through segregation in the South. There was no moral embarrassment evident in those who spoke of these actions, but rather indignation that they could be outlawed by the international community when in their own minds they were so clearly internal matters.[173]

As indicated, the ABA forged a strong alliance with sections of the Senate that unapologetically defended a rigid sovereignty over the domestic sphere in the U.S.A.[174] The Chairman of the Senate Foreign Relations Committee, Democratic Senator Connally from Texas, opposed any "treaties that bind us to do things in our domestic jurisdiction".[175] In 1950, Senator Alexander Wiley, a Republican from Wisconsin, "didn't think the peoples of the earth [were] in any position where they can tell this great people on morals, politics and religion how they should live".[176] Raphael Lemkin even had to endure Congressional slights in relation to his "foreign" background, and was denied the opportunity to testify at Congressional hearings related to the ratification of the Convention that was so much a product of his own thinking and tireless, obsessive labours.[177]

On December 9, 1948, 55 delegates voted for the Genocide Convention, none against. The following states ratified the Convention with no reservations whatsoever: Cambodia, Costa Rica, Ecuador, El Salvador, Ethiopia, Guatemala, Haiti, Israel, Jordan, Liberia, Panama, Monaco, Republic of Korea, Saudi Arabia, Sri Lanka and Turkey. However, in the U.S.A. a meeting of the Senate Foreign Relations Committee was adjourned without debate on September 17, 1951. The Convention was not considered again until fully two decades later. And it was not until 1986 that the Convention would be ratified by the U.S.A., albeit with a burden of many reservations and declarations that drastically weakened its potential impact.[178]

Notes

[1] Sources I have made some use of in developing my account in this chapter include the following: D. W. Wessner, "From Judge to Participant. The United States as Champion of Human Rights," in P. Van Ness (ed.), *Debating Human Rights: Critical Essays from the United States and Asia* (London and New York: Routledge, 1999), pp. 255–277; R. Breitman, *Official Secrets: What the Nazis Planned, What the British and Americans Knew* (Ringwood, Victoria: Viking/Penguin, 1998); P. G. Lauren, *Power and Prejudice: The Politics and Diplomacy of Racial Discrimination*, second edn. (Boulder, Colorado: Westview, 1996); L. B. Sohn, "Supplementary Paper: A Short History of United Nations Documents on Human Rights," in *The United Nations and Human Rights*, 18th Report of the Commission to Study the Organization of Peace (Dobbs Ferry, N.Y.: Oceana Publications, 1968), pp. 39–186; A. D. Renteln, *International Human Rights: Universalism Versus Relativism* (Newbury Park, California: Sage, 1990); P. M. Von Eschen, *Race Against Empire: Black Americans and Anticolonialism, 1937–1957* (Ithaca, N.Y.: Cornell University Press, 1997); P. G. Lauren, *The Evolution of International Human Rights: Visions Seen* (Philadelphia: University of Pennsylvania Press, 1998); A. Williams, *Failed Imagination? New World Orders of the Twentieth Century* (Manchester: Manchester University Press, 1998); M. G. Johnson, "The Contributions of Eleanor and Franklin Roosevelt to the Development of International Protection for Human Rights," *Human Rights Quarterly*, vol. 9 (1987), no. 1, pp. 19–48; H. Tolley, Jr., *The U.N. Commission on Human Rights* (Boulder, Colorado: Westview Press, 1987); J. Morsink, *The Universal Declaration of Human Rights: Origins, Drafting and Intent* (Philadelphia: University of Pennsylvania Press, 1999); A. C. Grammatico, "The United Nations and the Development of Human Rights," Ph.D. dissertation, Department of Government, N.Y.U., 1956; L. B. Sohn, "The New International Law: Protection of the Rights of Individuals Rather than States," *American University Law Review*, vol. 32 (1982), no. 1, pp. 1–64; S. K. Murumba, "The Cultural and Conceptual Basis of Human Rights Norms in International Law," Ph.D. thesis, Law, Monash University, Melbourne, 1986; J. Morsink, "World War II and the Universal Declaration," *Human Rights Quarterly*, vol. 15 (1993), no. 2, pp. 357–405; J. Morsink, "The Philosophy of the Universal Declaration," *Human Rights Quarterly*, vol. 6 (1984), no. 3, pp. 309–334; W. J. Bajor, "Discussing 'Human Rights': An Anthropological Exposition on 'Human Rights' Discourse," Ph.D. thesis, Department of Social Anthropology, University of St. Andrews, St.

Andrews, Scotland, 1997; J. Glover, *Humanity: A Moral History of the Twentieth Century* (London: Jonathan Cape, 1999); J. H. Burgers, "The Road to San Francisco: The Revival of the Human Rights Idea in the Twentieth Century," *Human Rights Quarterly*, vol. 14 (1992), no. 4, pp. 447–477; E. Borchard, "Historical Background of International Protection of Human Rights," *The Annals of the American Academy of Political and Social Science*, vol. 243 (January 1946), pp. 112–117; E. Luard, *A History of the United Nations Vol. 1: The Years of Western Domination, 1945–1955* (London and Basingstoke: Macmillan, 1982); A. L. Parrott, "Social Security: Does the wartime dream have to become a peacetime nightmare?," *International Labour Review*, vol. 131 (1992), no. 3, pp. 367–386; P. G. Lauren, "First Principles of Racial Equality: History and the Politics and Diplomacy of Human Rights in the United Nations Charter," *Human Rights Quarterly*, vol. 5 (1983), no. 1, pp. 1–26; T. Evans, *The Politics of Human Rights: A Global Perspective* (London: Pluto Press, 2001); I. Brownlie, *Principles of Public International Law*, fourth edn. (Oxford: Clarendon Press, 1990); J. L. Kunz, "The United Nations Declaration of Human Rights," *American Journal of International Law*, vol. 43 (April 1949), no. 2, pp. 316–323; R. Piotrowicz and S. Kay, *Human Rights in International and Australian Law* (Chatswood, N.S.W.: Butterworths, 2000); P. Malanczuk, *Akehurst's Modern Introduction to International Law*, seventh edn. (London: Routledge, 1997); D. Cohen, "Beyond Nuremberg: Individual Responsibility for War Crimes," in C. Hesse and R. Post (eds.), *Human Rights in Political Transitions: Gettysburg to Bosnia* (New York: Zone Books, 1999), pp. 53–92; K. Sellars, *The Rise and Rise of Human Rights* (Phoenix Mill: Sutton Publishing, 2002); R. A. Falk, *Human Rights Horizons: The Pursuit of Justice in a Globalizing World* (London and New York: Routledge, 2000); H. Lauterpacht, *International Law and Human Rights* (London: Stevens and Sons, 1950; reprinted, Hamden, Connecticut: Archon Books, 1968); H. Lauterpacht, *International Law and Human Rights* (New York: Praeger, 1950) ; J. Jhabvala, "The Drafting of the Human Rights Provisions of the UN Charter," *Netherlands International Law Review*, vol. XLIV (1992), no. 1, pp. 1–31; T. Evans, *US Hegemony and the Project of Universal Human Rights* (London: Macmillan, 1996); T. J. Farer, "The United Nations and Human Rights: More than a Whimper," in R. P. Claude and B. H. Weston (eds.), *Human Rights in the World Community: Issues and Action* (Philadelphia: University of Pennsylvania Press, 1989), pp. 194–206; S. Davidson, *Human Rights* (Buckingham: Open University Press, 1993); L. B. Sohn, "The Human Rights Law of the Charter," *Texas International Law Journal*, vol. 12 (1977), no. 2/3, pp. 129–140; G. A. Finch,

"The Nuremberg Trial and International Law," *American Journal of International Law*, vol. 41 (1947), no. 1, pp. 20–37; Q. Wright, "The Law of the Nuremberg Trial," *American Journal of International Law*, vol. 41 (1947), no. 1, pp. 38–72; F. B. Schick, "The Nuremberg Trial and the International Law of the Future," *American Journal of International Law*, vol. 41 (1947), no. 4, pp. 770–794; G. Robertson, *Crimes Against Humanity: The Struggle for Global Justice* (Ringwood, Victoria: Allen Lane/Penguin, 1999); J. P. Humphrey, *Human Rights and the United Nations: A Great Adventure* (Dobbs Ferry, New York: Transnational Publishers, 1984); G. J. Bass, *Stay the Hand of Vengeance: The Politics of War Crimes Tribunals* (Princeton: Princeton University Press, 2000); B. Weston, "Human Rights," *Human Rights Quarterly*, vol. 6 (1984), no. 3, pp. 257–282; H. J. Steiner and P. Alston, *International Human Rights in Context: Law, Politics, Morals: Text and Materials*, second edn. (Oxford: Oxford University Press, 2000); S. Power, *"A Problem from Hell": America and the Age of Genocide* (London: Harper Collins, 2003); J. Rosenberg, *How Far the Promised Land? World Affairs and the American Civil Rights Movement from the First World War to Vietnam* (Princeton: Princeton University Press, 2006); M. Carrel, "Australia's Prosecution of Japanese War Criminals: Stimuli and Constraints," Ph.D. thesis, Faculty of Law, University of Melbourne, c. 2005–2006; W. A. Schabas, *Genocide in International Law* (Cambridge: Cambridge University Press, 2000); A. Devereux, *Australia and the Birth of the International Bill of Human Rights* (Sydney: The Federation Press, 2005); A. W. B. Simpson, *Human Rights and the End of Empire: Britain and the Genesis of the European Convention* (Oxford: Oxford University Press, 2001). See also E. Borgwardt, *A New Deal for the World: America's Vision for Human Rights* (Cambridge, Massachusetts: Belknap/Harvard University Press, 2005).

[2] Glover, *Humanity*, pp. 69, 77–79, 95, 258. See also Wessner, "From Judge to Participant," p. 258; and Simpson, *Human Rights and the End of Empire*, pp. 71–74, on the British RAAF's use of so-called "frightfulness": the use of sustained "air control" (bombings) against "Uncivilised Tribes" and anticolonial insurgents from the 1920s through the 1950s in British Somaliland, Mesopotamia, India, Palestine, South Arabia, Southern Sudan, Malaya and Kenya.

[3] On the debate over whether the use of atomic bombs at Hiroshima and Nagasaki could be morally justified as a way of ending the war sooner than would otherwise be possible, and thereby preventing possibly much greater loss of life, see Glover, *Humanity*, pp. 94, 95, 105.

[4] Borchard, "Historical Background of International Protection of Human Rights," p. 115.

[5] For example, black soldiers on leave in the U.S. military were often excluded from certain towns or other areas in Europe, and suffered the discriminatory use of courts martial against some of their number (Rosenberg, *How Far the Promised Land?*, p. 152).

[6] See, for example, Simpson, *Human Rights and the End of Empire;* Devereux, *Australia and the Birth of the International Bill of Human Rights*; Rosenberg, *How Far the Promised Land?*

[7] Lauren, *The Evolution of International Human Rights*, pp. 148–150.

[8] Quoted in ibid., p. 155.

[9] Ibid., p. 148. See also Simpson, *Human Rights and the End of Empire;* Power, *"A Problem from Hell."*

[10] Breitman, *Official Secrets,* pp. 148, 171, 211 (quotations are from pp. 171, 211).

[11] Ibid., pp. 92, 100–102, 121 (quotations from pp. 92, 100, 102). See also Power, *"A Problem from Hell,"* chs. 2–5.

[12] Power, *"A Problem from Hell,"* pp. 31–37.

[13] Quoted in Breitman, *Official Secrets,* p. 102.

[14] Ibid., pp. 102–105. See also Simpson, *Human Rights and the End of Empire,* pp. 158–160.

[15] Quoted in Simpson, *Human Rights and the End of Empire,* p. 227 (see also note 24, p. 227). Simpson notes that in 1942 "many Foreign Office officials thought that the immediate priority was to win the war, not dream dreams of peace" (Simpson, *Human Rights and the End of Empire*, p. 176).

[16] Quoted in Breitman, *Official Secrets,* p. 200.

[17] Ibid., pp. 208, 212–213; Simpson, *Human Rights and the End of Empire,* p. 192 (the quotation comes from this page).

[18] Simpson, *Human Rights and the End of Empire,* pp. 163, 157–158, 160, 159, 164 (including note 33), 165–166 (the quotations are from these pages); Lauren, *The Evolution of International Human Rights*, pp. 151–153; Burgers, "The Road to San Francisco," pp. 464–468.

[19] Simpson, *Human Rights and the End of Empire*, pp. 169–171.

[20] Burgers, "The Road to San Francisco," p. 471.

[21] Lauren, *The Evolution of International Human Rights,* pp. 152–153; Burgers, "The Road to San Francisco," p. 473.

[22] Burgers, "The Road to San Francisco," p. 473. In 1943 the Joint Committee on Religious Liberty had also proposed a specialized human rights body to operate

under the U.N.'s ECOSOC – see Burgers, "The Road to San Francisco," p. 476. The American Jewish Congress had also advocated an "international human rights agency" in the United Nations, and an international Bill of Rights (Burgers, "The Road to San Francisco," p. 476).

[23] Lauren, *The Evolution of International Human Rights,* p. 159.

[24] Burgers, "The Road to San Francisco," p. 473.

[25] Quoted in Simpson, *Human Rights and the End of Empire,* p. 197 (see also p. 196).

[26] Ibid., p. 197; Lauren, *The Evolution of International Human* Rights, p. 158; Burgers, "The Road to San Francisco," p. 473.

[27] Grammatico, "The United Nations and the Development of Human Rights," p. 27.

[28] Ibid., p. 20.

[29] Lauren, *The Evolution of International Human Rights*, p. 158.

[30] Grammatico, "The United Nations and the Development of Human Rights," pp. 20–21.

[31] Morsink, *The Universal Declaration of Human Rights*, p. 1. On Gurvitch's declaration I rely on Simpson, *Human Rights and the End of Empire,* pp. 202–203 (quotations from p. 203).

[32] Lauren, *The Evolution of International Human Rights,* pp. 176–179.

[33] Ibid., pp. 154–155 (as described by Lauren). Jonathan Rosenberg identifies the origins of the campaign in an editorial and banner published in the *Pittsburgh Courier* on December 13, 1941 – see Rosenberg, *How Far the Promised Land?,* pp. 142–143, 279 (note 36 – citing L. Finkle, "The Conservative Aims of Militant Rhetoric: Black Protest during World War II," *Journal of American History*, vol. 60 (December 1973), pp. 692–713).

[34] *Race Against Empire*, pp. 1–2, 22. See also M. L. Dudziak, *Cold War Civil Rights: Race and the Image of American Democracy* (Princeton: Princeton University Press, 2000), especially chs. 1–3.

[35] "Jim Crow's Last Stand," *Chicago Defender*, October 31, 1942 – excerpted in Rosenberg, *How Far the Promised Land?*, p. 155.

[36] Burgers, "The Road to San Francisco," p. 469 (Burgers noted that Roosevelt "was personally convinced that internationalization of the care for human rights was the proper idea for uniting the American people against the forces of totalitarianism"); Simpson, *Human Rights and the End of Empire*, p. 172.

[37] Lauren, *The Evolution of International Human Rights,* p. 141; Johnson, "The Contributions of Eleanor and Franklin Roosevelt to the Development of International Protection for Human Rights," pp. 20–21; Burgers, "The Road to

San Francisco," p. 469. See also Borgwardt, *A New Deal for the World* (FDR "and his foreign policy planners", according to Borgwardt, p. 3, sought "to internationalize the New Deal.").

[38] Quoted in Lauren, *The Evolution of International Human Rights*, p. 141.

[39] Burgers, "The Road to San Francisco," p. 468.

[40] Johnson, "The Contributions of Eleanor and Franklin Roosevelt to the Development of International Protection for Human Rights," p. 21.

[41] Burgers, "The Road to San Francisco," p. 469.

[42] Evans, *The Politics of Human Rights,* pp. 20-21. See, *contra* Evans, Borgwardt, *A New Deal for the World*; and J. T. Kloppenberg, "Franklin Delano Roosevelt, Visionary," *Reviews in American History*, vol. 34 (2006), no. 4, pp. 509–520.

[43] Quoted in S. P. Marks, "From the 'Single Confused Page' to the 'Decalogue for Six Billion Persons': The Roots of the Universal Declaration of Human Rights in the French Revolution," *Human Rights Quarterly*, vol. 20 (1998), pp. 459–508, at p. 508 (note 228).

[44] Evans, *The Politics of Human Rights,* p. 22.

[45] Burgers, "The Road to San Francisco," p. 470, referred to the fact that Roosevelt "must have been encouraged" by the work of H. G. Wells, whom he knew well (see also p. 469). See also Johnson, "The Contributions of Eleanor and Franklin Roosevelt to the Development of International Protection for Human Rights," p. 20.

[46] Burgers, "The Road to San Francisco," p. 469; and pp. 469–470; Simpson, *Human Rights and the End of Empire,* pp. 187–188.

[47] Simpson, *Human Rights and the End of Empire*, pp. 187–188. See also Borgwardt, *A New Deal for the World* and Kloppenberg, "Franklin Delano Roosevelt, Visionary." On the status of economic and social rights in the U.S.A. in more recent years, see C. Sunstein, "Why Does the American Constitution Lack Social and Economic Guarantees?," in M. Ignatieff (ed.), *American Exceptionalism and Human Rights* (Princeton: Princeton University Press, 2005), ch. 4.

[48] Simpson, *Human Rights and the End of Empire*, p. 188.

[49] Ibid., p. 173.

[50] Ibid., p. 179 (on the drafting of the Charter, see also pp. 179–183). Borgwardt, (*A New Deal for the World*, p. 4) attributes the appellation "Atlantic Charter" to "an enterprising British journalist" of the time).

[51] Lauren, *The Evolution of International Human Rights*, pp. 142–143; Simpson, *Human Rights and the End of Empire*, p. 180. The quotations from the Atlantic

Charter come, respectively, from Lauren, *The Evolution of International Human Rights*, p. 142; Simpson, *Human Rights and the End of Empire*, p. 180; Lauren, *The Evolution of International Human Rights*, p. 142; Simpson, *Human Rights and the End of Empire*, p. 180.

[52] Simpson, *Human Rights and the End of Empire*, pp. 181, 235–238 (with quotations from pp. 181, 236).

[53] Quoted in Lauren, *The Evolution of International Human Rights*, p. 144 (emphasis added). See also Lauren, *The Evolution of International Human Rights*, p. 160; N. R. Mandela, " 'No Easy Walk to Freedom, Presidential Address (1953)," and "Statement during the Rivonia Trial (1964)," in W. Laqueur and B. Rubin (eds.), *The Human Rights Reader*, rev. edn. (New York: Meridian/Penguin, 1990), pp. 314–319; and pp. 320–324, respectively.

[54] Lauren, *The Evolution of International Human Rights*, p. 144. See, further, Borgwardt, *A New Deal for the World*.

[55] Lauren, *The Evolution of International Human Rights*, pp. 145, 160; Borgwardt, *A New Deal for the World*, pp. 40, 55.

[56] Lauren, *The Evolution of International Human Rights*, p. 145 (original emphasis removed).

[57] Ibid., p. 150.

[58] Ibid., p. 151.

[59] Quoted in ibid., p. 151.

[60] See, for example, Lord Halifax's (U.K. Ambassador to the U.S.A.) response on March 25, 1941 to FDR's "Four Freedoms" speech, cited in Simpson, *Human Rights and the End of Empire*, p. 174.

[61] Quoted in ibid., p. 185 (emphasis added).

[62] Ibid., pp. 22–23, 204–205, 221, 231.

[63] Ibid., pp. 208–209 (quotation from latter page).

[64] Quoted in ibid., p. 213.

[65] Minute, June 1944, quoted in ibid., p. 212.

[66] Lauren, *The Evolution of International Human Rights*, pp. 112, 143, 156, 161, 162. See also Steiner and Alston, *International Human Rights in Context*, pp. 242–245; P. Hunt, *Reclaiming Social Rights: International and Comparative Perspectives* (Aldershot: Ashgate/Dartmouth, 1996), pp. xvii–xviii, 1–8; Parrott, "Social Security"; S. Morphet, "Economic, Social and Cultural Rights: The Development of Governments' Views, 1941–88," in R. Beddard and D. M. Hill (eds.), *Economic, Social and Cultural Rights: Progress and Achievement* (London: Macmillan, 1992), pp. 74–92; R. M. Brucken, "A Most Uncertain Crusade: The United States, Human Rights and the United Nations, 1941–1954",

Ph.D. dissertation, History, Ohio State University, 1999; C. Palley, *The United Kingdom and Human Rights*, The Hamlyn Lectures, Forty-second Series (London: Stevens and Sons/Sweet and Maxwell, 1991). On American exceptionalism regarding economic and social rights, see, further, Sunstein, "Why Does the American Constitution Lack Social and Economic Guarantees?" ; and Moravcsik, "The Paradox of U.S. Human Rights Policy," in Ignatieff (ed.), *American Exceptionalism and Human Rights*, chs. 4 and 6. For the view that the U.S.A. is less laissez-faire and libertarian than it is usually characterized, see Borgwardt, *A New Deal for the World*; and Kloppenberg, "Franklin Delano Roosevelt, Visionary." Anne-Marie Devereux's study has recently shown that free-market libertarianism, calls for "small government" and resistance to "socialistic" economic and social rights had significant support within at least Liberal governments in Australia during the 1950s and 1960s – see *Australia and the Birth of the International Bill of Human Rights*.

[67] Lauren, *The Evolution of International Human Rights,* p. 162; Lauren, "First Principles of Racial Equality," p. 7.

[68] Lauren, *The Evolution of International Human* Rights, pp. 162–163.

[69] Quoted in ibid., p. 163 (emphasis added).

[70] Ibid., p. 163; Simpson, *Human Rights and the End of Empire,* pp. 185–186.

[71] Quoted in Lauren, *The Evolution of International Human Rights,* p. 163 (emphasis added). See Eleanor Roosevelt, quoted in J. F. Green, *The United Nations and Human Rights* (Washington, D.C.: The Brookings Institution, 1956), pp. 30–31.

[72] Quoted in Lauren, *Power and Prejudice,* p. 156.

[73] Ibid., pp. 156–158. See also Lauren, *The Evolution of International Human Rights*, pp. 165–170.

[74] Lauren, *The Evolution of International Human Rights,* p. 165.

[75] G. Williams, *Human Rights under the Australian Constitution* (Oxford: Oxford University Press, 2002), p. 58. On the positivistic tendencies of both the U.K. and Australia, I rely, also, on C. A. Gearty, *Can Human Rights Survive?* (Cambridge: Cambridge University Press, 2006); Devereux, *Australia and the Birth of the International Bill of Human Rights*; and Simpson, *Human Rights and the End of Empire*.

[76] Lauren, *The Evolution of International Human Rights,* p. 164.

[77] Ibid., p. 166; Lauren, "First Principles of Racial Equality," pp. 9–13; Simpson, *Human Rights and the End of Empire,* p. 239.

[78] Quoted in Lauren, "First Principles of Racial Equality," p. 10.

[79] Quoted in Sohn, "Supplementary Paper," p. 47.

[80] Jhabvala, "The Drafting of the Human Rights Provisions of the UN Charter," p. 3.

[81] Quoted in Simpson, *Human Rights and the End of Empire*, p. 243. See also Lauren, "First Principles of Racial Equality," p. 10, and *passim*.

[82] Quoted in Lauren, "First Principles of Racial Equality," p. 10.

[83] Andrei Gromyko, quoted in Lauren, *Power and Prejudice*, p. 159 (emphasis added). Simpson's account is that "the Chinese proposal was never pressed, and was not discussed," but due "presumably" to "pressure ... put on China by the USA" – *Human Rights and the End of Empire*, p. 243.

[84] Lauren, "First Principles of Racial Equality," p. 10; Lauren, *The Evolution of International Human Rights*, pp. 164–170; Lauren, *Power and Prejudice*, p. 159.

[85] Quoted in Lauren, *Power and Prejudice*, pp. 148–149.

[86] Ibid., pp. 159–161; Tolley, Jr., *The U.N. Commission on Human Rights*, p. 4; Lauren, "First Principles of Racial Equality," pp. 10–11; Lauren, *The Evolution of International Human Rights*, pp. 166–170.

[87] Quoted in Lauren, *The Evolution of International Human Rights*, p. 167.

[88] Quoted in Lauren, "First Principles of Racial Equality," p. 11. See also Lauren, *The Evolution of International Human Rights*, pp. 167–168.

[89] Lauren, *The Evolution of International Human Rights*, pp. 168–170; Lauren, *Power and Prejudice*, pp. 160–161; Lauren, "First Principles of Racial Equality," p. 12.

[90] Lauren, *The Evolution of International Human Rights*, p. 166.

[91] W. E. B. Du Bois castigated Dumbarton Oaks for its failure to represent the world's 750 million black people, and, more generally, for the distorted priority it gave to states over human beings – Von Eschen, *Race Against Empire*, p. 75.

[92] For this section, I have relied on the following sources: Lauren, *Power and Prejudice*, pp. 160-163; Lauren, *The Evolution of International Human Rights*, pp. 175–178; Burgers, "The Road to San Francisco," pp. 475–476.

[93] Simpson, *Human Rights and the End of Empire*, p. 238.

[94] For my account of trials preceding Nuremberg, and for the Nuremberg trials themselves, I rely principally on Bass, *Stay the Hand of Vengeance*.

[95] See ibid., pp. 15, 16, 18, 20, 25, 200–201, 296, 298–300, 322 (note 108); Robertson, *Crimes Against Humanity*, pp. 201–204, 207–211; C. L. Blakesley, "Obstacles to the Creation of a Permanent War Crimes Tribunal," in C. Ku and P. Diehl (eds.), *International Law: Classic and Contemporary Readings* (Boulder, Colorado: Lynne Rienner, 1998), pp. 281–303, at pp. 283, 291–292; Falk, *Human Rights Horizons*, ch. 12 and especially pp. 200–201, 211, 215, 261 (note 1, ch. 12); Sellars, *The Rise and Rise of Human Rights*, ch. 2 and especially

pp. 48–52, 54–64; Cohen, "Beyond Nuremberg," pp. 53–92 (and especially pp. 53–55, 59–61, 69–76, 77ff, 78, 89); Davidson, *Human Rights*, p. 12. On the distorted application of the war crime of "aggression" in the context of the trials at Nuremberg and in the Far East, see Robertson, *Crimes Against Humanity*, p. 201 and ch. 6; Finch, "The Nuremberg Trial and International Law"; and Schick, "The Nuremberg Trial and the International Law of the Future."

[96] On the precedents of the Leipzig and Ottoman trials at the end of the Great War, see Bass, *Stay the Hand of Vengeance*. Bass has little to say about war crimes trials in the Far East.

[97] Lloyd George, September 1918, quoted in Bass, *Stay the Hand of Vengeance*, p. 65.

[98] Id.

[99] Bass, *Stay the Hand of Vengeance*, p. 22.

[100] Ibid., pp. 61, 63, 64, 65, 66, 69, 72, 74–75.

[101] Wright, "The Law of the Nuremberg Trial," pp. 38–72, at pp. 57, 60, 61. See also Malanczuk, *Akehurst's Modern Introduction to International Law*, p. 435; Bass, *Stay the Hand of Vengeance*, pp. 116, 349 (note 73); Blakesley, "Obstacles to the Creation of a Permanent War Crimes Tribunal," p. 285 (where he reports, regarding the 1915 Armenian massacre, that "those who committed such atrocities knew they were committing a crime. Moreover, a review of some state practices and of the views of scholars demonstrates that there was an understanding that crimes against humanity existed" at that time). On Wright's academic background, I rely on Simpson, *Human Rights and the End of Empire*, p. 191.

[102] Malanczuk, *Akehurst's Modern Introduction to International Law*, pp. 112–114, 353–360, ch. 20. See also Robertson, *Crimes Against Humanity*, pp. 211–224; M. Shaw, *International Law*, fourth edn. (Cambridge: Cambridge University Press, 1997), pp. 209–212, 470–473; R. Piotrowicz and S. Kaye, *Human Rights in International and Australian Law* (Chatswood, N.S.W.: Butterworths, 2000), chs. 6, 7, 9 and especially at pp. 165–168.

[103] Malanczuk, *Akehurst's Modern Introduction to International Law*, p. 113.

[104] Ibid., pp. 112–114, 353–355. The full citations for the cases referred to are as follows: *Eichmann v Att.-Gen. of Israel* (1962), 36 ILR 277; *Filartiga v Peña-Irala* (1980) 630 F.2d 876 (2d Cir. 1980) (cited and discussed in ibid., pp. 113–114).

[105] Wright, "The Law of the Nuremberg Trial," p. 39 (note 4).

[106] Bass, *Stay the Hand of Vengeance*, pp. 149-150 (quotations are from this source).

[107] W. B. Cowles, "Universality of Jurisdiction Over War Crimes," *California Law Review*, vol. 33, no. 2 (June 1945), p. 218, quoted in Carrel, "Australia's Prosecution of Japanese War Criminals," p. 63.

[108] Bass, *Stay the Hand of Vengeance*, pp. 149–150.

[109] Piotrowicz and Kaye, *Human Rights in International and Australian Law*, pp. 161–165. See also Robertson, *Crimes Against Humanity*, p. 207.

[110] Robertson, *Crimes Against Humanity*, p. 207.

[111] Ibid., pp. 204–206.

[112] Bass, *Stay the Hand of Vengeance*, pp. 22, 60–82, 92–105.

[113] Robert Lansing, quoted in ibid., p. 93.

[114] Bass, *Stay the Hand of Vengeance*, pp. 93–94.

[115] Quoted in ibid., p. 100. For biographical and other information concerning the Kaiser and the Crown Prince, I have relied on the entries on them in *Encyclopedia Britannica* (Chicago: William Benton, 1962), vol. 23, pp. 620–624, 626; and on Bass, *Stay the Hand of Vengeance*, pp. 60–82 and especially at pp. 78–80.

[116] Bass, *Stay the Hand of Vengeance*, pp. 92–104.

[117] Ibid., 92–105.

[118] Prime Minister Hughes, quoted in ibid., pp. 66–67.

[119] Lauren, *The Evolution of International Human Rights*, p. 87. See also Schabas, *Genocide in International Law*, pp. 16–22. See also Power, *"A Problem from Hell,"* ch. 1.

[120] Blakesley, "Obstacles to the Creation of a Permanent War Crimes Tribunal," pp. 281–303, at p. 285.

[121] Quoted in ibid., p. 285.

[122] Bass, *Stay the Hand of Vengeance*, pp. 60–82, 92–104. *Encyclopedia Britannica*, pp. 620–624, 626.

[123] *Encyclopedia Britannica*, pp. 620–624, 626; Bass, *Stay the Hand of Vengeance*, pp. 66, 74, 76–77, 82–92, 336. On the Leipzig trials, see Bass, *Stay the Hand of Vengeance*, pp. 59, 76, 78, 80–82.

[124] Bass, *Stay the Hand of Vengeance*, pp. 106–108, 110, 114–117, 119–144.

[125] Ibid., *passim*; pp. 12, 147; Robertson, *Crimes Against Humanity*, pp. 198–199.

[126] Robertson, *Crimes Against Humanity*, pp. 198–199 (quotations are from this source); Bass, *Stay the Hand of Vengeance*, pp. 61–62.

[127] Bass, *Stay the Hand of Vengeance*, especially pp. 16, 20–28, 147, 155–157, 181, 184–203. See also Robertson, *Crimes Against Humanity*, pp. 198–200, 207–208.

[128] Quoted in Robertson, *Crimes Against Humanity*, p. 199.

[129] Bass, *Stay the Hand of Vengeance,* p. 154.

[130] Quoted in ibid., pp. 157–158 (I also rely on pp. 12, 150–181, 203–204). Mary Ann Glendon seems to make Prime Minister Churchill the sole villain in this drama. She notes that "Churchill still wanted to shoot them [Nazis]," but she neglects to mention that this was also the U.S. approach under the Morgenthau Plan – see *A World Made New: Eleanor Roosevelt and the Universal Declaration of Human Rights* (New York: Random House, 2001), p. 16.

[131] Bass, *Stay the Hand of Vengeance*, pp. 148, 173–180; 191–194. British Attorney-General Somervell said on one occasion that engaging in a war of aggression was "not a 'war crime' as recognised by International Law" (quoted in ibid., p. 368, note 185). Bass (*Stay the Hand of Vengeance*, p. 368) pointed out "an obvious irony here, with Britain renouncing a principle it had itself established in the Versailles treaty."

[132] Ibid., pp. 175–177. Robertson (*Crimes Against Humanity,* pp. 210–211) has noted that the nexus was eroded by customary international law, the Genocide Convention (1948), draft codes by the International Law Commission, the statutes for the Yugoslavian and Rwandan war crimes tribunals, and the *Tadic* case. He describes (p. 211) the present legal position as follows: "Crimes against humanity may therefore be committed in peacetime, and irrespective of any internal conflict (although the requirement for widespread and systemic oppression will normally mean that such crimes will be committed at times of civil unrest)."

[133] Quoted in Bass, *Stay the Hand of Vengeance,* p. 177.

[134] Ibid., pp. 149 (quotation from this page), 293.

[135] Ibid., pp. 178, 193 (quotation from this page; see also pp. 290–293).

[136] Quoted in ibid., p. 193 (see also p. 16). Note, however, that Somervell's position on this seems inconsistent with his rejection of "waging aggressive war" as an international war crime.

[137] Ibid., pp. 194, 179.

[138] Ibid., p. 194.

[139] Ibid., pp. 147, 14, 160, 19, 24–26, 104, 147–148, 161, 164–168, 176–177. Robertson, *Crimes Against Humanity*, pp. 198–200.

[140] Bass, *Stay the Hand of Vengeance,* pp. 148, 171, 173–180.

[141] Ibid., p. 180.

[142] Robertson, *Crimes Against Humanity*, pp. 201–202. See also Steiner and Alston, *International Human Rights in Context*, p. 125; Sellars, *The Rise and Rise of Human Rights*, ch. 2.

[143] Robertson, *Crimes Against Humanity*, pp. 201–202; Blakesley, "Obstacles to the Creation of a Permanent War Crimes Tribunal," p. 283 (referring to Soviet mistreatment of "national minorities" as a crime against humanity).

[144] Quoted in Bass, *Stay the Hand of Vengeance*, p. 322 (note 108).

[145] Robertson, *Crimes Against Humanity*, pp. 201–202. Consider, also, Stalin's political purges, forced collectivization, and "deportations and forced labour" in Soviet occupied territories (Robertson, *Crimes Against Humanity*, pp. 201–202); Davidson, *Human Rights*, p. 12; Bass, *Stay the Hand of Vengeance*, pp. 200–201.

[146] Robertson, *Crimes Against Humanity*, pp. 208–209; Sellars, *The Rise and Rise of Human Rights*, ch. 2. See also Falk, *Human Rights Horizons*, pp. 201, 215.

[147] Carrel, "Australia's Prosecution of Japanese War Criminals: Stimuli and Constraints", ch. 2 and especially pp. 19, 23–27. See also Falk, *Human Rights Horizons*, ch. 12. For statistics, I rely on Carrel, "Australia's Prosecution of Japanese War Criminals," p. 23, Table A.

[148] Carrel, "Australia's Prosecution of Japanese War Criminals," pp. 2, 19.

[149] Cohen, "Beyond Nuremberg," pp. 59–60; Sellars, *The Rise and Rise of Human Rights*, pp. 48, 50, 52, 63; Falk, *Human Rights Horizons*, ch. 12 (and especially p. 201).

[150] Sellars, *The Rise and Rise of Human Rights*, pp. 48 (quotation from this page), 62.

[151] Ibid., p. 55.

[152] Ibid., pp. 54–55; Falk, *Human Rights Horizons*, p. 201 (where he also notes that the number of Japanese prosecuted for war crimes was reduced because of the Cold War).

[153] Carrel, "Australia's Prosecution of Japanese War Criminals," pp. 7–8, 255–256.

[154] Sellars, *The Rise and Rise of Human Rights*, pp. 48–49. Cf. Falk, *Human Rights Horizons*, p. 200 (that the Tokyo trial amounted to "redress imposed by the victors in the war … and remained characterized in Japanese society as little more than a kangaroo court").

[155] See Carrel, "Australia's Prosecution of Japanese War Criminals," ch. 7.

[156] Ibid., p. 101, Tables C and D; and pp. 29–30, 32, 34.

[157] For example, in the Cairo Declaration of December 1, 1943, the Allies declared that "territories 'stolen' from the Chinese, such as Manchuria, Formosa and the Pescadores should be restored to China, that she [Japan] should be expelled from 'all other territories which she has taken by violence and greed',

and that 'in due course' Korea should become free and independent" (Paul Hasluck, quoted in ibid., p. 34). The Chungking Far-Eastern and Pacific Sub-Commission concentrated on crimes committed against Chinese nationals (Carrel, "Australia's Prosecution of Japanese War Criminals," p. 32). The Australian trial R127 (May 23–24, 1946) concerned a charge against Lt. Gen. Ito Takeo of murdering in Pacific New Ireland "in or about 1944–1945 ... a number of Chinese civilians, half-caste civilians and natives" (Carrel, "Australia's Prosecution of Japanese War Criminals," p. 192, quoting from the original charge).

[158] Cohen, "Beyond Nuremberg," p. 58.

[159] Bass, *Stay the Hand of Vengeance,* p. 119.

[160] Ibid., ch. 4 and especially pp. 106–108, 119–125.

[161] Ibid., pp. 124–125 (see also p. 122).

[162] Quoted in ibid., p. 125. Bass (*Stay the Hand of Vengeance,* p. 125) observes that "Decades before Nuremberg and the *Yamashita* case, this was a command-responsibility conviction on something very close to crimes against humanity. Echoing the 1915 Allied declaration, the court convicted the two men of acting 'against humanity and civilization.'"

[163] Power, *"A Problem from Hell,"* pp. 17–20, 48.

[164] Simpson, *Human Rights and the End of Empire,* p. 205.

[165] Power, *"A Problem from Hell,"* p. 48.

[166] Quoted in ibid., p. 19.

[167] Ibid., pp. 27–28, 53, 44; Brucken, "A Most Uncertain Crusade: The United States, Human Rights and the United Nations, 1941–1954", Ph.D. dissn., History, Ohio State University, 1999, pp. 286–287.

[168] Schabas, *Genocide in International Law,* pp. 63, 68–69.

[169] As summarized by Power, *"A Problem from Hell,"* p. 20.

[170] Schabas, *Genocide in International Law,* p. 69.

[171] Power, *"A Problem from Hell,"* p. 64. On the ABA, McCarthyism, Southern senators, Jim Crow laws and opposition to internationalism and multilateralism, see Brucken, "A Most Uncertain Crusade," pp. 213, 215, 218, 272, 303–310, 345.

[172] Brucken, "A Most Uncertain Crusade," p. 304; Power, *"A Problem from Hell,"* pp. 68–69. According to Brucken, "A Most Uncertain Crusade," p. 218, of the ABA's membership of 41,000 in 1949, only 13 were African Americans.

[173] Power, *"A Problem from Hell,"* pp. 65, 68, 69–70; Brucken, "A Most Uncertain Crusade," pp. 303–304, 242, 298–300 (quotations are from p. 304).

[174] Power, *"A Problem from Hell,"* p. 69.

[175] Quoted in Brucken, "A Most Uncertain Crusade," p. 316; see also pp. 295–296.

[176] Quoted in ibid., p. 311.

[177] Power, *"A Problem from Hell,"* p. 68.

[178] Ibid., pp. 59, 530 (note 2), 60; Brucken, "A Most Uncertain Crusade," pp. 316, 406.

CHAPTER 3

The U.N. Charter and the Universal Declaration of Human Rights

The United Nations Conference on International Organization in San Francisco in 1945 provided the many critics of the plans decided upon at Dumbarton Oaks with an historic opportunity – one that the critics seized, despite the resistance they faced. The conference was notable for its improved representativeness and for the critical role played by NGOs.[1] There were 300 official delegates and 2,500 advisers present. Historian Paul Lauren has concluded that "[n]ever before in the history of the world had so many nations of such various sizes been so widely represented at such a high-level international conference. Never before had Asia and the Pacific Rim been given so much recognition."[2]

While the use of committees and "working commissions" meant that the conference was unusually democratic,[3] this view must balanced by acknowledgement of the reality of the Great Powers' influence. This influence was ultimately seen in the preeminence of the Security Council and the predominance of the Permanent Five within it. Nevertheless, far from being a hegemonic imposition by the Western powers on an unwilling world, the recognition of human rights in the U.N. Charter was the hard-fought, and none too certain, result of the advocacy and lobbying of small and middle powers (especially Latin American countries) and NGOs, and of the impetus from world public opinion.[4]

What, then, was the attitude of the Great Powers, and, in particular, the U.S.A., toward human rights, culminating at San Francisco? The American historian Rowland Brucken, in a work based on extensive archival research, has traced a shift in the early 1940s in the U.S.A.'s stance on human rights, from the more sympathetic and expansive views of President Wilson (though we have to remember the significant blind spots in them) and the early Roosevelt administration, to the latter's more conservative years and those of the Harry Truman and Dwight Eisenhower presidential administrations.[5]

It is a complex task to determine the nature and authenticity of Franklin Roosevelt's and the U.S. State Department's support for human rights, given internal divisions and changes over time, as well as the difference between human rights rhetoric and actors' underlying motives and real policy intentions.[6] One aspect of the internal divisions in the State Department was the rivalry between the more conservative Secretary of State Cordell Hull and the more progressive Undersecretary Sumner Welles. Another conflict revolved around State Department resistance in the summer of 1943 to "pleas by scholars and activists to grant some measure of jurisdiction over human rights issues to an international organization."[7]

Human rights invocations by Roosevelt during the war, as well as the Atlantic Charter, were inspirational rallying calls. But the focus on winning the war, its accompanying devastation, American domestic racial politics[8] (and the racial politics of the British Empire), and the lessons of the League of Nations (especially the U.S.A.'s failure to join it), contributed to the U.S.A.'s dilution of its stated commitments to human rights. Instead, non-intervention, national sovereignty, and an emphasis on national and international security became key themes. In 1944, the postwar Informal Political Agenda Group made only one reference to human rights, and decided not to include reference to them in the list of purposes of the proposed postwar International Organization. This was an indication of internal departmental and Allied reluctance. The pursuit of an international bill of rights and commission on human rights became less pressing for Roosevelt and was met, respectively, with "indifference" and "opposition" from Churchill and Stalin. The U.S.S.R., for example, wanted the postwar organization to devote itself almost exclusively to peace and security issues, with non-intervention a governing principle.[9] The British were anxious that their imperial interests not be interfered with.[10]

Early in 1944, U.S. Secretary of State Cordell Hull retreated from a commitment to human rights, referring to "self-government" only for peoples who were "qualified," and laying stress on "non-intervention" and "national sovereignty." On December 19, 1944, Roosevelt cast doubt on the Atlantic Charter as a source of real obligation. A deal was also struck between the State Department and leading conservative senators, including an assurance to them that there would be no "domestic interference" with local state race laws.[11]

As previously discussed, there was only a very modest provision in relation to human rights in the Dumbarton Oaks proposals. Brucken has, I think, explained one of the puzzles of the Dumbarton Oaks conference – that is, American opposition to, and support for, human rights. He notes the claim by some historians[12] that the U.S.A. battled for inclusion of a human rights clause in the face of British and Soviet opposition.[13] However, he concludes that "the Americans never favored a strong human rights plank,"[14] were uncertain about whether there should even be an Economic and Social Council, and emphasized that "[t]he international organization should refrain from intervention in the internal affairs of any state ..."[15] So, because the American delegation wanted to minimize incursions into American sovereignty, their lobbying for "the inclusion of a general, inconspicuous human rights clause somewhere in the outline for an international organization"[16] was perfectly consistent. Nevertheless, domestic pressure from organizations such as the American Jewish Committee led to some changes to the Dumbarton Oaks proposals: including the "promotion of human rights" as a purpose of the United Nations Organization, a role for the General Assembly in making "human rights recommendations," and in sponsoring a bill of rights, and the proposed establishment of an expert human rights commission which could receive individual petitions. In response to further pressure, and to the necessity of "selling" the idea of the U.N. to the American public, U.S. Undersecretary of State Edward Stettinius, Jr., invited 42 private organizations to participate in the San Francisco Conference as "consultants." The two critical factors in the achievement of the human rights clauses in the U.N. Charter were the advocacy and pressure of diverse states *other than* the Great Power Allies; and the activism of a multitude of NGOs. The Great Powers focused their attention on securing the dominance of the Security Council (and their dominance in it), the rights of states, and the continuation of colonialism.[17]

Latin American states provided passionate support for the human rights cause. Guatemala and Paraguay (together with Egypt and Mexico) argued for human rights to be recognized as an essential purpose of the United Nations. Brazil, the Dominican Republic and Mexico called for "respect for human rights and fundamental freedoms without discrimination against race, sex, condition or creed."[18] Bolivia, Cuba, Panama and Mexico sought to include a bill of rights in the U.N. Charter. Chile declared that human rights ought to prevail over national sovereignty. India, New Zealand, Norway and Lebanon, like Cuba, agreed that explicit, universal human rights should be included at the start of the U.N. Charter. China took the baton from Japan in arguing for the recognition of principles of racial equality and self-determination, and Australia and New Zealand, surprisingly (even given their governments' mildly socialist leanings) advocated a Trusteeship Committee to concern itself with the human rights of people in colonies and dependent territories. And, in the perhaps safer language of "development" (encompassing "welfare," "social," "economic" and "political" aspects), Dr. Herbert Evatt of Australia and Peter Fraser of New Zealand drew attention to the U.N.'s obligation to address the condition of indigenous peoples. Australia and New Zealand were prominent, also, in advocating the recognition of economic and social rights, including a right to "full employment" which was branded by the U.S.A. as "too communistic." In contrast to the U.S.A.'s position, most delegates at the San Francisco Conference closely examined a wide range of economic and social rights.[19]

Delegates of medium and small powers were given solid backing from a variety of NGOs.[20] The NGO consultants at San Francisco ranged from religious groups to internationalist organizations and those concerned with racial issues.[21] They had "extraordinary and unprecedented influence,"[22] a "remarkable impact ... exerted on the very genesis of human rights in the U.N. system."[23]

In contrast, true to the period leading up to San Francisco, the U.S.A. had remained very focused on security issues, a position held by leading U.S. delegate Virginia Gildersleeve.[24] In response to her views a letter was drafted by representatives from the American Jewish Committee and a consultant from the American Association of the United Nations. It called on the American delegation to include human rights in the purposes of the U.N. and to create a human rights commission, and was signed by 21 consultants. The U.S. delegation relented to the pressure brought to bear upon it and brought the proposals before the Big Four on May 2, 1945. They accepted that the U.N. should promote "respect for human rights and fundamental freedoms," that the General Assembly would have a role in advancing them without discrimination, and that the U.N.'s Economic and Social

Council (ECOSOC) would be able to establish a human rights commission.[25] Brucken argues that "Stettinius and the American delegation knew that securing the agreement of the forty-two other nations present might be hard to achieve, for several governments and American pressure groups thought the Big Four amendments *too conservative*."[26] Thus, far from the Charter's proposed human rights being foisted on an unwilling world by the U.S.A., the U.S.A. was criticized for *not going far enough* in protecting human rights. Indeed, the U.S.A. continued to oppose the more radical proposals of Latin America and the U.S.S.R., and lobbied for a domestic jurisdiction clause (which is now Article 2(7) of the U.N. Charter).[27] William Korey, the author of a large-scale study of human rights NGOs, seems to imply that it was really only the *American* NGOs that were responsible for the inclusion of human rights provisions in the U.N. Charter,[28] but this is a lopsided account. For a start, many American consultants had international links, including the National Association for the Advancement of Colored People (NAACP) and groups from other countries also had an influence: the World Trade Union Congress, Provisional World Council of Dominated Nations, West Indies National Council, Sino-Korean People's League, and Non-European United Committee (based in Cape Town, South Africa) among them.[29]

Historian Carol Anderson has, further, persuasively documented the impact of an African American internationalism in the lead-up to the creation of the U.N., and in its early days. As this book has demonstrated, African American groups in the U.S.A. were able to expose parallels between the plight of those living under the yoke of imperialism and colonialism in nearer or far-flung lands (and, indeed, regarding the condition of all people of color), and that of African Americans, from slavery to segregation. African Americans were suffering not only as blacks in a United States stained by racism, but as "coloreds in a white dominated world." Their suffering, empathetic capacity, solidarity and fate were, on this view, inextricably linked with the persistence and perishing of "white colonialism." National civil rights and international human rights had to be fought for in a double struggle: "the struggles for human and civil rights were interwoven, and African Americans were determined to bring about human rights and decolonization in the postwar world."[30]

An example of this linked struggle was the "Third World's" rejection of American attempts to forestall India's complaint to the

U.N. (dated June 22, 1946) over South African discrimination against Indian workers in South Africa. The U.S.A. had tried to take the complaint completely outside the jurisdiction of the U.N. The U.N. General Assembly rejected the U.S. proposal based on Article 2(7) ("domestic jurisdiction") of the Charter, reiterating that every state signatory of it had "made a certain renunciation of their sovereignty," and that it "imposed upon each [U.N.] member an obligation to refrain from policies based upon race discrimination." South Africa, in a victory for the Third World in coalition with the Soviet Union, and to the bafflement of the U.S.A., was formally censured in a 1947 General Assembly resolution for breaching the human rights standards of the U.N. Charter. As Anderson observed, the "UN action seemingly set an outstanding precedent. If the emerging system of apartheid was a violation of human rights, then certainly Jim Crow [segregation in the U.S.A.] had to be as well."[31]

Dr. W. E. B. Du Bois of the NAACP had earlier criticized the Dumbarton Oaks Conference and organized a "colonial conference" on April 6, 1945 to prepare for San Francisco. It brought together scholars and other representatives hailing from Indonesia, British Guiana, Uganda, the Gold Coast, Burma, Puerto Rico, India, Jamaica, and from other regions of Asia, Africa and the Caribbean. The conference proposed the establishment of a colonial commission which would set a timetable for the move toward independence of every colonial territory, and have the U.N. enforce adequate economic, political and social standards in every territory, whether a mandate or not. Moreover, the U.N. would be required to ensure that any Mandatory Power exercising discrimination in such a territory would have its administering power stripped from it. The commission was also to "secure industrialization, economic advancement, and social services in *all* colonial areas," an anticipation in a sense of Third World advocacy of a right to development.[32]

American and Allied resistance to the recognition of human rights in the U.N. Charter, together with the fact that the views of the NGOs ultimately largely prevailed, are sufficient to rebut historian Kristen Sellars' thesis that the American government had all along been committed to human rights and a commission, and simply manipulated the NGOs; giving them a false sense of autonomy as they "pressured" the U.S. government to do what it had already intended to do.[33]

When formally agreed, the U.N. Charter[34] referred to human rights in a number of its provisions. The Preamble reaffirms "faith in fundamental human rights, in the dignity and worth of the human person, in the equal rights of men and women ... to promote social progress and better standards of life in larger freedom." Article 1(3) urges "international cooperation in solving international problems of an economic, social, cultural, or humanitarian character" and the promotion and encouragement of "respect for human rights and for fundamental freedoms for all without distinction as to race, sex, language or religion ..." Articles 10, 11 and 13 concern the General Assembly. Article 13 empowers the General Assembly to initiate studies and make recommendations to promote "international cooperation in the economic, social, cultural, educational, and health fields," and to assist "in the realization of human rights and fundamental freedoms for all without distinction as to race, sex, language, or religion." Article 22 describes the General Assembly's power to establish "subsidiary organs," including those relating to human rights. Articles 58, 60, 62 and 66(2) concern specialized agencies and the responsibilities of the General Assembly and Economic and Social Council (ECOSOC). Article 62, for example, provides that ECOSOC "may make recommendations for the purpose of promoting respect for, and observance of, human rights and fundamental freedoms for all"; and authorizes the drafting of conventions (3) and the arrangement of conferences (4). Article 68 requires that ECOSOC "set up commissions in economic and social fields and for the promotion of human rights." Article 73 mandates respect for "the interests of the inhabitants" of non-self-governing territories; and Article 76 similarly refers to the encouragement of "respect for human rights" in the context of the trusteeship system.[35]

Article 55 provides that, in order to foster stable, peaceful and friendly international relations ("based on respect for the principle of equal rights and self-determination of peoples"), the United Nations shall promote:

a. higher standards of living, full employment, and conditionsof economic and social progress and development;

b.   solutions of international economic, social, health, and related problems; and international cultural and educational co-operation; and

c.   universal respect for, and observance of, human rights and fundamental freedoms for all without distinction as to race, sex, language or religion.

The article is significant in drawing attention to links between human rights violations within a state, international dysfunctions of various kinds, and instability predisposing the world to conflict. Domestic tyranny, oppression or deprivation could increase the likelihood of aggressive foreign policy.[36] Anticolonialist struggles and Wilsonian ideals are reflected in the reference to the "equal rights and self-determination of peoples." The article also embodies the concerns at the time of many social-democratic welfare states such as Australia and New Zealand, by referring to socio-economic conditions, standards of living, employment, development and health. All of this is consistent with the burgeoning of international cooperation and organizations in the nineteenth century. Article 55 also includes a long-sought non-discrimination clause.

These provisions are not at all confined to Western or European experience, or, in particular, to a narrow statist focus on "Enlightenment" civil and political liberties as conventionally conceived. Their attention to "macro" international dilemmas makes recent debates over the global *problématique*, for example, seem much less novel. Unfortunately these provisions have not always been taken seriously.

Article 56 states that all U.N. members "pledge themselves to take joint and separate action in cooperation with" the U.N. "for the achievement of the purposes set forth in Article 55."

Common criticisms of the human rights provisions in the Charter are that the language used is uncertain and that there is much doubt about whether they create international legal obligations, and, if so, of what kind.[37] On the first point, the breadth of the language has some advantages: allowing for the evolution of standards over time, for instance in relation to unforeseen circumstances and new insights, and in maximizing cultural inclusiveness. In terms of the second point, the use of the word "shall" in Article 55 and "pledge" in Article 56 clearly suggests legal obligation[38]; the U.N. Charter is, after all, an international treaty.[39] Any weakness is to be found in the nature or substance of the obligation, "promotion" being a matter of degree. International lawyer Peter Malanczuk concludes that "the vagueness of the language probably leaves a wide discretion to states about the speed and means of carrying out their obligations." He also argues that the provisions do not give individuals rights, but rather only confer *benefits* on them – a resurrection of the old line on individuals as at best "objects" of international law.[40] However, he cites no legal authorities for his conclusion, which is inconsistent with the plain words "human *rights*" (emphasis added) and the overall tenor of Article 55.

As we have seen, the U.S.A. was particularly concerned that any international organization not interfere in domestic issues. Article 2(7) provides that:

> Nothing contained in the present Charter shall authorize the United Nations to intervene in matters which are essentially within the domestic jurisdiction of any state or shall require the Members to submit such matters to settlement under the present Charter; but this principle shall not prejudice the application of enforcement measures under Chapter VII.

Any supranationalism in the Charter could thus be undermined by this commitment to national sovereignty or non-intervention, consistent with a realist model of independent states acting upon each other like impenetrable billiard balls. Nevertheless, over time the language of Article 2(7) has proven to be elastic, and compatible with at least the legal doctrine (if not always the realization) of the protection of human rights. A state's conformity to its own law will not excuse a violation of law at the international level.[41] Moreover, the cry of "domestic jurisdiction" is much less likely to be accepted these days as a defence to a charge that a state has violated human rights. This fact helps to advance the Nuremberg principle. Over time the extent of what can be considered a "domestic" issue has contracted, as has the traditional supremacy accorded to state sovereignty, as former U.N. Secretary-General Boutros Boutros-Ghali once announced. Concurrently, the understanding of what constitutes a "threat to the peace, breach of the peace, or act of aggression" (U.N. Charter, Article

39) has expanded. The impact of this has been that intrastate conduct, such as gross human rights abuses, may be adjudged a threat to international peace and security (for example, by resulting in a civil war that spills across borders, provoking reprisals, or prompting military and/or humanitarian (or other) intervention in or against the offending state). These developments are evident in the humanitarian interventions since the 1990 Gulf War, with Security Council backing, in, for example, Haiti, Somalia, the former Yugoslavia, Rwanda and Kosovo under Chapters VI and VII of the U.N. Charter. In any event, on its face Article 2(7) does not suggest that a state or other official body committing human rights violations is not acting unlawfully; rather it declares that the *United Nations* may not *intervene* (except under Chapter VII) in such matters. What is meant by "intervene" is obviously ambiguous, and it is not clear that it would preclude, say, diplomatic representations. So Article 2(7), even on a fairly conservative reading, does not deny that a state's actions may be in violation of international human rights law, although acting within its domestic jurisdiction; nor does it give a state immunity from legal consequence or sanction for its violations.[42]

Despite these newer constructions, Article 2(7) remains something of an obstacle to punishment of human rights violations. The undemocratic nature of the Security Council, the relative weakness of the General Assembly, the lack of independent funding and military forces, the absence of compulsory international adjudication (in which individuals would have standing) and enforcement mechanisms, and the limitations of the trusteeship scheme[43] are among the familiar criticisms of the constitution of the U.N. Nor was there yet an international bill of rights.

The UDHR[44] has been criticized for, among other things, the lack of representativeness of the process that led to its creation, as well as the supposedly "Western" nature of the norms it contains. The legal scholar Makau Mutua,[45] for example, has argued that the philosophy behind the UDHR and the human rights regime is "essentially European," with "non-Western" views being "largely unrepresented." According to Mutua, the "West" imposed its human rights philosophy on the world, able to do so because of its dominance in the U.N. in 1948. He argues that "most African and Asian states" were not able to participate in the drafting process because of the impediments of colonialism. Further, economic, social and cultural rights were, on his view, "downgraded" in the UDHR, compared with the (presumed to be) Western civil and political rights; despite what he terms the "ineffectual resistance" of the "minority socialist bloc." And he alleges that the individual drafters of the UDHR were mainly Europeans or "Westerners," or were non-Western in only a nominal or tokenistic sense. This last-mentioned point is commonly made by those who wish to argue against the apparent cultural diversity of the drafters. Mutua quotes international legal scholar Virginia Leary as emphasizing that the non-Europeans Pen-Chung Chang (China) and Charles Malik (Lebanon) were "educated in the West."[46] Leary's view raises questions of cultural authenticity and representation as well as cultural determinism: is a particular worldview transmitted by education in "the West" (a term which can suggest a dangerous, misleading homogenization); one which cannot be evaluated or transcended – if need be – by a person so educated?

Mutua, himself a graduate of Harvard Law School and, at the time of writing, Director of the Human Rights Center at S.U.N.Y. at Buffalo, New York, wrote that while the drafters seemed to be a "culturally diverse" group (three from Latin America, two from Asia, and two from Europe) "it was in reality Eurocentric" because Chang had studied at Clark College and Malik at Harvard University, where he had also spent some time teaching.[47] The irony, if one accepts *his own* argument about Western education, of the Western-educated Mutua advocating a "non-Western" view of human rights should be evident.

The drafters were in fact a diverse lot, neither illegitimately aligned with nor able to be readily manipulated by the West. In addition to Malik and Chang, the drafters included Félix Nieto del Rio and Hernán Santa Cruz from Chile, Osman Ebeid and Omar Loufti of Egypt, Ghasseme Ghani from Iran, German Gil Guardia of Panama, General Carlos P. Romulo from the Philippines, Hansa Mehta representing India and Otero J. Mora of Uruguay. Hansa Mehta, educated at the University of Bombay and then the L.S.E., was hardly a puppet of Western imperial designs. She had been the head of the All India Women's Conference, had written a pamphlet (*Civil Liberties* (1945)) decrying Britain's use of emergency powers in her country, and the censorship, confiscation of property and detention without trial that was associated with it. Indeed, she had even endured imprisonment in the years 1930, 1932 and 1940–1941 at the hands of colonial authorities for her civil disobedience activities in India. As the Harvard legal scholar Mary Ann Glendon reports, General Romulo thought of himself as a "third world soldier." He was one of the strongest and most outspoken critics of colonialism, and a persistent advocate for the entrenchment of the principle of equality of treatment of persons under international law. A Lebanese Arab, Malik was influenced by growing up in a country where he was exposed to Christian, Islamic, Arabic and French cultures. With regard to the claim that he was liable to be manipulated by Western forces, the lonely Malik was a fiercely independent member of the Commission on Human Rights. Moreover, he came to be heavily engaged in Middle East politics, especially through his role as the main spokesman for the Arab League. Chang had been Dean of Tsing Hua College and a professor at Nankai University in China. He was familiar with Islamic culture, having been China's ambassador to Turkey from 1940 to 1942. He had also held an ambassadorial post in Chile during the war. He was a committed anti-imperialist. As Glendon emphasizes, Chang "deplored the efforts of colonial powers to impose on other peoples a standardized way of thinking and a single way of life. That sort of uniformity could be achieved, he said, only by force at the expense of truth. It could never last." Both Chang and Santa Cruz were staunch supporters of economic and social rights. According to the U.N.'s John Humphrey, Chang and Malik were the dominant intellectual forces when it came to the drafting the UDHR. This evidence regarding the diverse background of the drafters can be deployed to rebut claims similar to Mutua's that have been made by other scholars[48]

British political scientist Tony Evans has been one of the principal exponents of the view of "the Project of Universal Human Rights" as a projection of "US Hegemony."[49] Evans proceeds on the basis that the UDHR was a result of the exercise of hegemonic power by the U.S.A. in its own interests. Evans' argument can be broken down into three main phases. In the first phase, Evans describes the U.S.A. as a hegemon that put "universal" human rights to the forefront internationally. Influenced by Gramscian hegemonic and regime theories, Evans argues that such human rights were in the interests of, and provided a legitimating cloak for, the United States. Some of the key interests he identifies include the following: the role of the rhetoric of human rights as a moral mobilizer of American society during World War II (principally as a way of countering popular American isolationist resistance to the U.S.A.'s becoming involved in a "foreign" war); the legitimation of American intervention internationally, particularly in order to establish a global free-trade regime; as a symbol for the "Americanizing" of the world in the image of liberal capitalism; and as a propaganda weapon against the communist bloc as the Cold War intensified.[50] For Evans, universal human rights were used by the U.S.A. as a "symbol of solidarity" to gain popular approval of "a new international political and economic order with the United States actively at its centre."[51]

In the second phase (arguably dating, for Evans, from the mid-1950s, but he is unclear on this), human rights expanded in directions that the U.S.A. did not approve of, and that conflicted with its interests. Communist states, for example, pressed for recognition in the UDHR of rights to work, to social security, and for a strong role for the state in realizing rights; despite, also, the U.S.S.R. giving these a strongly positivist character, and providing a staunch defence of state sovereignty and non-intervention. What Evans calls less developed states (including the Latin American "bloc") advocated that human rights be legally guaranteed, that humanitarian intervention in the cause of human rights not be frustrated by any doctrine of state sovereignty, and – especially critical for the U.S.A. – that economic, social and cultural rights be accorded a respect equal to that given to civil and political rights with which they were intertwined. Evans argues that while economic, social and cultural rights found a place in the UDHR, they were degraded relative to civil and political rights by special qualifications. Other international developments described by Evans as contrary to American interests included the leadership role of the U.S.S.R. in relation to developing states' claims for equality of states, racial equality, self-determination and decolonization.[52]

Evans seems baffled that the American hegemon was not able to prevail on the question of the nature of the international human rights regime. In relation to the contrary developments just described, Evans concludes that:

> [f]inding such demands unacceptable *and irresistible*, the United States withdrew its early support for a human rights regime, leaving the regime without hegemonic leadership ...[53]
> [F]ollowing the attempt by the USA to establish the idea of human rights in the immediate postwar years, it became increasingly difficult to limit the debate to those areas that best

suited America's interests ... [There were] features of the early debates on human rights [that] weakened both the will *and the capacity* of the USA to develop a strong [human rights] regime ... [So the] United States became increasingly aware that it *could not hope to limit* the extent of the regime to its own interests ... [A]ttempts to construct a regime were conducted within the context of the Cold War and rapid decolonisation. Taken together, these political conditions meant that the USA *could not resist* the growing movement to cast human rights *in a way that challenged its interests* ... To avoid [the] risk [of being outvoted by the developing countries' bloc in the U.N. General Assembly], with its attendant perceived loss of status and increasing unrest among domestic groups ... the United States calculated that the withdrawal from the debate was politically preferable ... These forces caused the hegemon to change its emphasis in an attempt to marginalize an issue [human rights] that promised to gain an importance *beyond its control and against its own interests.*[54]

My point in recording some of Evans' statements, as the added emphasis in the quotations no doubt implies, is to stress the extent to which he acknowledges that the U.S.A. did not get its own way in setting the agenda for an international human rights regime. If a "hegemon" has not been successful in constructing a regime that coincides with its principal interests, is it still hegemonic with regard to that regime? I would have thought not. Evans accepts that all states, even hegemonic ones, operate under certain "constraints,"[55] but he nevertheless urges that such constraints can be "ameliorated if the hegemon is successful in gaining legitimacy for a set of rights that reflect its own existing social order, beliefs and practices."[56] But, on his own account, that is precisely what the U.S.A. was *unable* to do. The international community embraced a conception of human rights that went well beyond Evans' construction of them as a liberal, capitalist American phenomenon. It is inconsistent to say that the U.S. approach was not entrenched in the U.N. system (that is, it was *not* "successful in gaining legitimacy for a set of rights that reflect its own existing social order, beliefs and practices")[57] but that U.S. hegemonic power was fundamentally undiminished. Moreover, Evans underestimates the degree of diversity within the U.S.A. on the issue of human rights.

Evans' creative solution to this dilemma can be described in the context of what I have called the third phase of his argument: that because the international human rights regime expanded in a direction contrary to U.S. interests, the U.S.A. determined to exercise hegemonic power by undermining that regime, by making the UDHR non-binding, by emasculating economic, social and cultural rights (for example, the creation of separate covenants for civil and political and economic, social and cultural rights), and by withdrawing from U.N. processes of human rights norm-creation.[58] It is true that these American influences had a weakening effect on the human rights regime; but, overall, it is more consistent to conclude, as Evans himself does in several places, that the U.S.A. was *not* successful in installing a human rights regime that dovetailed with its interests, at least as those interests are characterized by Evans.

As we have seen, and as I will further elaborate, part of the bafflement Evans experiences comes from his exaggeration of the U.S.A.'s wartime and postwar "early enthusiasm for human rights."[59] While recognizing domestic forces hostile to human rights as pressures on the American hegemon, he underestimates the extent to which those hostile forces (combined with traditions of understandable respect for America's constitutional system, and with isolationism, libertarianism and racism) were at times explicitly, at other time implicitly, *consistent with* the interests of the American state. We have seen this in relation to the limits of Wilsonian idealism, American wariness of humanitarian intervention and war crimes trials, and reluctance to address human rights at Dumbarton Oaks and at San Francisco. My point here is that the entrenchment of a diverse human rights regime at the international level was achieved at times *despite* American and Western resistance to it.

Incidentally, Evans often falls into the trap of equating the "Western" approach with that of the liberal-capitalist U.S.A. However, as we will see, that is a grave mistake. There were differences between the various Western states. For example, on the question of economic and social rights, while there was some American resistance (but this is still more complex than Evans seems to understand – especially considering the continuing influence of the spirit of the New Deal kept alive by Eleanor Roosevelt) to some conceptions and forms of implementation in relation to these rights, other Western states wholeheartedly embraced them (for example, France, whose 1946 constitution protected such rights; Australia; New Zealand; the British, though less consistently; and much of Europe).[60]

Moreover, it is a misrepresentation, as the debates on the UDHR bear out,[61] to imply, as Evans does, that the developing states were not really interested in so-called "traditional" civil and political rights.[62] Having suffered violations of these rights in an acute form under colonial rule (for example, lack of political participation in a democratic system, racial discrimination, slavery and slave labour), again and again one finds representatives of developing states lending support to the recognition of these rights.[63] What, after all, is a right to equal treatment, and, especially, the right not to be subject to racial discrimination (which Japan and China, for instance, advocated, backed by a vast array of national, international and transnational forces against racism and colonialism), if not a *civil* right? So it is crude to conclude in relation to the UDHR, as Evans does, that "it is important to note that only Articles 22–27 deal with the group of rights of central concern to socialist and less developed states. The remainder are of an overwhelmingly political and civil nature and reflect the dominant view of the western majority in the Assembly."[64]

One might also note here a common criticism of the UDHR on the basis that there are *fewer* economic, cultural and social rights provisions in the UDHR. This is true, but again a rather crude point. The recognition of economic, social and cultural rights cannot simply be determined by the relative *number* of articles devoted to them. For example, one could make the obvious point, necessary given how often reference is made in the literature to the number of articles in criticism of the UDHR, that one might have, for the sake of argument, a single, but very detailed, article on economic, social and cultural rights in a declaration, but several articles on, say, the rights of prisoners. One could not, surely, conclude from this that the rights of prisoners have been given a priority over economic, cultural and social rights in this hypothetical declaration. One would have to look, for example, at the *content* of the respective articles, and the overall tenor of the declaration. We will return to such issues later in this chapter, but we should keep in mind the robustness and breadth of some of the economic, social and cultural rights that do appear in the UDHR. Take, for example, Article 22, which provides, *inter alia*, that

> [e]veryone, as a member of society, has the right to social security and is entitled to realization ... of the economic, social and cultural rights indispensable for his dignity and the free development of his personality.

Consider, also, Article 25(1), which declares, in part, that

> [e]veryone has the right to a standard of living adequate for the health and well-being of himself and of his family ...

Ironically, despite Evans' call for scholars to pay more attention to the politics of human rights, his account seems to have been influenced by taking some of the Cold War human rights propaganda, or at least rhetoric, on "both" sides at face value. For example, he says:

> According to the socialist countries those [civil and political rights] developed in the US and Europe during the seventeenth and eighteenth centuries were nothing less than a reactionary attempt to legitimate a set of outmoded, middle-class, bourgeois values that did little for the interests of the poor and excluded.[65]

In fact, as Stephen Marks has shown, at least various French declarations of the eighteenth century included proto-socialist notions and rights guarantees for the poor.[66]

As an alternative to Evans' three-phase argument, I want to provide one of my own as a brief summation of my critique of his approach (which is not to say that I do not see the value of his exploration, nor that there is no common ground between our views).

The first phase of the argument accepts that the U.S.A. was a hegemonic power at the end of World War II, but one that was often *resistant* to international human rights. This resistance was consistent with a long history of isolationism. Even under the relatively internationalist Wilson administration there had been, as we have seen, resistance to humanitarian intervention, to the Japanese-sponsored racial equality clause, and to war crimes trials. There was much opposition to the trial of those accused of committing war crimes during World War Two. Official U.S. government support for international human rights at Dumbarton Oaks and at San Francisco was weak at best. There was also resistance to the Genocide Convention (1948). The U.S.A. was not enthusiastic about decolonization, and racism was a pivotal force in domestic politics. The U.S. Government was strongly committed to the principles of state sovereignty and non-intervention, arguing successfully (along with the U.S.S.R.) for the "domestic jurisdiction" clause in the U.N. Charter. Segregation, lynchings and restrictive immigration supported by a combination of racism, libertarianism and a strong anti-communist federalism played their part: "liberals" criticizing American race relations were accused of being in league with "socialistic" central government tyranny or even "world government" dictatorship under the cover of the United Nations. Constitutional arguments were also called in aid by organizations such as the American Bar Association. All of these tendencies were given expression in the U.S. Senate, which had earlier excluded the U.S.A. from the League of Nations.[67]

In speaking of U.S. resistance to human rights, however, we must keep in mind the complexity involved here. For while there was substantial resistance to international human rights in the U.S. State Department and from a variety of conservative organizations and actors (including U.S. Senators and the American Bar Association),[68] there were the contrasting supportive efforts of Eleanor Roosevelt and a coalition of home-grown human rights activists.[69] My primary focus here is on official American government resistance.

The examples of American government resistance to international human rights are many. The U.S.A. pressured Eleanor Roosevelt to push for a non-binding human rights declaration rather than a treaty, and the U.S. State Department often undermined her efforts.[70] It unsuccessfully opposed the reference to "rebellion against tyranny and oppression" in the Preamble of the UDHR. Eleanor Roosevelt suggested that such a phrase "could be interpreted as conferring a legal character on uprisings against a government that was in no way tyrannical," or, similarly, it could be "invoked by subversive groups wishing to attack or undermine genuinely democratic Governments." Ironically it was a Cuban representative who retorted that such a right to rebellion was to be found in the speeches of Thomas Jefferson.[71] The U.S.A. also opposed the inclusion of economic and social rights. From his unmatched archival research into the drafting of the UDHR, Johannes Morsink concluded that the U.S.A. was alone in interpreting the distinction between civil and political and economic and social rights in a "malignant" fashion, in a way that undermined the latter rights. With the possible exception of the U.K., but only upon occasion, the other drafters accepted the unity, equality and synergy between all human rights in the UDHR.[72] The U.S. delegation, according to one scholar, also tried to emasculate human rights relating to healthcare, social security, tertiary education, labour standards, and immigration and asylum.[73] It assisted in thwarting plans for a system to conduct human rights investigations based on individual petitions,[74] and helped influence the U.N. Commission on Human Rights' judgment that it lacked power to act on the approximately 1000 petitions it had received (the so-called "self-denying rule").[75] It advocated a "federal," "non-self-executing" clause. Such a clause would have precluded international human rights obligations applying locally unless they had been specifically implemented by legislation.[76] The U.S. Senate, in particular, was a vociferous opponent of the Genocide Convention (1948), fearing that its provisions might apply to lynchings and to vilification of, and other discrimination toward, African Americans. The U.S. State Department opposed the category of "cultural genocide," the principle of universal jurisdiction, and the Convention's possible application to the treatment of African Americans. These facts are striking and tragic given how recently Allied troops had been trudging on the cold dirt of Dachau, Belsen and Auschwitz. Its arm strengthened by the American Bar Association and other conservative groups, the U.S. Senate failed to ratify the Convention. It thus resisted the entreaties of the Truman Administration, strong domestic support from NGOs in the U.S.A. and the overwhelming international approval of the Convention. The Senate was not swayed by James Rosenberg (leader of the U.S. Committee for a Genocide Convention), who had presented to Undersecretary of State Robert Lovett an inventory of groups in favour of the Convention with an aggregate of more than twenty million members. The Genocide Convention was unanimously adopted by the U.N. General Assembly, but it would not be until four decades later that the U.S. Senate would ratify it.[77]

The second phase of the argument suggests that the U.S.A. and its allies were pushed to keep the promises they had made during the war, and even to go beyond them. Those who pushed the Allies included the Latin American states, the socialist bloc, China, other smaller powers, domestic and international organizations (for example, the ILO), NGOs, social movements, and committed idealists, activists and scholars, including leading lights from the American civil rights and Pan-African movements. These actors were able to transform the weak recognition of international human rights into the stronger acknowledgement in the U.N. Charter, and still more robust protections of the UDHR. The U.S. hegemon, contrary to Evans' view, was not able to win out on fundamental issues regarding universal human rights. Evans argued that "the hegemon must sustain a view of human rights that demands little change to existing social practices."[78] Clearly, the U.S.A. was *not* able to sustain such a view. The character of the international human rights regime that emerged was not a simple outline of an American hegemonic footprint. The sources of vociferous American domestic opposition to that regime are perfectly consistent with this view: the American view as described by Evans did not prevail on decolonization, racial equality or economic and social rights.

The third phase of the argument is that the U.S.A. was effectively defeated in its efforts (on Evans' view) to reduce the UDHR to a mere copy of the American Bill of Rights. An emerging transnational civil society supporting human rights, the interventions of small states, the socialist bloc, and the nascent "Third World" ensured that the UDHR accommodated decolonization, racial equality and the *duties* of the individual, and paid attention to world conditions required for the realization of universal human rights (see Article 28, UDHR). That is why American withdrawal from the international human rights regime (including the long delay in the U.S.A.'s ratification of international human rights instruments) is more plausibly understood as being what it looks like: not an innovative exercise of hegemonic power to undermine the existing regime, but a defeat of the hegemon on a number of its interests (at least at the level of normative standards).

As an elaboration of this argument, I now want to examine more closely the drafting of the UDHR. Johannes Morsink, whose work on the origins and drafting of the UDHR is probably the most detailed archive-based study in English,[79] concluded as follows:

> The lingering allegation of ethnocentrism [against the UDHR] is in part caused by the fact that very few people seem to know what was said and done during the drafting process. This ignorance has led to numerous misconceptions about how the document was written and what it and its various parts

mean ... [T]he two-year-long process of drafting the Declaration was a very inclusive one ...[80]

Morsink identifies a preparatory phase followed by seven further drafting "stages." In the preparatory phase, a "nuclear" committee received contributions from many NGOs on the question of human rights, as well as human rights bill drafts from a number of Latin American states.[81] The Nuclear Committee recommended that the Economic and Social Council (ECOSOC) "should at all times pay due regard to equitable geographical distribution,"[82] and this was reflected in the appointments to the Commission on Human Rights responsible for developing the UDHR, namely: Australia, Belgium, Byelorussian Soviet Socialist Republic (B.S.S.R.), Chile, China, Egypt, France, India, Iran, Lebanon, Panama, Philippine Republic, U.K., U.S.A., U.S.S.R., Uruguay and Yugoslavia.[83]

Stage 1 of the drafting process involved the first session of the Commission on Human Rights (January–February 1947). The Chairman (Eleanor Roosevelt – U.S.A.), Vice-Chairman (Pen-Chung Chang – China), and Rapporteur (Charles Malik – Lebanon) were to "undertake, with the assistance of the [U.N.] Secretariat, the task of formulating a preliminary draft international bill of human rights."[84] They were authorized to "consult any document or person deemed by them of relevance to their work."[85] There was criticism by the U.S.S.R., Canada, Chile, Czechoslovakia and France that the initial drafting group of Roosevelt, Malik, Chang and Humphrey was too small and unrepresentative. In response, the drafting committee was increased to eight members: Australia, Chile, China, France, Lebanon, U.S.S.R., U.K., U.S.A. John Humphrey, a Canadian, was appointed Director of the Secretariat's Division on Human Rights and was asked in the first instance by Roosevelt, and then more formally by ECOSOC, to complete a draft international bill of rights.[86] Humphrey was heavily influenced by Latin American jurists[87] and by his own socialist commitments. Humphrey's draft became the "basic" one for discussion as a model for the UDHR.[88]

Humphrey based his draft on a number of drafts the U.N. Secretariat had at its disposal. These included the "Sankey Bill,"[89] which had been inspired by H. G. Wells' activism in London, and ones by international law scholar Hersch Lauterpacht, the American Law Institute and the *Institut de droit international*. Humphrey observed in his memoirs that "[w]ith two exceptions, all these texts came from English-speaking sources and all of them from the democratic West. The documentation which the Secretariat brought together *ex post facto* in support of my draft included texts extracted from the constitutions of many countries. But I did not have this before me when I prepared my draft."[90] It is misleading, however, to emphasize the predominance of English-language human rights drafts as examples for Humphrey's draft. For instance, while Humphrey found the American Law Institute's draft to be "the best of the texts on which I worked," the American Law Institute was not a U.S. organization. We may recall that the *Statement of Essential Human Rights* produced by that Latin American Institute was the result of "two years' worth of work by a committee of advisers representing the major cultures of the world."[91] Humphrey himself emphasized that the American Law Institute draft had been proposed without success by Panama at San Francisco, and that it had been written "by a distinguished group representing many cultures ..."[92] These drafts, then, were not merely reflections of the interests and values of European, developed states. Further, the fact that the draft could be correlated with so many constitutional provisions around the world, albeit *ex post facto*, is not without significance.

In Stage 2, the enlarged drafting committee of eight was appointed (April 8, 1947). It discussed a number of drafts, including ones from a range of countries and NGOs, but agreed to use Humphrey's. It became known as the Secretariat Outline. A Temporary Working Group comprised of representatives from France, Lebanon, and the U.K. asked René Cassin (France) to polish Humphrey's draft.[93]

Stage 3, for Morsink, covered the second session of the full Commission on Human Rights, at which, in addition to being present at meetings of the Drafting Committee, many NGOs[94] participated. NGOs, individuals and various states (China, U.K., France, Chile, Ecuador, Cuba, Panama, India and the U.S.A.) presented their own human rights bill drafts. The Commission produced the so-called "Geneva Draft" in this session. Of thirty-eight states given the opportunity to respond to the Geneva Draft, fourteen did so: Egypt, Norway, South Africa, Pakistan, Canada, the Netherlands, Australia, U.S.A., New Zealand, India, Sweden, Brazil, France and Mexico. Stages 4 and 5, covering May–June 1948, involved sessions of the Drafting Committee and Commission. Stage 6 refers to the Third (Social and Humanitarian) Committee of the General Assembly's meetings between September and December 1948. Finally, Stage 7 covers the final debate in the Plenary Session of the Third General Assembly which adopted the UDHR unanimously on December 10, 1948.[95]

While Morsink acknowledges the impact of eighteenth-century declarations on the UDHR, and especially the Preamble and Article 1, he argues that it is a mistake to conclude that the UDHR simply mirrored those declarations. While the phraseology of the Virginia Declaration of Rights (1776), the American Declaration of Independence and French Declaration (1789) found its way into the UDHR, Morsink emphasizes the UDHR's more complete embrace of secularism.[96] The most important underlying features of UDHR rights according to Morsink are their inalienability, universality and what he calls "inherence"[97]:

> [H]uman ... rights ... [are] located in human beings simply by virtue of their own humanity and for no other extraneous reason, such as social conventions, acts of governments, or decisions of parliaments or courts.[98]

Article 1 of the UDHR declares that "All human beings are born free and equal in dignity and rights. They are endowed with reason and conscience and should act towards one another in a spirit of brotherhood." The first recital of the Preamble similarly declares that "recognition of the inherent dignity and of the equal and inalienable rights of all members of the human family is the foundation of freedom, justice and peace in the world." These provisions embody principles of the "moral equality" of people and inalienability. The UDHR *recognizes* human rights – they are not *given* by anyone and thus cannot be taken away. They are inherent. It pays to note that it was in accordance with a proposal from China that "conscience" was included in Article 1. The Chinese equivalent of the word implied "two-man-mindedness," or an empathetic disposition toward a fellow human being. It was not an exclusively Western conception.[99]

Morsink concludes that despite the obvious Enlightenment influences, precedents from the Enlightenment did not have a "great role" in the UDHR's drafting.[100] Instead, throughout his major work on the making of the UDHR he emphasized the significance of the

Holocaust, national and international NGOs, Latin American countries, and socialist states.

Stephen Marks, a Harvard human rights scholar who has undertaken a great deal of primary research into French Revolution documents on rights, treats them as having a significant "impact on the form and content of the UDHR."[101] In part I think his view is a result of where he was looking, but, nevertheless, even Marks identifies a range of other significant influences on the UDHR from ancient thought, the natural law tradition, Marxism and socialist philosophy, practice and state systems, and views that had their genesis outside the West.[102] In answer to a frequently cited article by the historian of religion Elaine Pagels,[103] Marks notes that "certain ideas of equality, fairness, charity, and dignity have origins far earlier and culturally less confined than the Enlightenment."[104] As far as French Revolution documents are concerned, Marks concludes that "the heritage of those texts, while strongly felt in twentieth century texts, has been enriched by other streams of thinking to the extent that it would be erroneous to dismiss internationally recognized human rights as a product of Western cultural imperialism."[105]

Moreover, Marks' research is important in counteracting the stunted, inaccurate view that the Enlightenment overall, and especially French Revolution documents, embodied a narrow, disconnected liberal individualism (in tune with other "straw persons" of liberalism).[106] This misleading view, which Marks challenges, could be said to neglect *égalité* and *fraternité* in the revolutionary slogan. He draws attention to elements of "solidarity" in the declarations, to limits on rights, and to duties to the community, to proto-socialist values emerging out of the Rousseauian tradition, and to economic, social, welfare and cultural rights.[107] He concludes that the "complexity of the debate in the eighteenth century, and the balancing of Locke and Rousseau in the spirit of that age, should raise considerable suspicion over the reductionism by which human rights come under attack as privileging egoism over the needs of society."[108]

Let us look more closely at the heritage of the French Revolution. Specific articles of the 1789 French Declaration were used as "points of reference" during the drafting of the UDHR, especially in relation to the Preamble and Article 1 of the UDHR, and concerning criminal "due process" (including the presumption of innocence – which, it must be said, was also well known to the common law world), and "resistance to oppression." Reference was made to the 1789 Declaration not only because of its obvious fame and clarion tone, but because it had constitutional status at the time of the creation of the UDHR, incorporated (via the 1791 French constitution) in France's 1946 constitution.[109]

Equality was given pride of place over liberty by the French Constituent Assembly, Article 1 of the 1789 Declaration stating, in part, that "[m]en are born and remain free and equal in rights ..." The 1789 Declaration also referred to equality in "public employment, taxation, and ownership of property." However, as this book has already noted, the Declaration did not attempt to deal with gender or racial equality – two large gaps that the UDHR sought to fill.[110]

In the spirit of this seriously limited egalitarianism, various French declarations of the eighteenth century sought to protect economic, social and cultural rights. In so doing, they anticipated what we now call the "indivisibility" of human rights. It has often been claimed, inaccurately as I have argued, that the UDHR was mainly a reflection of Enlightenment thought, which meant that civil and political rights (in a Cold War caricature, the "real" human rights) dominated it, and were only supplemented by "new," "second generation" (nineteenth- and twentieth-century) economic rights at the behest of the socialist bloc.[111] But this view is doubly mistaken: first, in attributing too much to the influence of the Enlightenment on the UDHR; and second, in characterizing that Enlightenment influence as a narrowly "liberal" or libertarian one that knew little, if anything, of economic (with the exception of property) and social rights. Indeed, social, cultural and economic rights were well known in the Enlightenment and represented in eighteenth-century declarations in France. They answered the revolutionary call for *égalité*.[112] According to Marks, "[i]n the mind of many representatives of the Third Estate, human rights began with the rights that today we call economic, social and cultural ..." And the writers of the Declaration of 1789 conceived of the enmeshing of social, cultural, economic and civil and political rights, not their distinction.[113]

The 1789 Declaration provided rights to education, work and "public assistance." The French constitution of 1791 includes a Title I, "Fundamental Provisions Recognized by the Constitution," which demonstrates the breadth of rights protections acknowledged by France in the eighteenth century. Equal access to employment, equal taxation "in proportion to means," equal punishment of offences, "public relief for abandoned children, infirm paupers, and persons who have not found work" and "free public basic education" were all recognized in 1791.[114] Other French draft declarations of the late eighteenth century, and the 1793 Declaration reinforced a broad conception of human rights. For example, a draft by Abbé Sieyès (a representative from Nemours in the Estates General) included a human right of a citizen "unable to satisfy his needs ... [to] the assistance of his fellow citizens."[115] Similarly, the 1793 Declaration proclaimed that "public assistance" was a "sacred debt" that meant, in practical terms, finding work for, or publicly assisting, unfortunates. The Declaration also made reference to a notion of "social protection": which spoke of society's obligation to ensure its members' enjoyment of rights.[116]

The Preamble of the UDHR refers to the "disregard and contempt for human rights [that] have resulted in barbarous acts which have outraged the conscience of mankind." Morsink has argued that the "moral outrage" of the drafters toward the Nazi regime and the Holocaust lay "behind the acceptance of the entire range of rights" in the UDHR.[117] The UDHR was, on this view, a systematic response to the lessons of Nazism. Articles 1 and 2 of the UDHR reflect the inherent, equal dignity of all human beings without discrimination, the "unity of the human race"[118] in contrast to the radical, racist dehumanization of Nazism.[119] Articles 3 and 4 proclaim rights to "life, liberty and security of the person" and a prohibition on slavery and servitude, motivated partly by the Nazi attitude of contempt for human life, its slave labour, forced prostitution and exploitation of POWs. Article 5 prohibits "torture, cruel and inhuman treatment or punishment" of which Nazi medical experimentation on humans was just one gruesome example.[120] Articles 6, 7, 8, 9, 10 and 11 declared various rights related to legalism, rule of law and constitutionalism. Jews had been deprived of rights on the basis of German courts holding them to be "legally dead" and "incompetent." Thus, Article 6 recognizes a right to legal personality (it is useful to recall here my discussion of the personality of individuals under international law). Linked to this, Article 15 of the UDHR provides that everyone has the right to a nationality, and that no one is either to be arbitrarily deprived of it, nor denied a right to change it. This article was in part a response to the cynical Nazi cancellation of the nationality of Jews before they were killed or deported as "stateless" persons. The Nazi Adolf

Eichmann, of the obscenely named Bureau of Jewish Affairs, explained this Nazi strategy as follows:

> [T]he legal experts drew up the necessary legislation for making the victims stateless, which was important on two counts: it made it impossible for any country to inquire into their fate, and it enabled that state in which they were resident to confiscate their property.[121]

Article 7 speaks of "equality before the law," flagrantly violated under the racist Nazi "legal" system. The inclusion of Article 7 had been opposed by both the U.K. and the U.S.A, ironically most likely for reasons of race, which we have already discussed in a number of places. Articles 9, 10 and 11 were an understandable response in part to the capricious, corrupt and politicized Nazi "legal" and "judicial" systems.[122] For example, Nazi prosecutors used the warped pseudo-biological classification of "criminal 'type.'"[123] Morsink elaborated on this issue as follows:

> The Nazi model of criminals as sick people dismissed the need for ... the presumption of innocence, the need for a public trial, the right to the means for one's defense and protection from being charged under a retroactive law.[124]

Articles 19 and 20 on freedom of expression and of assembly and association were a response to the intolerant, repressive Nazi regime where political opponents were brutally attacked or eliminated. Article 16 acknowledges a right to marry and establish a family, unlike the Nuremberg Laws (1935) which prohibited sexual relations or marriages between Jewish and non-Jewish Germans. Article 26 set the limits of acceptable education: it "shall be directed to the full development of the human personality and to the strengthening of respect for human rights and fundamental freedoms. It shall promote understanding, tolerance and friendship among all nations, racial or religious groups ..." The article rejected the Nazi state's totalitarian monopoly of education as indoctrination, and its intrusion into families.[125]

The Nazi system and the Holocaust made the contours of human dignity and rights based on an inherent, universal humanity clearer through their tragic negation. Philosopher and psychologist John

Glover has given an illuminating account of how Nazis attacked the humanity of perpetrators and victims by numbing proper human empathetic relations, not to mention moral impulses and requirements. Victims were humiliated, degraded and stripped of their dignity. Nazis distanced and dehumanized their victims, deploying corrosive stereotypes. This removal of the protective layers of human dignity "breached a moral barrier" and made it "easier to go the whole way in atrocity."[126]

The economic and social rights in the UDHR are the result of wide-ranging influences and support: including social-democratic and socialist ideas, the revolutionary experiences of the eighteenth, nineteenth and twentieth centuries, the ILO and other international and transnational organizations, Latin American constitutional experience, and even American experience (despite subsequent official state resistance to the rights).[127] The principal drafters René Cassin (France) and John P. Humphrey (Canada) were committed to many socialist and social-democratic values. The reformed Latin American constitutions of the 1930s and 1940s, as well as the Mexican constitution of 1917, became useful models for Humphrey, as did draft human rights bills from Panama, Chile and Cuba. There is also a significant overlap between the provisions of the UDHR and the Latin American Bogotá Declaration (1948).[128] In his memoirs, Humphrey recalled that he "did not need to be told" that "civil and political rights ... can have little meaning without ... economic, social and cultural rights."[129]

Were Humphrey ever to waver from this imperative he would have been quickly brought back into line by the character and content of one of the main drafts he had before him, the so-called "Sankey Bill" (formally styled, in a truly Victorian formulation, as " 'A Declaration of the Rights of Man': A Charter prepared in 1940, under the Chairmanship of Lord Sankey, and originally drafted for discussion by H. G. Wells"). A lawyer, Sankey had been President of the House of Lords and involved with the *Académie diplomatique internationale*.[130] The Declaration's "Introduction" refers to "men's ability either to co-operate with, or to injure and oppress one another, and to consume, develop or waste the bounty of nature." It condemns governments that have fallen "under the sway of monopolist productive and financial organizations," as well as inveighing against "war and monstrous exploitation." The Sankey Bill has socialist, collectivist or communitarian qualities. A nascent environmentalism was even linked to economic and social justice and to a concern for human welfare. Article 1 (Right to Live), for example, provided in part that

> Every man is a joint inheritor of all the natural resources and of powers, inventions and possibilities accumulated by our forerunners. He is entitled, within the measure of these resources and without distinction of race, colour or professed belief or opinions, to the nourishment, covering and medical care needed to realize his full possibilities and mental development from birth to death ...

The Sankey Bill places importance on the fulfilment of basic human needs through the reciprocal duties of the individual, the community and the state. It is strong evidence to contradict the notion that Humphrey had before him only narrowly liberal-capitalist Western documents. The individual had the duty, under Article 3, "not only to respect but to uphold and to advance the rights of all other men throughout the world," and to contribute service to (and services for) the community. Fulfilment of this duty would "ensure the performance of those necessary tasks for which the incentives which will operate in a free society do not provide." This constitutes not only a reinforcement of civic and social duties, but an implicit critique of any principal reliance on profit incentives to deliver necessary social services. It was only by "doing his quota of service that a man can justify his partnership in the community." The Declaration also guaranteed rights to knowledge, information and education (Article 4), and a right to work (with pay according to the contribution it made to "the welfare of the community" (Article 6)), as well as constraints on "anti-social activities" by speculators, profiteers and corporations (Article 6). And if a child were "without parental protection in whole or in part, the community, having due regard to the family traditions of the child" would "accept or provide alternative guardians" for her or him.[131]

Naturally, also, FDR's Four Freedoms speech (1941) and a 1942 draft bill of rights (including Article II, which provided that "[a]ll persons ... have the right to enjoy such minimum standards of economic, social and cultural well-being as the resources of the country, effectively used, are capable of sustaining")[132] were influences kept alive by Eleanor Roosevelt's advocacy, despite her own State Department's attempts to hobble her, and the further retreat from support for international human rights in the middle and later stages of President Roosevelt's government, and under the Truman and Eisenhower administrations. The retreat was in part a response to various domestic social, economic, legal and political pressures but it was also, as this book has argued, because the government and the various anti-human rights lobbies often shared common interests.[133] But, despite being opposed by her own government and monitored by the F.B.I. for her "communistic" views, Eleanor Roosevelt continued to articulate the importance of economic and social rights, and to emphasize the necessity of a "New Deal" for the world if there were to be a real and enduring peace.[134] Consistent with this emphasis, Eleanor Roosevelt had a long interest and involvement in relieving the miseries of poverty for those living in slum conditions or being exploited in sweatshops. She also had a keen interest in the welfare of women and children.[135]

Eleanor Roosevelt also saw clearly that domestic and international failures on these issues made it very difficult for the U.S.A. to "win the hearts and minds" of those in developing countries during the Cold War: she declared that "our great struggle today is to prove to the world that democracy has more to offer than communism."[136] Her voice was a rare, and sometimes a lone, voice on these issues in official American circles, although one that sometimes prevailed.[137]

While the U.S.A., and at times the U.K., were the states most reluctant to embrace economic and social rights, it is inaccurate to conclude that the inclusion of economic and social rights was simply the result of Soviet bloc and Latin American pressure. As Mary Ann Glendon concludes, "support for these ideas was very broad-based."[138] For instance, the substance of Articles 23 and 24 of the UDHR was "already the common stuff of labor legislation in most liberal democracies (decent working conditions including paid vacations and limits on working hours; protection against unemployment; the right to form and join trade unions)."[139] Indeed, Sir Hersch Lauterpacht, a Cambridge law professor, and not particularly noted for social radicalism, recognized in very clear terms the interdependence (and what came to be called the indivisibility) of civil and political rights and economic and social rights; and, moreover, he recognized the socially embedded and contextualized nature of property rights and market freedoms. "There is," he wrote:

a wide and growing acceptance of the view that personal and political freedom is impaired – if not rendered purely nominal – unless its enjoyment is made practicable by a reasonable guarantee of social and economic freedom ... [Rights] of personal liberty and political freedom may become a hollow mockery for those whom the existing social and economic order leaves starving, insecure in their livelihood, illiterate and deprived of their share in the progress and well-being of the society as a whole ...[140]

I now want to analyze some of the economic and social rights more closely, beginning with the right to property.[141] Article 17(1) of the UDHR declares that "Everyone has the right to own property alone as well as in association with others." The concept of property in this article is an expansive one; even owning property "alone" is not confined to private property. The phrase "alone as well as in association with others" had its origins in a U.S.S.R. proposal, the purpose of which was to make it clear that the article could accommodate capitalist, communist or hybrid economies.[142] Moreover, the right to property was not an unlimited one. Of course, even classical liberal and neo-classical theorists rarely espoused such an unlimited right. The right is limited by Article 29, as well as by its location in the context of other economic, social and cultural rights.[143] As Morsink concludes:

[T]he deep impulse behind property rights in the Universal Declaration is not the one so often associated with Western "possessive individualism," but one that has deeper communitarian roots than is normally thought ...[144]

Socialist traditions again played their part in work-related rights in the UDHR. Countries making important contributions to discussion and formulation of these rights included Chile, Cuba, New Zealand, U.S.S.R., B.S.S.R., Panama, Australia, the Philippines and Argentina. In contrast, the U.S.A., in a 1951 U.N. debate, resisted a right to work, believing that it augured a centralized economy in which the workforce would be centrally controlled in pursuit of the goal of full employment.[145]

Article 24 – "Everyone has the right to rest and leisure, including reasonable limitation of working hours and periodic holidays with pay." – has sometimes been derided as exemplifying just how utopian a document the UDHR is.[146] Yet, in this regard, it is salutary to note that a right to leisure was protected in the constitutions of several states (for example, Brazil, Costa Rica, Cuba, Ecuador, Guatemala, Honduras, Mexico, Nicaragua, Panama). Article 25 recognizes that "Everyone has the right to a standard of living adequate for the health and well-being of himself and of his family, including food, clothing, housing and medical care ..." China, the U.S.S.R., the ILO and Australia were especially prominent in their support of this article.[147] Pen-Chung Chang (China) asserted that he "did not see what possible objection there could be to that phrase [in the proposed Article 25] when millions of people throughout the world were deprived of food and clothing."[148] An Australian representative urged that "Freedom from want, the third of the Four Freedoms, had been widely accepted in the world: At the present stage in world history people were especially interested in economic and social as well as political rights ..."[149] This sentiment was supported by Chile, China and France.[150] Some resistance to the character of the article came from the U.S.A. and the U.K. Uncharacteristically, it was Eleanor Roosevelt who implied that Article 25 perhaps went too far because the "covenant" was intended for every state, "not only for a progressive state like Australia."[151] Likewise, a British delegate insisted upon the necessity to distinguish "between human rights and fundamental freedoms on the one hand, and those things which were necessary for the development of the full life of the individual."[152]

The U.S.S.R. lent vital support to the rights to housing and medical care. Many countries provided domestic rights protections in relation to healthcare, in contrast to the U.S.A. They included several Latin American countries, China, U.S.S.R. and Yugoslavia. There was a right to housing in at least ten of the constitutions of Latin American countries. Despite British and American resistance, the Chinese proposal on food, clothing, housing and medical care was adopted as part of Article 25.[153]

Johannes Morsink has concluded that the human being identified in the UDHR is not an isolated, self-centred, disengaged individual outside cultural and social contexts, indifferent to society. Human beings are not like those asocial, calculating, competitive, possessive individualists one finds in caricatures of liberal theory. Humans are connected to a range of communities and have duties toward them. We might reiterate here the long-running connections between human rights and duties from the classical period onward which I have traced in this book. Article 29(1) declares that

> Everyone has duties to the community *in which alone* the free and full development of his personality is possible [emphasis added].

Strong support for the inclusion of duties in the UDHR came from Cuba, China (although, interestingly, along with the U.S.A., it opposed Australia's proposal for the inclusion of the word "alone" in Article 29), Australia, the U.S.S.R., France and even the U.K.[154] Corbet (U.K.) considered that

> [having the word "alone" in the clause] stressed the essential fact that the individual could attain the full development of his personality only within the framework of society.[155]

René Cassin (France) emphasized that

> man must be envisaged not only in his relations with the state, but with the social groups of all sorts to which he belongs: family, tribe, city, profession, confession, and more broadly the global human community.[156]

In his memoirs, John Humphrey reported that delegate Charles Dukes, a British trade unionist and Labour Party member, "retorted [to opponents of Article 29] that unrestricted individual liberty was impossible in any modern community," and that there was a "coexistence" and "closely knit interdependence" between the individual and the state.[157] An Australian representative considered that the purpose of allowing a limitation of rights in Article 29 was "to emphasize that every right had its obligations."[158] Under the UDHR individuals are to be respected as ends in themselves, as unique human beings. But individuals are not characterized in the UDHR as decontextualized: "'everyone'" is "situated in families, communities, workplaces, associations, societies, cultures, nations, and an international order." Indeed, the UDHR "begins and ends with exhortations to solidarity."[159]

Glendon has further explained that the UDHR does not limit *"responsibility* for protecting human rights" to the nation-state. It extends, rather, "to persons and groups below and above the nation level."[160] This is evident in the Preamble of the UDHR, which calls on "every individual and *every organ of society* [emphasis added]" to "secure" the "universal and effective recognition and observance" of the human rights in it.[161]

The UDHR gave limited and only indirect protection to minorities.[162] The orthodox view is that the UDHR does not recognize human rights directly and collectively held and exercised by a minority, but, rather, relevant human rights are held by individual members of minorities.[163] There is no explicit mention of minorities in the UDHR, but the theme of non-discrimination, embodied in provisions such as Articles 2 and 7, is obviously relevant to sustaining a minority.[164] Other rights that facilitate minority cultures include rights of association and assembly, to freedom of conscience and religion, and of "Everyone's ... right freely to participate in the cultural life of the community ..." (Article 27).[165]

Conceivably, Article 29(2) could allow for limitations to rights in the interests of minorities, providing that such limitations are "determined by law solely for the purpose of securing due recognition for the rights and freedoms of *others* and of meeting the just requirements of *morality, public order* and *the general welfare* in a democratic society," and not "aimed at the destruction of any of the rights and freedoms" (Article 30) in the UDHR (emphasis added). It is not unreasonable to argue that a sophisticated, multicultural, "federal," democratic, pluralist society might seek to protect minorities from oppression, discrimination, assimilation or other mistreatment under Articles 29 and 30 of the UDHR. Nevertheless, clearly it would have been better had specific clauses on minorities (and on indigenous peoples) been included in the UDHR.

Indeed, Humphrey *had* included an article on minorities in his first draft of the UDHR, based on arguments by Lauterpacht that the UDHR should at least offer equivalent protection to that which had been promised under the League of Nations regime.[166] The U.S.A. was "the sole strong opponent" of Humphrey's minority clause.[167] Eleanor Roosevelt warned, somewhat surprisingly given her activism on behalf of African Americans, that "provisions relating to rights of minorities had no place in a declaration of human rights" and that "in the United States, there was no minority problem."[168] There was also opposition from China, Australia, some Latin American countries (worried about its potential abuse by immigrants), and colonial powers.[169] Some Australian representatives were particularly resistant to minority rights. A. J. D. Hood, for example, was sceptical about giving rights to "groups as such." He argued that "assimilation of all groups ... [was] in the best interest of all in the long run." Another Australian representative, still more menacingly, saw "the dispersal of groups rather than the formation of minorities" as the goal.[170] Given the existence of the "White Australia" policy and the history of the mistreatment of indigenous peoples, and of immigrant groups such as the Chinese, these disturbing sentiments were not exceptional for the time at which they were expressed. A B.S.S.R. delegate, one Kaminsky, was scathing in responding to claims of this ilk:

> Australia had carried out a policy of forceful elimination of its aboriginal groups and ... the North American Indian had almost ceased to exist in the United States ... [I]n colonial territories too there were no signs that indigenous culture was being developed and encouraged ...[171]

In contrast to the view that the UDHR was an American hegemonic project, we may now draw further attention to the many and culturally diverse states that contributed to its development. While Asia and Africa were not adequately represented, the drafters nevertheless came from countries with diverse religious, political, economic and cultural experience.[172] In addition to the principal drafters from Canada, France, China, Lebanon, Chile, U.S.S.R. and the U.S.A., many other countries were represented as secondary drafters: Argentina, Australia, Belgium, Bolivia, Brazil, B.S.S.R., Cuba, Denmark, Dominican Republic, Egypt, Ecuador, Greece, Haiti, India, Lebanon, Mexico, the Netherlands, New Zealand, Pakistan, Panama, Philippines, Poland, Saudi Arabia, Syria, Turkey, Ukrainian Soviet Socialist Republic, Union of South Africa, U.S.S.R., U.K., Uruguay, Venezuela and Yugoslavia.[173] Glendon[174] describes the delegates coming from 58 states as representing four-fifths of the global population. She gives a geographical breakdown as follows: the Americas (21), Europe (16),

Asia (14), Africa (4), Oceania (3). In politico-cultural terms, she gives a different distribution: socialist bloc (6), Islamic (11), Buddhist (4), Judeo-Christian (37). Consider, also, Philippe De La Chappelle's estimate of U.N. membership in 1948:

> North and South America with 21 countries represented 36% of the total, Europe with 16 countries 27%, Asia with 14 countries 24%, Africa with 4 countries a mere 6%, and the South Sea Islands with three countries 5%.[175]

For two years, the UDHR was dissected and debated in the U.N. by these many states.[176]

At least four particular contributions were made by smaller states to the final character of the UDHR.[177] Latin American, Asian, Middle Eastern and socialist bloc states were committed to socio-economic rights. The rights of women were advanced by representatives from countries such as India, Dominican Republic, Pakistan and Denmark in conjunction with the U.N. Commission on the Status of Women. Despite opposition from the U.S.A. and China, the strenuous efforts of a number of delegates (and particularly women delegates) from Denmark, the U.S.S.R., India and the Dominican Republic ensured that the UDHR would apply to all persons – men and women – equally and without discrimination. The UDHR refers to "human beings" (Article 1) and throughout to "all," "everyone" and "no one". Nevertheless, there is, unfortunately, some use of generic male language in the UDHR – for example, the reference to "spirit of brotherhood" in Article 1, to "man" in the Preamble; and the use of "he" and "his" in various articles. But these references are not sufficient to shake the conclusion that the UDHR was to apply to men and women equally.[178] This conclusion is certainly consistent with Eleanor Roosevelt's impeccable commitment to the human rights of women, and to feminist causes from her involvement in the New York Consumers' League and the League of Women Voters to her role as Director of Women's Activities in the Democratic Party in 1928.[179] Smaller states were also critical to the adoption of an anti-discrimination clause in the UDHR, with South Asian delegates to the forefront. And the cause of decolonization was supported by Syria, Haiti, Pakistan, Egypt and Yugoslavia, among others. Yugoslavia's proposal that the UDHR apply to all, even to those living in "dependent" areas, was adopted despite the vigorous opposition of colonial powers.[180]

Famously, the UDHR was adopted without a single dissenting vote, but there were eight abstentions, six from the Soviet socialist bloc as well as South Africa and Saudi Arabia. What is the significance of these abstentions? Certainly, we must conclude that not all states were prepared at this time to endorse the UDHR. South Africa refused to endorse the UDHR principally because its contents challenged the racist political, legal and social organization of apartheid. Saudi Arabia's abstention turned on its opposition to Article 16 (equality of marriage rights) and Article 18 (freedom to change religion or belief).[181] Concerning Article 18, at least, however, the Saudi view should not be taken to represent a typical stance from Arabic and/or Islamic states. Article 18 received endorsement from Karim Azkoul (Lebanon) in the following terms: the article was necessary to allow

> the possibility of each individual to determine his own destiny. That was the reason for the special mention … of the freedom for an individual to change his belief, as such change might be at the root of a new spiritual impulse.[182]

Muslim states such as Syria, Iran, Turkey and Pakistan voted in favour of the UDHR.[183]

The abstentions of the Soviet bloc were tainted by Cold War politics, and by the fear, ironically shared with the U.S.A., that the UDHR could erode state sovereignty. The U.S.S.R. often pushed for *the state* to *guarantee* the respective rights in accordance with a state's laws; claiming that this was better than espousing "bourgeois" ideals that would not be implemented. However, the majority of delegates saw this approach as a Trojan horse for a kind of positivism that would likely leave human rights at the mercy of a state – that such rights could be given and taken away as laws are passed, repealed or amended.[184] Other specific criticisms from the socialist abstainers included the following: that there was no condemnation of "war-mongering and fascist ideas," that a right to street protests should have been included, that there was no explicit protection of minorities, that "[t]here was no mention of the duties which an individual owed to his neighbors, his family, his group, or his nation," and that collective rights needed to be acknowledged.[185] But "none of these countries voted against the

Declaration. If any thought that there was no such thing as human rights, their behavior and most of what they said did not show it."[186]

The UDHR was not the result of a U.S. hegemonic project. The advancement of universal human rights depended on widespread support from myriad states, organizations and individuals from around the world, and on sometimes surprising coalitions. Indeed, the UDHR was achieved in the face of often staunch U.S. resistance, at the official level and from many conservative groups domestically.

Notes

[1] P. G. Lauren, *The Evolution of International Human Rights: Visions Seen* (Philadelphia: University of Pennsylvania Press, 1998), pp. 184–189; R. M. Brucken, "A Most Uncertain Crusade: The United States, Human Rights and the United Nations, 1941–1954," Ph.D. dissertation, History, Ohio State University, 1999, pp. 1–116; E. Borgwardt, *A New Deal for the World: America's Vision for Human Rights* (Cambridge: Cambridge University Press, 2005), p. 172.

[2] Lauren, *The Evolution of International Human Rights*, p. 184.

[3] Ibid., p. 185.

[4] See ibid., generally; Brucken, "A Most Uncertain Crusade"; W. Korey, *NGOs and the Universal Declaration of Human Rights: "A Curious Grapevine"* (New York: St. Martins, 1988), pp. 1–50.

[5] Brucken, "A Most Uncertain Crusade," pp. ii–iii, 2–5, 17–18, 23–116 (especially at pp. 65–66), and generally.

[6] Ibid., pp. 6, 63, 65–66.

[7] See ibid., pp. 1–107 (and generally), and p. 63 (the quotation is taken from this page).

[8] See, further, M. L. Dudziak, *Cold War Civil Rights: Race and the Image of American Democracy* (Princeton: Princeton University Press, 2000).

[9] Brucken, "A Most Uncertain Crusade," pp. 84–86, 94–95, 76, 81–83, 85–86, 77.

[10] Lauren, *The Evolution of International Human Rights,* p. 198.

[11] Brucken, "A Most Uncertain Crusade," pp. 83–84, 101.

[12] See, for example, K. Sellars, *The Rise and Rise of Human Rights* (London: Sutton Publishing, 2000), pp. xii-xiii: "[T]he Americans made sure that the issue [of human rights] did not fall off the international agenda. At the

Dumbarton Oaks conference of 1944 ... its delegates insisted on inserting a reference to it in the final conference proposal, despite Soviet and British objections."

[13] Brucken, "A Most Uncertain Crusade," pp. 88–91.

[14] Ibid., p. 89.

[15] Ben Cohen (FDR's personal representative), quoted in ibid., p. 91.

[16] Brucken, "A Most Uncertain Crusade," p. 93.

[17] Ibid., pp. 105–107, 94–95, ii, 17, 77, 106–116; Lauren, *The Evolution of International Human Rights,* p. 185. See, further, C. Anderson, "From Hope to Disillusion: African Americans, the United Nations, and the Struggle for Human Rights, 1944–1947," *Diplomatic History*, vol. 20, no. 4 (Fall 1996), pp. 531–563, especially at p. 538 (where she notes the U.S. Senate's pressure on the U.S. San Francisco delegation *not* to have a strong human rights provision in the Charter) and A. W. B. Simpson, *Human Rights and the End of Empire: Britain and the Genesis of the European Convention* (Oxford: Oxford University Press, 2001), pp. 252–253 (noting that it was the Zionist Joseph Proskauer, a former superior judge in New York and Chairman of the Committee on Peace Problems of the American Jewish Committee, who helped to persuade the reluctant Stettinius by reminding him of millions of voters associated with the human rights organizations).

[18] Lauren, *The Evolution of International Human Rights,* pp. 188, 190 (the quotation comes from this page); Brucken, "A Most Uncertain Crusade," pp. 103, 111. See also A.W. B. Simpson, *Human Rights and the End of Empire*, p. 261.

[19] Brucken, "A Most Uncertain Crusade," pp. 103, 111; Lauren, *The Evolution of International Human Rights*, pp. 187–192, 195. The quotations come from Lauren, *The Evolution of International Human Rights*, pp. 191–192.

[20] Lauren, *The Evolution of International Human Rights*, p. 188.

[21] Brucken, "A Most Uncertain Crusade," pp. 94–98; Lauren, *The Evolution of International Human Rights*, p. 188.

[22] Lauren, *The Evolution of International Human Rights*, p. 188.

[23] Korey, *NGOs and the Universal Declaration of Human Rights,* p. 41.

[24] Brucken, "A Most Uncertain Crusade," p. 108.

[25] Ibid., pp. 108–111.

[26] Ibid., p. 111 (emphasis added).

[27] Ibid., pp. 112–116.

[28] Korey, *NGOs and the Universal Declaration of Human Rights*, p. 31.

[29] Lauren, *The Evolution of International Human Rights*, p. 188. See also Anderson, "From Hope to Disillusion," especially at pp. 531–534, 548–551.

[30] Anderson, "From Hope to Disillusion," pp. 531–532. On the British Colonial Office's opposition in the 1940s to the inclusion of specific political rights in any international bill of rights because it would aid the cause of anticolonialists in British colonies and undermine the shield of "domestic jurisdiction" under article 2(7) of the U.N. Charter, see Simpson, *Human Rights and the End of Empire*, pp. 374, 385–386 (see also pp. 303–304, 306).

[31] Anderson, "From Hope to Disillusion," pp. 548–551.

[32] Ibid., pp. 533–534.

[33] Sellars, *The Rise and Rise of Human Rights*, pp. 1–11.

[34] *Charter of the United Nations and Statute of the International Court of Justice* (New York: U.N. Office of Public Information, n.d. [1945]). See also: I. Brownlie and G. S. Goodwin Gill (eds.), *Basic Documents on Human Rights*, fourth edn. (Oxford: Oxford University Press, 2002), pp. 1–2; Center for Study of Human Rights, Columbia University, *Twenty-five Human Rights Documents* (New York: Center for the Study of Human Rights, Columbia University, 1994), pp. 1–5; H. Hannum, "Human Rights," in C. C. Joyner (ed.), *The United Nations and International Law* (Cambridge: Cambridge University Press, 1997), pp. 133–134; A. Dundes Renteln, *International Human Rights: Universalism Versus Relativism* (Newbury Park, California: Sage, 1990), pp. 21–27; R. Piotrowicz and S. Kaye, *Human Rights in International and Australian Law* (Chatswood, N.S.W.: Butterworths, 2000), pp. 22–27; P. Taylor, "The United Nations and International Organization," in J. Baylis and S. Smith (eds.), *The Globalization of World Politics: An Introduction to International Relations* (Oxford: Oxford University Press, 1997), pp. 264–285. For subsequent references to the U.N. Charter's articles I have typically consulted *Charter of the United Nations and Statute of the International Court of Justice* and Center for the Study of Human Rights, Columbia University, *Twenty-five Human Rights Documents*.

[35] P. Malanczuk, *Akehurst's Modern Introduction to International Law*, seventh edn. (London: Routledge, 1997), pp. 211–215.

[36] See Taylor, "The United Nations and International Organization," generally, and at pp. 264, 269.

[37] See Malanczuk, *Akehurst's Modern Introduction to International Law*, p. 212; Piotrowicz and Kaye, *Human Rights in International and Australian Law*, p. 24; Renteln, *International Human Rights*, pp. 21–22. The eminent international lawyer Hersch Lauterpacht (quoted in A.W. B. Simpson, *Human*

Rights and the End of Empire, p. 354) concluded that the U.N. Charter was indeed "a legal document" and its references to the human rights of individuals "must of necessity be deemed to refer to legal rights ... recognized by international law and independent of the law of the state."

[38] Malanczuk, *Akehurst's Modern Introduction to International Law,* p. 212.

[39] Renteln, *International Human Rights,* p. 22, notes that "the principle of good faith in treaty interpretation requires states to observe human rights." But see, *contra,* Louis Henkin, quoted in H. J. Steiner and P. Alston, *International Human Rights in Context: Law, Politics and Morals: Text and Materials,* second edn. (Oxford: Oxford University Press, 2000), p. 142. Cf. Kaufman J in *Filartiga v. Pena-Irala* (U.S. Court of Appeals, Second Circuit, 1980, 630 F.2d876), quoted in Steiner and Alston, *International Human Rights in Context,* p. 1052: "The United Nations Charter ... makes it clear that in this modern age a state's treatment of its own citizens is a matter of international concern ..."

[40] Malanczuk, *Akehurst's Modern Introduction to International Law,* p. 212.

[41] S. Taylor, "Reconciling Australia's International Protection Obligations with the 'War on Terrorism,'" *Pacifica Review,* vol. 14 (2002), no. 2, pp. 121–140, pp. 121–122 ("It is, of course, a principle of customary international law that, *on the international plane,* a state cannot defend a claim that it has breached its international obligations by saying that its conduct was permitted or even mandated under its national law."). See also M. Shaw, *International Law,* fourth edn. (Cambridge: Cambridge University Press, 1997), pp. 102–103, 455, citing Article 27 of the Vienna Convention of the Law of Treaties 1969 and the *Alabama Claims* arbitration (1872).

[42] See, further, Renteln, *International Human Rights,* pp. 22–23; Malanczuk, *Akehurst's Modern Introduction to International Law,* p. 212: Article 2(7) "was later interpreted as not preventing U.N. bodies from addressing human rights violations in member states." See also Malanczuk, *Akehurst's Modern Introduction to International Law,* p. 220, and ch. 22; J. Chopra and T. G. Weiss, "Sovereignty is No Longer Sacrosanct: Codifying Humanitarian Intervention," in C. Ku and P. F. Diehl (eds.), *International Law: Classic and Contemporary Readings* (Boulder, Colorado: Lynne Rienner, 1998), pp. 369–387; Shaw, *International Law,* pp. 454–455, 202 (note 34) ("the question of the extent and content of domestic jurisdiction is a matter for international law, see *Nationality Decrees in Tunis and Morocco* cases, PCIJ, Series B, No. 4, 1923; 2 ILR, p. 349 ..."). See also Simpson, *Human Rights and the End of Empire,* pp. 310–311, 314 (on the meaning of "intervention"), 310, 311 (quoting the view in 1951 of the expert Gerald Fitzmaurice of the British Foreign Office that

"it is difficult if not impossible to maintain that questions of human rights are purely domestic questions and have not become international in character" – Simpson's emphasis removed), 355.

[43] Lauren, *The Evolution of International Human Rights*, pp. 191–193, 197, 198, identifies the "exploitation" of "colonial possessions" by Britain, France, Portugal, Spain, the Netherlands, Belgium and the U.S.A.; and the fact that the Trusteeship Council was not able to undertake independent investigations or to "compel reports" from administering powers. See also Piotrowicz and Kaye, *Human Rights in International and Australian Law*, pp. 26–27. On U.N. reform, see, for example, R. A. Falk, *Predatory Globalization: A Critique* (Cambridge: Polity Press, 1999), ch. 7.

[44] In developing my account of the origins of the UDHR, I have drawn upon, among others, the following sources: S. Morphet, "Economic, Social and Cultural Rights: The Development of Governments' Views, 1941–88," in R. Beddard and D. M. Hill (eds.), *Economic, Social and Cultural Rights: Progress and Achievement* (London: Macmillan, 1992), pp. 74–92; B. W. Cook, "Eleanor Roosevelt and Human Rights: The Battle for Peace and Planetary Decency," in E. P. Crapol (ed.), *Women and American Foreign Policy: Lobbyists, Critics, and Insiders*, second edn. (Wilmington, Delaware: Greenwood Press/Scholarly Resources, 1992), pp. 91–118; J. Morsink, *The Universal Declaration of Human Rights: Origins, Drafting and Intent* (Philadelphia: University of Pennsylvania Press, 1999); H. Lauterpacht, *International Law and Human Rights* (First published: London: Stevens and Sons, 1950; reprinted, Hamden, Connecticut: Archon Books, 1968); Y. Arieli, "On the Necessary and Sufficient Conditions for the Emergence of the Doctrine of the Dignity of Man and His Rights" and K. Dicke, "The Founding Function of Human Dignity in the Universal Declaration of Human Rights," in D. Kretzmer and E. Klein (eds.), *The Concept of Human Dignity in Human Rights Discourse* (The Hague: Kluwer Law International, 2002), pp. 1–17, and 111–120 respectively; S. P. Marks, "From the 'Single Confused Page' to the 'Decalogue for Six Billion Persons': The Roots of the Universal Declaration of Human Rights in the French Revolution," *Human Rights Quarterly*, vol. 20 (1998), no. 3, pp. 459–514; Lauren, *The Evolution of International Human Rights;* M. A. Glendon, "Knowing the Universal Declaration of Human Rights," *Notre Dame Law Review*, vol. 73 (1998), pp. 1153–1176; E. Pagels, "The Roots and Origins of Human Rights" and C. E. Wyzanski, Jr., "The Philosophical Background of the Doctrines of Human Rights," in A. H. Henkin (ed.), *Human Dignity: The Internationalization of Human Rights* (New York:

Aspen Institute for Humanistic Studies; Dobbs Ferry, New York: Oceana Publications; Alphenaan den Rijn, Netherlands: Sijthoff and Noordhoff, 1979), pp. 1–8, 9–13, respectively; Lord Steyn, *Human Rights: The Legacy of Mrs Roosevelt*, Presidential Address to The Holdsworth Club of the Faculty of Law in the University of Birmingham (Birmingham: Holdsworth Club, University of Birmingham, 2001); L. B. Sohn, "The New International Law: Protection of the Rights of Individuals Rather than States," *American University Law Review*, vol. 32 (1982), no. 1, pp. 1–64; E. Brems, *Human Rights: Universality and Diversity* (The Hague: Martinus Nijhoff Publishers / Kluwer Law International, 2001), pp. 1–25; T. Evans, *US Hegemony and the Project of Universal Human Rights* (London and New York: Macmillan/St. Martin's, 1993); J. Morsink, "The Philosophy of the Universal Declaration," *Human Rights Quarterly*, vol. 6 (1984), no. 3, pp. 309–334; J. Morsink, "Women's Rights in the Universal Declaration," *Human Rights Quarterly*, vol. 13 (1991), no. 2, pp. 229–256; J. Morsink, "World War II and the Universal Declaration," *Human Rights Quarterly*, vol. 15 (1993), no. 2, pp. 357–405; A. C. Grammatico, "The United Nations and the Development of Human Rights," Ph.D. dissertation, Department of Government, N.Y.U., 1956; H. Tolley, Jr., *The U.N. Commission on Human Rights* (Boulder, Colorado: Westview Press, 1987); J. Glover, *Humanity: A Moral History of the Twentieth Century* (London: Jonathan Cape, 1999); S. Waltz, "Universalizing Human Rights: The Role of Small States in the Construction of the Universal Declaration of Human Rights," *Human Rights Quarterly*, vol. 23 (2001), pp. 44–72; Brucken, "A Most Uncertain Crusade"; Lord Ritchie-Calder, *On Human Rights*, H. G. Wells Memorial Lectures, Inaugural Lecture, December 7, 1967 (London: H. G. Wells Society, 1968); M. Svensson, *The Chinese Conception of Human Rights: The Debate on Human Rights in China, 1898–1949* (Lund, Sweden: Lund University Press, 1996): T. J. Farer, "The United Nations and Human Rights: More than a Whimper," in R. P. Claude and B. H. Weston (eds.), *Human Rights in the World Community: Issues and Action* (Philadelphia: University of Pennsylvania Press, 1989), pp. 194–206; T. Evans (ed.), *Human Rights Fifty Years On : A Reappraisal* (Manchester and New York: Manchester University Press, 1998); T. Evans *The Politics of Human Rights: A Global Perspective* (London: Pluto Press, 2001); P. Von Eschen, *Race Against Empire: Black Americans and Anticolonialism, 1937–1957* (Ithaca, New York: Cornell University Press, 1997); J. L. Kunz, "The United Nations Declaration of Human Rights," *American Journal of International Law*, vol. 43 (April 1949), no. 2, pp. 316–323; S. K. Murumba, "The Cultural and Conceptual Basis of

Human Rights Norms in International Law," Ph.D. thesis, Law, Monash University, Melbourne, 1986; J. P. Humphrey, "The Memoirs of John P. Humphrey, The First Director of the United Nations Division of Human Rights," *Human Rights Quarterly*, vol. 5 (1983), no. 4, pp. 387–439; W. J. Bajor, "Discussing 'Human Rights': An Anthropological Exposition on 'Human Rights' Discourse," Ph.D. thesis, Department of Social Anthropology, University of St. Andrews, St Andrews, Scotland, 1997; J. P. Humphrey, "The Universal Declaration of Human Rights: Its History, Impact and Juridical Character," in B. G. Ramcharan (ed.), *Human Rights: Thirty Years after the Universal Declaration* (Dordrecht: Martinus Nijhoff, 1979), pp. 21–37; D. W. Wessner, "From Judge to Participant: The United States as Champion of Human Rights," in P. Van Ness (ed.), *Debating Human Rights: Critical Essays from the United States and Asia* (London and New York: Routledge, 1999), pp. 255–277; K. Mühlahn, "China, the West and the Question of Human Rights: A Historical Perspective," *asien afrika lateinamerika*, vol. 24 (1996), pp. 287–303; H. J. Steiner and P. Alston, *International Human Rights in Context;* Renteln, *International Human Rights;* T. Buergenthal, "Remembering the Auschwitz Death March," *Human Rights Quarterly*, vol. 18 (1996), no. 4, pp. 874–876; J. Donnelly, "Human Rights: A New Standard of Civilization?," *International Affairs*, vol. 74 (1998), no. 1, pp. 1–24; M. G. Johnson, "The Contributions of Eleanor and Franklin Roosevelt to the Development of International Protection for Human Rights," *Human Rights Quarterly*, vol. 9 (1987), no. 1, pp. 19–48; G. Best, "One World or Several? Reflections on the Modern History of International Law and Human Rights," *Historical Research*, vol. LXI (1988), no. 145, pp. 212–226; J. Gordon, "The Concept of Human Rights: The History and Meaning of Its Politicization," *Brooklyn Journal of International Law*, vol. XXIII (1998), no. 3, pp. 689–701; A. Pollis and P. Schwab, "Human Rights: A Western Construct with Limited Applicability," in A. Pollis and P. Schwab (eds.), *Human Rights: Cultural and Ideological Perspectives* (New York: Praeger, 1979), pp. 1–18; A. Pollis, "Cultural Relativism Revisited: Through a State Prism," *Human Rights Quarterly*, vol. 18 (1996), no. 2, pp. 316–344; J. P. Humphrey, *Human Rights and the United Nations: A Great Adventure* (Dobbs Ferry, New York: Transnational Publishers, 1984); Malanczuk, *Akehurst's Modern Introduction to International Law*, especially at pp. 211–213; Brownlie and Goodwin-Gill (eds.), *Basic Documents on Human Rights*; H. B. Holmes, "A Feminist Analysis of the Universal Declaration of Human Rights," in C. C. Gould (ed.), *Beyond Domination: New Perspectives on Women and Philosophy* (Totowa, New

Jersey: Rowman and Allanheld, 1984), pp. 250–264; L. Henkin, "Human Rights Standards and Their 'Generations,'" in L. Henkin, *International Law: Politics and Values* (Dordrecht: Martinus Nijhoff, 1995), pp. 184–202; O. Schachter, "International Human Rights," in O. Schachter, *International Law in Theory and Practice* (Dordrecht: Kluwer Academic, 1991), pp. 330–361; B. H. Weston, "Human Rights," *Human Rights Quarterly*, vol. 6 (1984), no. 3, pp. 257–282; S. Davidson, *Human Rights* (Buckingham: Open University Press, 1993); A. L. Parrott, "Social Security: Does the wartime dream have to become a peacetime nightmare?," *International Labour Review*, vol. 131 (1992), no. 3, pp. 367–386; A. Moravcsik, "The Origins of Human Rights Regimes: Democratic Delegation in Postwar Europe," *International Organization*, vol. 54 (2000), no. 2, pp. 217–252 (on the European human rights regime); B. P. Meighen, "The Universal Declaration of Human Rights and the Democratic Representative: A Study of Coming to Agree," Ph.D. dissertation, Columbia University, 1953. See also: M. A. Glendon, *A World Made New: Eleanor Roosevelt and the Universal Declaration of Human Rights* (New York: Random House, 2001); E. Roosevelt, "The Promise of Human Rights," *Foreign Affairs*, vol. 26 (1948), no. 3, pp. 470–477; M. Ganji, *International Protection of Human Rights* (Geneva; Paris: Librairie E. Droz; Librairie Minard, 1962); J. F. Green, *The United Nations and Human Rights* (Washington, D.C.: The Brookings Institution, 1956); H. Lauterpacht, *An International Bill of Rights* (New York: Columbia University Press, 1945); M. Neal, *The United Nations and Human Rights, International Conciliation*, no. 489 (New York: Carnegie Endowment for International Peace, 1953); E. Schwelb, *Human Rights and the International Community: The Roots and Growth of the Universal Declaration of Human Rights 1949–1963* (Chicago: Quadrangle Books, 1963): L. B. Sohn, "Supplementary Paper: A Short History of United Nations Documents on Human Rights," in *The United Nations and Human Rights*, 18th Report of the Commission to Study the Organization of Peace (Dobbs Ferry, New York: Oceana Publications, 1968); J. Wronka, *Human Rights and Social Policy in the 21st. Century: A History of the Idea of Human Rights and Comparison of the United Nations Universal Declaration of Human Rights with United States Federal and State Constitutions* (Lanham, Maryland: University Press of America, 1992); T. Buergenthal, "International Human Rights in an Historical Perspective," in J. Symonides (ed.), *Human Rights: Concepts and Standards* (Aldershot: Ashgate/Dartmouth/UNESCO Publishing, 2000), pp. 3–30; J. Berger, "Eleanor Roosevelt and the Framing of the United Nations Declaration of Human Rights," in J. Berger, *A New Deal for the World: Eleanor Roosevelt and American Foreign Policy* (New York: Social Science Monographs/Columbia University Press, 1981), pp. 67–74; Simpson, *Human Rights and the End of Empire*. For the UDHR, I have commonly made reference to the reprint in Center for the Study of Human Rights, Columbia University, *Twenty-five Human Rights Documents*, pp. 6–9.

[45] M. W. Mutua, "The Ideology of Human Rights," *Virginia Journal of International Law*, vol. 36 (1996), no. 3, pp. 589–657.

[46] Ibid., pp. 592–593, 605–606.

[47] Ibid., p. 606 (note 49). Cf. Mary Ann Glendon's view that Charles Malik's fluency in languages such as Arabic, French, German and English "enabled him to move easily between East and West, and between large and small nations" ("Knowing the Universal Declaration of Human Rights," p. 1161). She also referred to his regular defence of "Arab and Palestinian views in the early 1950s" (Glendon, "Knowing the Universal Declaration of Human Rights," p. 1160 (note 37)), which is contrary to Mutua's implication that he was a lackey of the West. Note also Brian Simpson's view (*Human Rights and the End of Empire*, p. 298) that "anti-colonial feeling in colonial territories" was "particularly" strong "amongst *Western*-educated elites" (emphasis added)

[48] See, for example, Bajor, "Discussing 'Human Rights,'" p. 44 ("the concept of 'Human Rights' employed in drafting the Universal Declaration of Human Rights … is largely based on the past experiences of only three nations: France, the United Kingdom and the United States."). But, note that he also concludes (at p. 46) that "no 'people' or 'place' can lay sole claim to inventing the notion of 'Human Rights.'" See also M. S'Anchez-Zamorano, "Postfoundationalism, Human Rights, and Political Cultures," Ph.D. dissertation, Graduate Department of Philosophy, University of Toronto, 1996, pp. 37–38; Brems, *Human Rights: Universality and Diversity*, pp. 6–8; Svensson, *The Chinese Conception of Human Rights,* p. 26 ("Since the idea of human rights arose in Europe, the question arises of whether an idea of indisputable Western origin can be applied or rendered meaningful in other cultures."), and pp. 9–46; Evans, *US Hegemony and the Project of Universal Human Rights*; Evans, *The Politics of Human Rights*; T. Evans, "Introduction: power, hegemony and the universalization of human rights," in T. Evans (ed.), *Human Rights Fifty Years On,* pp 1–23; Pollis and Schwab, "Human Rights: A Western Construct with Limited Applicability." For the backgrounds of the drafters, I rely principally on Simpson, *Human Rights and the End of Empire*, pp. 88, 353, 362–367, 377, 521–522 and Glendon, *A World Made New*, especially at pp. 10–13, 33, 38, 44, 53, 82, 84, 124–125, 128, 133, 147, 185. See also Z. Arat, "Forging a Global

Culture of Human Rights: Origins and Prospects of the International Bill of Rights," *Human Rights Quarterly*, vol. 28 (2006), no. 2, pp. 416–437; and S. Waltz, "Universal Human Rights: The Contribution of Muslim States," *Human Rights Quarterly*, vol. 26 (2004), pp. 799–844.

[49] Evans, *US Hegemony and the Project of Universal Human Rights*, and other works. My critique of Evans has been influenced by Waltz, "Universalizing Human Rights."

[50] Evans, "Introduction," at p. 7 ("As a self-proclaimed protector of universal human rights, the USA sought to legitimate its role as leader of the new world order and to justify intervention wherever and whenever it was necessary."); Evans, *US Hegemony and the Project of Universal Human Rights*, pp. 8, 50–53, 54 ("Roosevelt saw that human rights offered an issue that served America's future economic needs while simultaneously allowing full expression of the values associated with being American."), 72–73 ("Since the United States was the only major power … it assumed the dominant role in determining the character of the new order. Consequently, the United States was well placed to promote those elements that supported its new hegemonic role while excluding those that appeared to offer a threat … [F]rom the end of the war until the mid-1950s, American and Western values predominated. The norms of the human rights regime were negotiated during this earlier period … What is seen in the process leading to the Declaration is the predominance of western values."); Evans, *The Politics of Human Rights*.

[51] Evans, *The Politics of Human Rights*, p. 20.

[52] Evans, *US Hegemony and the Project of Universal Human Rights*, pp. 40, 74–75, 79, 10, and generally; Evans, *The Politics of Human Rights*, pp. 23–25, and generally.

[53] Evans, *US Hegemony and the Project of Universal Human Rights*, p. 9 (emphasis added).

[54] Ibid., pp. 40–41 (emphasis added).

[55] Evans, *The Politics of Human Rights*, p. 21.

[56] Id.

[57] Id.

[58] Evans, *US Hegemony and the Project of Universal Human Rights*, pp. 10, 41; Evans, *The Politics of Human Rights*, p. 25.

[59] Evans, *US Hegemony and the Project of Universal Human Rights*, p. 73.

[60] See, generally, Morsink, *The Universal Declaration of Human Rights*; Lauterpacht, *International Law and Human Rights*. See also C. Palley, *The United Kingdom and Human Rights*, The Hamlyn Lectures, Forty-second

Series (London: Stevens and Sons / Sweet and Maxwell, 1991), especially at pp. 25–27, 55–68. See also the preamble to the French Constitution, quoted in Lauterpacht, *International Law and Human Rights*, p. 284: "... The nation ensures to the individual and the family the conditions necessary to their development. It guarantees to all, and notably the child, the mother and the aged worker, protection of health, material security, rest and leisure. Every human being who, because of his age, his physical or mental condition, or because of the economic situation, finds himself unable to work has the right to obtain from the community the means to lead a decent existence." Cf. Article 151 in the German Constitution of 1919, quoted in Lauterpacht, *International Law and Human Rights*, p. 285 (note 35): "the organization of economic life must correspond to the principles of justice and be designed to ensure for all a life worthy of human beings." See also Glendon, "Knowing the Universal Declaration of Human Rights," pp. 1166–1167. Eleanor Roosevelt had written (quoted in Glendon, *A World Made New*, p. 43) that "Freedom without bread ... has little meaning. My husband always said that freedom from want and freedom from aggression were twin freedoms which had to go hand in hand."

[61] See Morsink, *The Universal Declaration of Human Rights*.

[62] Evans is not consistent regarding this matter. While on one occasion he recognized that "civil and political rights remained important" for "the less developed countries" (*The Politics of Human Rights*, p. 24), on another he argued (in *US Hegemony and the Project of Universal Human Rights*, p. 28) that "[t]he idea for most non-western states concerns establishing justice for their community as a whole. This looks not to individual rights within a state but the rights of peoples and communities to participate in a global economic, social and political system on a basis of equality and fairness." Interestingly, Evans makes no reference in this regard to Article 28 of the UDHR, which reads as follows: "Everyone is entitled to a social and international order in which the rights and freedoms set forth in this Declaration can be fully realized."

[63] See Morsink, *The Universal Declaration of Human Rights*.

[64] Evans, *US Hegemony and the Project of Universal Human Rights*, p. 92. Cf. Anderson, "From Hope to Disillusion," p. 542: "the fight for colonial self-determination paralleled the battle to overturn the [American] South's racist voting restrictions. The efforts to revise the UN's 'domestic jurisdiction' clause matched the assault on the states' rights philosophy of the South. And the dissatisfaction with a trusteeship plan that denied colonies the right to lay their grievances before an international tribunal mirrored the opposition to

America's separate and unequal system of justice. The organizations representing over eight million African Americans, vowed to move on all fronts to secure civil and human rights."

[65] Evans, *The Politics of Human Rights*, p. 23.

[66] Marks, "From the 'Single Confused Page' to the 'Decalogue for Six Billion Persons.'"

[67] See Evans, *US Hegemony and the Project of Universal Human Rights*, pp. 10, 40, 77, 108ff., 111, and generally; Evans, *The Politics of Human Rights*, p. 22–26, and generally.

[68] See, for example, Evans, *The Politics of Human Rights*, pp. 22–25 (On conservative fears that the U.N. would become a "World Government"; and that international human rights could threaten American naturalization and immigration laws, and provide a basis for civil rights laws). Note, also, Waltz, "Universalizing Human Rights," pp. 69–70, especially at p. 69 ("If put to popular referendum in the United States in 1948, it is doubtful that the ... [UDHR] would have been endorsed by the electorate.").

[69] See, generally, Brucken, "A Most Uncertain Crusade"; Waltz, "Universalizing Human Rights."

[70] Steyn, *Human Rights,* p. 5, refers to the fact that President Truman "wanted to remove that indomitable campaigner [Eleanor Roosevelt] from involvement in progressive domestic causes"; ironically the attempted relegation of her to a supposed political backwater at the U.N. actually allowed her to have a critical role in the development of human rights. Waltz ("Universalizing Human Rights," p. 70 (note 114)) argues that "Cold War concerns abroad and the defense of states' rights at home easily eclipsed the World War II rhetoric of human rights ... Almost immediately following [Franklin] Roosevelt's death – and just two weeks before the opening of the meeting in San Francisco that chartered the United Nations – the United States began to backpedal on its commitment to human rights ... *Eleanor Roosevelt...did become an ardent and formidable champion of human rights, but she had her own battles to fight with the US State Department.*" (emphasis added). See also Brucken, "A Most Uncertain Crusade," pp. 169, 217; Humphrey, *Human Rights and the United Nations,* p. 5 (Eleanor Roosevelt "was soon exploited for short-term Cold War objectives"); Johnson, "The Contributions of Eleanor and Franklin Roosevelt to the Development of International Protection for Human Rights," pp. 34, 44; Lauren, *The Evolution of International Human Rights,* pp. 231–232; Berger, "Eleanor Roosevelt and the Framing of the United Nations Declaration of Human Rights," especially at pp. 68 ("Domestic politics ... explain Mrs

Roosevelt's refusal to support the passage of more ambitious [binding] conventions. She and the administration anticipated that the Senate would oppose treaties binding the United States to honor the civil rights of its people or to guarantee full employment."), 70. See also Evans, *US Hegemony and the Project of Universal Human Rights*, pp. 77, 90, 123.

[71] Morsink, *The Universal Declaration of Human Rights,* pp. 310-212.

[72] Ibid., pp. 225, 228, 230, 235–238.

[73] Brucken, "A Most Uncertain Crusade," pp. 131, 155, 148 (where he quotes a representative of the U.S. State Department (Hendrick) declaring that "Our policy was to get a declaration which was a carbon copy of the American Declaration of Independence and Bill of Rights.").

[74] Ibid., pp. 133, 213, 217, 231–232, 244.

[75] Ibid., pp. 131, 143, 156, 217, 231–232, 244.

[76] Lauterpacht, *International Law and Human Rights*, p. 302; Brucken, "A Most Uncertain Crusade," p. 215. Cf. the notorious Bricker Amendment that would have amended the U.S. Constitution to "prohibit a president from entering treaties and agreements without the express consent from the ... states." It failed by a single vote in the Senate (Waltz, "Universalizing Human Rights: The Role of Small States in the Construction of the Universal Declaration of Human Rights," p. 71 (note 119)). See, further, Tolley, Jr., *The U.N. Commission on Human Rights*, ch. 2 (on general U.S. resistance to international human rights); pp. 25–27, 29 (on "federal–state" clause).

[77] Brucken, ibid., pp. 275–291, 294-295, and ch. 6. On the U.S.A.'s poor record of ratification of international human rights instruments, see, further, Wessner, "From Judge to Participant." Wessner ("From Judge to Participant," pp. 256, 260) argues that the U.S.A. has tended to see human rights abuses as a "foreign" (and one could say a "foreign policy") problem, and that "[t]his pattern of hesitancy stretches back to ante-bellum federal–state sovereignty tensions, and has been steadfastly maintained through much of this century by a combined lobby of anti-Communists, states' rights activists, isolationists, and segregationists."

[78] Evans, "Introduction," p. 7.

[79] See in this regard the works of Johannes Morsink.

[80] Morsink, *The Universal Declaration of Human Rights,* p. xiii.

[81] Ibid., pp. xiii, 4.

[82] Quoted in ibid., p. 4.

[83] Ibid., p. 4.

[84] Quoted in ibid., p. 5.

[85] Quoted in id.

[86] Ibid., pp. 5-6. See, also, Tolley, Jr., *The U.N. Commission on Human Rights*, p. 14; Roosevelt, "The Promise of Human Rights," p. 472.

[87] Morsink, *The Universal Declaration of Human Rights*, especially at p. 6; Humphrey, *Human Rights and the United Nations*.

[88] Morsink, *The Universal Declaration of Human Rights*, p. 6.

[89] Ibid., pp. 6-7.

[90] Humphrey, "The Memoirs of John P. Humphrey," pp. 406-407.

[91] Lauren, *The Evolution of International Human Rights*, p. 158. See also Glendon, *A World Made New*, pp. 49-50, 56-59.

[92] Humphrey, "The Memoirs of John P. Humphrey," p. 407.

[93] Morsink, *The Universal Declaration of Human Rights*, pp. 7-9.

[94] Ibid., p. 9.

[95] Ibid., pp. 9-12.

[96] Ibid., pp. 281-284.

[97] Ibid., p. 290.

[98] Ibid., p. 281 (see also p. 292). Cf. Arieli, "On the Necessary and Sufficient Conditions for the Emergence of the Doctrine of Dignity of Man and His Rights," pp. 1-17, who concludes that the UDHR "is therefore defined in the meta-language of a universal secular order," focused on "the inherent Dignity of all human beings" (p. 8). See also Dicke, "The Founding Function of Human Dignity in the Universal Declaration of Human Rights," pp. 111-120, especially at pp. 114, 115, 117.

[99] Morsink, *The Universal Declaration of Human Rights*, pp. 292, 293, 297, 299. See also Glendon, *A World Made New*, p. 67, referring to cognate expressions such as "sympathy," "consciousness of one's fellow man," and "compassion."

[100] Morsink, *The Universal Declaration of Human Rights*, p. 320.

[101] Marks, "From the 'Single Confused Page' to the 'Decalogue for Six Billion Persons,'" especially at p. 460.

[102] Ibid., p. 471.

[103] See Pagels, "The Roots and Origins of Human Rights."

[104] Marks, "From the 'Single Confused Page' to the 'Decalogue for Six Billion Persons,'" p. 473.

[105] Ibid., p. 465.

[106] Cf. the liberal egalitarianism or welfare liberalism of the English scholar T. H. Green (1836-1882), as described by Palley, *The United Kingdom and Human Rights*, p. 67: "Green emphasised that the personality was realised by

playing a part in society; that politics was about creating social conditions for moral development; and that it was the duty of the state to safeguard all social interests relating to the general welfare. Green was an advocate of compulsory education, of extension of sanitary regulations, of higher standards of living and of the right of individuals to share in the goods produced by society."

[107] Marks, "From the 'Single Confused Page' to the 'Decalogue for Six Billion Persons,'" pp. 465, 475–478. At p. 475, he remarks that the Third Estate "included voices that challenged the economic injustices of the Old Order and anticipated socialist theory and practice of the nineteenth and twentieth centuries."

[108] Ibid., p. 494.

[109] Ibid., pp. 491, 489.

[110] Ibid., pp. 494–496.

[111] Marks, ibid., p. 489, argues that the focus on the 1789 Declaration, to the neglect of the 1793 one, "left the erroneous impression that concern with work, education, and social protection arose as new features of socialist thinking or of the emergence of the welfare state."

[112] Ibid., p. 503 (emphasis added).

[113] Ibid., p. 499.

[114] Ibid., pp. 466, 487–488 (particularly in note 135).

[115] Ibid., p. 503.

[116] Ibid., p. 506.

[117] Morsink, *The Universal Declaration of Human Rights,* p. 37; see also pp. 300, 313, and chs. 2 and 8. And, see, further, Morsink, "The Philosophy of the Universal Declaration" and "World War II and the Universal Declaration."

[118] René Cassin quoted in Morsink, *The Universal Declaration of Human Rights,* p. 38.

[119] Morsink, ibid., p. 38. See also Glover, *Humanity.*

[120] Morsink, *The Universal Declaration of Human Rights*, pp. 39–42, 42–43.

[121] Ibid., pp. 45–58; 80.

[122] Ibid., pp. 45–47, 49–57.

[123] Ibid., pp. 50–51.

[124] Ibid., p. 53.

[125] Ibid., pp. 65–66, 88, 90.

[126] Glover, *Humanity,* pp. 327, 337–341, and generally.

[127] Marks, "From the 'Single Confused Page' to the 'Decalogue for Six Billion Persons,'" pp. 475–509.

[128] Morsink, *The Universal Declaration of Human Rights,* pp. 130–134; Marks, "From the 'Single Confused Page' to the 'Decalogue for Six Billion Persons,'" especially at pp. 480, 506–509; Lauren, *The Evolution of International Human Rights,* p. 113.

[129] Humphrey, "The Memoirs of John P. Humphrey," p. 407; Humphrey, *Human Rights and the United Nations,* p. 2: "Human rights without economic and social rights have little meaning for most people, particularly on empty bellies."

[130] Lauren, *The Evolution of International Human Rights,* p. 152; A. W. B. Simpson, *Human Rights and the End of Empire,* p. 164. See also Burgers, "The Road to San Francisco," pp. 465–467 (especially at p. 465).

[131] Lord Ritchie-Calder, *On Human Rights,* Appendix One, pp. 15–18 (all the quotations in this section come from this source).

[132] Quoted in Marks, "From the 'Single Confused Page' to the 'Decalogue for Six Billion Persons,'" p. 508.

[133] See, further, Brucken, "A Most Uncertain Crusade"; *Eleanor Roosevelt* (Parts I and II), WGBH Educational Foundation television documentary, aired on SBS Television, Australia, September–October, 2003.

[134] There was, for example, reportedly a 3,000 page file on her prepared under Herbert Hoover's directorship of the F.B.I. (see *Eleanor Roosevelt*); Cook, "Eleanor Roosevelt and Human Rights," pp. 91–118, especially at pp. 91, 107, 113. See also Berger, "Eleanor Roosevelt and the Framing of the United Nations Declaration of Human Rights," ch. 6.

[135] *Eleanor Roosevelt.* See also Glendon, *A World Made New,* p. 90 (on her support for southern African Americans, the unemployed, "slum dwellers," and the "rural poor," which influenced her positions on health, education, housing and racial equality).

[136] Quoted in Cook, "Eleanor Roosevelt and Human Rights," p. 115.

[137] See, further, Johnson, "The Contributions of Eleanor and Franklin Roosevelt to the Development of International Protection for Human Rights.'"

[138] Glendon, "Knowing the Universal Declaration of Human Rights," p. 1166.

[139] Ibid., p. 1167. See also Morphet, "Economic, Social and Cultural Rights," p. 74: In the 1940s, "the differences within each group [First, Second and Third Worlds] have often been just as fierce as those between groups." She also noted (at p. 80) that the "First World (apart from the United States) has been particularly consistent about accepting civil and political and economic, social and cultural rights." Palley, in *The United Kingdom and Human Rights,* pp. 56–62, and *passim,* gives an illuminating account of key European and English

figures in the development of the right to work, communal property rights, redistributive tax schemes, state education and state relief of poverty such as Abbé Morellet (in his *Code of Nature* of 1755), Turgot (1727–1781), Louis Blanc (1811–1882), Ferdinand Lasssalle (1825–1864), Thomas Paine (1737–1809), Condorcet (1743–1794), Fichte (1762–1814), Jeremy Bentham (1748–1832), Robert Owen (1771–1858) and T. H. Green (1836–1882).

[140] H. Lauterpacht, *International Law and Human Rights* (New York: Praeger, 1950), p. 285.

[141] See Morsink, *The Universal Declaration of Human Rights,* ch. 4.

[142] Ibid., pp. 139–140, 147, 150, 155–156.

[143] Ibid., pp. 139, 154–155.

[144] Ibid., p. 139. A UNESCO conference of philosophers, which circulated a questionnaire to a diverse group of philosophers and other thinkers, endorsed the right to own property as a universal human right (Lauren, *The Evolution of International Human Rights,* pp. 223–225).

[145] Morsink, *The Universal Declaration of Human Rights,* ch. 5; M. C. R. Craven, *The International Covenant on Economic, Social and Cultural Rights: A Perspective on its Development* (Oxford: Clarendon Press, 1995), pp. 195, 198.

[146] Such scepticism is consistent with Maurice Cranston's view that human rights must be manifested in positive law – see the discussion in Evans, *US Hegemony and the Project of Universal Human Rights,* p. 35; in A. Belden-Fields, *Rethinking Human Rights for the New Millennium* (New York: Palgrave Macmillan, 2003), p. 42; and Morsink, *The Universal Declaration of Human Rights,* p. 364 (note 58). And see M. Cranston, "What Are Human Rights?," in W. Laqueur and B. Rubin (eds.), *The Human Rights Reader,* rev. edn. (New York: Penguin / Meridian, 1990), pp. 17–25.

[147] Morsink, *The Universal Declaration of Human Rights,* pp. 185, 192–198 (on Article 25, UDHR), 224. On the right to leisure, see Morsink, *The Universal Declaration of Human Rights,* pp. 181, 185–190.

[148] Quoted in ibid., p. 197.

[149] Quoted in ibid., p. 224.

[150] Id.

[151] Quoted in ibid., p. 225.

[152] Wilson (U.K.), quoted in id.

[153] Ibid., pp. 192, 193, 198.

[154] Ibid., pp. 239–240; Humphrey, "The Memoirs of John P. Humphrey," p. 399; Meighen, "The Universal Declaration of Human Rights and the Democratic Representative," p. 145.

[155] Quoted in Morsink, *The Universal Declaration of Human Rights,* p. 248.

[156] Quoted in Glendon, "Knowing the Universal Declaration of Human Rights," p. 1169 (see also pp. 1170, 1172).

[157] Humphrey, "The Memoirs of John P. Humphrey," p. 399. Dukes had been General Secretary of the National Union of General and Municipal Workers up to 1946, and Chairman of the Trade Union Congress. Previously, he was an M.P. for Warrington in the U.K. (Simpson, *Human Rights and the End of Empire*, p. 351).

[158] Meighen's paraphrase in "The Universal Declaration of Human Rights and the Democratic Representative," p. 145. Cf. H. Lauterpacht, *International Law and Human Rights* (first published London: Stevens and Sons, 1950; reprinted Hamden, Connecticut: Archon Books, 1968), pp. 326–327.

[159] Glendon, "Knowing the Universal Declaration of Human Rights," p. 1172 (see also p. 1170).

[160] Ibid., p. 1170 (emphasis added).

[161] Id.

[162] In this section I rely on the following references: P. Alston, "Introduction," in P. Alston (ed.), *Peoples' Rights* (Oxford: Oxford University Press, 2001), pp. 1–6; J. Crawford, "The Right of Self-Determination in International Law: Its Development and Future," in Alston (ed.), *Peoples' Rights*, pp. 7–67, at pp. 14–15; P. Thornberry, "Self-Determination, Minorities, Human Rights: A Review of International Instruments," in C. Ku and P. F. Diehl (eds.), *International Law: Classic and Contemporary Readings* (Boulder, Colorado: Lynne Rienner, 1998), pp. 135–153; Malanczuk, *Akehurst's Modern Introduction to International Law*, pp. 105–108, 338–340; Steiner and Alston, *International Human Rights in Context*, pp. 491–493, 1289–1292; H. Steiner, "Ideals and Counter-Ideals in the Struggle Over Autonomy Regimes for Minorities" [*Notre Dame Law Review*, vol. 66 (1991)], extracted in Steiner and Alston, *International Human Rights in Context*, pp. 1292–1297; Shaw, *International Law*, pp. 210–223; P. Alston, "People's Rights: Their Rise and Fall," in Alston (ed.), *Peoples' Rights*, pp. 259–293, at p. 273; Morsink, *The Universal Declaration of Human Rights,* pp. 261–263, 269–280, and especially at pp. 269–277, 280.

[163] Malanczuk, *Akehurst's Modern Introduction to International Law*, p. 106; Crawford, "The Right of Self-Determination in International Law," p. 15.

[164] Morsink, *The Universal Declaration of Human Rights,* p. 270; Crawford, "The Right of Self-Determination in International Law."

[165] Steiner, "Ideals and Counter-Ideals in the Struggle Over Autonomy Regimes for Minorities," pp. 1292–1297, especially at p. 1293; Steiner and Alston, *International Human Rights in Context,* pp. 1291–1292.

[166] Morsink, *The Universal Declaration of Human Rights,* pp. 270–271.

[167] Ibid., p. 272.

[168] Quoted in ibid., pp. 274, 272. See also Glendon, *A World Made New,* pp. 86, 161.

[169] Morsink, *The Universal Declaration of Human Rights,* pp. 269–80.

[170] Quoted in ibid., pp. 274, 277.

[171] Quoted in ibid., pp. 277.

[172] Ibid., pp. 21, 36.

[173] Ibid., pp. 4–5, 28–31, 31–33, and generally.

[174] Glendon, "Knowing the Universal Declaration of Human Rights," p. 1155.

[175] Quoted in Morsink, *The Universal Declaration of Human Rights,* p. 96. See, further, on non-Western contributions to the UDHR, P. Alston, "The Universal Declaration at 35: Western and Passé or Alive and Universal," *Review: International Commission of Jurists,* no. 1 (December 1983), pp. 60–70, at pp. 60–61 (noting the strong contributions of Cuba, India, China, Lebanon, Egypt, Ethiopia, Liberia, Afghanistan, the Philippines, Thailand, Pakistan and the Americas).

[176] Morsink, *The Universal Declaration of Human Rights,* p. 40

[177] I rely here principally on Waltz, "Universalizing Human Rights," p. 21. Glendon (*A World Made New,* p. 74) cites a Harvard History honours thesis by Shirin Sinnar that argues that India was committed to universal human rights as part of its struggle against European colonialism and discrimination (including the discriminatory treatment of Indians in South Africa).

[178] Morsink, *The Universal Declaration of Human Rights,* pp. 95, 117–120; pp. 116–129.

[179] *Eleanor Roosevelt.* For a less forgiving assessment of the use of gender-specific language in the UDHR, see Holmes, "A Feminist Analysis of the Universal Declaration of Human Rights."

[180] Waltz, "Universalizing Human Rights," p. 64–66; Article 2, UDHR.

[181] Morsink, *The Universal Declaration of Human Rights,* pp. 24–28.

[182] Quoted in ibid., p. 25.

[183] Ibid., p. 26. See, further, Humphrey, "The Memoirs of John P. Humphrey," pp. 428, 432–435. For a fuller treatment of the significant contribution of

Muslim states to the International Bill of Rights (the UDHR and the 1966 Covenants), see Waltz, "Universal Human Rights." See also Z. Arat, "Forging a Global Culture of Human Rights."

[184] Morsink, *The Universal Declaration of Human Rights,* pp. 21–24, and generally.

[185] Humphrey, "The Memoirs of John P. Humphrey," pp. 433–434.

[186] Morsink, *The Universal Declaration of Human Rights,* p. 21.

CHAPTER 4

The 1966 Covenants

The U.N. Commission on Human Rights (CHR) from the Economic and Social Council (ECOSOC) was originally charged with three drafting responsibilities in relation to human rights: the creation of a non-binding declaration, of a binding convention and of an instrument concerning implementation or enforcement machinery for realizing human rights. As is commonly known, the "triptych" ultimately came in another form: the "side panels" reflecting legally binding covenants on civil and political, and economic, social and cultural, rights, flanking the UDHR.[1] Together, the UDHR, International Covenant on Civil and Political Rights (ICCPR) and International Covenant on Economic, Social and Cultural Rights (ICESCR) came to be known colloquially as the International Bill of Rights. The CHR worked simultaneously on a binding human rights covenant (convention or treaty) and the UDHR, especially intensively between 1949 and 1954. The Covenants were adopted by the U.N. General Assembly in 1966, and came into force in 1976. In this chapter I trace the development of the Covenants and assess the implications for the universality of international human rights law.[2]

At the first session of the CHR (January–February 1947) it was decided to pursue the writing of an international bill of rights encompassing a non-binding human rights declaration (ultimately the UDHR), a covenant (binding treaty) and an instrument relating to implementation or enforcement of human rights.[3] As Czech scholar Vratislav Pechota notes, "[t]his conception enabled the General Assembly first to set general principles or standards and then, building upon those general principles, to define in a convention signed and ratified by states specific rights as well as limitations or restrictions on the exercise of those rights."[4]

A drafting committee was established to work on the declaration, a convention, and an instrument relating to implementation, with a working group associated with each undertaking. By the end of the second session of the CHR (1947), a draft covenant on human rights, focused on civil and political rights, had been completed, and was then circulated to governments for their responses. In answer to the General Assembly's resolution adopting the UDHR on December 10, 1948 (General Assembly resolution 217 (III), Part E), the CHR rededicated itself in its fifth session to finalizing a human rights convention.[5] Although the initial draft Covenant was based on civil and political rights, the CHR had before it additional suggested articles on economic, social and cultural rights for which the U.S.S.R. was one of the principal sources. The CHR asked the Secretariat to "survey" U.N. agencies and other organs relevant to these suggested rights so that it might be better informed to analyze the rights.[6]

Pechota has given a useful chronology and summary of the main stages of the drafting of the Covenants from 1949 to 1954. At its fifth session (May–June 1949), the CHR discussed the critical draft Covenant line by line. The draft covered in some detail most of the civil and political rights in the UDHR.[7] At the next session (March–May 1950), the CHR reconsidered the draft, taking into account the governments' responses. It also devised suggested means of implementation. In the seventh session (April–May 1951), the CHR spent most of its time discussing proposed articles on social and economic rights and the question of whether they were to be included in a single, comprehensive, covenant or separate covenants. The CHR decided in its eighth session (April–June 1952) to create two covenants, one on civil and political, another on economic, social and cultural rights; reversing its earlier decision in favour of a single, comprehensive covenant. The ninth session (April–May 1953) concentrated on the creation, nature and functioning of the proposed Human Rights Committee. At the tenth session, drafts of both covenants were completed, including a "federal–state" clause and territorial (or colonial) clause.[8] The completed drafts were then, as already mentioned, rigorously and vigorously debated and revised over the next twelve years, and were adopted in 1966.

The drafting of the 1966 Covenants revolved around four main issues with implications for the universality of human rights: the question of whether one covenant or two covenants ought to be created (and the way in which economic, social and cultural rights might bear on that question); the debate over the so-called "colonial clause"; the issue of self-determination; and the "federal–state" clause.

The initial draft Covenant travelled a tortuous path, forking into the 1966 Covenants that were ultimately adopted. Debates whether to create one or two covenants were often intertwined with debates over whether economic and social (and cultural) rights ought to be included in *any* legally binding international instrument, and over which, if any, international implementation or enforcement machinery was suitable for human rights. This was despite the fact that neither logic nor good policy necessarily dictated such an entanglement of issues.

The drafting and debating process in relation to the question of "one or two covenants" resembled a crowded, and sometimes unfriendly, game of volleyball. Various drafts, amendments, proposals, recommendations, resolutions, reports and pieces of advice floated and ricocheted between the U.N. General Assembly (and its Third Committee), ECOSOC, the CHR, specialized agencies and governments. I do not intend to give a point-by-point description here of this "game", but to set out the main features of it.

In 1947 the U.N. decided to produce a tripartite International Bill of Rights.[9] A First Draft Covenant focused on political and civil rights for individuals in line with British and American predilections.[10] International legal scholar Kitty Arambulo claims that the U.N. originally intended to have one legally binding covenant containing economic and social as well as civil and political rights.[11] At the fifth session of the CHR (June 23, 1949) the U.S.S.R. and Australia proposed having economic and social rights recognized in any covenant agreed upon.[12] France, along with some other Western states, supported the recognition of such rights but in another covenant.[13] In November 1950, the Third Committee of the General Assembly urged the CHR, via ECOSOC, "in accordance with the spirit of the Universal Declaration of Human Rights to include in the Covenant a clear expression of economic, social and cultural rights in a manner which would relate them to the civic and political freedoms to be proclaimed by the Covenant."[14] But in December 1950 the U.N. General Assembly determined that the U.N. would draft one Covenant containing civil and political rights only;[15] albeit anticipating later covenants "dealing with economic, social, cultural ... and other categories of human rights."[16] In 1951–1952, the U.N. decided to draft two separate covenants on civil and political, and economic, social and cultural rights respectively.[17] In Resolution 543 (VI) the U.N. General Assembly "requested the ECOSOC to ask" the CHR[18]

> [t]o draft two covenants on human rights ... one to contain civil and political rights and the other to contain economic, social and cultural rights, in order that the General Assembly may approve the two covenants simultaneously and open them at the same time for signature, the two Covenants to contain, in order to emphasise the unity of the aim in view and to ensure respect for and observance of human rights, as many similar provisions as possible.[19]

In 1951 the CHR began to work on a covenant recognizing economic, social and cultural rights, drafting fourteen articles, and taking account of input from the ILO, UNESCO and WHO.[20] By 1954, Draft Covenants on Economic, Social and Cultural Rights and on Civil and Political Rights were completed and submitted to ECOSOC and the General Assembly for consideration, debate and ultimate adoption.[21]

During the preparation of the 1966 Covenants some of the leading states of the developed Western world were resistant to the recognition of economic and social rights. This resistance usually coloured the views of those who advocated separate covenants. The U.K. and the U.S.A. were among the chief advocates of separate covenants along these lines. But advocacy of separate covenants did not necessarily mean opposition *simpliciter* to the validity of economic and social rights generally. For the British, in particular, their resistance to including such rights in a legally binding covenant was due especially to a legalism and positivism in accordance with which it was doubted whether such rights were justiciable. In Benthamite spirit, it was felt better to have fewer "real" legal rights than extravagant goals that could not be adjudicated and enforced in any sensible way. For example, according to one tradition of the common law, there can be no effective rights without "remedies," and there was some British scepticism about whether there were effective remedies to sanction a state breaching economic and social rights.[22] Furthermore, so the argument went, there might be better ways to advance social and economic welfare than through *legal* devices. This approach may be contrasted with the Eisenhower administration's rather more cynical 1953 commitment to a human rights "Action Plan" – depending on education and the like – in place of the ratification of international, legally binding human rights covenants.[23] Nonetheless, the generalization that leading Western powers tended to resist the inclusion of economic and social rights in a single, comprehensive human rights covenant is largely accurate. On the other hand, Afro-Asian, Latin American, and other developing states, the U.S.S.R. and the socialist bloc (together with social-democratic Western states such as Australia) strongly supported the recognition of all kinds of human rights, and, in particular, economic and social rights, in a single, comprehensive covenant.[24]

Even before the avalanche of decolonization in the early 1960s, non-Western states came to have significant majorities in a number of U.N. institutions. Political scientist Howard Tolley, Jr. calculates that in the years 1947 to 1954, Latin America and Asia provided 40 per cent of the total number of representatives in the CHR, compared with a Western representation of 34 per cent. In this period the following countries were represented on the CHR: Egypt, China, India, Iran, Lebanon, Pakistan, Philippines, B.S.S.R., Poland, Ukraine, U.S.S.R., Yugoslavia, Chile, Guatemala, Panama, Uruguay, Australia, Belgium, Denmark, France, Greece, Norway, Turkey, U.K. and U.S.A.[25] Of "Near Eastern", Asian and Latin American states in the U.N., American scholar James Green wrote in 1956, in a study for The Brookings Institution, that "[t]his group, which usually controls a majority of votes, has succeeded in including in the draft covenants [of 1954] many provisions about which they feel deeply."[26] Among "underdeveloped countries," together with the U.S.S.R. and satellites, there was tenacious support for the recognition of economic, social, cultural, civil and political rights in a single covenant.[27] As early as 1951, the U.S. State Department recognized that there was majority support in the U.N. General Assembly for the inclusion of economic and social rights in a single covenant, and it even seemed that it might respect that majority:[28]

> To press for the separation of those provisions in the face of majority opposition in the Assembly would only invite a great deal of ill-will against the United States and rebound unfavourably with respect to the general political position of the United States *vis-à-vis* other countries, particularly in the

case of the many underdeveloped countries urging the inclusion of these provisions in the Covenant.[29]

Despite the caution shown by the U.S. State Department on this occasion, it joined the U.K. in opposing the inclusion of economic and social rights in any covenant, and, if that opposition were not successful, in calling for a separate (and preferably later) covenant to contain them. The U.K. and the U.S.A. would have preferred any covenant to contain predominantly, if not exclusively, civil and political rights. In this stance they were joined by some European and Commonwealth countries, despite widespread constitutional and ordinary legal recognition of certain economic and social rights in Europe and Latin America.[30] It must noted, however, that the U.S.A. had at times contemplated international provision for economic and social rights.[31] But, as Green says, the U.S.A. would "find it difficult to accept a *treaty* containing economic, social and cultural rights, because these went far beyond the rights contained in the United States Constitution and were not enforceable – apart from particular legislation – by the federal and state courts in the United States."[32] On the other hand, as Tolley observed, "[s]ome representatives of Western liberal regimes accepted as consistent with emerging welfare state ideals promises of free public education, food, clothing, housing, medical care and necessary social services, the right to work, and to paid holidays."[33] Even so, there was significant Western resistance at the official level to the inclusion of economic and social rights in any covenants. Obviously, Cold War politics abroad and at home was central to the U.S.A.'s position, as it sought to undercut the U.S.S.R.'s propaganda about its success in the economic and social arena, with a state that claimed to provide for all the needs of its citizens from "cradle to grave." Additionally, the U.S.S.R. proclaimed this state responsibility as an important dimension of its understanding of "socialist," compared with "bourgeois," democracy. The U.S.A. also had to deal with an inflammatory combination of anti-communism, anti-collectivism and states' rights at home.[34]

But the U.N. decided to include economic, cultural and social rights in any covenant it adopted – and on that position it was immovable. In the face of this, the U.S.A. sought, especially in 1951–1952, to persuade the U.N. to overturn its decision to have only one comprehensive human rights covenant.[35] Green refers to the "intensive efforts by the United States in foreign capitals and in United Nations lobbies and committee rooms, in favor of the two covenants."[36]

Arguments in favour of two covenants centred on the supposed differences between civil and political rights on one hand, and economic, social and cultural rights on the other. On this basis, it was argued that it was necessary to have different implementation methods and machinery for each kind of right. Were these different methods and machinery contained in the one instrument, it was argued that such a "covenant within a covenant" would create incoherence.[37]

A series of dichotomies was employed by the U.S.A., U.K. and some other Western states, which were intended to demonstrate why separate covenants were needed. Civil and political rights were said to be "absolute," "enforceable," fundamental, "immediately applicable", justiciable, focused on the rights of the individual against the state, not resource-intensive, within a state's power to achieve, and suitable for implementation via an inter-state complaints system. By contrast, economic and social rights were characterized as conditional, unenforceable, secondary, to be progressively fulfilled, non-justiciable, requiring "positive action" from the state, expensive, dependent on forces outside the state's power (for example, upon global economic forces) and suited to a "soft" system of regular state reporting.[38]

There has been an extensive debate in the literature over these contrasts. I find the differentiation crude and often unpersuasive. There is, for example, a failure to identify precisely which rights are being analyzed and compared. For every argument made by proponents of separate covenants there is a rebuttal. The UDHR provides for limitations of certain *civil and political* rights in certain circumstances. Further, the protection and realization of many civil and political rights is resource-intensive and dependent on positive state action (for example, the infrastructure necessary to ensure fair and free elections, a fair trial, lawful policing and so forth). Economic rights can also, like civil and political rights, be immediately applicable, even if their fulfilment might be a matter of degree dependent on "available resources." Moreover, many economic and social rights are readily justiciable. One thinks, for example, of countries with constitutional or legislative protection of such rights, and with anti-discrimination and industrial tribunals to adjudicate upon them. And the maintenance of civil and political rights can also be vulnerable to international forces (for example, a government might be undermined or overthrown by outside forces). U.N. Special Rapporteur Danilo Turk has confirmed that the violation of social, economic and cultural rights can have legal consequences, and that states should set up administrative and judicial review machinery in relation to them. Under the so-called Limburg principles the ICESCR Committee has determined that certain ICESCR rights are "capable of immediate application by judicial and other organs in many national legal systems." Examples of such rights include equality of rights for men and women, "equal pay for equal work," trade union rights and the right to free primary education. The idea of justiciable economic and social rights is hardly an implausible or heterodox one. Doctrines, rules and remedies relating to economic rights (for example, in property, contract, family, tort, corporations, and commercial law) are pervasive in most legal systems.[39]

At the thirteenth session of ECOSOC (30 July–21 September 1951) a resolution put forward by Belgium, the U.K. and the U.S.A. was passed.[40] It proposed that ECOSOC "invite the General Assembly to reconsider its decision in resolution 421(V) to include in one Covenant articles on economic, social and cultural rights together with civil and political rights."[41] There was a vociferous response to this proposal from many non-Western states. A number of states, among them the U.S.S.R., Iraq, Pakistan and Yugoslavia, doubted whether it was legal for ECOSOC to seek to disturb an already established General Assembly resolution.[42] And non-Western states (for example, Mexico, Saudi Arabia and Syria) pressed arguments in favour of economic and social rights and of a single, comprehensive covenant. They argued that economic and social rights were of equal status to civil and political rights, were not easily distinguished, and were dependent on each other for their utility. They also argued that one ought not try to put them in some kind of hierarchical relation.[43] Such states, also, and with good reason, doubted the bona fides of Western states' arguments in favour of separate covenants, seeing them as rationalizations for the undermining of the protection of economic and social rights.[44] A representative from Iraq even declared that "no great harm would be done if some countries used the inclusion of articles on economic, social, and cultural rights as a pretext not to ratify the covenant".[45]

As it turned out, however, it was a compromise on the part of non-Western states that led to the outcome of separate covenants. The compromise was motivated by the dual objectives of ensuring the widest possible ratification of civil and political rights and saving the prospects for economic and social rights.[46] As Green put it in 1956, some non-Western states were prepared "to acquiesce, reluctantly, in the separation of the two covenants in order to make it possible for the United States, the British Commonwealth, and others to ratify at least a covenant on civil and political rights."[47] As it happened, of course, the U.S.A. failed to ratify either covenant, under the new policy of the Eisenhower administration.[48]

The General Assembly resolution proposing the drafting of two separate covenants was adopted on February 4, 1952.[49] It stressed the interdependence, interconnectedness, unity and equality of both kinds of rights, and "insisted on ... simultaneous preparation and approval of the two documents."[50] The resolution also required the CHR "to include as many similar provisions as possible in the two documents to illustrate their unity of purpose."[51] Despite the fact that separate covenants were now proposed, the recognition of wide-ranging economic, cultural and social rights in the drafts completed in 1954 was of significant benefit normatively to the non-Western world.[52] Their recognition was assessed by the U.S.A. as such a challenge to its economic interests and national sovereignty that it set its jaw still more strongly against international human rights treaties. Green concludes[53] that

> [t]he economic, social and cultural rights [in the draft covenants] follow the general pattern of the Universal Declaration, but they are far more detailed. This resulted in part from the overriding concern of the majority with this category of rights and their determination to spell them out at length.

In this regard, it is telling that the U.S.A. failed in its various attempts to include a right to own property in the covenants.[54]

During the drafting of the 1966 Covenants, key colonial and administering powers sought through the device of a so-called "colonial" or "territorial" clause to limit and control the extension of human rights protections to inhabitants of relevant colonies or territories.[55] The U.K., France and other colonial powers, supported by the U.S.A., sponsored the inclusion of a colonial clause that would make the application of the Covenants to their territories dependent upon accession to the treaties by a metropolitan power on their behalf. This would effectively make human rights protections for inhabitants of colonial and equivalent territories dependent on the decision of an administering power. Initial drafts (including one produced in 1947) of the Covenant, as it then was, contained such an article.[56] This article, refined in 1949 by the CHR, meant that the covenant would apply to all Non-Self-Governing, Colonial and Trust Territories, but only if the relevant metropolitan, administering state "acceded to the covenant on behalf of such colony or territory."[57]

Colonial or so-called "administering powers"[58] put forward a number of arguments in favour of a colonial clause. First, they argued that they needed to have discretion over which territories would come under the covenant[59] given that such territories had various levels of development.[60] While states sponsoring the clause claimed to be committed to assisting territories' transition to independence, this was said to be an evolutionary process involving gradual education and the development of the required institutions.[61] Second, and relatedly, they argued that premature, automatic and universal application of the covenant to such territories ran the serious risk of undermining the human rights regime. They argued that the standards embodied in any human rights covenant would have to be lowered so that poorer territories would be able to fulfil its demands. It was better, so it was said, "to allow developed states to ratify, while also giving less developed countries time to realise their aspirations. In short, the Covenant should be applied immediately and in its entirety in those countries where suitable conditions already prevailed, but should be introduced by degrees in those countries that the [U.N.] Charter recognised as presently unfit for full independence."[62] Third, the powers argued that were they to subject the territories to human rights obligations, effectively without their consent (since international relations was usually the province of metropolitan powers), they would be interfering with the domestic autonomy and democracy of such territories. It was argued that the question of undertaking human rights obligations ought to be left to such territories themselves to decide, upon gaining their independence.[63] This was an argument particularly favoured by the U.K.[64] It explained that "[a]lthough it retains an ultimate sovereignty in regard to its colonial territories, and, although, of course, it speaks for and represents its colonial territories in international matters, the United Kingdom Government is not, in general, responsible for legislation in the colonial territories."[65]

Opponents of the colonial clause from the non-Western world argued, however, that it was hypocritical for administering powers to espouse respect for democratic processes in relation to colonial and quasi-colonial inhabitants, when these processes had been strongly resisted in relation to self-determination.[66] To such opponents, the clause simply maintained racist, imperialistic values that rationalized the vested economic interests of the administering powers.[67] Non-Western states opposed to the clause further argued that "human rights were universal and that the effectiveness of the Covenant would be diminished if it was [*sic*] not made applicable to dependent territories, which needed human rights protection even more than the metropolitan states."[68] Regarding the argument that automatic and universal applicability of the human rights Covenant would impinge upon the autonomy of the territories, states that opposed the colonial clause urged the colonial powers to commit to the implementation of the Covenant and come to agreement with the territorial authorities.[69] Representatives from India, Pakistan and Haiti reinforced this argument by referring to the fact that no local legislature would refuse to enact laws mandated by a colonial power.[70] An alternative to the proposed colonial clause was one attributed to the U.S.S.R.[71]:

the present Covenant shall extend or be applicable both to the metropolitan territory which is signatory to the present Covenant, as well as to all the other territories (non-self-governing, trust, and colonial territories) which are being administered or governed by the metropolitan power in question.[72]

After various internal U.N. machinations[73] and a slight rewording, this alternative clause was passed (December 4, 1950) as General Assembly resolution 422(V):

The provisions of the present Covenant shall extend to or be applicable equally to a signatory metropolitan State and to all the territories, be they Non-Self-governing, Trust or Colonial Territories, which are being administered or governed by such metropolitan State.[74]

The CHR agreed to this clause for the Covenant with no debate.[75]

Ultimately the clause was not, however, included in the 1966 Covenants because so much had occurred to advance the principle of self-determination and the practice of decolonization by the time of the adoption of the Covenants that such a clause was seen by most U.N. states as unnecessary.[76] By 1960, for example, the General Assembly had adopted the Declaration on the Granting of Independence to Colonial Countries and Peoples.[77]

The experience of the attempted inclusion of a colonial clause, and its ultimate failure, demonstrates yet again that the U.S. and other leading Western powers were unable to impose their will regarding a critical part of the international human rights regime. The Soviet resolution that became 422(V) was, as Evans concedes,[78] "a resolution diametrically opposing the intentions of the United Kingdom and other colonial powers ... [I]t was an anticolonial clause ..." Western "hegemonic" powers were defeated by the anti-colonialist majority in the U.N. Inconsistently with his characterization of the early years of the U.N. as dominated by the West, Evans[79] wrote that

[w]ith the mood in the [U.N. General] Assembly growing avowedly anticolonial by 1950, the colonial clause offered even greater opportunities for less developed and socialist countries to denounce colonial powers.

He further accepted that by

1950 the membership of the Assembly included a large bloc of Arab and Muslim states who were in regular contact with Algerian and Moroccan leaders. During the debate on the colonial clause, members of this bloc would often read out extracts of communications from these leaders detailing the contempt with which France treated its North African colonies. Vociferous among those who spoke regularly against the colonial clause were Afghanistan, Egypt, Ethiopia, Iraq, Lebanon, Pakistan, Saudi Arabia, Syria, Turkey and the Yemen.[80]

States voting in favour of the anti-colonial clause were Afghanistan, Burma, B.S.S.R., U.S.S.R., Chile, China, Cuba, Czechoslovakia, Egypt,

Ethiopia, Guatemala, Haiti, India, Indonesia, Iran, Iraq, Israel, Lebanon, Liberia, Mexico, Pakistan, Philippines, Poland, Saudi Arabia, Syria, Ukrainian S.S.R., Uruguay, Venezuela, Yemen and Yugoslavia. Those voting against were the Netherlands, New Zealand, Turkey, South Africa, U.K., U.S.A., Australia, Belgium, Canada and Greece.[81]

Green,[82] writing in 1956, expressed some dismay that the U.S.A. and the rest of the "Western world" were unable to prevail on the colonial issue:

> The [Soviet anti-colonial] article was vigorously opposed by the administering powers, which warned that inclusion of this provision would make it difficult for them to accept the covenant; but they were decisively defeated by a vote ... This decision of the Assembly was accepted without debate by the Commission on Human Rights ... These decisions, like the inclusion of the article on self-determination, reflect the desire of the majority of nonadministering members to write their own views of the colonial problem into the covenants even though this may make ratification impossible for the minority of administering members. This would hardly seem to be the most satisfactory method of concluding a treaty that is supposed to represent the whole world community.

Self-determination had been recognized in the Atlantic Charter of 1941, and the United Nations accepted an obligation in its Declaration of 1942 to "respect the right of all peoples to choose the form of government under which they will live."[83] Article 1(2) of the U.N. Charter declared one of the purposes of the U.N. to be the development of "friendly relations among nations based on the respect for the principle of equal rights and self-determination of peoples ..."[84] Chapters XI, XII and XIII regarding the transition of dependent territories to "self-government" are also relevant.[85] Although the UDHR did not refer to self-determination by name, in Article 2 it did proclaim that

> no distinction shall be made on the basis of the political, jurisdictional or international status of the country or territory to which a person belongs, whether it be independent, trust,

non-self-governing or under any other limitation of sovereignty.

Also relevant are provisions relating to rights of participation ("The will of the people shall be the basis of the authority of government ...": Article 21(3)) and to "a social and international order in which the rights and freedoms" of the UDHR could be "fully realized" (Article 28).

From 1950 to 1954, the idea of self-determination was discussed and propelled forward in the U.N. by an anticolonialist momentum. At the 311th meeting of the Third Committee, Afghanistan and Saudi Arabia asked the CHR to "study ways and means which would ensure the rights of peoples and nations to self-determination". Not a single European state gave its support for the proposal.[86] In contrast, many non-Western, "Third World" countries urged the introduction of self-determination to a covenant or covenants, including Afghanistan, Saudi Arabia, Chile, Burma, Egypt, India, Indonesia, Iran, Iraq, Lebanon, Pakistan, Philippines, Syria and Yemen.[87] In 1952, Chile added a new element to the right of self-determination:

> The right of the peoples to self-determination shall also include permanent sovereignty over their natural wealth and resources. In no case may a people be deprived of its own means of subsistence on the grounds of any rights that may be claimed by other states.[88]

The opposing colonial and administering powers criticized self-determination on a number of counts. Self-determination was characterized as a contentious and conditional political *principle* rather than an individual legal *right*. It was further contended that a collective right such as self-determination was out of place in a covenant or covenants predominantly committed to *individual* rights. Self-determination was also regarded as a threat to national unity, sovereignty and territorial integrity (for example, it was argued that minorities might seek for themselves territory and the apparatus of the state). The doctrine was also said to be plagued by uncertainty: What did "self-determination" and "peoples" mean? *Which* peoples had a right to it? The opposing powers also asserted that many societies were unprepared to assume the responsibilities self-determination brings.

Finally, it was strongly urged that civil and political rights should be entrenched before the granting of self-determination.[89]

Supporters of self-determination argued in response that it enabled individuals to avail themselves of the full range of human rights in the UDHR and the covenant(s). It is true that simple independence for a country does not guarantee a democratic system and protection of human rights, but the doctrine of self-determination has for a considerable time now, if not always, been much more than simple independence. In its combination with the value of self-government, it has for a considerable period at least favoured, if not presupposed, democracy.[90] This was certainly the case following the writing of the U.N. Charter, although this value has always been in tension with other constitutive norms such as sovereignty, non-intervention and domestic jurisdiction as reflected in Article 2(7).[91] During the covenant debates an Indian delegate captured the reinforcing relationship between self-determination and an individual's well-being by insisting that "the individual could not enjoy his full rights unless he was a member of a self-determined society." Article 55 of the U.N. Charter guards against individual human rights being undermined by self-determination claims. On its face, it is open to the interpretation that "universal respect for ... human rights" is the "underpinning" for "stability," "well-being" and "peaceful and friendly" international relations "based on respect for the principle of equal rights and self-determination of peoples," rather than the other way around.[92] We should also recall the communitarian and collectivist dimensions of the human rights regime, including the UDHR, described earlier. A further defence against any undermining of an individual's human rights in the pursuit or maintenance of self-determination can now be found in common Article 5(1) of the 1966 Covenants:

> Nothing in the present Covenant may be interpreted as implying for any State, group or person any right to engage in any activity or perform any act aimed at the destruction of any of the rights and freedoms recognized herein or at their limitation to a greater extent than is provided for in the present Covenant.

Regarding the argument that self-determination was a political *principle* rather than a legal *right*, we may observe that this formalistic distinction is not persuasive given the room for interpretation of the relevant articles, the fluid nature of international law, the role of the practice of states and international organizations in the development, specifically, of customary international law, and the inconsistency in making precision of terminology a criterion for whether a claim can be considered a legal right.[93]

As far as interpretation of Article 1(2) of the U.N. Charter is concerned, it can be read as requiring concurrent respect for the self-determination of peoples *and* for the equal rights not just of individuals but also of peoples. It refers to the *principle* of equal rights and self-determination, not principles, which lends some plausibility to this, perhaps unorthodox, interpretation. In full, it describes one of the purposes of the U.N.:

> 2. To develop friendly relations among nations based on respect for the principle of equal rights and self-determination of peoples, and to take other appropriate measures to strengthen universal peace ...

Falk[94] has questioned the materiality of the contrast between a principle and a right in this context, arguing that the realization of any principle under international law will inevitably impose and confer relevant duties and rights. To similar effect, Pechota has argued that

> [t]he futility of the debate, which centred on the question of whether self-determination was a political principle or a legal right, is demonstrated by the fact of decolonization and by later developments in the political organs of the United Nations, where a series of resolutions gave practical effect to the right and declared it to be a legally binding principle of the Charter. The arguments made against the right, as well as the assertion that a covenant on human rights was not the place to enunciate collective rights, were brushed aside by the majority, and the provision was formulated in a forceful and unambiguous manner.[95]

On the question of uncertainty regarding the conceptualization of self-determination, non-Western proponents wondered why imprecision was not considered fatal in other debates over terms such as "fair wages," "adequate standard of living," "aggression" and "peace."[96]

In addition to Western powers' resistance to self-determination because of its potential to cause fragmentation in a state (through secessionist claims by, for example, competing nationalist splinter groups, historic ethno-nations or minorities of various kinds),[97] they were very anxious over the economic dimension of self-determination. Tony Evans has gone so far as to suggest that during the debates over a human rights covenant, "economic arguments were the cause of most concern for western industrialized countries."[98]

Recall that in 1952 Chile put forward a self-determination proposal that incorporated a people's right of permanent sovereignty over their country's natural wealth and resources so that its subsistence could be maintained.[99] Western states, and especially colonial and administering powers, regarded this proposal as a threat to their economic interests. It had the potential, so they thought, to legitimate a "new" state's nationalization of industries (especially mining industries), expropriation of foreign property without proper compensation, and/or revocation or repudiation of international treaties and contracts respectively.[100]

In answer, non-Western states rightly pointed out that the economic dimension was vital to self-determination and to the fulfilment of human rights. They also drew attention to the unfair economic advantages imperial powers had long gained through mercantilism, including "cheap raw materials," cheap labour and strategic spheres of influence.[101] They argued that "the purpose of the article was not to threaten foreign investment as suggested but to prevent such foreign exploitation as would deprive the local population of its means of subsistence."[102] It was inconsistent for Western powers to use a paradigm of sovereignty based on values of non-intervention, territorial integrity, domestic jurisdiction, political supremacy and so on, to deny claims for political self-determination, and then to use another model of limited "sovereignty" to deny newly independent states full control of their economies and resources (subject only to relevant international legal regulation).

If Western states had been consistent, and employed the understanding of sovereignty they believed applicable to themselves, they would not have been able to deny economic self-determination to non-Western states. One can imagine the answer Western states would be likely to give to a stipulation that *they* could not "for their own ends, freely dispose of their natural wealth and resources," and that *they* could be "deprived of ... [their] own means of subsistence." Their answer would in all likelihood be that such a stipulation would be in violation of their sovereignty. For example, the International Commission of Jurists (Aaland Islands dispute) advised in 1920 that "in the absence of express provisions in international treaties, the right of disposing of national territory is essentially an attribute of the sovereignty of every State."[103]

Indeed, control of a territory, national sovereignty as a form of proprietorship or dominion over territory (for example, over land, territorial sea, airspace), is essential to the definition of a state under international law. Following the Montevideo Convention on the Rights and Duties of States (1933), the Restatement of the Foreign Relations Law of the United States defines a state as "an entity that has a *defined territory* and permanent population, *under the control of its own government*, and that engages in, or has the capacity to engage in, formal relations with other such entities."[104] So, in calling for economic self-determination of the kind that Chile proposed, non-Western states were only making explicit a standard feature of state sovereignty, while adding a modest minimum regarding subsistence (one entirely consistent with the commitments of the U.N. Charter, UDHR and Covenants to social and economic rights and to improving human development).[105]

In any event, supporters of economic self-determination sought to allay some of the fears of Western states by removing the phrase "permanent sovereignty" and adding the qualification that a "people's" free disposal of their wealth and resources would be "without prejudice to any obligations arising out of international economic cooperation, based upon the principle of mutual benefit, and international law" (common Article 1(2), ICCPR, ICESCR). What are we to make of this rather opaque language? On its face, it seems to be reassuring "non-disposing" states that the principle of *pacta sunt servanda*[106] (that treaties obligations bind) will generally be complied with, and that such states, along with all others, will be subject to international law. This might then be an embodiment of "economic sovereignty"[107] as "*responsibly conceived.*"[108]

I want to emphasize that, in criticizing some Western powers for being inconsistent in relation to their use of conveniently differing conceptions of sovereignty to respond to arguments for political and economic self-determination by non-Western states (resisting fragmentation of Western states by defending their sovereign control over their territory while denying *non-Western* states control of their "natural wealth and resources" because that was somehow beyond the power of their sovereignty), I do not endorse any conception of state sovereignty that makes it a paramount norm of international relations. A parochial state sovereignty that is indifferent or hostile to international regulation has done much to impede the work of the global body politic. The development of universal human rights (including humanitarian intervention, *erga omnes* obligations, declarations and treaties, international criminal law and universal jurisdiction) is vital in overcoming such an obstacle. In this sense, although Weston discusses responsibility in the context of developing countries, I am sure that he would agree that a goal of international law should be to make *all* states' exercise of sovereignty responsible.[109]

International law seems to recognize this requirement of responsibility. While a state is entitled to *independence*, as a subject of international law (for example, through the doctrine of recognition), that independence is to be exercised *subject to the law*. To use a sporting analogy, a coach might release a soccer player to "follow the ball" (and thus not to play in a designated position), to play freely and independently, but this is no licence to play outside the laws of the game. The laws of the game are outside and superior to the coach's power: just as (supranational) international law is outside and normatively superior to the power of any state. One must remember, however, that just as the laws of the game of soccer seek to accommodate (and allow some freedom, autonomy, discretion, decision-making and power to) various actors in the game (for example, coaches, referees and players), so too has international law (for example, in the contracting "domestic jurisdiction" clause). One could think of the interplay of forces in a federal constitutional system or the principles of "margin of appreciation" and "subsidiarity" in European Union law. As Shaw has put it:

> [I]nternational law permits freedom of action for states, unless there is a rule constraining this. However, it must be emphasized that such freedom exists within and not outside the international legal system and it is therefore international

law which dictates the scope and content of the independence of states and not the states themselves individually and unilaterally.[110]

The issues discussed here have been particularly keenly debated in the context of the international law relating to a state's expropriation of foreign property.[111] Despite Article 47 of the ICESCR ("Nothing in the present Covenant shall be interpreted as impairing the inherent right of all peoples to enjoy and utilize fully and freely their natural wealth and resources")[112] (see, also, Article 25, ICESCR), the implied reassurance to non-Western states regarding expropriation was well supported in international law up to at least the adoption of the Covenants, and, arguably, up to the present day. Any expropriation of foreign property was required to be lawful (according to international law and, arguably, more generally, in the sense that it complied with notions of the rule of law that precluded vengeful, venal or arbitrary expropriations), for a public purpose or in the public interest, non-discriminatory (and not in violation of international human rights law) and compensated for.[113] More radical communist and/or Third World perspectives argued that the history of colonial exploitation and the detrimental impact of many transnational corporations on developing countries' economies, quality of life, environment, political autonomy and stability, and human rights meant that compensation was not mandatory. This stance is consistent with the critical views of a wide range of schools of thought that have criticized the inequity in North–South relations, especially regarding the economic realm. These schools have included Marxists and socialists, "dependency" theorists, World System theorists, World Order theorists and Critical Theorists. But certainly a complete rejection of the compensation principle has not found strong roots in international law.[114]

The prevailing law is better captured in the 1962 Declaration on Permanent Sovereignty over Natural Resources (UNGAA Res. 1803 (XVII)).[115] Paragraph 4 of the Declaration provides as follows:

Nationalization, expropriation or requisitioning shall be based on grounds or reasons of public utility, security or the national interest which are recognized as overriding purely individual or private interests, both domestic and foreign. In such cases the owner shall be paid *appropriate* compensation, in accordance with the rules in force in the State taking such measures in the exercise of its sovereignty and in accordance with international law.[116]

While the Declaration is notable for its reinforcement of the main pillars of the orthodox conception of international law in this area, to a significant degree it also promoted the interests of developing countries; including the references to "permanent sovereignty," to public, societal or national interests that may prevail over "purely individual or private interests," to the rules of a state in this field, and to "appropriate" rather than to "adequate" compensation (which was the criterion Western states had traditionally preferred).[117] We might note, however, that, subsequently (and outside the period this book examines) developing countries presented a forceful challenge to the supremacy of traditional principles relating to expropriation, particularly in their push for a New International Economic Order in 1974.[118]

Even with the qualifications to the economic self-determination embodied in Article 1(2) of the Covenants, the majority of Western states still perceived it as a grave threat to their economic interests. But it was the *non*-Western states, as we know, that largely prevailed on this issue.[119]

Common Article 1(1) of the 1966 Covenants refers to the right of all peoples to "freely pursue their economic, social and cultural development." Article 1(2) declares that "In no case may a people be deprived of its own means of subsistence." Article 2(1), ICESCR, provides, in part:

Each State Party to the present Covenant undertakes to take steps, individually *and through international assistance and cooperation, especially economic* and technical, to the maximum of its available resources, with a view to achieving progressively the full realization of the rights recognized in the present Covenant by all appropriate means ... [emphasis added]

Article 6, ICESCR, refers to the "steps" that states are obliged to take in pursuit of "steady economic, social and cultural development." Article 11, ICESCR, recognizes "the right of everyone to an adequate standard of living" ("including adequate food, clothing and housing," and freedom from hunger). Article 12, ICESCR, recognizes "the right of everyone to the enjoyment of the highest attainable standard of physical and mental health." Article 13, ICESCR, recognizes "the right of everyone to education." Article 15, ICESCR, recognizes "the right of everyone ... to take part in cultural life." Louis B. Sohn, a pioneering human rights scholar, has persuasively discerned in provisions of this nature a right to development; a right that has often been considered as a recent innovation, as a "third generation" right. This latter perspective makes sense if one conceives of the right to development as "merely" a right of a developing state to modernization, equitable participation in the global economy, international aid, and so forth; but a right to development need not be so circumscribed. It is best regarded as a right to human development. It can be understood as a synthesis of all the ways in which the realization of human rights fulfils human needs and promotes human flourishing (which obviously, on my view, would still require equitable participation in the global economy, and so on). In this way, the indivisibility of civil and political and economic social and cultural rights is preserved, and economic development is not set up in competition with human rights protection (the so-called rights–development trade-off).[120] An exclusive focus on development and economic growth does not guarantee just distributive outcomes, nor the realization of social and economic rights. It is telling that the greatest ambition for this model is that wealth will "trickle down" to the poverty-stricken in society, in circumstances that demand a steady and substantial flow. And civil and political rights ought not to be jettisoned in development's name. As political scientist Jack Donnelly says, the "ultimate purpose of development is to lay the basis for realizing human dignity." In recent years, the notion of "sustainable development" has emerged in a phrase that tries to capture something of holistic human development: economic development, social and economic justice, respect for human rights and environmental stability. In this it echoes the specification of "World Order Values" by scholars such as Richard Falk of the WOMP (World Order Models Project), which flourished in the 1960s and 1970s and continues to this day. The notion of sustainable development has been elaborated and discussed through the U.N. Development program and in a series of U.N. and regional conferences, along with the idea of "governance" (for example, at the 1992 Rio Conference on the environment and the 1993

Vienna Conference on human rights). These values have even entered the rhetoric of some actors in the international economic regime (for example, the World Bank), although they often sit uneasily with an aggressively neo-liberal agenda (privatization, deregulation, free "marketization" and so on).[121] This holistic approach[122] to human development has, however, a long lineage; examples include ancient religious norms of economic justice, and ideals of economic and social rights and human welfare during the Enlightenment and among early socialists. The holistic approach is reflected in a number of provisions of the Covenants. For example, the Preamble of the ICESCR provides that the "ideal of free human beings enjoying freedom from fear and want can only be achieved if *conditions are created* whereby everyone may enjoy his economic, social and cultural rights, as well as his civil and political rights" [emphasis added]. Article 4 of the ICESCR provides that any limitations on the rights must be "determined by law" and extend "only in so far as this may be compatible with the nature of these rights and solely for the purpose of promoting the general welfare in a democratic society." It clearly answers in the negative those who would argue that human rights can be sacrificed at the altar of a state's economic development:

> Nothing in the present Covenant may be interpreted as implying for *any State, group or person* any right to engage in any activity or perform any act aimed at the destruction of any of the rights and freedoms recognized herein, or at their limitation to a greater extent than is provided for in the present Covenant [emphasis added].

According to Sohn, with whom I agree, a link is present between self-determination and development, though I cast it as *human* development, as discussed above. Sohn cites provisions of the Declaration of Philadelphia (1944) (now part of the ILO Constitution (1946)), the U.N. Charter, UDHR, the Teheran Declaration (1968), UNESCO's Declaration on Race and Racial Prejudice (1978) and the African Charter on Human and Peoples' Rights (1981), among other instruments, in support of his view.[123] The 1960 Declaration on the Granting of Independence to Colonial Countries and Peoples provided the model for common Article 1 of the 1966 Covenants, which is identically worded.[124] The link between self-determination and development is also evident in the 1970 Declaration on Principles of International Law Concerning Friendly Relations[125] (to use a short title), the 1986 Declaration on the Rights of Development[126], Principle 3 of the Rio Declaration (1992) and the Vienna Declaration (1993).[127] The Vienna Declaration sums up the symbiotic relationship between development and human rights. While "the right to development is a 'universal and inalienable right and an integral part of fundamental human rights,'" the Declaration warns that "the lack of development may not be invoked to justify the abridgement of ... human rights."[128]

The U.N. Draft Declaration on the Rights of Indigenous Peoples (1994)[129] similarly attempts to reconcile development, cultural autonomy and environmental concerns in a non-assimilationist fashion. For example, Article 4 provides:

> Indigenous peoples have the right to maintain and strengthen their distinct political, economic, social and cultural characteristics, as well as their legal systems, while retaining their rights to participate fully, if they so choose, in the political, economic, social and cultural life of the State.

Article 26 declares, in part, that

> [i]ndigenous peoples have the right to own, develop, control and use the lands and territories, including the total environment ... and other resources which they have traditionally owned or otherwise occupied or used. This includes the right to full recognition of their laws, traditions and customs, land-tenure systems and institutions for the development and management of resources ...

Article 30 provides that indigenous peoples have "the right to determine and develop priorities and strategies for the development or use of their lands, territories and other resources." It also provides that indigenous peoples can insist upon "their free and informed consent prior to the approval of any project" having an impact upon their resources, "particularly in connection with the development, utilization or exploitation of mineral, water, or other resources," and, with such peoples' "agreement," to receive "just and fair compensation ... to mitigate adverse environmental, economic, social, cultural or spiritual impact." Article 31 recognizes, "as a specific form of exercising their right to self-determination," that indigenous peoples "have the right to autonomy or self-government in matters relating to their internal and local affairs including [*inter alia*] culture, religion, education ... health, housing, employment, social welfare, economic activities, land and resources management, environment and entry by non-members, as well as ways and means for financing these autonomous functions."

In light of the criticism that the International Bill of Rights is too individualistic, and thus does not adequately cater for collective claims, I will now assess the potential for the 1966 Covenants to accommodate cultural rights and group claims, paying particular attention to the realization of the rights of minorities and indigenous peoples under the banner of self-determination or otherwise.

Given the great messiness of the definition, applicability, significance and extent of the right of self-determination under international law, it will be useful to try to identify its main characteristics. Before doing so, however, it is critical to appreciate the great fluidity and ambiguity regarding the conceptualization and experience of self-determination under international law.[130] As Falk[131] has observed:

> [T]he contours of the right of self-determination have never been and aren't now fixed in the concrete of rigid legal doctrine. The right has been continuously evolving conceptually and experientially in response to the pressure of events, geopolitical priorities and the prevailing moral and political climate. This combination of factors tends to produce a confusing pattern of historically conditioned precedents, leaving considerable room for widely disparate interpretations bearing on legal doctrine ... The law of self-determination is in flux, especially pertaining to indigenous peoples, and is likely to remain so for the indefinite future, reflecting the ebb and flow of both practice on the ground, doctrine interpreted by various concerned actors, and above all the realities of power and the vagaries of geopolitics.

Of course, such fluidity is not unique to this field of international law, nor to international law compared with other kinds of law; and some contours can be discerned in sharper and more resilient relief than others. With these cautions in mind, we may now attempt to identify some of the leading dimensions of self-determination under international law.[132]

First, it is clear that the self-determination of peoples includes a right of "external" self-determination. This right is intended to ensure that an entire people within a defined territory is free from "alien," colonial rule. When a people formerly under a colonial power obtains independence it assumes the full apparatus of a state under international law (independence, equality, self-government, national unity, territorial integrity, and so on). Nevertheless, the territorial boundaries of the former colony are preserved (*uti possidetis juris* doctrine).[133]

Second, at least since the coming into force of the 1966 Covenants (common Article 1), the right applies to all peoples, and is thus not confined to the colonial situation, but can also apply to independent states. However, generally, self-determination must not be used as a legal instrument to dismantle sovereign states.[134]

Third, one can, nevertheless, find in international instruments, doctrine and practice support for a dual right to self-determination and secession in circumstances of the continuation of colonialist practices despite formal independence, and/or where there is no democratic, representative government in a state representing the "whole people" (since, on one view, territorial integrity is only guaranteed to such a state). Arguably, gross denials of human rights or of political participation to *a* people (within the "whole people") might also qualify – as in the case of a country operating an apartheid-like system. Further, a right of secession is similarly more likely to be recognized in "colonialist" situations where there is continuing, gross, irremediable discrimination, persecution or genocidal threats or practices.[135]

Fourth, conventionally international law has not regarded minorities (members of which collectivities are accorded rights under Article 27, ICCPR) or indigenous peoples as "peoples" within Article 1 of the 1966 Covenants. And because they do not come within the article, self-determination, let alone secession, is not available to them. But this view has increasingly come under challenge, as it should.[136]

Fifth, the norm, law and practice of self-determination can and do include much more than a possible right of secession.[137] The anxiety of national governments over secession, and the fetishization of it by ethno-nationalist groups (sometimes accompanied by exclusivist, racist and genocidal mentalities, identities and practices) has tended to obscure this aspect of self-determination. In this regard, there is much to commend a sophisticated norm of internal self-determination, together with the practices, constitutions and laws of "autonomy regimes."[138] These regimes can often advance the interests and rights of indigenous peoples alike – accommodating territorial, political, cultural, legal and economic claims, while developing a tolerant, diverse polity that applies international human rights to all "citizens" (in the broadest sense of that word).

This approach to self-determination, which extends the view beyond secessionist myopia, has a number of other virtues. It does not promote and entrench some of the unhealthier dimensions of statism and nationalism, especially when they are joined with an exclusive, monocultural outlook. It does not hold out the state as a symbolic trophy for a particular "people," and as a vehicle of power. Thus, there is potential for the recommended kind of self-determination to enhance the respect for common *human* needs within a state. Additionally, it does not fragment the state as a political and economic entity.[139] While human rights advocates are justified in constraining the state's power and propensity to harm human beings, it is also important to protect the state as an enhancer of human well-being. The fragmentation of a state through secession can undermine the *capacity* (for example, through education, law, resources, and so on) for a strong but "humane" state that can promote human rights values and embody them in relevant institutions.[140] Think, for example, of a stable and healthy democratic, welfare state that can strengthen anti-discrimination regimes; facilitate multiculturalism; regulate government and the private sector; help fulfil political, economic, social and cultural rights; and ameliorate harsh impacts due to globalization. A fragmented state might find it much harder to sustain these values and to work toward these goals. This weakening effect is of particular concern given that a secessionist group succeeding to state power might well reject the values of the humane state (in this, an analogy with the way in which federalism has sometimes undermined human rights protections is instructive). Of course my support here for a more creative approach to self-determination assumes the existence of a state/government with a democratic character and a commitment to human rights that, realistically, will always be a matter of degree.

Probably the best-known definition of a minority – and there is no clear, formal definition in international law[141] – comes from Professor Capotorti:

> [A] ... group numerically inferior to the rest of the population of a State, in a non-dominant position, whose members – being Nationals of the State – possess ethnic, religious or linguistic characteristics differing from the rest of the population and show, if only implicitly, a sense of solidarity, directed towards preserving their culture, traditions, religion or language.[142]

Of course, as Steiner and Alston have pointed out, describing a group in a state as a minority still leaves undetermined the question of what its cultural, political and economic character, identity and circumstances are. It could have friendly relations with the majority or not, be more or less "integrated" with other cultures within the state (in a more or less voluntary way), and its differentiation from the majority (in terms of values and practices, and so forth) may be stark or minimal.[143] There has also been an at times frustrating, but nevertheless important, debate over whether indigenous peoples are subsumed in the term "minorities." Certainly indigenous peoples usually constitute a small fraction of any country's population. Malanczuk refuses to accept that indigenous peoples have characteristics that warrant their being conceived of and treated in a different way from "other minorities."[144] But, as we will see, understandings of indigenous peoples in international law have moved in the direction of a three-fold hybridity: that for certain purposes (for example, under the principles of non-discrimination) indigenous peoples may be regarded as "ordinary" minorities, for others as "special" minorities, and, for others still, as indigenous *peoples* capable of exercising rights of at least internal (and, in exceptional circumstances, external) self-determination.[145]

Having defined minorities, we may then ask do they have any self-determination rights? Traditional international-law doctrine after World War II has tended to deny external self-determination (including a right of secession) to a minority, treating the matter as one entirely different from that of the emergent but subjugated nation-state. It is interesting to note that this is quite different from the earlier doctrine of the Wilsonian era, which was *characteristically* concerned with captive ethnic nations within state borders obtaining their independence, equality of status and just treatment.[146] As international lawyer Diane Orentlicher has observed:

> By defining the 'self' entitled to exercise the right in strictly territorial terms, the postwar rendering of self-determination drained the principle of its rich interwar meaning. Self-determination was thus transformed from a principle for state-making into a corrective to the historical injustice of alien subjugation.[147]

This is a reasonably accurate description if it is remembered that the interwar principle she describes often did not come into fruition, as the Aaland Island dispute shows.

It is clear from the historical record of the debates over the 1966 Covenants that the majority of states, including non-Western states, were not prepared to grant full self-determination, conceived of as involving the automatic grant of a right of secession, to minorities, but rather more limited rights.[148] For example, during the debates a New Zealand representative declared that the

> principle [of self-determination] was opposed to the idea of colonialism and related to the wishes of the majority occupying a given area or territory, and it should not be confused with rights of minorities scattered throughout the territory who might be seeking equality of treatment with the majority, but not political separation.[149]

It should be noted, however, that the representative overlooks something here: what if a minority is not "scattered" but consolidated in a territory with which it has historic connections? What if, as in the usual case that causes controversy, a minority *is* seeking "political separation"? A representative from India put the matter more starkly and clearly:

> the problem of minorities should not be raised in connexion with the implementation of the right to self-determination, as it was completely different.

A Syrian delegate explained that

> the word "people" which was the keyword in the statement of
> the principle of the right to self-determination, meant the
> multiplicity of human beings constituting a nation, or the
> aggregate of the various national groups governed by a single
> authority.

To similar effect, a Greek representative said that "it should be made
clear that the problem at issue was that of national majorities not of
minorities."[150]

We have already mentioned a possible exception to the doctrine
that a right of secession is unavailable to a minority. This exception
may be termed external self-determination *in extremis*. As the
commissions involved in determining the Aaland Islands dispute
hinted, secession may be a possibility when a minority is subjected to
gross denial of its (human) rights within a state (especially in the
postwar period, and if it involves discrimination or genocidal actions).
In this we can see an overlap between self-determination *in extremis*,
humanitarian intervention, the Nuremberg principles and the
prohibition on genocide, and endorsement of general human rights
protections.[151] The Aaland Island Rapporteurs explained that

> [t]he idea of justice and of liberty, embodied in the formula of
> self-determination, must be applied in a reasonable manner to
> the relations between States and the minorities they included
> … [T]he ethnical character and the ancient traditions of these
> minorities should be respected as much as possible, and …
> they should be especially authorised to practise freely their
> religion and to cultivate their language … The separation of a
> minority from the State of which it forms part … can only be
> considered as an altogether exceptional solution, a last resort
> when the State lacks either the will or the power to enact and
> apply just and effective guarantees.[152]

Thus, as early as 1921, the right of a minority to protection of its civil
and cultural rights and autonomy was recognized, building on the
heritage of earlier treaties (which, for example, granted rights related to
religious belief and practice) and the League of Nations. To put it

another way, minorities have a right to *internal* self-determination, and, exceptionally, to secession. In a similar, but more generous, vein than the Rapporteurs, Alan Buchanan[153] understands "the right to secede" as a last-resort remedy to address the following injustices: "(1) persistent and serious violations of individual human rights"; "(2) past unredressed seizure of territory"; and, less certainly, [3] "discriminatory redistribution (or, as it is sometimes called, internal colonialism or regional exploitation)." Probably only (1) and [3] have some foundation in international law, with (2) being left to the fate of a civil war or revolution, and the international community's recognition of a minority's control of any relevant territory (re)seized by it. However, such a matter is complex and might fall foul of the U.N. prohibition on the use of force under Article 2(4) of the Charter.[154]

Generally a minority can hope to have its rights and interests protected through some kind of "autonomy regime" or internal self-determination, buttressed by general and specific (such as Article 27, ICCPR) human rights provisions.[155] An early, but still valuable, account of some of the goals of such autonomy regimes in relation to minorities can be found in the *Minority Schools in Albania* case (1935) (Permanent Court of International Justice – PCIJ) concerning the League of Nations system. A principal goal in such a regime is

> to secure for certain elements incorporated in a State, the population of which differs from them in race, language or religion, the possibility of living peaceably alongside that population and co-operating amicably with it, while at the same time preserving the characteristics which distinguish them from the majority, and satisfying the ensuing special needs.[156]

At another point, the PCIJ argued that

> [i]n order to attain this object, two things were regarded as particularly necessary … The first is to ensure that nationals belonging to racial, religious or linguistic minorities shall be placed on a footing of perfect equality with other national[s] of the State. The second is to ensure for the minority …

suitable means for the preservation of their ... peculiarities, their traditions and their national characteristics.[157]

Autonomy regimes offer sophisticated, flexible potential to safeguard and facilitate the rights and interests of minorities – a spectrum along which are arrayed cultural rights, forms of self-government, access to state resources, development of local law, territorial controls and resource management, conferral of membership, and so on.[158] International jurists Steiner and Alston identify three main kinds of autonomy regimes: "personal law regimes," often involving the application of traditional, religious or cultural law peculiar to a group or to members of that group, and to those members only; "territorial" regimes, where a minority exercises some power over a territory through a federation, regional governance or other devolution; and "power-sharing regimes" which provide ethnic groups with distinctive opportunities for participating in political, economic or other domains (for example, representation in a national or local legislature; or the requirement of special majorities if various legal, constitutional or administrative protections of their rights and interests are to be disturbed). There are innumerable possibilities for these regimes to be combined in various ways, giving a minority varying kinds and degrees of autonomy within a state.[159]

Various human rights provisions have a bearing on the parameters and content of autonomy regimes: for example, the non-discrimination provisions in the UDHR, the 1966 Covenants, the 1965 Convention on the Elimination of Racial Discrimination, and customary international law; civil and political rights to free expression, assembly, association, religious expression and to political participation; to cultural rights; and principles prohibiting genocide and endorsing humanitarian intervention. In combination, these provisions and principles assist a minority in the creation and maintenance of various institutions and "ways of life."[160]

In addition to these general human rights provisions, there are a number of specific provisions that bear upon the rights of minorities. Chief among them are Article 27, ICCPR, and the Declaration on the Rights of Persons Belonging to National or Ethnic, Religious or Linguistic Minorities (U.N. General Assembly, 1992).[161] Article 27, ICCPR, reads:

> In those States in which ethnic, religious or linguistic
> minorities exist, persons belonging to such minorities shall not
> be denied the right in community with the other members of
> their group, to enjoy their own culture, to profess and practice
> their own religion, or to use their own language.

Just by looking at the words of the article, one can grasp its *apparently*
individualistic orientation ("*persons* belonging to such minorities,"
rather than the minorities themselves), its negative formulation (a state
"shall not" deny to such persons), and the apparently limited nature of
the rights enumerated. But upon another interpretation, one that has
received some support from the U.N. Human Rights Committee (see
General Comment No. 23 on Article 27), collective dimensions can be
identified. The relevant persons have to *belong* to a particular minority,
and a "minority" is obviously a collective entity. Every right is to be
exercised "*in community* with the other members of the *group*," and the
specific rights enumerated (religion, language and culture) are all
characteristically communal enterprises or social phenomena.
Moreover, the conferral of a right on a person to enjoy the culture of
"their" group presupposes the existence and continuing vitality (or at
least functioning) of that culture. In all of this, international legal
scholar Malcolm Shaw's observations[162] are apt:

> In recent years [in the U.N.] ... more attention has been given
> to various expressions of the concept of collective rights,
> although it *is often difficult to maintain a strict differentiation
> between individual and collective rights.*

In any event, the U.N. Human Rights Committee, in its General
Comment No. 23, indicated that under Article 27 a state was
responsible to act *positively* to protect a minority's "way of life" and its
"identity" and to "ensure the effective participation of members of
minority communities in decisions which affect them."[163]

After noting that the 1966 Covenants give "explicit
acknowledgement of group claims as a specific and distinct dimension
of human rights,"[164] Falk assesses that there is much potential for the
U.N. to create "policy instruments for the realization of affirmative
group rights, and schemes for devolution, autonomy, self-government,
federalism, and self-administration."[165] A modest contribution to this

cause has been made by the U.N. Declaration on the Rights of Persons Belonging to National or Ethnic or Linguistic Minorities (1992).[166] Elaborating or responding to Article 27, ICCPR, the Declaration provides in Article 1 that

1. States shall protect the *existence* and the national or ethnic, cultural, religious and linguistic *identity of minorities* within their respective territories and shall *encourage conditions for the promotion of that identity.*

2. States shall adopt appropriate legislative and other measures to achieve those ends. [167]

Under Article 4(4), "States should, where appropriate, take measures in the field of education, in order to encourage knowledge of the history, traditions, language and culture of the minorities ..."[168] One could argue that such attention to education is not directed *only* toward members of a particular minority, but also toward collectivist objectives. These include the enhancement of the knowledge, understanding and tolerance of the wider community; and the facilitation of the cultural resources that a minority transmits to its members as a way of maintaining the group's existence and identity. These objectives are compatible with some of the provisions of the Genocide Convention (1948).[169]

The status of indigenous peoples under international law is unclear: sometimes they are regarded as "peoples," sometimes as "minorities." In 1994, the U.N. Human Rights Committee referred to "certain *minority* rights, in particular, those pertaining to indigenous peoples, [that] might consist of a way of life closely associated with territory and the use of resources, such as fishing, hunting and the right to live" in enclaves "protected by law."[170] Indicia associated with the definition of indigenous peoples include the following: their ancient connections with the natural environment; their continuous connections with "premodern practices and institutions";[171] their common suffering under colonialism, neo-colonialism, genocidal and assimilationist policies; and their unique place as *First* Peoples of the territory they inhabit.[172] However, while there is a basis for solidarity among indigenous groups nationally and transnationally, it is well to keep in mind their great diversity, including the way in which they respond to modernity.[173] J. R. Martinez (U.N. Special Rapporteur) has provided an extended definition of indigenous peoples that includes their "historical continuity with pre-invasion and pre-colonial societies," their "non-dominant" place in society today, their desire "to preserve, develop and transmit to future generations their ancestral territories, and their ethnic identity," as well as their individual recognition of themselves (which is duly recognized internally) as indigenous.[174]

There remains some doubt over the existence of a right of indigenous peoples in international law to claim the full rights of self-determination (including secession), except *in extremis*, along the lines I have discussed in relation to minorities. There is also some doubt in relation to the practicality or desirability of a right to secession.[175] However, there is absolutely no doubt regarding indigenous peoples' right to *internal* self-determination, embodied in autonomy regimes, to the same extent as for minorities.[176] As with minorities, such a right has been enhanced by general human rights provisions concerning non-discrimination and civil, political, economic and cultural rights; by Article 27, ICCPR; and by specific instruments such as the ILO's Convention No. 169 and the U.N. Draft Declaration on the Rights of Indigenous Peoples (1994).[177]

The latter instruments can be used as frameworks for domestic autonomy regimes of various kinds.[178] ILO Convention No. 169[179] is an important, wide-ranging instrument binding upon those ILO members that have ratified it (Article 38). It reaffirms the applicability of general human rights provisions (and especially, as noted in the preamble, those relating to "the prevention of discrimination"), and seeks to address present inequalities regarding indigenous peoples' participation in the dominant society, while rejecting assimilationist models of development. Instead, indigenous peoples should have "control over their own institutions, ways of life and economic development and [be able] to maintain and develop their identities, languages and religions, within the framework of the States in which they live ..." It seeks to foster and institutionalize cultural autonomy, self-development and management, political, economic and social participation, equitable treatment, and degrees of self-government, though it does not explicitly guarantee indigenous peoples a full right of self-determination. For example, Article 1(3) provides that "[t]he use of the term 'peoples' in this Convention shall not be construed as having any implications as regards the rights which may attach to the term under international law." The Convention (Preamble) also notes "that in many parts of the world these peoples are unable to enjoy their fundamental human rights to the same degree as the rest of the population of the States in which they live, and that their laws, values, customs and perspectives have often been eroded ..."

In support of these objectives, the Convention contains articles on governments' responsibilities to "protect the rights of these peoples and to guarantee respect for their integrity" (Article 2(1)), including their "social, economic and cultural rights ... with respect for their social and cultural identity, their customs and traditions and their institutions" (Article 2(2)(b)) "without hindrance or discrimination" (Article 3(1)). To this end, governments must take "[s]pecial measures ... as appropriate for safeguarding the persons, institutions, property, labour, cultures and environment of the peoples concerned" (Article 4(1)) (see, also, Articles 2–5).

Indigenous peoples are to be consulted ("in particular through their representative institutions") in relation to laws or "administrative measures" that would affect them (Article 6(1)(a)), to be given equal opportunity to participate in a country's "decision-making" processes, and to have "means for the full development" of their own "institutions" (Article 6(1)(b) and (c)).

Under the Convention, indigenous peoples have "the right to decide their own priorities for the process of development as it affects their lives, beliefs, institutions and spiritual well-being and the lands they occupy or otherwise use, and to exercise control, to the extent possible, over their own economic, social and cultural development ... [and to] participate in the formulation, implementation and evaluation of plans and programs for national and regional development which may affect them directly" (Article 7(1)). Development projects must be carried out with due regard for "the social, spiritual, cultural and environmental impact" on indigenous peoples (Article 7(3)). The national legal system is to take account of, and give a place to, indigenous peoples' "customs or customary laws" (Article 8(1)) provided they are compatible with the "national legal system" and "internationally recognised human rights" (Articles 8(2), 9).

Provision is made for what has compendiously been known as indigenous peoples' "land rights" in all their forms (Articles 13–14), for self-management of natural resources (including rights to be consulted, to have their consent or its withdrawal taken into account (Articles 15(2), 16, 17), and for "fair compensation for any damages they may sustain" as a result of development (Articles 15(2), 15–19 generally).

Further, the Convention contains provisions on economic and social rights, including: conditions of recruitment and the workplace, training programs (Articles 20–21); indigenous "[h]andicrafts, rural and community-based industries, and subsistence economy and traditional activities ... such as hunting, fishing, trapping and gathering" (Article 23; and see, generally, Parts III and IV); and social security, health and education (Parts V, VI).

Part VI of the Convention stipulates that "[e]ducation programs and services" for indigenous peoples "shall be developed and implemented in co-operation with them to address their special needs, and shall incorporate their histories, their knowledge, and technologies ... [and] their value systems ..." (Article 27). Part VI also refers to the maintenance of indigenous peoples' languages and to the development and sustaining of their own educational institutions (Articles 27–28). Article 31 prescribes that "[e]ducational measures shall be taken among *all sections of the national community* [emphasis added] " to combat "prejudices" against indigenous peoples and to prevent distorted accounts of them.

The Convention has interesting international and transnational dimensions: "Governments ... [are to] take appropriate measures, including by means of international agreements, to facilitate contacts and co-operation between indigenous and tribal peoples across borders, including activities in the economic, social, cultural, spiritual and environmental fields" (Article 32).

The non-binding U.N. Draft Declaration on the Rights of Indigenous Peoples (1994) has reiterated and further developed the kinds of norms and rights to be found in ILO Convention No. 169. The Draft Declaration was largely the work of a Working Group on Indigenous Populations, created from the U.N. Sub-commission on Prevention of Discrimination and Protection of Minorities, which answered to the U.N. Commission on Human Rights. It was staffed by "independent expert members." The annual meetings of the Group are said to be "among the most broadly participatory in the entire UN system."[180]

Article 3 of the Draft Declaration recognizes that "[i]ndigenous peoples have the right of self-determination" through which "they freely determine their political status and freely pursue their economic, social and cultural development." Key Article 4 provides that "[i]ndigenous peoples have the right to maintain and strengthen their distinct political, economic, social and cultural characteristics, as well as their legal systems, while retaining their rights to participate fully, if they so choose, in the political, economic, social and cultural life of the State." Other articles relate to indigenous peoples' rights to participation, in decisions affecting them, through their own and other institutions (Articles 19, 20); their "free and informed consent" to measures having an impact on them (Article 20); and their rights relating to land, resources and development (Articles 25–27, 30). Article 31, going beyond ILO Convention No. 169, declares that indigenous peoples, "as a specific form of exercising their right to self-determination, have the right to autonomy or self-government in matters relating to their internal and local affairs", including: religion, culture, education, media, information, housing, health, social welfare, employment, land and resources management, economic matters, environment, access given to non-members, and the financing of these "autnomous functions". Article 34 states that indigenous peoples have "the *collective* right to determine the responsibilities of individuals to their communities" [emphasis added].[181]

We should recall here, also, the relevance of the U.N. Declaration on the Rights of Persons Belonging to National or Ethnic, Religious and Linguistic Minorities. Other instruments and doctrines with significance for the human rights of indigenous peoples have emerged out of the contexts of standard-setting for the protection of the environment and for so-called "sustainable development" – see, for example, the Rio Declaration and Agenda 21 (1992), and the U.N. Declaration on the Right of Development (1986).[182]

To recapitulate, the efforts to include articles relating to self-determination in the 1966 Covenants met with staunch resistance from a number of Western states that saw it as a threat to colonial interests, to national unity and territorial integrity, and to their economic interests. Nevertheless, non-Western states succeeded in having self-determination included in the 1966 Covenants. Despite its limitations, the doctrine of self-determination has proven to be a useful normative and legal framework within which collective human rights claims can be made. The rights of minorities and of indigenous peoples have been discussed here as instructive examples.

The final issue I will explore in relation to the 1966 Covenants concerns the so-called federal–state clause that the U.S.A., Canada and Australia, in particular, sought to include.[183] The intended purpose and effect of a federal clause was to differentiate between federal and unitary states regarding their international human rights obligations. The intended differentiation has been well summarized by Pechota:

> A proposed federal clause would have enabled the governments of federal states to apply those [human rights] articles they regarded as appropriate for federal action and to accept the obligation to bring those provisions they considered appropriate for action by their constituent units [states, provinces and so on] to the latter's attention with a favorable recommendation.[184]

Part of the argument on behalf of a federal clause was that, in certain federal states, constitutionally authority, power, responsibility or jurisdiction were said to be split between the federal (central) unit and the constituent units, so that many human rights provisions would come within the competence of the constituent units. That being the case, so it was argued, the central government would not be able to guarantee the adoption, fulfilment or enforcement of human rights provisions in that field. Federal states (and their governments) in this position were thus being asked, on this view, to accept international legal obligations in a covenant or covenants that they would lack the power to guarantee. Thus, such federal nation-states claimed that they would not be able to ratify such a covenant or covenants without the inclusion of a federal clause.[185]

The U.S.A. was the chief proponent of a federal clause, and "fought vigorously" to have it in any human rights covenant.[186] One American representative, for example, drew attention to a range of issues that were said to be within the jurisdiction of the states under the U.S. Constitution, including "due process," freedom of expression, freedom of religion, equality before the law, freedom of assembly and legal sanction for violations of rights by private persons in a constituent state.[187] International law scholar Manouchehr Ganji insightfully notes that those nation-states which had supported the inclusion of a "colonial clause" (discussed above) in any covenant also sponsored the inclusion of a federal clause.[188]

In 1947, the U.N. Commission on Human Rights accepted in its draft Covenant a federal clause produced by the relevant Working Group. It was apparently modelled on a provision in the ILO Constitution (1946) (Article 19(7)).[189] The clause was as follows:

> In the case of a Federal State, the following provisions shall apply:

> (a) With respect to any Articles of this [human rights] Covenant which the federal Government regards as wholly or in part appropriate for federal action, the obligations of the federal government shall, to this extent, be the same as those parties which are not federal States;

> (b) In respect of Articles which the Federal government regards as appropriate under its constitutional system, in whole or in part, for action by the constituent States, Provinces or Cantons, the federal government shall bring such provisions, with a favourable recommendation, to the notice of the appropriate authorities of the States, Provinces and Cantons.[190]

There seems to be some uncertainty in the literature as to when momentum in the U.N. turned against a federal clause. Evans claims that "as early as 1950 it was clear that the majority in the Assembly would not tolerate any special considerations for federal states."[191] Nevertheless, on December 4, 1950 a General Assembly resolution asked ECOSOC to produce

> recommendations which will have as their purpose the securing of the maximum extension of the Covenant to the constituent units of federal States, and the meeting of the constitutional problems of federal States. [192]

Still, it does seem that the General Assembly placed more importance on the former over the latter consideration. A wide range of arguments was marshalled against the federal clause. They generally focused on the view that it would undermine the universality, binding quality and effectiveness of any covenant's human rights provisions, and discriminate unfairly between unitary and federal states.[193] Such a clause could also "cause disputes, differences and uncertainties concerning the exact obligations of federal states."[194] Additionally, serious doubts were also expressed about the constitutional (and, indeed, one could add, international legal) basis for arguments in favour of a federal clause.[195] Under the U.S. Constitution (Article VI),[196] a treaty that has properly become a part of American federal law is "supreme law" and would prevail over inconsistent state laws. This was a consideration which motivated conservative "states' rights" groups to agitate for a federal clause.[197]

The American approach to the relationship between international law and municipal law can be characterized as a seriously qualified monism. That is, it is monist only in relation to so-called "self-executing" treaties (the criteria for which it determines) and effectively dualist in relation to "non-self-executing" treaties. Non-self-executing treaties require implementing legislation for a party to pursue relief in an American court. The nebulous distinction between self-executing and non-self-executing treaties has some similarity to the doctrine of justiciability or standing, the "political questions" doctrine, and related conceptions of the separation of powers (with concomitant understandings of the proper functions, in democratic and constitutionalist terms, of the legislature and judiciary).[198]

It is all very well for a court to answer the question "What is a self-executing treaty?" with "One that is not enforceable in a domestic court of law without implementing legislation"; but that does not tell us either what *kinds* of treaties are not to be justiciable in this way, or *why* certain treaties attracting automatic applicability in courts do so.[199] The test outlined in *Sei Fujii* (1952 (38 Cal. 2d 718, 742, P. 2d 617))[200] is as follows:

> In determining whether a treaty is self-executing courts look to the intent of the signatory parties as manifested by the language of the instrument, and, if the instrument is uncertain, recourse may be had to the circumstances surrounding its

> execution ... In order for a treaty provision to be operative
> without the aid of implementing legislation and to have the
> force and effect of a statute, it must appear that the framers of
> the treaty intended to prescribe a rule that, standing alone,
> would be enforceable in the courts ...[201]

To this test, Section III of the Restatement (Third) Foreign Relations
Law of the United States (1987) adds that a treaty is non-self-executing

> (b) if the Senate in giving consent to a treaty or Congress by
>   resolution, requires implementing legislation, or

> (c) if implementing legislation is constitutionally required.[202]

Overall, it is reasonable to conclude that the U.S. federal government
has the authority to enact legislation that incorporates a treaty in the
domestic legal system, overriding existing or prior legislation.[203]

Regarding Australia, another supporter of the federal clause, it also
has, and had at the time, the power to enact federal legislation
implementing international treaties. But Australia takes a consistently
dualist approach to the relationship between international and
municipal law (originally following the approach of the U.K.).[204] At the
time of the debate over the Covenant(s), Australia was less willing to
use federal legislation under the "external affairs" power
(*Commonwealth of Australia Constitution Act* (1900) (Imp.), s.
51(xxix))[205] to implement a treaty in a way that would encroach on the
states' powers than it would be now. However, the trend of
constitutional interpretation in Australia had for a long time been
toward centralization of power in the Commonwealth (federal)
government, eroding state jurisdiction, resources, and power – a trend
accelerated by the necessities of World War II, the development of a
welfare state, the domination of taxation power and so on. The
relevance of all this to the federal clause is that Australia could have
legislated to bind constituent states, using s. 51(xxix) of the constitution
in combination with s. 109 (which, to put it roughly, provides that in
the event of a conflict between a Commonwealth (federal) law and a
state law, the Commonwealth law prevails to the extent of
inconsistency between them). Like the U.S.A., the push for a federal

clause can be better understood in light of the traditionally conservative role of constituent states' rights.[206] This is seen in the "races power" in the Australian Constitution (s. 51(xxvi)) which, before its amendment in 1967, provided (emphasis added):

> The Parliament shall, subject to this Constitution, have power to make laws for the peace, order, and good government of the Commonwealth with respect to:- ... (xxvi) The people of any race, *other than the aboriginal race in any State* for whom it is deemed necessary to make special laws.

The italicized words were deleted in 1967. The provision was a compromise between the Commonwealth and the states at the time of the constitution's creation in 1900. While the federal government would regulate, in particular, immigrant labour, the "welfare" of indigenous peoples would be left to the states (whose economies benefited from the exploitation of Aboriginal labour, particularly in the pastoral sector).[207] A Royal Commission on the Constitution considered whether s. 51 (xxvi) ought to be extended to "the aboriginal race," but concluded:

> We recognize that the effect of the treatment of aborigines [*sic*] on the reputation of Australia furnishes a powerful argument for a transference of control to the Commonwealth [Federal Government]. But we think that on the whole the States are better equipped for controlling aborigines than the Commonwealth. The States control the police and the lands, and they to a large extent control the conditions of industry.[208]

Thus, the role of states in Australia can be compared with the role of some American states in seeking to maintain, and shield from international scrutiny or regulation, the structures of racial segregation and economic exploitation.[209]

In terms of international-law arguments, it was clear, under public international law of the time, that a nation-state could not use its own laws or constitutional tribulations in relation to compliance with international legal obligations as a defence to a violation of human rights (a principle later embodied in the Vienna Convention on Treaties (1969), Article 27).[210] Steiner and Alston have concluded:

Generally it is not relevant from an international-law perspective whether a treaty is self-executing, since a state is obligated under international law to do whatever may be required under its internal law (such as legislative enactment) to fulfil its treaty commitments.[211]

In 1950, the U.S.A. had proposed a federal clause, again without success.[212] In 1952, and again in 1954, versions of a federal clause were presented but were defeated.[213]

Meanwhile, during the years 1951–1954, the battle of the notorious "Bricker Amendment" was fought in the U.S. Senate and in American politics generally. There was a loose coalition of conservative forces in the U.S.A. who were alarmed by international and domestic human rights and civil rights developments. Among these forces were the American Bar Association, the U.S. Chamber of Commerce, the National Association of Manufacturers and conservative senators. Among the developments that provoked such groups were President Franklin's Roosevelt's "New Deal" legislation, the human rights articles in the U.N. Charter, the Presidential Commission on Civil Rights (1946), the UDHR (and its influence on various legal systems), the Genocide Convention (1948), other regional and treaty human rights protections, and the character of the proposed human rights covenant(s).[214]

Regarding the U.N. Charter and the UDHR, conservative opponents of international human rights in the U.S.A. were not satisfied with assurances, official and otherwise, that these instruments would not intrude upon the domestic political, legal and social scene. A legal adviser to the U.S. Department of State stated in 1947 that Articles 55 and 56 of the U.N. Charter were not considered "as imposing a legal obligation to guarantee observance of specific human rights and fundamental freedoms without distinction as to race, sex, language or religion."[215] *Sei Fujii v State*, 1952 (38 Cal. 2d 718, 242, P. 2d 617)[216] is sometimes cited in support of that view. But in *Fujii*, the Supreme Court of California accepted that

[i]t is not disputed that the [U.N.] charter is a treaty, and our federal Constitution provides that treaties made under the authority of the United States are part of the supreme law of the land and that judges in every state are bound thereby: U.S.

Const., art. VI ... [M]ember nations have *obligated*
themselves to cooperate with the international organization in
promoting respect for and observance of human rights ...
[emphasis added][217]

Thus, the judgment was not based on the understanding that the U.N.
Charter did not create legal obligations regarding human rights – rather,
it recognized the opposite. It was based on the interaction of those
obligations with the American legal system in the form of the
distinction between self-executing and non-self-executing treaties. The
court concluded that the U.N. Charter was a non-self-executing treaty.
This conclusion, however, only has significance at the domestic level.
In stronger terms than in *Fujii*, Murphy J in *Oyama v California* (332
U.S. 633) (U.S. Supreme Court) (1948) – a case concerning the
position of aliens under land law in California – emphasized that

> this nation has recently pledged itself, through the United
> Nations Charter, to promote respect for, and observance of,
> human rights and fundamental freedoms for all without
> distinction as to race, sex, language and religion. The Alien
> Land Law [which prohibits aliens from owning real property
> in California] stands as a barrier to the fulfillment of that
> national pledge. Its inconsistency with the Charter, which has
> been duly ratified and adopted by the United States, is but one
> more reason why the statute must be condemned.[218]

Some commentators have confused the question of whether there is a
legal obligation in the Charter regarding human rights with the question
of what its nature is (if it exists).[219] While I am not convinced that the
language in the Charter referring to human rights is impossibly vague
compared with language that abounds in innumerable other treaties, or
that it could not be justiciable, neither of these cases supports the view
of the State Department legal adviser that there is no "legal obligation
to guarantee observance of specific human rights." That is one reason
why conservative fears were not allayed; together with the fact that
later human rights instruments have achieved greater specification of
the human rights referred to in the Charter, in addition to customary
law entrenchment of some human rights. Article 2(7) of the Charter on
"domestic jurisdiction" does not doctrinally (regardless of its practical

impact) preclude or prevent monitoring of a state's treatment of its own citizens, of municipal laws and practices, in the way that the U.S. Government had intended it to. "Thus, the investigation, discussion and condemnation ('droit de regard') of human rights violations in a state, has become compatible with the sovereignty of that state ..."[220]

In 1948, Eleanor Roosevelt, seeking to alleviate domestic anxieties in the U.S.A., and no doubt under the direction of the State Department, explained:

> In giving our approval to the declaration today, it is of primary importance that we keep clearly in mind the basic character of the document. It is not a treaty; it is not an international agreement. It is not and does not purport to be a statement of law or of legal obligation. It is a declaration of basic principles of human rights and freedoms, to be stamped with the approval of the General Assembly by formal vote of its members and to serve as a common standard of achievement for all peoples of all nations.[221]

Despite this understanding, the UDHR quickly came to have an impact on the laws and constitutions of many countries, a trend that has continued to the present day. The UDHR was reflected in: the constitutions of Indonesia, Costa Rica, Syria, El Salvador, Haiti, Jordan, Federal Republic of Germany, Puerto Rico; instruments for Eritrea, Libya, Somaliland; and the peace treaty with Japan. The UDHR has also been cited in the International Court of Justice and in municipal courts.[222] The Charter of the Organization of American States (put before the U.S. Senate in 1949) included reference to "cooperation on economic, social and cultural standards." This prompted a reservation by the U.S.A. in terms similar to the proposed federal clause.[223] The degree to which the U.S.A. was resistant to international human rights provisions is demonstrated in starkly ironic fashion by the Japanese peace treaty. The treaty was subjected to criticism in a ratification debate in the U.S. Senate because its preamble proclaimed *Japan's* pledge to comply with the UDHR.[224] The State Department even produced an official memorandum on the issue, which demonstrated American anxiety that the formerly fascist state's (whose military had committed atrocities on a large scale during World War II) new commitment to human rights could constitute a dangerous precedent for international interference in the U.S.A. on the basis of *its* human rights record.[225] The memorandum emphasized, with an eye on the U.S.A., that

> [t]here is nothing in the peace treaty which makes human rights a matter of international contract or which gives any Allied nations the right to interfere in Japan's internal affairs on account of human rights. There is no article of the treaty which mentions human rights ... [t]he preamble of the treaty contains a number of declarations of intention as is customary ... Japan [states] that she intends 'to strive to realize the objectives of the universal declaration of human rights and fundamental freedoms.' Some wanted the treaty to include a legal obligation to respect human rights and fundamental freedoms. This was done in the case of the Italian satellite treaties. However, there has developed in the United States considerable objection to trying to make human rights a matter of enforceable treaty obligation because, under our Constitution, treaties become 'the supreme law of the land' and a treaty on human rights might perhaps impair states' rights in relation to this subject. Therefore, we did not make human rights a matter of treaty obligation.[226]

When it became clearer to American conservatives that a federal clause was unlikely to be accepted,[227] they pushed still harder for what became known as the Bricker Amendment. In short, this amendment sought to achieve at the *domestic* level, through constitutional amendment, what the federal clause was designed to achieve at the *international* level: namely, to prevent the imposition of human rights obligations on constituent states through the simultaneous overriding of local laws (especially those relating to race).[228]

Senator John Bricker (Rep., Ohio), an unsuccessful Vice-Presidential candidate in the 1944 presidential election, put forward a resolution in the Senate that would declare the human rights Covenant in violation of the American Bill of Rights.[229] It also called on the president to reject the Covenant, and for the U.S.A. "to withdraw from further negotiations with respect to the Covenant on Human Rights, and all other covenants, treaties, and conventions ... which if passed by Congress as domestic legislation would be unconstitutional."[230] The so-called "Bricker Amendment" was put forward in final form on January 7, 1953. It was supported by 62 senators. The amendment aimed to amend the Constitution with regard to the executive's treaty-making powers, and in relation to the effect of a ratification of a treaty. In effect, if passed, it would have transformed the U.S.A. from a partially dualist to a completely dualist state: international law would be valid and take effect in the U.S.A. *only* through implementing legislation.[231] The Amendment was ultimately narrowly defeated in the Senate on February 25, 1954.[232] The defeat was due, in part, to a pragmatic concern in the new Eisenhower administration that the amendment could jeopardize authority for U.S. membership in the U.N. and NATO. It was also due to Eisenhower's new policy on human rights, which took some of the heat out of the debate as far as conservative opponents were concerned.[233]

The new policy jettisoned any possibility of U.S. support for legally binding U.N. international human rights covenants. Instead, the U.S.A. proposed an "Action Plan" that involved the promotion of human rights outside international law, through such vehicles as self-reporting of human rights by states, consultation, research (making use of experts), education and training.[234] U.S. Secretary of State Dulles announced the new policy to the Senate, on April 6, 1953,[235] in the following terms:

> The present administration intends to encourage the promotion everywhere of human rights and individual freedoms, but to favor methods of persuasion, education, and example rather than formal undertakings which commit one part of the world to impose its particular social and moral standards upon another part of the world community, which has different standards. That is the point of view I expressed in 1951 in relation to the Japanese peace treaty. Therefore, while we shall not withhold our counsel from those who seek to draft a treaty or covenant on human rights, we do not ourselves look upon a treaty as the means which we would now select as the proper and most effective way to spread throughout the world the goals of human liberty to which this nation has been dedicated since its inception. We therefore do not intend to become a party to any such covenant or present it as a treaty for consideration by the Senate.[236]

Eleanor Roosevelt, too independent for the new administration's liking, was replaced by the more pliant Oswald B. Lord, who was drilled on the new policy by Secretary of State Dulles.[237] The international community was sorely disappointed by the U.S.A.'s announcement that it would not ratify any U.N. human rights covenant, nor participate much in the further drafting of the covenants.[238] According to Green[239], the new U.S. policy "reflected the basic philosophy ... that the promotion of human rights is essentially a matter for the state and local community in the United States and not ordinarily a matter for federal legislation or for international treaties." Most other countries rightly doubted the bona fides of the U.S.A. regarding its new policy direction,[240] some describing it frankly as camouflage for racist laws and policies.[241]

With opposition to any federal clause increasing, and the U.S.A. having taken itself off-stage, so to speak, the arguments of states such as Pakistan, Poland, China and Egypt prevailed in 1954 against the proposed clause.[242] Sounding somewhat wounded, Green[243] gave the following account of its demise:

> The [predominantly non-Western] majority was consistently unable or unwilling to understand the constitutional problems of the [predominantly Western] minority and insisted that the federal states, which had adhered to many different kinds of treaties in the past, should not insist on special privileges with respect to the covenants. The Soviet bloc did not hesitate to charge that it was primarily the problem of racial discrimination that led the United States to demand the special privileges, a charge that probably had some influence on many of the delegations that were especially color-conscious.

A Soviet proposal in 1954 that the Covenants "shall extend to all parts of federal States without any limitations or exceptions" was adopted, and now finds its place in Article 28, ICESCR, and Article 50, ICCPR.[244] So, on another issue of critical importance to their interests (as defined by their governments), key Western states, including the U.S.A., were not able to impose their will upon the Covenants.

If the U.S.A. and other Western powers were unable to prevail on issues of key importance to them as early as the mid–1950s, this was truer still of subsequent years, as the wave of decolonization crashed over them. In 1955 the so-called Bandung Conference was held in Indonesia, bringing together 29 countries from Asia and Africa. The delegates were said to represent 1.5 billion people, "united," said President Sukarno of Indonesia, by "a common detestation" of racism and colonialism. The conference consolidated the rise of the Third World and ushered in its Non–Aligned Movement. In the postwar period many countries received their independence, including the following: Ghana, Guinea, the Philippines, India, Pakistan, Burma, Sri Lanka, Indonesia, Laos, Cambodia, South Vietnam, Tunisia and Morocco. In 1960 alone many African states emerged, including Cameroon, Central African Republic, Chad, Congo, Côte d'Ivoire, Dahomey, Gabon, Senegal, Mauritania, Togo, Upper Volta and Zaire. In the early 1960s, Sierra Leone, Tanganyika, Algeria, Burundi, Kenya, Malawi, Rwanda, Uganda, Zambia, Cyprus, Jamaica, Kuwait, Mongolia and Trinidad and Tobago realized their right to self-determination. These developments had an immediate and dramatic impact as the non-Western states obtained and consolidated majority control of U.N. institutions, especially the General Assembly. Afro-Asian states endorsed the U.N. Charter, the UDHR, and the Covenants, and helped secure the adoption of the International Convention on the Elimination of All Forms of Racial Discrimination in 1965. An extremely diverse set of states contributed to the development of the Covenants and adopted them. They were not cast from the hegemonic mould of the U.S.A. nor of any other Western state; which is why a frustrated Eisenhower administration walked further away from legally binding international human rights standards. As early as 1953, John Hickerson, at the time the U.S. Assistant Secretary of State for U.N. Affairs, wrote that the "Covenants will no doubt serve as accepted standards of conduct after their approval by the UN, *whether the United States does or doesn't ratify them.*" His assessment has proven to be accurate.[245]

Notes

[1] T. Evans, *US Hegemony and the Project of Universal Human Rights* (London: Macmillan, 1996), p. 90.

[2] In developing my account in this chapter, I have relied, principally, on the following sources: Evans, ibid.; United Nations Blue Book Series, vol. VII, *The United Nations and Human Rights: 1945–1995* (New York: Department of Public Information, U.N., 1995), pp. 3–47; Brucken, "A Most Uncertain Crusade: The United States, Human Rights and the United Nations, 1941–1954," Ph.D. dissn., History, Ohio State University, 1999; H. Tolley, Jr., *The U.N. Commission on Human Rights* (Boulder, Colorado: Westview Press, 1987), especially at pp. 14–32; A. Cassese, "The General Assembly: Historical Perspective 1945–1989," in P. Alston (ed.), *The United Nations and Human Rights: A Critical Appraisal* (New York: Oxford University Press, 1992), pp. 25-54; P. Alston "The Commission on Human Rights," in Alston (ed.), *The United Nations and Human Rights*, ch. 5, at pp. 126–145, 187–197; A. H. Robertson and J. G. Merrills, *Human Rights in the World: An Introduction to the Study of the International Protection of Human Rights*, fourth edn. (Manchester: Manchester University Press, 1996), pp. 30–34; A. Eide, "Economic, Social and Cultural Rights as Human Rights," in A. Eide, C. Krause and A. Rasas (eds.), *Economic, Social and Cultural Rights: A Textbook* (Dordrecht: Martinus Nijhoff, 1995), ch. 2, especially at pp. 21–23; L. B. Sohn, "The New International Law: Protection of the Rights of Individuals Rather than States," *American University Law Review*, vol. 32 (1982), no. 1, pp. 1–64, especially pp. 19–64; S. Waltz, "Universalizing Human Rights: The Role of Small States in the Construction of the Universal Declaration of Human Rights," *Human Rights Quarterly*, vol. 23 (2001), pp. 44–72; Marks, "From the 'Single Confused Page' to the 'Decalogue for Six Billion Persons': The Roots of the Universal Declaration of Human Rights in the French Revolution," *Human Rights Quarterly*, vol. 20 (1998), no. 3, pp. 459–514; Lord Steyn, *Human Rights: The Legacy of Mrs Roosevelt*, Presidential Address to The Holdsworth Club of the Faculty of Law in the University of Birmingham (Birmingham: The Holdsworth Club of the University of Birmingham, 2001); T. Evans, *The Politics of Human Rights: A Global Perspective* (London: Pluto Press, 2001); E. Roosevelt, "The Promise of Human Rights," *Foreign Affairs*, vol. 26, no. 3, (April 1948), pp. 470–477; M. Ganji, *International Protection of Human Rights* (Geneva: Paris: Librairie E. Droz; Librairie Minard, 1962), especially ch. vi; J. F. Green, *The United Nations and Human Rights* (Washington D.C.: The Brookings Institution, 1956); H. Lauterpacht, *An International Bill of the Rights of Man* (New York: Columbia University Press, 1945); P. G. Lauren, *The Evolution of International Human Rights: Visions Seen* (Philadelphia: University of Pennsylvania Press, 1998); P. Hunt,

Reclaiming Social Rights: International and Comparative Perspectives (Aldershot: Ashgate, 1996; reprinted 1998, 1999), especially "Introduction"; H. Lauterpacht, *International Law and Human Rights* (London: Stevens and Sons, 1950; reprinted, Hamden, Connecticut: Archon Books, 1968); P. Malanczuk, *Akehurst's Modern Introduction to International Law*, seventh rev. edn. (London: Routledge, 1997); R. Piotrowicz and S. Kaye, *Human Rights in International and Australian Law* (Chatswood, N.S.W.: Butterworths, 2000), pp. 22–27; I. Brownlie, *Principles of Public International Law*, fourth edn. (Oxford: Clarendon Press, 1990); H. J. Steiner and P. Alston, *International Human Rights in Context: Law, Politics, Morals: Text and Materials*, second edn. (Oxford: Oxford University Press, 2000); M. N. Shaw, *International Law*, fourth edn. (Cambridge: Cambridge University Press, 1997); M. C. R. Craven, *The International Covenant on Economic, Social and Cultural Rights: A Perspective on its Development* (Oxford: Clarendon Press, 1995); D. McGoldrick, *The Human Rights Committee: Its Role in the Development of the International Covenant on Civil and Political Rights* (Oxford: Clarendon Press, 1991), especially ch. 1; V. Pechota, "The Development of the Covenant on Civil and Political Rights," in L. Henkin (ed.), *The International Bill of Rights: The Covenant on Civil and Political Rights* (New York: Columbia University Press, 1981), ch. 2; K. Arambulo, *Strengthening the Supervision of the International Covenant on Economic, Social and Cultural Rights: Theoretical and Procedural Aspects*, School of Human Rights Research Series, Volume 3 (Antwerpen, Groningen, Oxford: Intersentia/Hart, 1999); S. Joseph, J. Schultz and M. Castan, *The International Covenant on Civil and Political Rights: Cases, Materials, and Commentary* (Oxford: Oxford University Press, 2000). I have variously used the reprinting of the U.N. Charter (extracts), UDHR, the ICCPR, and ICESCR in Center for the Study of Human Rights, *Twenty-five Human Rights Documents* (New York: Center for the Study of Human Rights, Columbia University, 1994) and *Charter of the United Nations and Statute of the International Court of Justice* (New York: Office of Public Information, U.N., n.d. [1945]). I have also found the following collection useful: I. Brownlie and G. S. Goodwin-Gill (eds.), *Basic Documents on Human Rights*, fourth edn. (Oxford: Oxford University Press, 2002). For a recent archive-based examination of the development of the 1966 Covenants, focused on Australia, see A. Devereux, *Australia and the Birth of the International Bill of Human Rights 1946–1966* (Sydney: The Federation Press, 2005). Devereux's study is largely consistent with my line of argument regarding Western resistance to international human rights norms. She finds, principally, that Australia began boldly as a supporter of human rights and continued to make important contributions to the development of an international human rights regime. However, she also concludes that with the long reign of conservative federal governments in the country through the 1950s and 1960s, Australia became increasingly resistant to strong international human rights norms and enforcement machinery. This was especially the case regarding economic and social rights and expansive welfare states, minority rights, the principles of equality and "equal protection" (and specifically anti-discrimination principles targeting racist laws and activities), immigration and refugee matters, self-determination and quasi-colonial issues. During this period, Australia, like the U.S.A., often sought to rely on the "domestic jurisdiction" clause in the U.N. Charter (Article 2(7)) to support its conception of state sovereignty. In Australia's case, Article 2(7) was most commonly relied upon by governments in an attempt to shield federal and state laws, policies and activities in relation to indigenous peoples, immigrants, asylum seekers, and even political dissenters (especially of the leftist variety), from what they regarded as international "interference."

[3] McGoldrick, *The Human Rights Committee*, pp. 4–5; Pechota, "The Development of the Covenant on Civil and Political Rights," pp. 33, 37.

[4] Pechota, "The Development of the Covenant on Civil and Political Rights," p. 37.

[5] McGoldrick, *The Human Rights Committee*, p. 5; Evans, *US Hegemony and the Project of Universal Human Rights*, p. 127.

[6] Evans, *US Hegemony and the Project of Universal Human Rights*, p. 127.

[7] Pechota, "The Development of the Covenant on Civil and Political Rights," p. 39.

[8] Ibid., pp. 39–40.

[9] Tolley, Jr., *The U.N. Commission on Human Rights*, p. 21, attributes this formulation to "China's P. C. Chang [who] proposed the ultimate solution, a tri-partite approach beginning with a declaration, followed by a convention, and finally implementation measures."

[10] Craven, *The International Covenant on Economic, Social and Cultural Rights*, pp. 16–17; Ganji, *International Protection of Human Rights*, pp. 168–169; Arambulo, *Strengthening the Supervision of the International Covenant on Economic, Social and Cultural Rights*, pp. 17–18.

[11] Arambulo, *Strengthening the Supervision of the International Covenant on Economic, Social and Cultural Rights*, p. 15.

[12] Ganji, *International Protection of Human Rights*, p. 169; Green, *The United Nations and Human Rights*, p. 39.

[13] Ganji, *International Protection of Human Rights*, p. 169.

[14] Quoted in Ganji, *International Protection of Human Rights*, p. 170 (author's emphasis removed).

[15] UNGA Resolution 421E(V), December 4, 1950 – cited in Arambulo, *Strengthening the Supervision of the International Covenant on Economic, Social and Cultural Rights*, p. 16.

[16] Report of the tenth session of the Commission on Human Rights (1954), quoted in Arambulo, *Strengthening the Supervision of the International Covenant on Economic, Social and Cultural Rights*, p.18.

[17] See "Preparation of two Draft International Covenants on Human Rights," UNGA Resolution 543(VI) (February 5, 1952) – cited in id.

[18] McGoldrick, *The Human Rights Committee*, p. 7.

[19] Quoted in id. (see also p. 11); Ganji, *International Protection of Human Rights*, pp. 171–172.

[20] Arambulo, *Strengthening the Supervision of the International Covenant on Economic, Social and Cultural Rights*, p. 18; Tolley, Jr., *The U.N. Commission on Human Rights*, p. 25.

[21] Robertson and Merrills, *Human Rights in the World*, p. 32; Ganji, *International Protection of Human Rights*, p. 172. The full texts of the Drafts can be found in Green, *The United Nations and Human Rights*, pp. 179–194.

[22] See B. H. Weston, "The Character of Economic Rights and Duties of States and the Deprivation of Foreign-Owned Wealth," in C. Ku and P. F. Diehl (eds.), *International Law: Classic and Contemporary Readings* (Boulder, Colorado: Lynne Rienner, 1998), pp. 519–548, at p. 528 ("as once suggested by Mr. Justice Holmes, a right without an effective remedy may be no right at all"). See also Tolley, Jr., *The U.N. Commission on Human Rights*, p. 25; Arambulo, *Strengthening the Supervision of the International Covenant on Economic, Social and Cultural Rights*, p. 17; McGoldrick, *The Human Rights Committee*, pp. 11–12; Pechota, "The Development of the Covenant on Civil and Political Rights," p. 42. See also Gary Bass' account of British legalism in *Stay the Hand of Vengeance: The Politics of War Crimes Tribunals* (Princeton: Princeton University Press, 2000).

[23] See, further, Lauren, *The Evolution of International Human Rights*, pp. 247–248; Tolley, Jr., *The U.N. Commission on Human Rights*, pp. 26, 29; Green, *The United Nations and Human Rights*, pp. 59–65.

[24] See, generally, Ganji, *International Protection of Human Rights*; Arambulo, *Strengthening the Supervision of the International Covenant on Economic, Social and Cultural Rights;* Green, *The United Nations and Human Rights*; Tolley, Jr., *The U.N. Commission on Human Rights*; Eide, "Economic, Social and Cultural Rights as Human Rights"; Pechota, "The Development of the Covenant on Civil and Political Rights"; McGoldrick, *The Human Rights Committee;* Sohn, "The New International Law"; Evans, *US Hegemony and the Project of Universal Human Rights.*

[25] Tolley, Jr., *The U.N. Commission on Human Rights*, pp. 14–15. See also B. Rajagopal, *International Law from Below: Development, Social Movements, and Third World Resistance* (Cambridge: Cambridge University Press, 2003), pp. 33, 191, 216–217; A. Cassese, *International Law in a Divided World* (Oxford: Clarendon Press, 1986), pp. 70, 72–73.

[26] Green, *The United Nations and Human Rights*, p. 38. James Green had been a U.S. State Department aide to Eleanor Roosevelt – see Brucken, " A Most Uncertain Crusade," p. 340.

[27] Green, *The United Nations and Human Rights*, p. 39. See also Ganji, *International Protection of Human Rights*, pp. 167–168.

[28] Evans, *US Hegemony and the Project of Universal Human Rights*, p. 130.

[29] Quoted in ibid., p. 130.

[30] See Arambulo, *Strengthening the Supervision of the International Covenant on Economic, Social and Cultural Rights,* p. 17. See also Green, *The United Nations and Human Rights*, pp. 38, 40. See, further, Annotations on the Text of the Draft International Covenants on Human Rights UN Doc. A/2929 (1955), at 7, quoted in Steiner and Alston, *International Human Rights in Context*, p. 245: It "was argued that not in all countries and territories were all civil and political rights 'legal' rights, nor all economic, social and cultural rights 'programme' rights. A civil or political right might well be a 'programme' right under one regime, an economic, social or cultural right a 'legal' right under another."

[31] Ganji, *International Protection of Human Rights*, in Footnote 12, pp. 170–171, has, for example, unearthed an American proposal to the CHR (January 28, 1947), which proposed recognition of "social rights, such as the right of employment and social security and the right to enjoy minimum standards of economic, social and cultural well-being." However, it is notable that this proposal pre-dates the UDHR, and so its relationship to any "covenant" might be considered tenuous: the term was at that time sometimes used interchangeably with terms referring to non-legally-binding "agreements", "Bills" or "declarations." See also E. Borgwardt, *A New Deal for the World:*

America's Vision for Human Rights (Cambridge: Belknap/Harvard University Press, 2005); and J. T. Kloppenberg, "Franklin Delano Roosevelt, Visionary," *Reviews in American History*, vol. 34 (2006), no. 4, pp. 509–520.

[32] Green, *The United Nations and Human Rights*, p. 40 (emphasis added).

[33] Tolley, Jr., *The U.N. Commission on Human Rights*, p. 23.

[34] See Evans, *US Hegemony and the Project of Universal Human Rights*, and my discussion in the previous chapter.

[35] Ibid., pp. 130–131.

[36] Green, *The United Nations and Human Rights*, p. 42.

[37] Arambulo, *Strengthening the Supervision of the International Covenant on Economic, Social and Cultural Rights*; Tolley, Jr., *The U.N. Commission on Human Rights*; United Nations Blue Book Series, vol. VII, *The United Nations and Human Rights: 1945–1995*; McGoldrick, *The Human Rights Committee*, generally, and especially at p. 11.

[38] Ganji, *International Protection of Human Rights*, especially at p. 171; Arambulo, *Strengthening the Supervision of the International Covenant on Economic, Social and Cultural Rights*, especially at p. 17; Tolley, Jr., *The U.N. Commission on Human Rights*, p. 25; Sohn, "The New International Law," p. 38; Pechota, "The Development of the Covenant on Civil and Political Rights," pp. 42–43; Eide, "Economic, Social and Cultural Rights as Human Rights," pp. 22–23; McGoldrick, *The Human Rights Committee*, p. 11; United Nations Blue Book Series, vol. VII, *The United Nations and Human Rights:1945–1995*, pp. 43–44; Steiner and Alston, *International Human Rights in Context Law*, ch. 4, and *passim*. Cf. Annotations on the Text of the Draft International Covenants on Human Rights, U.N. Doc. A/2929 (1955), at 7, quoted in Steiner and Alston, *International Human Rights in Context*, p. 245.

[39] See generally: United Nations Blue Book Series, vol. VII, *The United Nations and Human Rights: 1945–1995*; Steiner and Alston, *International Human Rights in Context;* Ganji, *International Protection of Human Rights*; Tolley, Jr., *The U.N. Commission on Human Rights*; Eide, "Economic, Social and Cultural Rights as Human Rights"; McGoldrick, *The Human Rights Committee;* Pechota, "The Development of the Covenant on Civil and Political Rights"; Green, *The United Nations and Human Rights*; Arambulo, *Strengthening the Supervision of the International Covenant on Economic, Social and Cultural Rights;* Sohn, "The New International Law." See also Marks, "From the 'Single Confused Page' to the 'Decalogue for Six Billion Persons,'" p. 501. On the question of justiciability, see, further, Hunt, *Reclaiming Social Rights*, pp. 24–34; U.N. Special Rapporteur Danilo Turk,

quoted in Hunt, *Reclaiming Social Rights*, p. 27; the ICESCR Committee on the Limburg Principles, quoted in Hunt, *Reclaiming Social Rights*, p. 26. See also Steiner and Alston, *International Human Rights in Context*, pp. 182–184 (on state obligations to provide public funds and infrastructure for elections; provide for policing; maintain the judicial system; and promote human rights); B. Rajagopal, *International Law from Below*, pp. 190–191, 192, 196, 229. But see, *contra*, Maurice Cranston, quoted in Steiner and Alston, *International Human Rights in Context*, p. 185.

[40] Evans, *US Hegemony and the Project of Universal Human Rights*, p. 131.

[41] Quoted in ibid., p. 131.

[42] Id.; Pechota, "The Development of the Covenant on Civil and Political Rights," p. 41.

[43] Evans, *US Hegemony and the Project of Universal Human Rights*, pp. 128–129; United Nations Blue Book Series, vol. VII, *The United Nations and Human Rights: 1945–1995*, p. 43; McGoldrick, *The Human Rights Committee*, p. 11; Arambulo, *Strengthening the Supervision of the International Covenant on Economic, Social and Cultural Rights*, pp. 17–18.

[44] Pechota, "The Development of the Covenant on Civil and Political Rights", pp. 41–42. See also Evans, *US Hegemony and the Project of Universal Human Rights*, p. 132 ("the United States and its western allies judged that the bifurcation of the covenant would help clarify their arguments against including economic and social rights in any legal binding form at all").

[45] Quoted in Pechota, "The Development of the Covenant on Civil and Political Rights," p. 42.

[46] Tolley, Jr., *The U.N. Commission on Human Rights*, p. 25.

[47] Green, *The United Nations and Human Rights*, p. 42.

[48] See, for example, ibid., pp. 59–65.

[49] Evans, *US Hegemony and the Project of Universal Human Rights*, p. 131.

[50] Sohn, "The New International Law," p. 38. See also Pechota, "The Development of the Covenant on Civil and Political Rights," pp. 42–43, on the Resolution's declaration of the unity and interdependence of all kinds of human rights.

[51] Tolley, Jr., *The U.N. Commission on Human Rights*, p. 25.

[52] Pechota, "The Development of the Covenant on Civil and Political Rights," p. 41. See also Evans, *US Hegemony and the Project of Universal Human Rights*, p. 132.

[53] Green, *The United Nations and Human Rights*, p. 45.

[54] Ibid., pp. 45–46.

[55] Pechota, "The Development of the Covenant on Civil and Political Rights";
Ganji, *International Protection of Human Rights*; Evans, *US Hegemony and the
Project of Universal Human Rights*; Green, *The United Nations and Human
Rights*.

[56] Ganji, *International Protection of Human Rights*, pp. 209–210; Pechota,
"The Development of the Covenant on Civil and Political Rights," pp. 51–52.

[57] Green, *The United Nations and Human Rights*, p. 56.

[58] Pechota, "The Development of the Covenant on Civil and Political Rights,"
p. 51; Green, *The United Nations and Human Rights*, pp. 55–56; Ganji,
International Protection of Human Rights, p. 211.

[59] Green, *The United Nations and Human Rights*, p. 56.

[60] Evans, *US Hegemony and the Project of Universal Human Rights*, pp. 138–
139.

[61] Id.

[62] Id.

[63] Ibid., pp. 138–141; Pechota, "The Development of the Covenant on Civil and
Political Rights", p. 51.

[64] Green, *The United Nations and Human Rights*, p. 56.

[65] Quoted in Ganji, *International Protection of Human Rights*, p. 211. See,
further, Green, *The United Nations and Human Rights*, p.56; Pechota, "The
Development of the Covenant on Civil and Political Rights," p. 51.

[66] Evans, *US Hegemony and the Project of Universal Human Rights*, p. 141.
See also B. Rajagopal, *International Law from Below*, pp. 216–217 (With "the
entry of developing countries into the UN Commission on Human Rights and
the politicization of the UNGA [U.N. General Assembly] from the 1960s …
[they] aggressively used human-rights discourse to counter racism and
colonialism – especially apartheid."). For an account of British suppression of
civil, political, procedural and economic rights of indigenous inhabitants in the
colonies (for example, through the use – as emergency powers or otherwise –
of exile, detention without trial, house arrest, *ad hominem* ordinances,
censorship and the banning of "seditious" organizations), see Simpson, *Human
Rights and the End of Empire*, pp. 75–76, 490; and pp. 491, 512–513 (on
British opposition to the anti-colonial movement's use of petitions to the U.N.
Trusteeship Council: between 1947 and 1959 the council responded to 16,232
petitions).

[67] Evans, *US Hegemony and the Project of Universal Human Rights*, pp. 138–
141.

[68] Pechota, "The Development of the Covenant on Civil and Political Rights," p. 51.

[69] Ibid., pp. 51–52.

[70] Ganji, *International Protection of Human Rights*, p. 211, Footnote 146 (and p. 211, generally).

[71] Ibid., p. 210.

[72] Quoted in id.

[73] See, further, ibid., p. 210.

[74] Quoted in Evans, *US Hegemony and the Project of Universal Human Rights*, p. 141.

[75] Pechota, "The Development of the Covenant on Civil and Political Rights," p. 52.

[76] Evans, *US Hegemony and the Project of Universal Human Rights*, p. 142.

[77] Id.

[78] Ibid., p. 141.

[79] Ibid., p. 138.

[80] Ibid., Footnote 71, pp. 146–147. See also "The Question of the Treatment of the People of Indian Origin in the Union of South Africa" (Internal Memorandum, U.S. Delegation to the U.N. General Assembly, 1950), quoted in Waltz, "Universalizing Human Rights," p. 69: "Many members of the Third Committee … [of the U.N. General Assembly] take very seriously the fact that the Third Committee deals with social, cultural, and humanitarian problems, and that they take pride in discussing these problems on their own merits without regard to political considerations … [I]n the Third Committee they take pleasure in voicing their independence and in functioning almost as though the 'cold war' did not exist." Cf. Simpson, *Human Rights and the End of Empire*, p. 534 ("As for the colonial applications clause, by 1950 anti-colonial feeling was so high that it was felt [by the U.K.] unlikely that such a clause would ever be included …").

[81] U.N. Doc. A/3.C/SR.302 (2 Nov. 1950), p. 206, cited in Ganji, *International Protection of Human Rights*, pp. 210–211, Footnote 143. See, generally, Ganji, *International Protection of Human Rights*, pp. 210–212.

[82] Green, *The United Nations and Human Rights*, pp. 56–57.

[83] Quoted in Sohn, "The New International Law," p. 48. See also Cassese, *International Law in a Divided World*, pp. 132–135, 288.

[84] See Sohn, "The New International Law," p. 49.

[85] R. A. Falk, *Human Rights Horizons: The Pursuit of Justice in a Globalizing World* (New York: Routledge, 2000), pp. 106–107; Shaw, *International Law*,

pp. 177–182; Malanczuk, *Akehurst's Modern Introduction to International Law*, pp. 326, 333; P. Thornberry, "Self-Determination, Minorities, Human Rights: A Review of International Instruments," in C. Ku and P. F. Diehl (eds.), *International Law*, pp. 135–153, at pp. 138–139; Sohn, "The New International Law," pp. 48–50.

[86] Evans, *US Hegemony and the Project of Universal Human Rights*, p. 133 (the quote comes from this page). And see, generally, Pechota, "The Development of the Covenant on Civil and Political Rights," p. 45; Lauren, *The Evolution of International Human Rights*, pp. 250–256; Sohn, "The New International Law," pp. 48–52; Ganji, *International Protection of Human Rights*, pp. 193–198; McGoldrick, *The Human Rights Committee*, pp. 14–15; Green, *The United Nations and Human Rights*, pp. 48–50.

[87] Ganji, *International Protection of Human Rights*, p. 193.

[88] Quoted in Evans, *US Hegemony and the Project of Universal Human Rights*, p. 136.

[89] Ibid., pp. 132–138; Pechota, "The Development of the Covenant on Civil and Political Rights," pp. 45, 56; Sohn, "The New International Law," p. 49; Ganji, *International Protection of Human Rights*, pp. 195–198; McGoldrick, *The Human Rights Committee*, pp. 14–15.

[90] See, for example, D. Orentlicher, "Separation Anxiety: International Responses to Ethno-Separatist Claims" [*Yale Journal of International Law*, vol. 23 (1998), pp. 1ff.], extracted in Steiner and Alston, *International Human Rights in Context*, pp. 1249–1257, at pp. 1250, 1257. See also Falk, *Human Rights Horizons*, p. 97. Shaw, *International Law*, pp. 217–218, has drawn attention to the U.N. Human Rights Committee's 1984 General Comment on self-determination which shows concern with the level of "participation in social and political structures" and with, to use Shaw's words again, the "right of self-determination ... [as] the overall framework for the consideration of principles relating to democratic governance." Cf. F. P. Walters, *A History of the League of Nations* (London: Oxford University Press, 1952; reprinted 1960, 1965), p. 44.

[91] See, for example, Sohn, "The New International Law," pp. 49–50; Falk, *Human Rights Horizons*, ch. 6, generally; Orentlicher, "Separation Anxiety," pp. 1252–1253. Consider, also, the commissions' opinions on the Aaland Islands Question in 1920–1921, under the auspices of the League of Nations: "Report of International Commission of Jurists on Legal Aspects of the Aaland Island Question" (1920), extracted in Steiner and Alston, *International Human Rights in Context*, pp. 1257–1260, at pp. 1257–1258; "Report of the

Commission of Rapporteurs on the Aaland Island Question" (1921), extracted in Steiner and Alston, *International Human Rights in Context*, pp. 1260–1263, at p. 1262.

[92] Indian delegate quoted in Ganji, *International Protection of Human Rights*, p. 196. See also Falk, *Human Rights Horizons,* p. 98; Evans, *US Hegemony and the Project of Universal Human Rights*, p. 137; Pechota, "The Development of the Covenant on Civil and Political Rights," p. 56; Sohn, "The New International Law," p. 49 ("Those who consider self-determination to be a collective right assert that without the right, neither a people nor the individual members thereof can be considered free."). Cf. The U.N. Human Rights Committee's Comment (1984) that the achievement of self-determination was "an essential condition for the effective guarantee and observance of individual human rights." (quoted in Shaw, *International Law*, p. 217). But Shaw, *International Law*, p. 217, argues that "[n]evertheless, the principle is seen as a collective one and not one that individuals could seek to enforce through ... individual petition ... [under the ICESCR]."

[93] See, generally, Falk, *Human Rights Horizons,* ch. 6, who makes some similar arguments. See also Evans, *US Hegemony and the Project of Universal Human Rights*, p. 136.

[94] Falk, *Human Rights Horizons,* p. 106

[95] Pechota, "The Development of the Covenant on Civil and Political Rights," pp. 45–46. See, for example, U.N. Charter, Articles 1(2), 55; Declaration on the Granting of Independence to Colonial Countries and Peoples (1960); Declaration on Principles of International Law Concerning Friendly Relations and Co-operation among States in Accordance with the Charter of the United Nations (1970); and the 1966 Covenants, common Article I, extracted and discussed in Steiner and Alston, *International Human Rights in Context,* pp. 1265–1268. See also Shaw, *International Law*, pp. 178–181, where he argues that self-determination could qualify as part of customary international law, or as a "general principle" of international law. See also *East Timor (Portugal v Australia)* (1995), cited, quoted and discussed in Shaw, *International Law*, p. 180.

[96] Evans, *US Hegemony and the Project of Universal Human Rights*, p. 136.

[97] See Falk, *Human Rights Horizons*; Evans, *US Hegemony and the Project of Universal Human Rights*, p. 135.

[98] Evans, *US Hegemony and the Project of Universal Human Rights*, p. 136.

[99] Id.

[100] Id.; Sohn, "The New International Law," pp. 50–51; McGoldrick, *The Human Rights Committee,* p. 15; Green, *The United Nations and Human Rights,* p. 49 (it "clearly reflected the historic conflict between the underdeveloped and developed countries over the issue of expropriation of private property").

[101] See, further, Evans, *US Hegemony and the Project of Universal Human Rights,* pp. 136–137.

[102] McGoldrick, *The Human Rights Committee,* p. 15.

[103] Quoted in Steiner and Alston, *International Human Rights in Context,* p. 1258.

[104] Cited, quoted and discussed in ibid., note 2, p. 1252 (emphasis added).

[105] See Shaw, *International Law,* pp. 140–141; Malanczuk, *Akehurst's Modern Introduction to International Law,* pp. 75–76, ch. 12, *passim* (and especially at pp. 183–184). See also Shaw, *International Law,* pp. 390, 361–362, 149–153, 333–334, 353, 458–459, 351–352, 215.

[106] On non-Western concessions, see McGoldrick, *The Human Rights Committee,* p. 15. See also Shaw, *International Law,* pp. 9, 25, 41, 81, 633 (citing the 1969 Vienna Convention on the Law of Treaties, the *Nuclear Tests* cases (1974)(ICJ), the *Nicaragua* case (1986)(ICJ), and the *Legality of the Threat of Use of Nuclear Weapons* (1996)(ICJ)).

[107] S. Zamora, "Economic Relations and Development," in C. C. Joyner (ed.), *The United Nations and International Law* (Cambridge: Cambridge University Press, 1997), pp. 232–286, at p. 259.

[108] B. H. Weston, "The Charter of Economic Rights and Duties of States and the Deprivation of Foreign-Owned Wealth," in C. Ku and P. Diehl (eds.), *International Law,* pp. 519–548, at p. 543 (emphasis in original). See also Pechota, "The Development of the Covenant on Civil and Political Rights," p. 56.

[109] Weston, "The Charter of Economic Rights and Duties of States and the Deprivation of Foreign-Owned Wealth," p. 546 (see also pp. 545–546). Cf. R. A. Falk, "Sovereignty and Human Dignity: The Search for Reconciliation" [in F. Deng and Lyons (eds.), *African Reckoning: A Quest for Good Governance*], extracted in Steiner and Alston, *International Human Rights in Context,* pp. 581–582 (at p. 582: arguing that there is "a clear trend away from the idea of unconditional sovereignty and toward a concept of responsible sovereignty").

[110] Shaw, *International Law,* p. 150 (emphasis added).

[111] In what follows, I rely principally on the following sources: Shaw, *International Law,* pp. 573–579, 583–584; Weston, "The Character of

Economic Rights and Duties of States and the Deprivation of Foreign-Owned Wealth"; Zamora, "Economic Relations and Development," p. 259.

[112] Cf. McGoldrick, *The Human Rights Committee,* p. 15: "It has been argued ... that ... article 47 ... [ICCPR] substantially altered the compromise reached on the content of the article 1 ... Article 47 attracted great opposition from the Western States who argued that it was designed to modify the effect of the substance of article 1 [(2)]. Some commentators have accepted that the purpose of article 47 was indeed to override the contents of article 1." My sense is, however, that such an interpretation is not required here: it is perfectly possible to reconcile the two provisions – "the inherent right of all peoples to enjoy and utilize fully and freely their natural wealth and resources" must still be exercised under international law.

[113] See Shaw, *International Law,* pp. 573–579, 583–584; Weston, "The Character of Economic Rights and Duties of States and the Deprivation of Foreign-Owned Wealth"; Zamora, "Economic Relations and Development," p. 259. See also Malanczuk, *Akehurst's Modern Introduction to International Law,* pp. 235–238; Shaw, *International Law,* p. 577. Cf. Weston, "The Character of Economic Rights and Duties of States and the Deprivation of Foreign-Owned Wealth," pp. 521, 545.

[114] Malanczuk, *Akehurst's Modern Introduction to International Law,* pp. 235–240, and especially at pp. 235–236; Weston, "The Character of Economic Rights and Duties and the Deprivation of Foreign-Owned Wealth," generally, and especially at pp. 528–531, 541–542, 544–545; Shaw, *International Law,* pp. 573–579; pp. 583–584. See also Weston, "The Character of Economic Rights and Duties of States and the Deprivation of Foreign-Owned Wealth," pp. 535, 541.

[115] Cited, quoted and discussed in Zamora, "Economic Relations and Development," p. 259; Malanczuk, *Akehurst's Modern Introduction to International Law,* p. 236.

[116] Quoted in Zamora, "Economic Relations and Development", p. 259 (emphasis added).

[117] Malanczuk, *Akehurst's Modern Introduction to International Law,* p. 236 (see, also, p. 237). And see Weston, "The Character of Economic Rights and Duties of States and the Deprivation of Foreign-Owned Wealth," pp. 527–528; Shaw, *International Law,* pp. 577–580; Zamora, "Economic Relations and Development," p. 259 ("the crucial issue of the level of compensation remains unsettled").

[118] Malanczuk, *Akehurst's Modern Introduction to International Law*, pp. 235–240; Shaw, *International Law*, p. 573; Weston, " The Character of Economic Rights and Duties of States and the Deprivation of Foreign-Owned Wealth."

[119] See Shaw, *International Law*; Malanczuk, *Akehurst's Modern Introduction to International Law*; Weston, "The Character of Economic Rights and Duties of States and the Deprivation of Foreign-Owned Wealth"; Pechota, "The Development of the Covenant on Civil and Political Rights," p. 56; Sohn, "The New International Law," p. 51; McGoldrick, *The Human Rights Committee*, p. 15; Green, *The United Nations and Human Rights*, pp. 49–50.

[120] Sohn, "The New International Law," pp. 52–56. On the "rights–development trade-off," see, for instance, J. Donnelly, *Universal Human Rights in Theory and Practice* (Ithaca, New York: Cornell University Press, 1989), chs. 9 and 10 and especially pp. 169, 202; R. J. Vincent, *Human Rights and International Relations* (Cambridge: Cambridge University Press, 1986), ch. 5.

[121] Donnelly, *Universal Human Rights in Theory and Practice*, p. 202. See also C. Thomas, "International Financial Institutions and Social and Economic Human Rights: An Exploration," in T. Evans (ed.), *Human Rights Fifty Years On,* ch. 7; A. G. McGrew, "Human Rights in a Global Age: Coming to Terms with Globalization," in Evans (ed.), *Human Rights Fifty Years On*, ch. 8; C. Thomas, "Poverty, Development and Hunger," in J. Baylis and S. Smith (eds.), *The Globalization of World Politics: An Introduction to International Relations* (Oxford: Oxford University Press, 1997), ch. 23; R. A. Falk, "Economic Aspects of Global Civilization: The Unmet Challenges of World Poverty," Center of International Studies, *World Order Studies Program Occasional Paper*, No. 22 (Princeton: Center of International Studies, Princeton University, 1992). See also World Bank, "Development and Human Rights: The Role of the World Bank" (1998), extracted in Steiner and Alston, *International Human Rights in Context Law,* p. 1337. For critiques of the role of international economic organizations in relation to human rights, see, for example: T. Evans, *The Politics of Human Rights* (London: Pluto Press, 2001), pp. 48, 97–101; Steiner and Alston, *International Human Rights in Context*, pp. 1334, 1349–1361; Zamora, "Economic Relations and Development," pp. 260–262; B. Rajagopal, *International Law from Below*, especially at pp. 196–197, 219–222; and (in a more conservative vein) Borgwardt, *A New Deal for the World*, pp. 257–260.

[122] See, for example, A. Belden-Fields, *Rethinking Human Rights for the New Millennium* (New York: Palgrave Macmillan, 2003), ch. 3.

[123] Sohn, "The New International Law," pp. 52–53.

[124] The Declaration is extracted in Steiner and Alston, *International Human Rights in Context*, pp. 1265–1266.

[125] Extracted in ibid., pp. 1266–1267.

[126] Malanczuk, *Akehurst's Modern Introduction to International Law*, p. 239.

[127] Id. (on both documents).

[128] Id. (quoting the Vienna Declaration).

[129] Extracted in Steiner and Alston, *International Human Rights in Context*, pp. 1302–1304.

[130] See Falk, *Human Rights Horizons*, chs. 6 and 7.

[131] Ibid., pp. 109, 118.

[132] In this section, I draw upon ibid.; Malanczuk, *Akehurst's Modern Introduction to International Law*; Shaw, *International Law*; Ganji, *International Protection of Human Rights*; Thornberry, "Self-Determination, Minorities, Human Rights"; F. Kirgis, Jr., "The Degrees of Self-Determination in the United Nations Era" [*American Journal of International Law*, vol. 88 (1994), pp. 304 ff.], extracted in Steiner and Alston, *International Human Rights in Context*, pp. 1270–1272; Orentlicher, "Separation Anxiety"; A. Buchanan, "Self-Determination, Secession, and the Rule of Law" [in R. McKim and J. McMahan (eds.), *The Morality of Nationalism* (1997)], extracted in Steiner and Alston, *International Human Rights in Context*, pp. 1286–1288; R. Higgins "Comments"[in C. Brölman, *et al.* (eds.), *Peoples and Minorities in International Law*], extracted in Steiner and Alston, *International Human Rights in Context*, pp. 1285–1286.

[133] Shaw, *International Law*, pp. 181–182; Declaration on the Granting of Independence to Colonial Countries and Peoples (U.N. General Assembly) (1960), Article 7, extracted in Steiner and Alston, *International Human Rights in Context*, pp. 1265–1266; Declaration on Principles of International Law Concerning Friendly Relations and Co-operation among States in Accordance with the Charter of the United Nations (1970), extracted in Steiner and Alston, *International Human Rights in Context*, pp. 1266–1267; Article III[3], Organization of African Unity Charter, cited in Shaw, *International Law*, p. 215; *Burkina Faso / Mali* case (1986) (ICJ), cited in Shaw, *International Law*, p. 216; Orentlicher, "Separation Anxiety," pp. 1255–1256; Kirgis, Jr., "The Degrees of Self-Determination in the United Nations Era," pp. 1270–1272; Malanczuk, *Akehurst's Modern Introduction to International Law*, pp. 326–327, 330–336; Falk, *Human Rights Horizons*, especially pp. 99–100.

[134] Shaw, *International Law*, pp. 216–217; Malanczuk, *Akehurst's Modern Introduction to International Law*, pp. 334–335; Sohn, "The New International Law," pp. 49–50.

[135] Aaland Commission of Jurists, "Report of International Commission of Jurists on Legal Aspects of the Aaland Islands Question," (1920), extracted in Steiner and Alston, *International Human Rights in Context,* pp. 1257–1260, at p. 1258. Antonio Cassese, the eminent international lawyer, has argued that "a racial or religious group may attempt secession, a form of external self-determination, when it is apparent that internal self-determination is absolutely beyond reach. Extreme and unremitting persecution and the lack of any reasonable prospect for peaceful challenge may make secession legitimate." – quoted in Shaw, *International Law*, p. 217. See also Buchanan, "Self-Determination, Secession, and the Rule of Law," p. 1287; Thornberry, "Self-Determination, Minorities, Human Rights," pp. 139–142. But cf. Malanczuk, *Akehurst's Modern Introduction to International Law*, p. 340. To similar effect, see Shaw, *International Law*, p. 217. See also Falk, *Human Rights Horizons*, p. 110; Malanczuk, *Akehurst's Modern Introduction to International Law*, pp. 332–333, especially at p. 333 (he considers but doubts whether "action to dismember an independent state is permitted if the government does not represent the whole people"); Shaw, *International Law*, pp. 217–218; Kirgis, Jr., "The Degrees of Self-Determination in the United Nations Era," p. 1271 ("one can thus discern degrees of self-determination, with the legitimacy of each tied to the degree of representative government in the State").

[136] Higgins, "Comments," pp. 1285–1286; Ganji, *International Protection of Human Rights*, pp. 197–198, 202; Shaw, *International Law*, p. 220–221; McGoldrick, *The Human Rights Committee,* p. 15; Thornberry, "Self-Determination, Minorities, Human Rights," p. 140, and generally; Declaration on the Rights of Persons Belonging to National or Ethnic, Religious or Linguistic Minorities (U.N. General Assembly) (1992), extracted in Steiner and Alston, *International Human Rights in Context,* pp. 1298–1299 (especially Article 8(4): "Nothing in the present Declaration may be construed as permitting any activity contrary to the purposes and principles of the United Nations, including sovereign equality, territorial integrity and political independence of States.").

[137] For my discussion here I have drawn upon the following sources: Falk, *Human Rights Horizons*; Steiner and Alston, *International Human Rights in Context*, ch. 15; Kirgis, Jr., "The Degrees of Self-Determination in the United Nations Era"; H. J. Steiner, "Ideals and Counter-Ideals in the Struggle over

Autonomy Regimes for Minorities" [*Notre Dame Law Review*, vol. 66 (1991)], extracted in Steiner and Alston, *International Human Rights in Context*, pp. 1292–1297; Buchanan, "Self-Determination, Secession, and the Rule of Law"; Thornberry, "Self-Determination, Minorities, Human Rights."

[138] Steiner and Alston, *International Human Rights, passim*, and especially at pp. 491–493, 1289–1305.

[139] Orentlicher, "Separation Anxiety," p. 1255, also emphasizes the difficulty of identifying the membership of a relevant group and its relationship to any territory in contention (a difficulty evident in the former Yugoslavia, in Middle-East politics, in the Kashmir, in religious conflicts in India, and in some indigenous peoples' land claims, for instance).

[140] Cf. R. A. Falk, *Predatory Globalization: A Critique* (Cambridge: Polity Press, 1999), p. 102 ("globalization, as shaped by a neo-liberal ideology, appears incompatible with the earlier project of the humane or compassionate state"). See also Rajagopal, *International Law from Below*.

[141] Steiner and Alston, *International Human Rights in Context*, p. 1291.

[142] Quoted in Thornberry, "Self-Determination, Minorities, Human Rights," pp. 142–143.

[143] Steiner and Alston, *International Human Rights in Context*, pp. 1290–1291.

[144] Malanczuk, *Akehurst's Modern Introduction to International Law*, p. 107.

[145] See, for example, Shaw, *International Law*, pp. 220–223.

[146] Orentlicher, "Separation Anxiety," p. 1256; McGoldrick, *The Human Rights Committee*, p. 15; Sohn, "The New International Law," p. 50; Malanczuk, *Akehurst's Modern Introduction to International Law*, pp. 338–339; Falk, *Human Rights Horizons*; Thornberry, "Self-Determination, Minorities, Human Rights," pp. 136, 139; Ganji, *International Protection of Human Rights*; Declaration on the Rights of Persons Belonging to National or Ethnic Minorities (U.N. General Assembly) (1992), extracted in Steiner and Alston, *International Human Rights in Context*, pp. 1298–1299.

[147] Orentlicher, "Separation Anxiety," p. 1256.

[148] Ganji, *International Protection of Human Rights*, pp. 197–198, 202; Thornberry, "Self-Determination, Minorities, Human Rights," pp. 136, 140; Higgins, "Comments," pp. 1285–1286.

[149] Quoted in Ganji, *International Protection of Human Rights*, p. 197.

[150] The Indian, Syrian and Greek representatives are quoted in ibid., p. 198.

[151] Falk, *Human Rights Horizons*; especially at pp. 133–136.

[152] "Report of the Commission of Rapporteurs on the Aaland Island Question" (1921), extracted in Steiner and Alston, *International Human Rights in Context*, pp. 1260–1263, at p. 1262.

[153] Buchanan, "Self-Determination, Secession, and the Rule of Law," p. 1287.

[154] As to (1) and (2), see ibid., p. 1287. On the question of civil war, I rely principally on Malanczuk, *Akehurst's Modern Introduction to International Law*, pp. 326–327, 334–336, 338–340, especially at p. 339.

[155] Steiner and Alston, *International Human Rights in Context*, pp. 1249, 1290; Malanczuk, *Akehurst's Modern Introduction to International Law*, pp. 338–339; Falk, *Human Rights Horizons*, generally and pp. 133–135; Kirgis, Jr., "The Degrees of Self-Determination in the United Nations Era," p. 1271; Thornberry, "Self-Determination, Minorities, Human Rights," pp. 149–150.

[156] Quoted in Thornberry, "Self-Determination, Minorities, Human Rights," p. 137 (and generally).

[157] Quoted in ibid., note 9, p. 151.

[158] See Falk, *Human Rights Horizons*, pp. 103–104 and note 16, p. 252 (on "Liechtenstein principles"); Steiner and Alston, *International Human Rights in Context*, pp. 491–492, 1289–1301, and ch. 15, generally.

[159] Steiner and Alston, *International Human Rights in Context*, pp. 491–492. See also Steiner, "Ideals and Counter-Ideals in the Struggle over Autonomy Regimes for Minorities," p. 1295.

[160] Steiner and Alston, *International Human Rights in Context*, pp. 492–493, 1290; Thornberry, "Self-Determination, Minorities, Human Rights," pp. 146–147; Shaw, *International Law*, p. 209–214; Falk, *Human Rights Horizons*, pp. 134–136 (the quotation is from p. 136), and generally. Falk, *Human Rights Horizons*, pp. 136, 141, 252 (note 15) has drawn attention to collective dimensions of the prohibition of discrimination and of genocide under international law. See also Declaration on the Elimination of all Forms of Intolerance and Discrimination Based on Religion or Belief (1981) (U.N. General Assembly), in Centre for the Study of Human Rights, *Twenty-five Human Rights Documents*, pp. 94–96.

[161] These are extracted in Steiner and Alston, *International Human Rights in Context*, pp. 1291–1292, 1298–1299.

[162] Shaw, *International Law*, p. 209 (emphasis added). See also Steiner and Alston, *International Human Rights in Context*, pp. 143, 492–493; Steiner, "Ideals and Counter-Ideals in the Struggle Over Autonomy Regimes for Minorities," p. 1293; Malanczuk, *Akehurst's Modern Introduction to International Law*, p. 339.

[163] Steiner and Alston, *International Human Rights in Context*, p. 1292 (emphasis added); Shaw, *International Law*, pp. 220–221; Malanczuk, *Akehurst's Modern Introduction to International Law*, p. 339 ("there is a tendency in the literature [on Article 27, ICCPR] to move towards a group-oriented view"). Cf. Falk, *Human Rights Horizons*, pp. 141–142.

[164] Falk, *Human Rights Horizons*, p. 134.

[165] Ibid., p. 142.

[166] Extracted in Steiner and Alston, *International Human Rights in Context*, pp. 1298–1299.

[167] Ibid., p. 1298 (emphasis added).

[168] Ibid., p. 1299.

[169] Cf. Falk, *Human Rights Horizons*, p. 252 (note 16).

[170] Summarized by Shaw, *International Law*, pp. 220–221 (emphasis added).

[171] Falk, *Human Rights Horizons*, p. 25 (note 16).

[172] Ibid., generally.

[173] Ibid., pp. 252 (note 16), 135.

[174] Quoted in Malanczuk, *Akehurst's Modern Introduction to International Law*, pp. 106–107 (see also, pp. 106–107). Cf. ILO Convention No. 169 on Indigenous and Tribal Peoples in Independent Countries (1989), Article 1(2) ("self-identification as indigenous or tribal shall be regarded as a fundamental criterion") – cited, quoted and discussed in Shaw, *International Law*, p. 222.

[175] Falk, *Human Rights Horizons*, p. 121, acknowledges that "[t]here is, to be sure, no binding formal instrument that establishes such a right," but argues it might yet find a place in international custom (pp. 121–122). In any event, he argues (chs. 6 and 7) that generally indigenous peoples do *not* seek complete state sovereignty internationally, accepting that such a goal may be undesirable (for example, in terms of the best use of available resources). See also M. Castan and S. Joseph, *Federal Constitutional Law: A Contemporary View* (Pyrmont, N.S.W.: Lawbook Co., 2001), pp. 347–366, *passim*; T. Blackshield and G. Williams, *Australian Constitutional Law and Theory: Commentary and Materials*, third edn. (Annandale, N.S.W.: The Federation Press, 2002), ch. 5; see also, especially, pp. 203–226, 175–202, 226–228, 232–233; Malanczuk, *Akehurst's Modern Introduction to International Law*, pp. 107–108.

[176] See, generally, Shaw, *International Law*, pp. 222–223; Falk, *Human Rights Horizons*; Steiner and Alston, *International Human Rights in Context*, pp. 1301–1304.

[177] See Falk, *Human Rights Horizons*, chs. 6 and 7; Shaw, *International Law*, pp. 222–224; Malanczuk, *Akehurst's Modern Introduction to International*

Law, pp. 106–108; Steiner and Alston, *International Human Rights in Context*, pp. 1301–1304.

[178] On suggested autonomy regimes in relation to indigenous peoples in Australia, see Council for Aboriginal Reconciliation, *Going Forward: Social Justice for the First Australians* (Canberra: AGPS, 1995), extracted in Blackshield and Williams, *Australian Constitutional Law and Theory*, pp. 234–235; Council for Aboriginal Reconciliation, *Recognising Aboriginal and Torres Strait Islander Rights*, (Canberra: AGPS, 2000), extracted in Blackshield and Williams, *Australian Constitutional Law and Theory*, pp. 236–237.

[179] In Centre for the Study of Human Rights, *Twenty-five Human Rights Documents*, pp. 97–105. See also Steiner and Alston, *International Human Rights in Context*, pp. 1301–1304; Falk, *Human Rights Horizons*, chs. 6 and 7; Shaw, *International Law*, pp. 222–223.

[180] Steiner and Alston, *International Human Rights in Context*, p. 1301.

[181] See Falk, *Human Rights Horizons*, especially pp. 124, 129, 133, 139, 142; Shaw, *International Law*, pp. 222–224. For the full text of the Declaration, see United Nations Draft Declaration on the Rights of Indigenous Peoples, 1994 in Brownlie and Goodwin-Gill (eds.), *Basic Documents on Human Rights*, pp. 72–81.

[182] Malanczuk, *Akehurst's Modern Introduction to International Law*, pp. 250–251; U.N. Declaration on the Right to Development (1986), extracted in Steiner and Alston, *International Human Rights in Context*, pp. 1420–1422; Steiner and Alston, *International Human Rights in Context*, ch. 16; Shaw, *International Law*, pp. 587–589. See also Falk, *Predatory Globalization*, pp. 17–20, 27–29, 101–102; Falk, *Human Rights Horizons*, ch. 7, especially at pp. 139–139.

[183] Pechota, "The Development of the Covenant on Civil and Political Rights," p. 49.

[184] Ibid., p. 49–50.

[185] See, generally, id.; Tolley, Jr., *The U.N. Commission on Human Rights*, p. 29; Green, *The United Nations and Human Rights*, pp. 16–17, 19–20, 53–55, 59–65; Ganji, *International Protection of Human Rights*, pp. 107–108, 110, 113–117, 105–114, 116, 118; McGoldrick, *The Human Rights Committee*, pp. 6, 7, 16–17; Pechota, "The Development of the Covenant on Civil and Political Rights," pp. 49–51.

[186] McGoldrick, *The Human Rights Committee*, p. 17. See also Ganji, *International Protection of Human Rights*, p. 212 (the U.S.A. "took the lead" in arguing for a federal clause).

[187] Ganji, ibid., p. 217. From Ganji's text it is not clear how much he is directly quoting from the U.S. representative because, while the relevant passage begins with a quotation mark, there is no closing quotation mark.

[188] Ibid., p. 216.

[189] I rely here on ibid., pp. 213 (and note 152), 214–215 (note 155).

[190] Quoted in ibid., p. 213. See also Green, *The United Nations and Human Rights*, p. 54.

[191] Evans, *US Hegemony and the Project of Universal Human Rights*, p. 107.

[192] Quoted in Ganji, *International Protection of Human Rights*, p. 213.

[193] Pechota, "The Development of the Covenant on Civil and Political Rights," p. 50; Ganji, *International Protection of Human Rights*, pp. 216–217.

[194] Ganji, *International Protection of Human Rights*, p. 217.

[195] Ibid., pp. 217–219; Pechota, "The Development of the Covenant on Civil and Political Rights," p. 50.

[196] See Constitution of the United States, extracted in Steiner and Alston, *International Human Rights in Context,* pp. 1462–1466.

[197] Evans, *US Hegemony and the Project of Universal Human Rights*, generally, and especially at pp. 107–110; Green, *The United Nations and Human Rights*, especially at pp. 59–65; Ganji, *International Protection of Human Rights*, pp. 217–219; Steiner and Alston, *International Human Rights in Context,* pp. 1022–1029, 1052–1054.

[198] Steiner and Alston, *International Human Rights in Context*, pp. 1022–1029, 1052–1054. See also Malanczuk, *Akehurst's Modern Introduction to International Law*, pp. 65–70; Shaw, *International Law*, pp. 102–103, 114–121. See also Borgwardt, *A New Deal for the World*, p. 267–268.

[199] Cf. Shaw, *International Law*, pp. 118–119.

[200] Extracted in Steiner and Alston, *International Human Rights in Context,* pp. 1026–1028.

[201] Per Gibson CJ, quoted in ibid., pp. 1027–1028.

[202] Cited, quoted and discussed in ibid., p. 1025.

[203] Pechota, "The Development of the Covenant on Civil and Political Rights", p. 50; Ganji, *International Protection of Human Rights*, pp. 218–219; Malanczuk, *Akehurst's Modern Introduction to International Law*, pp. 66–67. See also Brucken, "A Most Uncertain Crusade," p. 211 (citing the U.S. Supreme Court case of *Missouri v. Holland*, 252 U.S. 416 (1920) – see, also, other cases cited at p. 252, note 6).

[204] On monism, dualism, and the relationship between international and municipal law, see Shaw, *International Law*, pp. 100–103, 114–121;

Malanczuk, *Akehurst's Modern Introduction to International Law*, ch. 4; Steiner and Alston, *International Human Rights in Context,* pp. 573–582, 588–591, 986–990, 999–1008, 1012–1018, 1022, 1025–1029. On the position in Australia, see, for instance, Piotrowicz and Kaye, *Human Rights in International and Australian Law*, ch. 10; G. Williams, *Human Rights under the Australian Constitution* (Oxford: Oxford University Press, 2002), pp. 18–23.

[205] Reprinted in Blackshield and Williams, *Australian Constitutional Law and Theory,* pp. 1337–1357.

[206] On the "external affairs" power (s. 51 (xxix)), see Williams, *Human Rights under the Australian Constitution*, pp. 18–19. On s. 109 and the "federal balance," see Blackshield and Williams, *Australian Constitutional Law and Theory,* ch. 6; and especially pp. 370–372. On the often conservative implications of federalism in Australia, see H. Charlesworth, "Australia's Split Personality: Implementation of Human Rights Obligations in Australia," in P. Alston and M. Chiam (eds.), *Treaty-making and Australia: Globalization Versus Sovereignty?* (Sydney: The Federation Press, 1995), pp. 129–140, at p. 138.

[207] On the "races power" in the Australian Constitution (s. 51 (xxvi)), see Blackshield and Williams, *Australian Constitutional Law and Theory,* ch. 5, especially at pp. 181–202; Joseph and Castan, *Federal Constitutional Law,* pp. 347–366.

[208] I rely, here, on P. Hanks and D. Cass, *Australian Constitutional Law: Materials and Commentary*, sixth edn. (Melbourne: Butterworths, 1999), p. 91 (emphasis removed). On the extremely poor wages for indigenous workers, see N. O'Neill and R. Handley, *Retreat from Injustice: Human Rights in Australian Law* (Annandale, N.S.W.: The Federation Press, 1994), pp. 398–399, at p. 398.

[209] Cf. M. L. Dudziak, *Cold War Civil Rights: Race and the Image of American Democracy* (Princeton: Princeton University Press, 2000).

[210] Shaw, *International Law*, pp. 102–103.

[211] Steiner and Alston, *International Human Rights in Context*, p. 1026 (and see, further, pp. 588–591). See also Vienna Convention on the Law of Treaties (1969), Articles 26 ("'Pacta Sunt Servanda' Every treaty in force is binding upon the parties to it and must be performed by them in good faith."), 27 ("A party may not invoke the provisions of its internal law as justification for its failure to perform a treaty …"), 46(1) ("A State may not invoke that its consent to be bound by a treaty has been expressed in violation of a provision of its internal law regarding competence to conclude treaties invalidating its consent

unless that violation was manifest and concerned a rule of its internal law of fundamental importance.") – extracted in Steiner and Alston, this note, pp. 1458–1461. The prohibition in Article 27, Vienna Convention, is also "a general principle of international law" (according to Shaw, *International Law*, p. 662; citing *Applicability of the Obligations to Arbitrate under Section 21 of United Nations Headquarters Agreement* case (ICJ)(1988) and the *Alabama Claims* arbitration (1898)). See also Malanczuk, *Akehurst's Modern Introduction to International Law*, pp. 64 ("the general rule of international law is that a state cannot plead a rule of or a gap in its own municipal law as a defence to a claim"), 65, 81 ("it is the federal state which is regarded as responsible in international law"; *not* constituent states), 220; *Lockerbie* case (1992), cited and discussed in Shaw, *International Law*, p. 103 (and see, generally, Shaw, *International Law*, pp. 102–103); U.N. Committee on Economic, Social and Cultural Rights General Comment No. 9 (1998), extracted in Steiner and Alston, *International Human Rights in Context*, pp. 1013–1014, especially at p. 1013; D. J. Harris, *Cases and Materials on International Law*, sixth edn. (London: Sweet and Maxwell, 2004), p. 829.

[212] Evans, *US Hegemony and the Project of Universal Human Rights*, pp. 107–108.

[213] Ganji, *International Protection of Human Rights*, pp. 213–220.

[214] Evans, *US Hegemony and the Project of Universal Human Rights*, pp. 105–108, 110–112, and ch. 4; Green, *The United Nations and Human Rights*, pp. 4–5, 19–20, 25, 101, 108–109, 20–31, 35–36, 59–65. See also Brucken, "A Most Uncertain Crusade."

[215] Quoted in Green, *The United Nations and Human Rights*, p. 20.

[216] Extracted in Steiner and Alston, *International Human Rights in Context*, pp. 1026–1028.

[217] Ibid., pp. 1027–1028.

[218] Quoted in Green, *The United Nations and Human Rights*, p. 20 (note 23).

[219] Cf. Malanczuk, *Akehurst's Modern Introduction to International Law*, p. 212. See also Shaw, *International Law*, pp. 205–206 (Article 2(7), U.N. Charter, "has over the years been flexibly interpreted so that human rights issues are no longer recognised as being solely within the domestic jurisdiction of states."); Cf. Steiner and Alston, *International Human Rights in Context*, p. 138.

[220] Malanczuk, *Akehurst's Modern Introduction to International Law*, p. 220; Shaw, *International Law*, pp. 205–206.

[221] Quoted in Green, *The United Nations and Human Rights*, pp. 30–31.

[222] Ibid., pp. 35–36. See also Tolley, Jr., *The U.N. Commission on Human Rights*, p. 31, who refers to a report by the U.S. Department of Justice that found that the UDHR (during 1948–1973) had a definite influence on seventy-five states' constitutions or superior laws; and had been cited in sixteen national court decisions.

[223] Green, *The United Nations and Human Rights*, pp. 59–60. Note, also, U.S. Congressional condemnation of economic and social rights in the Constitution of Puerto Rico when it was before the U.S. Congress in 1952. The rights were described as unrealistic and "socialistic" – cited, quoted and discussed in Green, *The United Nations and Human Rights*, p. 61.

[224] Green, *The United Nations and Human Rights*, p. 60.

[225] "Memorandum Regarding the Reference in the Japanese Peace Treaty To The Universal Declaration of Human Rights." (Japanese Peace Treaty and Other Treaties Relating to Security in the Pacific, Hearings before the Senate Committee on Foreign Relations, 82 Cong. 2 sess., p. 153), cited, quoted and discussed in ibid., p. 60.

[226] Quoted in ibid., p. 60 (note 49).

[227] Evans, *US Hegemony and the Project of Universal Human Rights*, p. 107.

[228] Ibid., p. 11; pp. 110–118. Cf. Borgwardt, *A New Deal for the World*, pp. 192 (Federalism in the South "sheltered racist regimes from the reach of the US Constitution ..."), 288.

[229] Evans, *US Hegemony and the Project of Universal Human Rights*, pp. 109–110; Green, *The United Nations and Human Rights*, p. 61; Borgwardt, *A New Deal for the World*, pp. 267–268.

[230] Quoted in Green, *The United Nations and Human Rights*, p. 61.

[231] Evans, *US Hegemony and the Project of Universal Human Rights*, pp. 109–110, and, generally, pp. 109–118.

[232] Green, *The United Nations and Human Rights*, p. 63; Evans, *US Hegemony and the Project of Universal Human Rights*, p. 116.

[233] Evans, *US Hegemony and the Project of Universal Human Rights*, pp. 113–118; Green, *The United Nations and Human Rights*, pp. 63–64. Brucken, "A Most Uncertain Crusade," pp. 372–375, notes the Eisenhower administration's view that by interfering with executive agreements the Bricker amendment could undermine drug policing, disarmament and arms (including nuclear arms) control, international arbitration, multilateral defence arrangements and U.S. access to offshore military bases.

[234] Evans, *US Hegemony and the Project of Universal Human Rights*, pp. 115–116; Green, *The United Nations and Human Rights*, pp. 63–65; Ganji, *International Protection of Human Rights*, pp. 222–224.

[235] Green, *The United Nations and Human Rights*, p. 63.

[236] Quoted in id.

[237] Ibid., p. 64 (see also Lauren, *The Evolution of International Human Rights*, pp. 247–248). Mary P. Lord, also known as Mrs. Oswald B. Lord, represented the U.S.A. in the CHR and ECOSOC in the years 1953–1961 and in the U.N. General Assembly from 1953 until 1959 (Simpson, *Human Rights and the End of Empire*, p. 359 (footnote 180). She had been co-chair of the "Citizens for Eisenhower–Nixon movement" in the U.S.A. (Brucken, "A Most Uncertain Crusade," p. 371). On the question of the degree of independence of Eleanor Roosevelt from the State Department, see Simpson, *Human Rights and the End of Empire*, pp. 361–362.

[238] Green, *The United Nations and Human Rights*, p. 65; Evans, *US Hegemony and the Project of Universal Human Rights*, pp. 115–116. See also Tolley, Jr., *The U.N. Commission on Human Rights*, p. 29 ("the United States contributed nothing further to the drafting effort"); McGoldrick, *The Human Rights Committee*, pp. 16–17.

[239] Green, *The United Nations and Human Rights*, pp. 63–64.

[240] Evans, *US Hegemony and the Project of Universal Human Rights*, p. 117.

[241] Ganji, *International Protection of Human Rights*, p. 220 (see, also, at p. 222).

[242] Pechota, "The Development of the Covenant on Civil and Political Rights," p. 50; Evans, *US Hegemony and the Project of Universal Human Rights*, pp. 107-108.

[243] Green, *The United Nations and Human Rights*, pp. 53–54.

[244] Green, *The United Nations and Human Rights*, p. 55; Tolley, Jr., *The U.N. Commission on Human Rights*, p. 29; Pechota, "The Development of the Covenant on Civil and Political Rights," pp. 50-51; Evans, *US Hegemony and the Project of Universal Human Rights*, pp. 107–108. See also ICCPR Articles 2(2), 3(a), 3(b) and 3(c).

[245] Lauren, *The Evolution of International Human Rights*, pp. 250–254; Pechota, "The Development of the Covenant on Civil and Political Rights," pp. 54, 64; McGoldrick, *The Human Rights Committee*, p. 20; Craven, *The International Covenant on Economic, Social and Cultural Rights*, p. 23; Robertson and Merrills, *Human Rights in the World*, p. 34; Rosenberg, *How Far the Promised Land?*, p. 205. The UDHR was approved at Bandung, the

All-African People's Conference, the Summit Conference of Independent African States (which established the Organization of African Unity) and the Afro-Asian Peoples' Solidarity Organization (Lauren, *The Evolution of International Human Rights*, p. 253). As at January 31, 2002, the ICCPR had 148 States Parties while the ICESCR had 145 (Brownlie and Goodwin-Gill (eds.), *Basic Documents on Human Rights*, p. xiv). Sukarno is quoted in Rosenberg, *How Far the Promised Land?*, p. 205. Hickerson is quoted in Evans, *US Hegemony and the Project of Universal Human Rights*, p. 114 (emphasis added). In 1956, Hickerson wrote (*The United Nations and Human Rights*, p. 65) that the new U.S. human rights policy "did not deter the proponents of the covenants … and the [U.N. Human Rights] Commission continued … drafting. The United States participated in the debates and restated many of its previous positions on major issues, especially those in which efforts were made to *restrict* a right or introduce the concept of state control." (emphasis added). Hickerson (*The United Nations and Human Rights*, p. 65) also listed U.S. government failures regarding a private property article, the federal clause and petitions. Note, also, Evans' inconsistent admission (*US Hegemony and the Project of Universal Human Rights*, p. 116, emphasis added) that between 1953 and 1963, U.S. "involvement in the Covenant debate oscillated between total disinterest and cautious contributions motivated by an awareness that legally binding agreements were likely to become accepted standards *whether the United States contributed to them or not.*"

Conclusion

This book has provided an interdisciplinary account of the origins and development of universal human rights from the earliest days until the conclusion of the International Bill of Rights. It has drawn on historical, theoretical (and sometimes philosophical), political and legal developments and literature. It has answered some of the critics of human rights historiography by paying due regard to the interaction between domestic and international struggles for human rights, by examining the role of social movements and civil society, by emphasizing the role of the Third World in the context of colonialism, and by evaluating Western resistance to international human rights law.

It has taken universality as a systematic theme across a broad sweep of history. It has focused on the important question of whether the universal human rights embodied in the main corpus of international human rights law are really only the products of a Western hegemonic imposition, as scholars such as Tony Evans have argued. The book's principal findings are that such rights had diverse origins. They were not a Western hegemonic imposition. Indeed, their incorporation in international law was achieved in the face of widespread and persistent Western – including American – resistance.

This work examined early conceptions of human dignity, the unity of humankind and human rights that could be found in diverse, ancient Western and non-Western civilizations, religions and philosophies. In particular, it drew attention to collectivist and individualist aspects of these conceptions, as well as to the role of economic and social rights within them. It examined the universalist, natural law tradition that so heavily influenced the classical international law of the sixteenth and seventeenth centuries. It was a law that in principle applied equally to all states, peoples and individuals, not just those of the West. In this naturalistic tradition international law applied directly to individual human beings who were the bearers of human rights.

In this regard, the book discussed the importance of the attribution of international legal personality to individual human beings, as a necessary but not a sufficient condition for the fullest realization of human rights. The naturalistic doctrine concerning the recognition of individuals as subjects of international law was displaced by a new "orthodox," positivistic understanding of international law. Positivism in effect projected itself back to time immemorial; in the process erasing much of the international law that preceded its consolidation as an international law doctrine. Such was the power of this new positivism that the earlier naturalistic international law came to be portrayed in standard international law texts as a kind of utopia dreamt up by publicists cloistered in ivory towers. It must be emphasized, however, that the universalism of the classical international law of the sixteenth and seventeenth centuries remained unfulfilled, thwarted by religious intolerance, racism and colonialism (with especially harsh impacts upon the peoples of Africa and indigenous peoples in the Americas).

The discussion then turned to natural rights philosophy, constitutionalism, the Enlightenment, and the revolutionary experiences of the seventeenth and eighteenth centuries. Universalist ideals were again frustrated by racism, sexism, sectarianism, and class considerations. Nevertheless, I underscored the richness of the Enlightenment tradition (especially in relation to economic and social rights and the value of a supportive, regulatory state). This richness is very different from libertarian caricatures of the Enlightenment one finds in some contemporary debates on the universality of human rights.[1]

In the nineteenth century, science, positivism, nationalism, imperialism and an efflorescent capitalism produced a zeitgeist that was antagonistic toward naturalistic international law and the "rights of man." National sovereignty was augmented in international law, with the doctrinal effect that individuals were reduced to mere "objects." They were at the mercy of their own states. But, even in this period, there were countervailing developments that drew their life from a spirit of the "common rights of humanity."[2] This spirit was enlivened by the campaigns against slavery, by ad hoc humanitarian interventions (despite their serious defects), and even in the tolerance and accommodation of the diverse identities and cultures of various national minorities.

In the years 1900 to 1939, a period sometimes neglected by historians of human rights,[3] an anticolonial movement gave voice to non-Western critiques of the international order, and combined with a wider indigenous push for the recognition without discrimination of the full range of human rights. A variety of non-Western and Western NGOs made common cause on these critiques and mobilizations. To many, President Woodrow Wilson's elaboration of a new world – based on democracy, equality of nations, self-determination, the protection of minorities and the peaceful settlement of disputes through an international organization – seemed an answer to at least some of the more pressing grievances of smaller states and dependent peoples alike. But his new world order proved to be a limited one: it applied only to Europe, did not demand the urgent dismantling of empires, and rejected any notion of racial equality. The pattern of U.S. resistance to international, universal human rights, due to isolationism, libertarianism, states' rights, racial politics, a defensive national sovereignty and a constitutional chauvinism, was set in train.

Nevertheless, Wilsonian rhetoric gave some heart to a resilient internationalism in which African-American and "Third World" scholars and activists played a significant role in the interwar period. And this internationalism reemerged in wartime rhetoric, and in what the historian Elizabeth Borgwardt has recently called "Mandela's Atlantic Charter," a charter that, according to the South African lawyer, "reaffirmed faith in the dignity of each human being and propagated a host of democratic principles."[4] It was transformed into a rallying call in the "Third World" to hold Allied states accountable for the racist denial of human rights at home and abroad.

Racist attitudes, policies, laws and institutions of Allied countries were starkly ironic given that the "United Nations" soldiers were giving their lives to defeat the racist forces of Nazi Germany, fascist Italy and Japan and their allies. There was not only racial segregation in the U.S. armed forces, but the predominantly white, common law world (Britain, U.S.A., Canada and Australia) also maintained discriminatory immigration policies. And China's proposed principle of racial equality for the new postwar organization was defeated by leading Western states. These provocations, together with Britain's defence of its empire after the Atlantic Charter, spurred on the fight against racism in Western states and colonialism in the non-Western world. A distinctive embodiment of these concerns was African-American internationalism, which, consistent with Mandela's universalist conception, conceived of civil and political rights and economic and social rights as intertwined; as people of colour everywhere (whether African anticolonialists or African-American civil rights activists) were joined in the struggle against racism and colonialism. The right not to be discriminated against is, after all, a core civil *and* human right.

Western responses to atrocities committed during World War II were often weak. In contrast to the commonest account, the Western Allies did not endorse war crimes trials enthusiastically, but only grudgingly, as the Morgenthau Plan amply demonstrates. Moreover, war crimes trials were not the sole domain of Western powers. Western responses to the massacre of Armenians, the Holocaust, the notion of crimes against humanity and the Genocide Convention also betrayed racist and anti-Semitic prejudices. The Western resistance was made worse by the Big Three's staunch defence of the doctrines of state sovereignty and domestic jurisdiction. This resistance was particularly marked in the U.S.A. due to reverberations from the institutions of slavery, segregation and a resilient, libertarian federalism (which helped conservative states to quash any moves toward internationalism). On the other hand, there was strong non-Western support for the Genocide Convention, and non-Western actors were able to effectively criticize Western evasions regarding economic and social rights and racial equality.

The human rights provisions in the U.N. Charter, and specifically the non-discrimination provisions, did not result from American global leadership, but, principally, from the efforts of committed NGOs from around the world, backed by a range of states. Contrary to British political scientist Tony Evans' argument, neither the UDHR nor the 1966 Covenants were the outcomes of an American hegemonic imposition. Rather, the UDHR received wide-ranging support from numerous and diverse states, organizations, individuals and cultures. Indeed, the declaration that was finally adopted prevailed despite serious American resistance (all the more marked given the UDHR's formally non-binding status) in relation to many of its provisions, especially social and economic rights.

Furthermore, the UDHR is not simply Western in terms of its normative content. Its broad language accommodated the "dignitarian" values of many cultures.[5] It goes well beyond any putative "Enlightenment" heritage; a heritage that is, in any event, much richer and more complex than its detractors often suppose. The UDHR reflects the strong drafting contributions of developing countries from Latin America and Asia (as well as Muslim states); small and medium-sized social-democratic and welfare-capitalist states; and socialist states. When it was voted upon, the UDHR received overwhelming support.

This book has explored in considerable depth the origins of the 1966 Covenants. The Covenants have until recently been overlooked in debates concerning the universality of human rights. Perhaps in part this has been due to the perception among sceptical, relativist and postmodernist critics of the universalist claims of international human rights law that the UDHR is an easier target. In any case, there have been fewer interdisciplinary treatments of the origins of the 1966 Covenants: the majority of available works are technical, legal exegeses and guides.[6] In debates over economic and social rights, the proposed colonial and federal clauses, and self-determination, non-Western states were able to prevail in U.N. forums, despite determined opposition from a number of Western states. For the U.S.A., the omission of a federal clause from the Covenants was the last straw: the "hegemon" decided to walk away from any binding U.N. human rights instruments, and thus had very little say after 1953 in the character of the human rights covenants that were finalized in 1966.

This book has provided ample evidence to counter the provocative and highly influential claim by the social scientists Adamantia Pollis and Peter Schwab, in an essay published in 1979, that international human rights were a Western construct with limited applicability to the non-Western world (and in particular to developing countries). In this claim the scholars anticipated the critique by some authoritarian governments in Asia in the Bangkok Declaration of 1993. This declaration was at the centre of heated debates over universality at the U.N.'s international human rights conference in Vienna in that same year. Here I cannot discuss those complex debates (which came after the period this book examines).[7] However, it is clear that Pollis and Schwab's crude and confused claims about the conceptualization of human rights, the drafting of the International Bill of Rights and its normative content are not sustainable. The International Bill of Rights was not imposed on resistant non-Western states and peoples, is not simply based on Western culture and philosophy (which Pollis and Schwab reduce to a libertarian version of capitalistic democracy), does not prioritize civil and political rights over social and economic ones, and does not worship individualism. Moreover, Pollis and Schwab are wrong to suggest that the non-Western world was uninterested in civil and political rights, democracy and liberty. These entitlements and concepts were closely associated with the anticolonial movement and its struggle for racial equality and human dignity. As Mary Ann Glendon has argued, the dignitarian instruments that comprise the International Bill of Rights give a proper place to the family, the community, duties and egalitarian and welfare entitlements. The bill reflects a broad approach to human dignity, welfare and security. It recognizes, as did FDR in his Four Freedoms speech, that "want" can be as devastating to human dignity, welfare and rights as any number of violations of civil and political rights.[8]

This recognition has come to be linked to the right of self-determination that now incorporates notions of economic sovereignty and sustainable human development. Rather than the authoritarian statism and human rights–modernization "trade-off" that Pollis and Schwab tolerate (because they see it as more "applicable" to non-Western areas), the U.N. rightly rejects these approaches, instead endorsing human rights as universal, equal, interdependent and indivisible.[9] Furthermore, there is mounting evidence that democracy, political and civil rights *aid*, rather than retard, the growth of a modern, stable and successful economy. Thus, a trade-off between economic development and human rights is unnecessary. It is not at all difficult to think of examples of authoritarian states that are unstable and poverty-stricken, and of wealthy states with a strong democratic and human rights culture.[10]

Not only does the International Bill of Rights have diverse origins, but the distinctive (but not exclusive) emphasis of non-Western actors on economic and social rights, racial equality and global inequity also remains as relevant as ever in the present age of globalization. While forces of internationalization and globalization were not absent from the period this book covers, they have intensified since 1966. There is only space here to provide the briefest inventory of the key features of globalization: the information revolution (particularly computerization, the internet and telephone technology) and cultural hybridity; the weakening of state sovereignty; the existence of more open borders; the increased power of transnational corporations, regimes and supranational institutions; the globalization of trade and financial markets (including capital and labour mobility); the rise of neo-liberalism; the widening gap between the developed and developing worlds; the environmental crisis; and the consolidation of global civil society (including a web of international, regional, national and local NGOs).[11] Under these conditions, the social justice orientation[12] of the International Bill of Rights is a vital normative resource. Rights to food, healthcare, social security, education, shelter, clothing, decent labour conditions and an adequate standard of living can help to counter the worsening vulnerability of millions of people the world over (particularly in the developing world, but also in "Third World" enclaves in the First World).[13] While the dynamics of globalization have undoubtedly reduced the power of the state, it is not done for yet. Too often the forces of globalization – and of the unstoppable "free" market in particular – have been used by governments as a rationalization for the contraction of the welfare state, and/or violence and other coercive measures that lower working conditions, undermine trade unions, weaken the public sector and public infrastructure and suppress civil liberties and democratic rights (for example, freedoms of assembly and association) all in the name of "global competitiveness." While the state is more constrained than in the past, it has the potential to do much more to improve the welfare of its citizens than it has done, even in poorer states in the developing world (where systemic poverty is sometimes worsened by corruption and war). It needs to act, however, in conjunction with international and regional organizations, civil society and the public and private sectors.

As historians Micheline Ishay and Elizabeth Borgwardt have recently argued in their illuminating accounts, it is much too soon to pronounce the death of Keynesian economic planning, social democratic politics and the "humane" state.[14] A humane state is needed to provide something of an answer to neo-liberal market fundamentalism. Ishay and Borgwardt rightly argue that there is an indivisible relationship between socio-economic and civil and political rights, one that is essential to an expanded conception of human "security." This understanding of security goes well beyond the use of standard liberal, negative rights that shield citizens, for example, from a state's unlawful use of violence against them. Such an expanded notion of human security naturally has flow-on effects in terms of national and international stability.[15]

Ishay argues that although economic growth is important in the alleviation of poverty, so are the actions of state institutions. "In other words," she says, "realizing the advantage of a market economy ... call[s] for more state intervention, not less – to develop economic infrastructure, public health and education, and civil institutions."[16] The state cannot, however, be expected, even assuming the best of intentions on its part, to work toward the realization of human rights in isolation. This is where the critique and transformation of the global order is fundamental. As the much neglected Article 28 of the UDHR states: "Everyone is entitled to a social and international order in which the rights and freedoms set forth in this Declaration can be fully realized." Internationalists of various hues (for example, critical theorists, cosmopolitans, World Order and World System theorists, and even liberals), despite their differences, agree on the need to explore the ways in which the global order can enhance or undermine human welfare.

These concluding reflections have a particular relevance to the U.S.A. It has been at its weakest in guaranteeing economic and social rights, especially where systemic disadvantage is compounded by racial discrimination. It needs a more humane state to combat the dark side of its human rights "exceptionalism" – its wariness and even hostility toward international governance and international legal obligations.[17] As Borgwardt has argued in *A New Deal for the World*, the U.S.A. needs to recapture the fleeting multilateralist Keynesianism of the early New Deal.[18] But before the U.S.A. can play an effective part in bringing about such a deal for the world it must secure a New Deal for itself.

Notes

[1] A useful corrective to such caricatures is Micheline Ishay's recent history, *The History of Human Rights: From Ancient Times to the Globalization Era* (Berkeley, California: University of California Press, 2004).

[2] P. G. Lauren, *The Evolution of International Human Rights: Visions Seen* (Philadelphia: University of Pennsylvania Press, 1998), p. 39.

[3] But see the following notable exceptions: Ishay, *The History of Human Rights*; Lauren, *The Evolution of International Human Rights*; and A. W. B.

Simpson, *Human Rights and the End of Empire: Britain and the Genesis of the European Convention* (Oxford: Oxford University Press, 2001).

[4] E. Borgwardt, *A New Deal for the World: America's Vision for Human Rights* (Cambridge, Massachusetts: Belknap/Harvard University Press, 2005), p. 29 (see also pp. 28, 29–45).

[5] M. A. Glendon, *A World Made New: Eleanor Roosevelt and the Universal Declaration of Human Rights* (New York: Random House, 2001), p. 227 (see also pp. 111, 175, 227, 230–233).

[6] An exception is A. Devereux, *Australia and the Birth of the International Bill of Human Rights* (Sydney: The Federation Press, 2005).

[7] A. Pollis and P. Schwab, "Human Rights: A Western Construct with Limited Applicability," in A. Pollis and P. Schwab (eds.), *Human Rights: Cultural and Ideological Perspectives* (New York: Praeger, 1979), pp. 1–18. The literature concerning the "Asian values" debate, and other debates concerning the tension between universalist and relativist perspectives on human rights, is vast. The following is a selection of relevant works: C. A. Gearty, *Can Human Rights Survive?* (Cambridge: Cambridge University Press, 2006); M. Goodhart, "Origins and Universality in the Human Rights Debates: Cultural Essentialism and the Challenges of Globalization," *Human Rights Quarterly*, vol. 25 (2003), no.4, pp. 935–964; R. P. Churchill, *Human Rights and Global Diversity* (Upper Saddle River, New Jersey: Pearson Prentice Hall, 2006); A. Gutmann (ed.), *Human Rights as Politics and Idolatry* (Princeton: Princeton University Press, 2001); A. J. Langlois, *The Politics of Justice and Human Rights: Southeast Asia and Universalist Theory* (Cambridge: Cambridge University Press, 2001); T. Dunne and N. J. Wheeler (eds.), *Human Rights in Global Politics* (Cambridge: Cambridge University Press, 1999), part I; E. Brems, *Human Rights: Universality and Diversity* (The Hague: Martinus Nijhoff/Kluwer Law International, 2001).

[8] Glendon, *A World Made New*, pp. 28–45; Borgwardt, *A New Deal for the World*; T. Kloppenberg, "Franklin Delano Roosevelt, Visionary," *Reviews in American History*, vol. 34 (2006), no. 4, pp. 509–520.

[9] B. Rajagopal, *International Law from Below: Development, Social Movements and Third World Resistance* (Cambridge: Cambridge University Press, 2003), especially pp. 202–203, 212–214, 219, 221–222.

[10] See J. Donnelly, *Universal Human Rights in Theory and Practice* (Ithaca, New York: Cornell University Press, 1989); Churchill, *Human Rights and Global Diversity*.

[11] Ishay, *The History of Human Rights*, 251–258, 260–263, 287, 293–295; Borgwardt, *A New Deal for the World*, pp. 257–260; Goodhart, "Origins and Universality in the Human Rights Debates," especially pp. 935–937. See also J. A. Camilleri, *The End of Sovereignty? The Politics of a Shrinking and Fragmenting World* (Aldershot: Edward Elgar, 1992); T. Risse, S. C. Ropp and K. Sikkink (eds.), *The Power of Human Rights: International Norms and Domestic Change* (Cambridge: Cambridge University Press, 1999).

[12] Glendon, *A World Made New*, p. 175.

[13] See Richard Falk's useful discussion in "Economic Aspects of Global Civilization: The Unmet Challenges of World Poverty," Center of International Studies, *World Order Studies Program Occasional Paper*, no. 22, Princeton University (Princeton: Center of International Studies, Princeton University, 1992).

[14] Ishay, *The History of Human Rights*; Borgwardt, *A New Deal for the World*. Cf. Richard Falk's notion of "humane governance": *Human Rights Horizons: The Pursuit of Justice in a Globalizing World* (New York: Routledge, 2000), pp. 19–20, 34–35.

[15] Borgwardt, *A New Deal for the World*; Ishay, *The History of Human Rights*.

[16] Ishay, *The History of Human Rights*, p. 293. See also Rajagopal, *International Law from Below*, pp. 189, 190–192, 196, 225.

[17] Borgwardt, *A New Deal for the World*, pp. 150, 291–292 (see also p. 268 on the "diffuse Brickerite sensibility [that has] persisted in the law and politics of US foreign relations until at least the Vietnam War and possibly beyond ..."; and pp. 269–271). There is a growing literature concerning the U.S.A.'s human rights "exceptionalism." There is no space to discuss this concept further here, but see, for example: M. Ignatieff, "Introduction"; A. Moravcsik, "The Paradox of U.S. Human Rights Policy"; and C. R. Sunstein, "Why Does the American Constitution Lack Social and Economic Guarantees?," in M. Ignatieff (ed.), *American Exceptionalism and Human Rights* (Princeton: Princeton University Press, 2005), chs. 1, 6 and 4 respectively; Ishay, *The History of Human Rights*, pp. 226–228, 269, 280, 297, 283, 309; J. W. Dietrich, "U.S. Human Rights Policy in the Post-Cold War Era," *Political Science Quarterly*, vol. 121 (2006), no. 2, pp. 269–294; Kloppenberg, "Franklin Delano Roosevelt, Visionary."

[18] Borgwardt, *A New Deal for the World*, especially pp. 259–260.

Select Bibliography

Books

Alexandrowicz, C. H. *An Introduction to the History of the Law of Nations in the East Indies (16th, 17th and 18th Centuries)* (Oxford: Clarendon Press, 1967).

Alston, P. (ed.). *Peoples' Rights* (Oxford: Oxford University Press, 2001).

Alston, P. (ed.). *The United Nations and Human Rights: A Critical Appraisal* (New York: Oxford University Press, 1992).

Alston, P. and M. Chiam (eds.). *Treaty-making and Australia: Globalisation Versus Sovereignty?* (Annandale, N.S.W.: The Federation Press, 1994).

An-Na'im, A. (ed.). *Human Rights in Cross-Cultural Perspectives: A Quest for Consensus* (Philadelphia: University of Pennsylvania Press, 1992).

Anand, R. P. *Confrontation or Cooperation? International Law and the Developing Countries* (New Delhi: Banyan Publications, 1986).

Arambulo, K. *Strengthening the Supervision of the International Covenant on Economic, Social and Cultural Rights: Theoretical and Procedural Aspects*, School of Human Rights Research Series, vol. 3 (Antwerpen–Groningen–Oxford: Intersentia/Hart, 1999).

Bass, G. *Stay the Hand of Vengeance: The Politics of War Crimes Tribunals* (Princeton: Princeton University Press, 2000).

Baylis, J. and S. Smith (eds.). *The Globalization of World Politics: An Introduction to International Relations* (Oxford: Oxford University Press, 1997).

Belden-Fields, A. *Rethinking Human Rights for the New Millennium* (New York: Palgrave Macmillan, 2003).

Berger, J. *A New Deal for the World: Eleanor Roosevelt and American Foreign Policy* (New York: Social Science Monographs/Columbia University Press, 1981).

Bernhardt, R. (ed.). *Encyclopedia of Public International Law* (Amsterdam : Max-Planck-Institut Elsevier Science B.V., 1995).

Blackshield, T. and G. Williams. *Australian Constitutional Law and Theory: Commentary and Materials*, third edn. (Sydney: The Federation Press, 2002).

Blay, S., R. Piotrowicz and B. M. Tsamenyi (eds.). *Public International Law: An Australian Perspective* (Oxford: Oxford University Press, 1997).

Bloom, I. and W. L. Proudfoot (eds.). *Religious Diversity and Human Rights* (New York: Columbia University Press, 1996).

Borgwardt, E. *A New Deal for the World: America's Vision for Human Rights* (Cambridge, Massachusetts: Belknap/Harvard University Press, 2005).

Breitman, R. *Official Secrets: What the Nazis Planned, What the British and Americans Knew* (Ringwood, Victoria: Viking/Penguin, 1998).

Brems, E. *Human Rights: Universality and Diversity* (The Hague : Martinus Nijhoff Publishers/Kluwer Law International, 2001).

Brownlie, I. *Principles of Public International Law*, fourth edn. (Oxford: Clarendon Press, 1990).

Brownlie, I. and G. S. Goodwin-Gill (eds.). *Basic Documents on Human Rights*, fourth edn. (Oxford: Oxford University Press, 2000).

Camilleri, J. A. and J. Falk. *The End of Sovereignty? The Politics of a Shrinking and Fragmenting World* (Aldershot: Edward Elgar, 1992).

Carr, E. H. *The Twenty Years' Crisis: 1919–1939: An Introduction to the Study of International Relations*, second edn. (London: Macmillan, 1946).

Cassese, A. *International Law in a Divided World* (Oxford: Clarendon Press, 1986).

Castan, M. and S. Joseph. *Federal Constitutional Law: A Contemporary View* (Pyrmont, N.S.W.: Law Book Company, 2001).

Center for the Study of Human Rights, Columbia University. *Twenty-five Human Rights Documents* (New York: Center for the Study of Human Rights, Columbia University, 1994).

Chomsky, N. *The Umbrella of U.S. Power: The Universal Declaration of Human Rights and the Contradictions of U.S. Policy* (New York: Seven Stories Press, 1999).

Churchill, R. P. *Human Rights and Global Diversity* (Upper Saddle River, New Jersey: Pearson Prentice Hall, 2006).

Clark, D. *Principles of Australian Public Law* (Sydney: Lexis Nexis/Butterworths, 2003).

Clarke, J. J. *Oriental Enlightenment: The Encounter Between Asian and Western Thought* (London: Routledge, 1997).

Claude, R. P. and B. H. Weston (eds.). *Human Rights in the World Community: Issues and Action* (Philadelphia: University of Pennsylvania Press, 1989).

Cook, M. *Laying Down the Law: The Foundations of Legal Reasoning, Research and Writing in Australia*, fourth edn. (Sydney: Butterworths, 1996).

Craven, M. C. R. *The International Covenant on Economic, Social and Cultural Rights: A Perspective on its Development* (Oxford: Clarendon Press, 1995).

Davidson, S. *Human Rights* (Buckingham: Open University Press, 1993).

Davies, M. *Asking the Law Question: The Dissolution of Legal Theory*, second edn. (Sydney: Law Book Company, 2002).

Devereux, A. *Australia and the Birth of the International Bill of Human Rights* (Sydney: The Federation Press, 2005).

Donnelly, J. *Universal Human Rights in Theory and Practice* (Ithaca, New York: Cornell University Press, 1989).

Dudziak, M. L. *Cold War Civil Rights and the Image of American Democracy* (Princeton: Princeton University Press, 2000).

Dunne, T. and N. J. Wheeler (eds.). *Human Rights in Global Politics* (Cambridge: Cambridge University Press, 1999).

Eide, A., C. Krause and A. Rosas (eds.). *Economic, Social and Cultural Rights: A Textbook* (Dordrecht: Martinus Nijhoff, 1995).

Elias, T. O. *Africa and the Development of International Law*, second rev. edn. by R. Akinjide (Boston: Martinus Nijhoff, 1988).

Evans, T. *The Politics of Human Rights: A Global Perspective* (London: Pluto Press, 2001).

Evans, T. *US Hegemony and the Project of Universal Human Rights* (London: Macmillan, 1996).

Evans, T. (ed.). *Human Rights Fifty Years On: A Reappraisal* (Manchester and New York: Manchester University Press, 1998).

Falk, R. A. *Human Rights Horizons: The Pursuit of Justice in a Globalizing World* (London and New York: Routledge, 2000).

Falk, R. A. *On Humane Governance: Toward a New Global Politics: The World Order Models Project Report of the Global Civilization Initiative* (Cambridge: Polity Press, 1995).

Falk, R. A. *Predatory Globalization: A Critique* (Cambridge: Polity Press, 1999).

Forsyth, M. and M. Keens-Soper (eds.). *The Political Classics: A Guide to the Essential Texts from Plato to Rousseau* (Oxford: Oxford University Press, 1988, 1992).

Ganji, M. *International Protection of Human Rights* (Geneva; Paris: Librairie E. Droz; Librairie Minard, 1962).

Gearty, C. A. *Can Human Rights Survive?* (Cambridge: Cambridge University Press, 2006).

Glendon, M. A. *A World Made New: Eleanor Roosevelt and the Universal Declaration of Human Rights* (New York: Random House, 2001).

Glover, J. *Humanity: A Moral History of the Twentieth Century* (London: Jonathan Cape, 1999).

Gong, G. W. *The Standard of "Civilization" in International Society* (Oxford: Clarendon Press, 1987).

Gould, C. C. (ed.). *Beyond Domination: New Perspectives on Women and Philosophy* (Totowa, New Jersey: Rowman and Allanheld, 1984).

Green, J. F. *The United Nations and Human Rights* (Washington, D.C.: The Brookings Institution, 1956).

Gutmann, A. (ed.). *Human Rights as Politics and Idolatry* (Princeton: Princeton University Press, 2001).

Gutto, S. B. O. *Human and Peoples' Rights for the Oppressed* (Lund, Sweden: Lund University Press, 1993).

Hanks, P. and D. Cass. *Australian Constitutional Law: Materials and Commentary*, sixth edn. (Melbourne: Butterworths, 1999).

Harris, J. W. *Legal Philosophies* (London: Butterworths, 1980).

Heijden, van de B. and B. Tahzib-Lie (eds.). *Reflections on the Universal Declaration of Human Rights: A Fiftieth Anniversary Anthology* (The Hague : Martinus Nijhoff, 1998).

Henig, R. *Versailles and After: 1919–1933* (London and New York: Routledge, 1995).

Henkin, A. H. (ed.). *Human Dignity: The Internationalization of Human Rights* (Dobbs Ferry, New York: Oceana Publications, 1979).

Henkin, L. *International Law: Politics and Values* (Dordrecht: Martinus Nijhoff, 1995).

Henkin, L. (ed.). *The International Bill of Rights: The Covenant on Civil and Political Rights* (New York: Columbia University Press, 1981).

Hesse, C. and R. Post (eds.). *Human Rights in Political Transitions: Gettysburg to Bosnia* (New York: Zed Books, 1999).

Humphrey, J. P. *Human Rights and the United Nations: A Great Adventure* (Dobbs Ferry, New York: Transnational Publishers, 1984).

Hunt, P. *Reclaiming Social Rights: International and Comparative Perspectives* (Aldershot: Ashgate, 1996).

Ignatieff, M. (ed.). *American Exceptionalism and Human Rights* (Princeton: Princeton University Press, 2005).

Ishay, M. *The History of Human Rights: From Ancient Times to the Globalization Era* (Berkeley: University of California Press, 2004).

Janis, M. (ed.). *The Influence of Religion on the Development of International Law* (Dordrecht : Martinus Nijhoff, 1991).

Jenks, C. W. *The Common Law of Mankind* (London: Stevens and Sons, 1958).

Joseph, S., J. Schultz and M. Castan. *The International Covenant on Civil and Political Rights: Cases, Materials, and Commentary* (Oxford: Oxford University Press, 2000).

Joyner, C. C. (ed.). *The United Nations and International Law* (Cambridge: Cambridge University Press, 1997).

Keal, P. *European Conquest and the Rights of Indigenous Peoples: The Moral Backwardness of International Society* (Cambridge: Cambridge University Press, 2003).

Korey, W. *NGOs and the Universal Declaration of Human Rights: "A Curious Grapevine"* (New York: St. Martin's Press, 1998).

Koskenniemi, M. *The Gentle Civilizer of Nations: The Rise and Fall of International Law, 1870–1960* (Cambridge: Cambridge University Press, 2002).

Kretzmer, D. and E. Klein (eds.). *The Concept of Human Dignity in Human Rights Discourse* (The Hague: Kluwer Law International, 2002).

Krieger, J. (ed.). *The Oxford Companion to Politics of the World* (New York: Oxford University Press, 1993).

Ku, C. and P. Diehl (eds.). *International Law: Classic and Contemporary Readings* (Boulder, Colorado/London: Lynne Rienner, 1998).

Langlois, A. J. *The Politics of Justice and Human Rights: Southeast Asia and Universalist Theory* (Cambridge: Cambridge University Press, 2001).

Laqueur, W. and B. Rubin (eds.). *The Human Rights Reader*, rev. edn. (New York: Meridian/Penguin, 1990).

Lauren, P. G. *The Evolution of International Human Rights: Visions Seen* (Philadelphia: University of Pennsylvania Press, 1998).

Lauren, P. G. *Power and Prejudice: The Politics and Diplomacy of Racial Discrimination*, second edn. (Boulder, Colorado: Westview, 1996).

Lauterpacht, H. *An International Bill of the Rights of Man* (New York: Columbia University Press, 1945).

Lauterpacht, H. *International Law and Human Rights* (London: Stevens and Sons, 1950; reprinted Hamden, Connecticut: Archon Books, 1968).

Lauterpacht, H. *International Law and Human Rights* (New York: Praeger, 1950).

Long, D. and P. Wilson (eds.). *Thinkers of the Twenty Years' Crisis: Inter-war Idealism Reassessed* (Oxford: Clarendon Press, 1995).

Luard, E. *A History of the United Nations Vol. 1: The Years of Western Domination, 1945–1955* (London and Basingstoke: Macmillan, 1982).

Makonnen, Y. *International Law and the New States of Africa* (New York: UNESCO, 1983).

Malanczuk, P. *Akehurst's Modern Introduction to International Law*, seventh edn. (London: Routledge, 1997).

Mapel, D. R. and T. Nardin (eds.). *International Society: Diverse Ethical Perspectives* (Princeton: Princeton University Press, 1998).

Mayer, A. E. *Islam and Human Rights: Tradition and Politics* (Boulder, Colorado: Westview Press, 1991).

McGoldrick, D. *The Human Rights Committee: Its Role in the Development of the International Covenant on Civil and Political Rights* (Oxford: Clarendon Press, 1991).

Meron, T. *The Humanization of International Law* (Leiden ; Boston: Martinus Nijhoff, 2006).

Monshipouri, M. *Democratization, Liberalization and Human Rights in the Third World* (Boulder, Colorado: Lynne Rienner, 1995).

Morsink, J. *The Universal Declaration of Human Rights: Origins, Drafting and Intent* (Philadelphia: University of Pennsylvania Press, 1999).

Muschamp, D. (ed.). *Political Thinkers* (South Melbourne, Victoria: Macmillan, 1986).

Neal, M. *The United Nations and Human Rights, International Conciliation*, no. 489 (New York: Carnegie Endowment for International Peace, 1953).

Northedge, F. S. *The League of Nations: Its Life and Times* (Leicester: Leicester University Press, 1986).

Okoye, F. C. *International Law and the New African States* (London: Sweet and Maxwell, 1972).

O'Neill, N. and R. Handley. *Retreat from Injustice: Human Rights in Australian Law* (Annandale, N.S.W.: The Federation Press, 1994).

Palley, C. *The United Kingdom and Human Rights*, The Hamlyn Lectures, Forty-second Series (London: Stevens and Sons/Sweet and Maxwell, 1991).

Parkinson, P. *Tradition and Change in Australian Law* (Sydney: Law Book Company, 1994).

Piotrowicz, R. and S. Kaye. *Human Rights in International and Australian Law* (Chatswood, N.S.W.: Butterworths, 2000).

Pollis, A. and P. Schwab (eds.). *Human Rights: Cultural and Ideological Perspectives* (New York: Praeger, 1979).

Power, S. *"A Problem from Hell": America in the Age of Genocide* (London: Harper Collins, 2003).

Rajagopal, B. *International Law from Below: Development, Social Movements, and Third World Resistance* (Cambridge: Cambridge University Press, 2003).

Ramcharan, B. G. (ed.). *Human Rights: Thirty Years after the Universal Declaration* (Dordrecht: Martinus Nijhoff, 1979).

Renteln, A. D. *International Human Rights: Universalism Versus Relativism* (Newbury Park, California: Sage Publications, 1990).

Reus-Smit, C. *The Moral Purpose of the State: Culture, Social Identity, and Institutional Rationality in International Relations* (Princeton: Princeton University Press, 1999).

Risse, T., S. C. Ropp and K. Sikkink (eds.), *The Power of Human Rights: International Norms and Domestic Change* (Cambridge: Cambridge University Press, 1999).

Robertson, A. H. and J. G. Merrills. *Human Rights in the World: An Introduction to the Study of the International Protection of Human Rights*, fourth edn. (Manchester: Manchester University Press, 1996).

Robertson, G. *Crimes Against Humanity: The Struggle for Global Justice* (Ringwood, Victoria: Allen Lane/Penguin, 1999).

Robson, S. *The First World War* (London and New York: Longman, 1998).

Röling, B. V. A. *International Law in an Expanded World* (Amsterdam: Djambatan, 1960).

Rosenberg, J. *How Far the Promised Land? World Affairs and the American Civil Rights Movement from the First World War to Vietnam* (Princeton: Princeton University Press, 2006).

Schachter, O. *International Law in Theory and Practice* (Dordrecht: Kluwer Academic, 1991).

Schwelb, E. *Human Rights and the International Community: The Roots and Growth of the Universal Declaration of Human Rights 1949–1963* (Chicago: Quadrangle Books, 1963).

Sellars, K. *The Rise and Rise of Human Rights* (Phoenix Mill: Sutton Publishing, 2002).

Shaw, M. *International Law*, fourth edn. (Cambridge: Cambridge University Press, 1997).

Shute, S. and S. Hurley (eds.). *On Human Rights*: The Oxford Amnesty Lectures (New York: Basic Books, 1993).

Simpson, A. W. B. *Human Rights and the End of Empire: Britain and the Genesis of the European Convention* (Oxford: Oxford University Press, 2001).

Singer, P. (ed.). *A Companion to Ethics* (Oxford: Blackwell, 1999).

Sinha, S. P. *New Nations and the Law of Nations* (Leyden : A. W. Sijthoff, 1967).

Starke, J. G. *Introduction to International Law*, eleventh edn. (London: Butterworths, 1994).

Steiner, H. J. and P. Alston. *International Human Rights in Context: Law, Politics, Morals: Text and Materials*, second edn. (Oxford: Oxford University Press, 2000).

Svensson, M. *The Chinese Conception of Human Rights: The Debate on Human Rights in China, 1898–1949* (Lund, Sweden: Lund University Press, 1996).

Symonides, J. (ed.). *Human Rights: Concepts and Standards* (Aldershot: Ashgate/Dartmouth/UNESCO Publishing, 2000).

Talbott, W. *Which Rights Should Be Universal?* (Oxford: Oxford University Press, 2005).

Tester, K. *Moral Culture* (London: Sage Publications, 1997).

Tolley, H., Jr. *The U.N. Commission on Human Rights* (Boulder, Colorado: Westview, 1987).

Tuck, R. *The Rights of War and Peace: Political Thought and the International Order from Grotius to Kant* (Oxford: Oxford University Press, 1999).

United Nations Blue Book Series, vol. VII. *The United Nations and Human Rights: 1945–1995* (New York: Department of Public Information, 1995).

Van Asbeck, F. M. (ed.). *The Universal Declaration of Human Rights and Its Predecessors 1679–1948* (Leiden: E. J. Brill, 1949).

Van Ness, P. (ed.). *Debating Human Rights: Critical Essays from the United States and Asia* (London and New York: Routledge, 1999).

Vasak, K. and P. Alston (eds.). *The International Dimensions of Human Rights* (Westport, Connecticut: Greenwood Press/UNESCO, English edn., 1982), vol. 1.

Verzijl, J. H. *International Law in Historical Perspective: Vol. I: General Subjects* (Leyden : A.W. Sijthoff, 1968).

Vincent, R. J. *Human Rights and International Relations* (Cambridge: Cambridge University Press, 1986).

Von Eschen, P. *Race Against Empire: Black Americans and Anticolonialism, 1937–1957* (Ithaca, New York: Cornell University Press, 1997).

Waller, L. *Derham, Maher and Waller: An Introduction to Law*, eighth edn. (Pyrmont, N.S.W.: LBC Information Services, 2000).

Walters, F. P. *A History of the League of Nations* (London: Oxford University Press, 1952).

Wasserstrom, J. N., L. Hunt and M. B. Young (eds.), *Human Rights and Revolutions* (Lanham, Maryland: Rowman and Littlefield, 2000).

Williams, A. *Failed Imagination? New World Orders of the Twentieth Century* (Manchester: Manchester University Press, 1998).

Williams, G. *Human Rights under the Australian Constitution* (Oxford: Oxford University Press, 2002).

Wronka, J. *Human Rights and Social Policy in the 21st. Century: A History of the Idea of Human Rights and Comparison of the United Nations Universal Declaration of Human Rights with United States Federal and State Constitutions* (Lanham, Maryland: University Press of America, 1992).

Book Chapters, Articles, Reports and Papers

Aaland Commission of Jurists. "Report of International Commission of Jurists on Legal Aspects of the Aaland Islands Question," (1920), extracted in H. J. Steiner and P. Alston, *International Human Rights in Context: Law, Politics, Morals: Text and Materials*, second edn. (Oxford: Oxford University Press, 2000), pp. 1257–1260.

Alston, P. "The Commission on Human Rights," in P. Alston (ed.), *The United Nations and Human Rights: A Critical Appraisal* (New York: Oxford University Press, 1992), ch. 5.

Alston, P. "Introduction," in P. Alston (ed.), *Peoples' Rights* (Oxford: Oxford University Press, 2001), pp. 1–6.

Alston, P. "The 'Not-a-Cat Syndrome': Can the International Human Rights Regime Accommodate Non-State Actors?," in P. Alston (ed.), *Non-state Actors and Human Rights* (Oxford: Oxford University Press, 2005), ch. 1.

Alston, P. "The Universal Declaration at 35: Western and Passé or Alive and Universal," *Review: International Commission of Jurists*, no. 1 (1983), pp. 60–70.

Anand, R. P. "Sovereign Equality of States in International Law," in *Rd.C.*, vol. 197, 1986/II, pp. 9–228.

Anderson, C. "From Hope to Disillusion: African Americans, the United Nations and the Struggle for Human Rights, 1944–1947," *Diplomatic History*, vol. 20, no. 4 (Fall 1996), pp. 531–563.

Anghie, A. "Francisco de Vitoria and the Colonial Origins of International Law," *Social and Legal Studies*, vol. 5 (1996), no. 3, pp. 321–336.

Arat, Z. F. K. "Forging a Global Culture of Human Rights: Origins and Prospects of the International Bill of Rights," *Human Rights Quarterly*, vol. 28 (2006), no. 2, pp. 416–437.

Arieli, Y. "On the Necessary and Sufficient Conditions for the Emergence of the Doctrine of Dignity of Man and His Rights," in D. Kretzmer and E. Klein (eds.), *The Concept of Human Dignity in Human Rights Discourse* (The Hague : Kluwer Law International, 2002), pp. 1–17.

Azcárate, Pablo de. "Protection of Minorities and Human Rights," *The Annals of the American Academy of Political and Social Science*, vol. 243 (January 1946), pp. 124–128.

Balkin, R. "International Law and Domestic Law," in S. Blay, R. Piotrowicz and B. M. Tsamenyi (eds.), *Public International Law: An Australian Perspective* (Oxford: Oxford University Press, 1997), pp. 119–145.

Baxi, U. "Some remarks on Eurocentrism and the Law of Nations," in R. P. Anand (ed.), *Asian States and the Development of Universal International Law* (Delhi: Vikas Publications, 1972), pp. 3–9.

Berger, J. "Eleanor Roosevelt and the Framing of the United Nations Declaration of Human Rights," in J. Berger, *A New Deal for the World: Eleanor Roosevelt and American Foreign Policy* (New York: Social Science Monographs/Columbia University Press, 1981), pp. 67–74.

Best, G. "One World or Several? Reflections on the Modern History of International Law and Human Rights," *Historical Research*, vol. LXI (1988), no. 145, pp. 212–226.

Best, G. "Whatever Happened to Human Rights?," *Review of International Studies*, vol. 16 (1990), no. 1, pp. 3–18.

Blakesley, C. L. "Obstacles to the Creation of a Permanent War Crimes Tribunal," in C. Ku and P. Diehl (eds.), *International Law: Classic and Contemporary Readings* (Boulder, Colorado: Lynne Rienner, 1998), pp. 281–303.

Borchard, E. "Historical Background of International Protection of Human Rights," *Annals of the American Academy of Political and Social Science*, vol. 243 (1946), pp. 112–117.

Boyle, K. "Stock-taking on Human Rights: The World Conference on Human Rights, Vienna 1993," *Political Studies*, vol. XLIII (1995), pp. 79–95.

Buchanan, A. "Self-Determination, Secession, and the Rule of Law," in R. McKim and J. McMahan (eds.), *The Morality of Nationalism* (1997), extracted in H. J. Steiner and P. Alston, *International Human Rights in Context: Law, Politics, Morals: Text and Materials*, second edn. (Oxford: Oxford University Press, 2000), pp. 1286–1288.

Buckle, S. "Natural Law," in P. Singer (ed.), *A Companion to Ethics* (Oxford: Blackwell, 1999), pp. 161–174.

Buergenthal, T. "International Human Rights in an Historical Perspective," in J. Symonides (ed.), *Human Rights: Concepts and Standards* (Aldershot: Ashgate/Dartmouth/UNESCO Publishing, 2000), pp. 3–30.

Buergenthal, T. "Remembering the Auschwitz Death March," *Human Rights Quarterly*, vol. 18 (1996), no. 4, pp. 874–876.

Burgers, J. H. "The Road to San Francisco: The Revival of the Human Rights Idea in the Twentieth Century," *Human Rights Quarterly*, vol. 14 (November 1992), no. 4, pp. 447–477.

Carruthers, S. "International History 1900–1945," in J. Baylis and S. Smith (eds.), *The Globalization of World Politics: An Introduction to International Relations* (Oxford: Oxford University Press, 1997), pp. 49–69.

Carruthers, S. "International History 1945–1990," in J. Baylis and S. Smith (eds.), *The Globalization of World Politics: An Introduction to International Relations* (Oxford: Oxford University Press, 1997), pp. 71–87.

Cassese, A. "The General Assembly: Historical Perspective 1945–1989," in P. Alston (ed.), *The United Nations and Human Rights: A Critical Appraisal* (New York: Oxford University Press, 1992), pp. 25–54.

Charlesworth, H. "Australia's Split Personality: Implementation of Human Rights Treaty Obligations in Australia," in P. Alston and M. Chiam (eds.), *Treaty-making and Australia: Globalisation Versus Sovereignty?* (Leichhardt, N.S.W.: The Federation Press, 1995), pp. 129–140.

Charlesworth, M. "Augustine and Aquinas: Church and State," in D. Muschamp (ed.), *Political Thinkers* (South Melbourne, Victoria: Macmillan, 1986), pp. 43–50.

Chopra, J., and T. G. Weiss. "Sovereignty is no Longer Sacrosanct: Codifying Humanitarian Intervention," in C. Ku and P. F. Diehl (eds.), *International Law: Classic and Contemporary Readings* (Boulder, Colorado: Lynne Rienner, 1998), pp. 369–387.

Cmiel, K. "Review Essay: The Recent History of Human Rights," *American Historical Review*, vol. 109 (2004), no. 1, pp. 117–135.

Cohen, D. "Beyond Nuremberg: Individual Responsibility for War Crimes," in C. Hesse and R. Post (eds.), *Human Rights in Political Transitions: Gettysburg to Bosnia* (New York: Zone Books, 1999), pp. 53–92.

Cook, B. W. "Eleanor Roosevelt and Human Rights: The Battle for Peace and Planetary Decency," in E. P. Crapol (ed.), *Women and American Foreign Policy: Lobbyists, Critics, and Insiders*, second edn. (Wilmington, Delaware: Greenwood Press/Scholarly Resources, 1992), pp. 91–118.

Council for Aboriginal Reconciliation. *Going Forward: Social Justice for the First Australians* (Canberra: AGPS, 1995), extracted in T. Blackshield and G. Williams, *Australian Constitutional Law and Theory: Commentary and Materials*, third edn. (Sydney: The Federation Press, 2002), pp. 234–235.

Council for Aboriginal Reconciliation. *Recognising Aboriginal and Torres Strait Islander Rights* (Canberra: AGPS, 2000), extracted in T. Blackshield and G. Williams, *Australian Constitutional Law and Theory: Commentary and Materials*, third edn. (Sydney: The Federation Press, 2002), pp. 236–237.

Cranston, M. "What Are Human Rights?," in W. Laqueur and B. Rubin (eds.), *The Human Rights Reader*, rev. edn. (New York: Penguin/Meridian, 1990), pp. 17–25.

Crawford, J. "The Right of Self-Determination in International Law: Its Development and Future," in P. Alston (ed.), *Peoples' Rights* (Oxford: Oxford University Press, 2001), pp. 7–67.

Darian-Smith, E. "Postcolonialism: A Brief Introduction," *Social and Legal Studies*, vol. 5 (1996), no. 2, pp. 291–299.

Dicke, K. "The Founding Function of Human Dignity in the Universal Declaration of Human Rights," in D. Kretzmer and E. Klein (eds.), *The Concept of Human Dignity in Human Rights Discourse* (The Hague: Kluwer Law International, 2002), pp. 111–120.

Dietrich, J. W. "U.S. Human Rights Policy in the Post–Cold War Era," *Political Science Quarterly*, vol. 21 (2006), no. 2, pp. 269–294.

Donnelly, J. "Human Rights: A New Standard of Civilization?," *International Affairs*, vol. 74 (1998), no. 1, pp. 1–23.

Donnelly, J. "Human Rights at the United Nations 1955–1985: The Question of Bias," *International Studies Quarterly*, vol. 32 (1988), pp. 275–303.

Driscoll, J. "The Development of Human Rights in International Law," extracted in W. Laqueur and B. Rubin (eds.), *The Human Rights Reader* rev. edn. (New York: Meridian/Penguin, 1990), pp. 41–56.

Dunn, F. S. "The International Rights of Individuals," *Proceedings of the American Society of International Law* (1941) (April 25), pp. 14–22 (includes discussion).

Dunne, T. "Liberalism," in J. Baylis and S. Smith (eds.), *The Globalization of World Politics: An Introduction to International Relations* (Oxford: Oxford University Press, 1997), pp. 147–163.

Eide, A. "Economic, Social and Cultural Rights as Human Rights," in A. Eide, C. Krause and A. Rosas (eds.), *Economic, Social and Cultural Rights: A Textbook* (Dordrecht: Martinus Nijhoff, 1995), ch. 2.

Ermacora, F. "The Protection of Minorities Before the United Nations," in *Rd.C.*, vol. 182, 1983/IV, pp. 257–370.

Evans, T. "Introduction," in T. Evans (ed.), *Human Rights Fifty Years On: A Reappraisal* (Manchester: Manchester University Press, 1998), pp. 1–23.

Executive Board, American Anthropological Association. "Statement on Human Rights," (June 24, 1947), *American Anthropologist*, vol. 49 (October–December 1947), no. 4, pp. 539–543.

Falk, R. A. "Economic Aspects of Global Civilization: The Unmet Challenges of World Poverty," *World Order Studies Program Occasional Paper*, no. 22 (Princeton: Center of International Studies, Princeton University, 1992).

Falk, R. A. "False Universalism and the Geopolitics of Exclusion: The Case of Islam," *Third World Quarterly*, vol. 18 (1997), no. 2, pp. 7–23.

Falk, R. A. "Means and Ends in the Struggle against Global Terrorism," *Pacifica Review*, vol. 14 (2002), no. 1, pp. 49–56.

Falk, R. A. "The New States and International Legal Order," in *Rd.C.*, vol. 118, 1966/II, pp. 1–103.

Falk, R. A. "Sovereignty and Human Dignity: The Search for Reconciliation," in F. Deng and Lyons (eds.), *African Reckoning: A Quest for Good Governance*, extracted in H. J. Steiner and P. Alston, *International Human Rights in Context: Law, Politics, Morals: Text and Materials*, second edn. (Oxford: Oxford University Press, 2000), pp. 581–582.

Farber, D. "The Originalism Debate: A Guide for the Perplexed," *Ohio State Law Journal*, vol. 49 (1989), pp. 1085–1106.

Farer, T. J. "The United Nations and Human Rights: More than a Whimper," in R. P. Claude and B. Weston (eds.), *Human Rights in the World*

Community: Issues and Action (Philadelphia: University of Pennsylvania Press, 1989), pp. 194–206.

Finch, G. A. "The Nuremberg Trial and International Law," *American Journal of International Law*, vol. 41 (1947), no. 1, pp. 20–37.

Franck, T. "Is Personal Freedom a Western Value?," *American Journal of International Law*, vol. 91 (1997), no. 4, pp. 593–627.

Freeman, A. V. "Response [to Dunn]," *Proceedings of the American Society of International Law* (1941) (April 25), pp. 19–20.

George, R. "Natural Law and International Order," in D. R. Mapel and T. Nardin (eds.), *International Society: Diverse Ethical Perspectives* (Princeton: Princeton University Press, 1998), ch. 3.

Glendon, M. A. "Knowing the Universal Declaration of Human Rights," *Notre Dame Law Review*, vol. 73 (1998), pp. 1153–1176.

Goodhart, M. "Origins and Universality in the Human Rights Debates: Cultural Essentialism and the Challenge of Globalization," *Human Rights Quarterly*, vol. 25 (2003), no. 4. pp. 935–964.

Gordon, J. "The Concept of Human Rights: The History and Meaning of Its Politicization," *Brooklyn Journal of International Law*, vol. XXIII (1998), pp. 689–701.

Greig, D. W. "Sources of International Law," in S. Blay, R. Piotrowicz and B. M. Tsamenyi (eds.), *Public International Law: An Australian Perspective* (Melbourne: Oxford University Press, 1997), pp. 58–94.

Haldane, J. "Medieval and Renaissance Ethics," in P. Singer (ed.), *A Companion to Ethics* (Oxford: Blackwell, 1999), pp. 133–146.

Hambro, E. I. "Individuals before International Tribunals," *Proceedings of the American Society of International Law* (1941), pp. 23–29 (including discussion).

Hannum, H. "Human Rights," in C. C. Joyner (ed.), *The United Nations and International Law* (Cambridge: Cambridge University Press, 1997), pp. 131–154.

Henkin, L. "Human Rights Standards and their 'Generations,'" in L. Henkin, *International Law: Politics and Values* (Dordrecht: Martinus Nijhoff, 1995), pp. 184–202.

Higgins, R. "Comments," in C. Brölman, et al. (eds.), *Peoples and Minorities in International Law*, extracted in H. J. Steiner and P. Alston, *International Human Rights in Context: Law, Politics, Morals: Text and Materials*, second edn. (Oxford: Oxford University Press, 2000), pp. 1285–1286.

Higgins, R. "Conceptual Thinking About the Individual in International Law," *British Journal of International Studies*, vol. 4 (1978), pp. 1–19.

Holmes, H. B. "A Feminist Analysis of the Universal Declaration of Human Rights," in C. C. Gould (ed.), *Beyond Domination: New Perspectives on Women and Philosophy* (Totowa, New Jersey: Rowman and Allanheld, 1984), pp. 250–264.

Humphrey, J. P. "The Memoirs of John P. Humphrey: The First Director of the United Nations Division of Human Rights," *Human Rights Quarterly*, vol. 5 (1983), no. 4, pp. 387–439.

Humphrey, J. P. "The Universal Declaration of Human Rights: Its History, Impact and Juridical Character," in B. G. Ramcharan (ed.), *Human Rights: Thirty Years After the Universal Declaration* (Dordrecht: Martinus Nijhoff, 1979), pp. 21–37.

Hunt, L. "The Paradoxical Origins of Human Rights," in J. N. Wasserstrom, L. Hunt and M. B. Young (eds.), *Human Rights and Revolutions* (Lanham: Maryland: Rowman and Littlefield, 2000), pp. 3–17.

James, S. A. "*Freedom of Religion under the European Convention on Human Rights*, Carolyn Evans," *Global Change, Peace and Security*, vol. 15 (2003), no. 2, pp. 194–196.

James, S. A. "*Egalitarian Politics in the Age of Globalization*, Craig N. Murphy (ed.)," *Pacifica Review*, vol. 14 (2002), no. 3, pp. 254–256.

James, S. A. "*On Toleration*, Michael Walzer," *Pacifica Review*, vol. 10 (1998), no. 1, pp. 80–82.

Jhabvala, J. "The Drafting of the Human Rights Provisions of the UN Charter," *Netherlands International Law Review*, vol. XLIV (1992), no. 1, pp. 1–31.

Johnson, M. G. "The Contributions of Eleanor and Franklin Roosevelt to the Development of International Protection for Human Rights," *Human Rights Quarterly*, vol. 9 (1987), no. 1, pp. 19–48.

Kirgis, F., Jr. "The Degrees of Self-Determination in the United Nations Era," *American Journal of International Law*, vol. 88 (1994), extracted in H. J. Steiner and P. Alston, *International Human Rights in Context: Law, Politics, Morals: Text and Materials*, second edn. (Oxford: Oxford University Press, 2000), pp. 1270–1272.

Kloppenberg, T. "Franklin Delano Roosevelt, Visionary," *Reviews in American History*, vol. 34 (2006), no. 4, pp. 509–520.

Kunz, J. L. "The United Nations Declaration of Human Rights," *American Journal of International Law*, vol. 43 (April 1949), no. 2, pp. 316–323.

Lauren, P. G. "First Principles of Racial Equality: History and the Politics and Diplomacy of Human Rights Provisions in the United Nations Charter," *Human Rights Quarterly*, vol. 5 (1983), no. 1, pp. 1–26.

Lauterpacht, H. "The Subjects of the Law of Nations," *Law Quarterly Review*, vol. 63 (October 1947), pp. 438–460; vol. 64 (January 1948), pp. 97–119.

Leary, V. A. "Labour," in C. C. Joyner (ed.), *The United Nations and International Law* (Cambridge: Cambridge University Press, 1997), pp. 208–231.

Mandela, N. " 'No Easy Walk to Freedom,'" in W. Laqueur and B. Rubin (eds.), *The Human Rights Reader*, rev. edn. (New York: Meridian/Penguin, 1989), pp. 314–319.

Mandela, N. "Statement during the Rivonia Trial (1964)," in W. Laqueur and B. Rubin (eds.). *The Human Rights Reader*, rev. edn. (New York: Meridian/Penguin, 1989), pp. 321–324.

Marks, S. P. "From the 'Single Confused Page' to the 'Decalogue for Six Billion Persons': The Roots of the Universal Declaration of Human Rights in the French Revolution," *Human Rights Quarterly*, vol. 20 (1998), no. 3, pp. 459–514.

Mathew, P. "Human Rights," in S. Blay, R. Piotrowicz and B. M. Tsamenyi (eds.), *Public International Law: An Australian Perspective* (Oxford: Oxford University Press, 1997), pp. 271–300.

Mathew, P. "International Law and the Protection of Human Rights in Australia," *Sydney Law Review*, vol. 17 (1995), pp. 177–203.

McGrew, A. G. "Human Rights in a Global Age: Coming to Terms with Globalization," in T. Evans (ed.), *Human Rights Fifty Years On: A Reappraisal* (Manchester: Manchester University Press, 1998), ch. 8.

Minogue, K. "The History of the Idea of Human Rights," in W. Laqueur and P. Rubin (eds.), *The Human Rights Reader*, rev. edn. (New York: Meridian/Penguin, 1990), pp. 1–17.

Moravcsik, A. "The Origins of Human Rights Regimes: Democratic Delegation in Postwar Europe," *International Organization*, vol. 54 (2000), no. 2, pp. 217–252.

Morphet, S. "Economic, Social and Cultural Rights: The Development of Governments' Views, 1941–1988," in R. Beddard and D. M. Hill (eds.), *Economic and Social and Cultural Rights: Progress and Achievement* (London: Macmillan, 1992), pp. 74–92.

Morsink, J. "The Philosophy of the Universal Declaration," *Human Rights Quarterly*, vol. 6 (1984), no. 3, pp. 309–334.

Morsink, J. "Women's Rights in the Universal Declaration," *Human Rights Quarterly*, vol. 13 (1991), no. 2, pp. 229–256.

Morsink, J. "World War II and the Universal Declaration," *Human Rights Quarterly*, vol. 15 (1993), no. 2, pp. 357–405.

Mühlahn, K. "China, the West and the Question of Human Rights: A Historical Perspective," *asien afrika lateinamerika*, vol. 24 (1996), pp. 287–303.

Mutua, M. "The Ideology of Human Rights," *Virginia Journal of International Law*, vol. 36 (1996), no. 4, pp. 589–657.

No-hyoung Park. "The Third World as an International Legal System," *Boston College Third World Law Journal*, vol. 8 (1987), no. 1, pp. 37–60.

Orentlicher, D. "Separation Anxiety: International Responses to Ethno-Separatist Claims," *Yale Journal of International Law*, vol. 23 (1998), extracted in H. J. Steiner and P. Alston, *International Human Rights in Context: Law, Politics, Morals: Text and Materials*, second edn. (Oxford: Oxford University Press, 2000), pp. 1249–1257.

Otto, D. "Rethinking the 'Universality' of Human Rights Law," *Columbia Human Rights Law Review*, vol. 29 (1997), no. 1, pp. 1–46.

Otto, D. "Subalternity and International Law: The Problem of Global Community and the Incommensurability of Difference," *Social and Legal Studies*, vol. 5 (1996), no. 3, pp. 337–364.

Pagels, E. "The Roots and Origins of Human Rights," in A. H. Henkin (ed.), *Human Dignity: The Internationalization of Human Rights* (Dobbs Ferry, New York: Oceana Publications, 1979), pp. 1–8.

Parrott, A. L. "Social Security: Does the wartime dream have to become a peacetime nightmare?," *International Labour Review*, vol. 131 (1992), no. 3, pp. 367–386.

Partsch, K. "Individuals in International Law," in R. Bernhardt (ed.), *Encyclopedia of Public International Law* (Amsterdam: Max-Planck-Institut/Elsevier Science B.V., 1995), pp. 957–962.

Pechota, V. "The Development of the Covenant on Civil and Political Rights," in L. Henkin (ed.), *The International Bill of Rights: The Covenant on Civil and Political Rights* (New York: Columbia University Press, 1981), ch. 2.

Polakiewicz, J. "The Application of the European Convention on Human Rights in Domestic Law," *Human Rights Law Journal*, vol. 17 (1996), extracted in H. J. Steiner and P. Alston, *International Human Rights in Context: Law, Politics, Morals: Text and Materials*, second edn. (Oxford: Oxford University Press, 2000), pp. 1001–1004.

Pollis, A. "Cultural Relativism Revisited: Through a State Prism," *Human Rights Quarterly*, vol. 18 (1996), no. 2, pp. 316–344.

Pollis, A. and P. Schwab. "Human Rights: A Western Construct with Limited Applicability," in A. Pollis and P. Schwab (eds.), *Human Rights: Cultural and Ideological Perspectives* (New York: Praeger, 1979), pp. 1–18.

Rappard, W. E. "Human Rights in Mandated Territories," *The Annals of the American Academy of Political and Social Science*, vol. 243 (January 1946), pp. 118–123.

Raz, J. "The Rule of Law and Its Virtue," *Law Quarterly Review*, vol. 96 (1977), pp. 193–211.

"Report of the Commission of Rapporteurs on the Aaland Islands Question," (1921), extracted in H. J. Steiner and P. Alston, *International Human Rights in Context: Law, Politics, Morals: Text and Materials*, second edn. (Oxford: Oxford University Press, 2000), pp. 1257–1260.

Ritchie-Calder (Lord). *On Human Rights*, H. G. Wells Memorial Lectures, Inaugural Lecture, December 7, 1967 (London: H. G. Wells Society, 1968).

Roosevelt, E. "The Promise of Human Rights," *Foreign Affairs*, vol. 26 (1948), no. 3, pp. 470–477.

Sampford, C. "The Four Dimensions of Rights," in B. Galligan and C. Sampford (eds.), *Rethinking Human Rights* (Sydney: The Federation Press, 1997), pp. 50–71.

Schachter, O. "International Human Rights," in O. Schachter, *International Law in Theory and Practice* (Dordrecht: Kluwer Academic, 1991), pp. 330–361.

Schick, F. B. "The Nuremberg Trial and the International Law of the Future," *American Journal of International Law*, vol. 41 (1947), no. 4, pp. 770–794.

Schröder, H. "The Declaration of Human and Civil Rights for Women (Paris, 1791) by Olympe de Gouges," *History of European Ideas*, vol. 11 (1989), pp. 263–271.

Schwarzenberger, G. "The Standard of Civilisation in International Law," *Current Legal Problems*, vol. 8 (1955), pp. 212–234.

Sohn, L. B. "How American International Lawyers Prepared for the San Francisco Bill of Rights," *American Journal of International Law*, vol. 89 (1995), no. 2, pp. 540–553.

Sohn, L. B. "The Human Rights Law of the Charter," *Texas International Law Journal*, vol. 12 (1977), no. 2/3, pp. 129–140.

Sohn, L. B. "The New International Law: Protection of the Rights of Individuals Rather than States," *American University Law Review*, vol. 32 (1982), no. 1, pp. 1–64.

Sohn, L. B. "Supplementary Paper: A Short History of United Nations Documents on Human Rights," in *The United Nations and Human Rights*, 18th Report of the Commission to Study the Organization of the Peace (Dobbs Ferry, New York: Oceana Publications, 1968), pp. 39–186.

Steiner, H. "Ideals and Counter-Ideals in the Struggle over Autonomy Regimes for Minorities," *Notre Dame Law Review*, vol. 66 (1991), extracted in H. J. Steiner and P. Alston, *International Human Rights in Context: Law, Politics, Morals: Text and Materials,* second edn. (Oxford: Oxford University Press, 2000), pp. 1292–1297.

Steward, J. H. "Comments on the Statement on Human Rights," *American Anthropologist*, vol. 50 (1948), no. 2, pp. 351–352.

Steyn (Lord). *Human Rights: The Legacy of Mrs Roosevelt*, Presidential Address to the Holdsworth Club of the Faculty of Law in the University of Birmingham (Birmingham: Holdsworth Club, University of Birmingham, 2001).

Sucharitkul, S. "A Multi-Dimensional Concept of Human Rights in International Law," *Notre Dame Law Review*, vol. 62 (1987), pp. 305–317.

Szabo, I. "Historical Foundations of Human Rights and Subsequent Developments," in K. Vasak and P. Alston (eds.), *The International Dimensions of Human Rights* (Westport, Connecticut: Greenwood Press/UNESCO, English edn., 1982), vol. 1, pp. 11–40.

Tay, A. E. "The Western Legal Tradition and the Internationalization of Law," *Connecticut Journal of International Law*, vol. 6 (1991), pp. 529–545.

Taylor, S. "Reconciling Australia's International Protection Obligations with the 'War on Terrorism,'" *Pacifica Review*, vol. 14 (2002), no. 2, pp. 121–140.

Taylor, P. "The United Nations and International Organization," in J. Baylis and S. Smith (eds.), *The Globalization of World Politics: An Introduction to International Relations* (Oxford: Oxford University Press, 1997), pp. 264–285.

Thomas, C. "International Financial Institutions and Social and Economic Human Rights: An Exploration," in T. Evans (ed.), *Human Rights Fifty Years On: A Reappraisal* (Manchester: Manchester University Press, 1998), ch. 7.

Thomas, C. "Poverty, Development and Hunger," in J. Baylis and S. Smith (eds.), *The Globalization of World Politics: An Introduction to International Relations* (Oxford: Oxford University Press, 1997), ch. 23.

Thornberry, P. "Self-Determination, Minorities, Human Rights: A Review of International Instruments," in C. Ku and P. F. Diehl (eds.), *International Law: Classic and Contemporary Readings* (Boulder, Colorado/London: Lynne Rienner, 1998), pp. 135–153.

Waltz, S. "Universal Human Rights: The Contributions of Muslim States," *Human Rights Quarterly*, vol. 26 (2004), pp. 44–72.

Waltz, S. "Universalizing Human Rights: The Role of Small States in the Construction of the Universal Declaration of Human Rights," *Human Rights Quarterly*, vol. 23 (2001), pp. 44–72.

Wang Tieya. "International Law in China: Historical and Contemporary Perspectives," in *Rd.C.,* vol. 221, 1990/II, pp. 195–369.

Wasserstrom, J. N. "The Chinese Revolution and Contemporary Paradoxes," in J. N. Wasserstrom, L. Hunt and M. B. Young (eds.), *Human Rights and Revolutions* (Lanham, Maryland: Rowman and Littlefield, 2000), pp. 19–40.

Wessner, D. "From Judge to Participant: The United States as Champion of Human Rights," in P. Van Ness (ed.), *Debating Human Rights: Critical Essays from the United States and Asia* (London and New York: Routledge, 1999), pp. 255–277.

Weston, B. "Human Rights," *Human Rights Quarterly*, vol. 6 (1984), no. 3, pp. 257–282.

Weston, B. H. "The Charter of Economic Rights and Duties of States and the Deprivation of Foreign-Owned Wealth," in C. Ku and P. F. Diehl (eds.), *International Law: Classic and Contemporary Readings* (Boulder, Colorado: Lynne Rienner, 1998), pp. 519–548.

Weston, B. H. "Human Rights," in R. P. Claude and B. H. Weston (eds.), *Human Rights in the World Community: Issues and Action* (Philadelphia: University of Pennsylvania Press, 1989), pp. 12–28.

World Bank. "Development and Human Rights: The Role of the World Bank" (1998), extracted in H. J. Steiner and P. Alston, *International Human Rights in Context: Law, Politics, Morals: Text and Materials*, second edn. (Oxford: Oxford University Press, 2000), p. 1337.

Wright, C. "Revolution, Emancipation, and the State Definition of Human Status," *History of European Ideas*, vol. 11 (1989), pp. 51–82.

Wright, Q. "The Law of the Nuremberg Trial," *American Journal of International Law*, vol. 41 (1947), no. 1, pp. 38–72.

Wyzanski, C. E., Jr. "The Philosophical Background of the Doctrines of Human Rights," in A. H. Henkin (ed.), *Human Dignity: The Internationalization of Human Rights* (New York: Aspen Institute for Humanistic Studies; Dobbs Ferry, New York: Oceana Publications/Alphenaan den Rijn, The Netherlands, 1979), pp. 9–13.

Zamora, S. "Economic Relations and Development," in C. C. Joyner (ed.), *The United Nations and International Law* (Cambridge: Cambridge University Press, 1997), pp. 232–286.

Zarat, D. "Tradition, Human Rights, and the English Revolution," in J. N. Wasserstrom, L. Hunt and M. B. Young (eds.), *Human Rights and Revolutions* (Lanham, Maryland: Rowman and Littlefield, 2000), pp. 43–58.

Zuckert, M. "Natural Rights in the American Revolution: The American Amalgam," in J. N. Wasserstrom, L. Hunt and M. B. Young (eds.), *Human Rights and Revolutions* (Lanham, Maryland: Rowman and Littlefield, 2000), pp. 59–76.

Theses and Dissertations

Bajor, W. J. "Discussing 'Human Rights': An Anthropological Exposition on 'Human Rights' Discourse," Ph.D. thesis, Department of Social Anthropology, University of St. Andrews, St. Andrews, Scotland, 1997.

Brucken, R. M. "A Most Uncertain Crusade: The United States, Human Rights and the United Nations, 1941–1954," Ph.D. dissn., History, Ohio State University, 1999.

Carrel, M. "Australia's Prosecution of Japanese War Criminals: Stimuli and Constraints," Ph.D. thesis, Faculty of Law, University of Melbourne, c. 2005–2006.

Grammatico, A. C. "The United Nations and the Development of Human Rights," Ph.D. dissn., Department of Government, New York University, 1956.

Lavery, C. "The Classical Doctrine of Human Rights in International Law," Ph.D. dissn., Department of Political Science, University of Chicago, 1950.

Meighen, B. P. "The Universal Declaration of Human Rights and the Democratic Representative: A Study of Coming to Agree," Ph.D. dissn., Columbia University, 1953.

Murumba, S. K. "The Cultural and Conceptual Basis of Human Rights Norms in International Law," Ph.D. thesis, Law, Monash University, Melbourne, 1986.

Renteln, A. D. "A Conceptual Analysis of International Human Rights: Universalism Versus Relativism," Ph.D. dissn., Jurisprudence and Social Policy, University of California (Berkeley), 1987.

S'Anchez-Zamorano, M. "Postfoundationalism, Human Rights and Political Cultures," Ph.D. dissn., Graduate Department of Philosophy, University of Toronto, 1996.

International and National Instruments and Documents

American Declaration of the Rights and Duties of Man (1948), in I. Brownlie and G. S. Goodwin-Gill (eds.), *Basic Documents on Human Rights*, fourth edn. (Oxford: Oxford University Press, 2002) (hereafter *BDHR*), pp. 665–670.

Charter of the United Nations (1945) (excerpts), in Center for the Study of Human Rights, Columbia University, *Twenty-five Human Rights Documents* (New York: Center for the Study of Human Rights, Columbia University, 1994) (hereafter, *Twenty-five Human Rights Documents*), pp. 1–5.

Commonwealth of Australia Constitution Act 1900 (Imp.), in T. Blackshield and G. Williams, *Australian Constitutional Law and Theory: Commentary and Materials*, third edn. (Sydney: The Federation Press, 2002), pp. 1337–1357.

Constitution of the United States, extracted in H. J. Steiner and P. Alston, *International Human Rights in Context: Law, Politics, Morals: Text and Materials*, second edn. (Oxford: Oxford University Press) (hereafter, *IHRIC*), pp. 1462–1466.

Convention on the Prevention and Punishment of the crime of Genocide (1948), in *Twenty-five Human Rights Documents*, pp. 36–38.

Declaration Concerning the Aims and Purposes of the International Labour Organization (1944), in *BDHR*, pp. 307–309.

Declaration on the Elimination of all Forms of Intolerance and of Discrimination Based on Religion or Belief (1981), in *Twenty-five Human Rights Documents*, pp. 94–96.

Declaration on the Elimination of All Forms of Intolerance and of Discrimination Based on Religion or Belief (1981), in *BDHR*, pp. 33–36.

Declaration on the Granting of Independence to Colonial Countries and Peoples (1960), in *BDHR*, pp. 24–26.

Declaration on the Right and Responsibility of Individuals, Groups and Organs of Society to Promote and Protect Universally Recognized Human Rights and Fundamental Freedoms (1998), in *BDHR*, pp. 91–97.

Declaration on the Right to Development (1986), in *BDHR*, pp. 848–851; and extracted in *IHRIC*, pp. 1420–1422.

Declaration on the Rights of Persons Belonging to National or Ethnic, Religious and Linguistic Minorities (1992), in *BDHR*, pp. 59–62.

Draft United Nations Declaration on the Rights of Indigenous Peoples (1994), in *BDHR*, pp. 72–81.

International Convention on the Elimination of All Forms of Racial Discrimination (1965), in *Twenty-five Human Rights Documents*, pp. 39–47.

International Covenant on Civil and Political Rights (1966), in *Twenty-five Human Rights Documents*, pp. 17–29.

International Covenant on Economic, Social and Cultural Rights (1966), in *Twenty-five Human Rights Documents*, pp. 10–16.

Office of Public Information. *Charter of the United Nations and Statute of the International Court of Justice* (New York: United Nations, n.d. [1945]).

Optional Protocol to the International Covenant on Civil and Political Rights (1966), in *Twenty-five Human Rights Documents*, pp. 30–32.

The International Labor Organization Convention Concerning Indigenous and Tribal Peoples in Independent Countries (Convention 169) (1989), in *Twenty-five Human Rights Documents*, pp. 97–105.

Universal Declaration of Human Rights (1948), in *Twenty-five Human Rights Documents*, pp. 6–9.

Vienna Convention on the Law of Treaties (1967), extracted in *IHRIC*, pp. 1458–1461.

World Conference on Human Rights, *The Vienna Declaration and Programme of Action*, adopted 25 June 1993 (New York: United Nations, 1993).

Index